World Revolution
1917–1936
The Rise and Fall of
the Communist
International

C. L. R. JAMES

HUMANITIES PRESS
New Jersey

First paperback edition published 1993 by
Humanities Press International, Inc.,
Atlantic Highlands, New Jersey 07716.

© 1993 by Humanities Press International, Inc.

Introduction to the paperback edition © 1993 by Al Richardson

Reprinted 1994

Library of Congress Cataloging-in-Publication Data

James, C. L. R. (Cyril Lionel Robert), 1901–
World revolution, 1917–1936 : the rise and fall of the Communist
International / C. L. R. James.
p.   cm.—(Revolutionary studies)
Originally published: London : M. Secker and Warburg, 1937. With
new introd.
Includes bibliographical references and index.
ISBN 0–391–03790–0 (pbk.)
1. Communist International. 2. Communism. 3. Soviet Union—
Politics and government—1917–1936. I. Title. II. Series.
HX11.I5J25   1993
324.1′75—dc20   92–36830
                                              CIP

A catalog record for this book is available from the British Library.

Printed in the United States of America

To
The Marxist Group

World Revolution 1917–1936

REVOLUTIONARY STUDIES
Series Editor: PAUL LE BLANC

Contents

Introduction to
the Paperback Edition

C. L. R. JAMES'S *WORLD REVOLUTION*, HERE PRESENTED IN A
new edition, was one of the few attempts made at the time to
synthesize the experience of the revolutionary movement following the First World War. In judging the work's significance, both
in its own time and for ours, it is worth bearing in mind the
circumstances that gave rise to it.

The sheer weight of the Soviet Union's and the Comintern's
apparatuses had established a virtual monopoly over Marxist
thought by the mid 1930s. Dissident currents, whether of "right"
(Bukharinist or Brandlerite) or of "left" coloration (Bordigist,
Korschite or Trotskyist) had been successfully marginalized and
reduced to small group existence by massive propaganda, gang-
sterism, or terror.

Early in 1934 a dozen or so members of the Communist
League, the first British Trotskyist organization, at the instiga-
tion of Denzil Harber and Stewart Kirby, and with Trotsky's
support, left the parent body to set up a faction, later called the
Marxist Group, inside the Independent Labour Party, which had
parted company with the Labour Party a couple of years earlier.
By this time C. L. R. James had already arrived in Great Britain
and had made contact with members of the Labour Party in
Nelson, Lancashire; but when he came down to live on Boundary
Road in northwest London he was recruited into the Trotskyist
movement and joined the Marxist Group working in the ILP.[1]

In both groups the British Trotskyists were very few in number
at the time James encountered them, and while the main body
had been able, with difficulty, to sustain a monthly printed paper
from 1933 onwards, the entrist organization in the ILP had only
been able to issue a few duplicated pamphlets, and to put across
their viewpoint, had been obliged to sell the *Militant*, a journal
published by their American co-thinkers.

Trotskyism was not a popular standpoint during the mid 1930s in Great Britain. The wider Labour movement was more defensive than ever and was recovering from the painful split in the Labour Party at the time of the formation of the National Government in 1931. At the same time the Communist Party was just recuperating from its reduction to the rank of a tiny sect during the "Third Period" of the Comintern and was enjoying a period of rapid growth. The increase in the power of Nazi Germany made the U.S.S.R. seem an attractive ally, even in some establishment circles. Adoption of the Popular Front's policy enabled the party to make a far wider appeal than it had ever done before, setting the tone for the ideological life of the left for the next decade. The Communist Party was able to infiltrate or take over existing organizations, such as the Labour Party's student and youth groups, and to form a number of satellite bodies catering to the different interest groups in society.

The most effective of these was the Left Book Club, which came to enjoy a circulation of 57,000, and which was founded in May 1936 in partnership with the publisher Gollancz. Many of its titles were Soviet propaganda at its most mendacious; furthermore, they were virulently anti-Trotskyist in character. Examples of such books are Dudley Collard's *Soviet Justice and the Trial of Radek and Others*, the Webbs' *Soviet Communism: A New Civilisation*, and J. R. Campbell's *Soviet Policy and Its Critics*.

The Club's major programmatic book, *World Politics, 1918–1936*, justified the foreign policy of the Soviet Union. Written by the Communist Party's most cynical theorist, R. Palme Dutt, it appeared in 1936. Unable to match anything like this resource and others, the British Trotskyists felt very much on the defensive, so C. L. R. James decided to use his contacts with a rival publisher to mount a counter-operation. As he later described it:

> There were no books in English, only pamphlets, so after a time I said "Why haven't we a book in English?", and they said that it was about time they had one. I finally picked myself up and got hold of Frederick Warburg. . . . I told Warburg and he thought that there was scope for the publication of books that were Marxist but not C. P. So I went away to Brighton and wrote this book in three or four months.[2]

In the 1960s, although oral tradition in South Wales still pointed to a house where James allegedly worked on this book while campaigning for the ILP at the time of the Abyssinian War, it was largely put together, as he says, on the south coast. The local Communist Party bookshop in Brighton served as the basis for some of his material, though many of his earlier sources came from French and American non-Stalinist Marxists, and particularly from the rich collection brought back by Harry Wicks from his course at the Lenin School in Moscow. He thanks Wicks for his expertise in his preface.[3]

In early 1937 the book finally came out to a less than enthusiastic reception.[4] In the press dominated by the Communist Party advertisements for the book were not allowed.[5] In cases where the Communist Party was obliged to recognize its existence, such as in Gollancz's Left Book Club, it attacked the book with great hostility.[6] No less hostile was the reaction of the British colonial authorities, who forbade the export of copies to India.[7] This did not prevent it from being smuggled in and from exercising some influence. G. Selvarajatnan, who later became leader of the great strike in the Madras textile mills, was converted to Trotskyism upon reading it, and Leslie Goonewardene's *Rise and Fall of the Comintern*, published ten years afterwards in Bombay, was largely based on it.[8]

World Revolution has continued to suffer from neglect, being the least disseminated and commented on of all James's full-length works. The residue of Stalinist hostility towards the work remains, even in New Left circles which are otherwise inclined to idolize its author. For James's biographer, Paul Buhle, it is "James' least original major work," its "dogmatic weakness" being that it makes Stalinism "the deus ex machina for the failure of world revolution."[9]

Such criticisms are based upon the view that *World Revolution* is largely a summary of Trotsky's world view and the movement that followed him. Buhle, for example, saw differences between James and Trotsky only in James's treatment of the German crisis.[10] The book is far more original than it is given credit for, and neither James nor Trotsky thought they agreed on the basic argument contained in it. As James himself recalled:

> When I began to attack the Trotskyist position, some people in the United States said, "When we read your book *World Revolution* we said that it won't be long before James is attacking the Trotskyist movement". In this book it was pointed out to me in a particular

xiii

paragraph. I agreed with the interpretation. I was told, "James, when some of us read that quotation, we said that ultimately James will go".[11]

These doubts were also shared by Trotsky himself. While calling *World Revolution* "a very good book," he criticized it for "a lack of dialectical approach." He considered James's theory of the development of Soviet politics as wanting "to begin with the degeneration complete." While James's chapter on the German events of 1923 is entitled "Stalin Kills the German Revolution," Trotsky argued to the contrary that "the German Revolution had more influence on Stalin than Stalin on the German Revolution. In 1923 the whole party was in a fever over the coming revolution." While considering the policy of the German Communist Party during Hitler's accession to power ten years later, James asks "Why did Stalin persist in this policy?" and, "How could the Soviet bureaucracy possibly conceive that any useful purpose could be served by letting Hitler into Power?" Trotsky on the other hand argued that "Stalin hoped that the German Communist Party would win a victory, and to think that he had a 'plan' to allow Fascism to come to power is absurd."[12] This suggestion, that the blunders of the Comintern and the KPD (Kommunistische Partei Deutschlands) during the period of 1930 through 1933 were part of a deliberate plan, was to cause considerable embarrassment to the British Trotskyists, for their Communist opponents immediately seized the occasion to discredit the book.[13] Trotsky thus considered that the weaknesses of James's book were in its not allowing for the development of Soviet politics, in its allowing no movement within Soviet politics, and in its having a telescoping effect and intention—a sort of historical *post hoc ergo propter hoc* argument.

The reason for this difference becomes apparent when we examine the secondary sources used by James to construct the book, and the major models that influenced his thinking at the time. We can dismiss straightaway the suggestion made in Paul Buhle's biography, that he was in any way indebted to the "proletarian science" developed in the British Communist Party.[14] This was precisely the party against whom he was polemicizing. His main historical models were the classical historians and the great modern historians of the classical world, such as Grote, whose works remained on his bookshelf until his death.

They also included the classic Marxist histories, particularly *The Eighteenth Brumaire*, which James regarded as "an indispensable book for the student of any period of History" (32n. 1, below), and Trotsky's *My Life* and the *History of the Russian Revolution*. At the same time he was reading the works of the great French radical historians about the revolution of 1789 as preliminary research for his own future book, *Black Jacobins* (cf. 22–25, below). He must also have been acquainted with the historical labors of F. A. Ridley (for whom he maintained an affection to the end of his life), since they were both being published by Secker and Warburg at about the same time.

But it is the literature of the French and American non-Stalinist and non-Trotskyist left that supplies the key to understanding the distinctive features of *World Revolution*, in that they share a common assumption that the degeneration of the Russian Revolution began much earlier and proceeded at a more rapid rate than Trotsky would allow. One reference shows that James was acquainted with the literature of the *Que Faire*[15] group, and we may note that Souvarine's book, which he often cites, supported the Kronstadt insurrection against Soviet power as early as 1921.[16] We know from other indications that at this time James was acquainted with the "State Capitalist" theories about the U.S.S.R. held by the French Union Communiste group led by Henri Chazé,[17] as well as being in touch with some of B. J. Field's supporters in Canada, and conversant with the material of Weisbord, Oehler, and Erwin Ackernecht.[18]

James was particularly open to theories of the sort dismissed at the time by Trotskyists as "ultra left," for after a long and sterile experience with entry activity within the ILP he came to reject the tactic of entry altogether, refused to join the group pursuing such a course in the Labour Party, and entered into a dispute with the Trotskyist International Secretariat.[19] After a fragile unity was forced upon the British groups in 1938 he was sent to the USA, partly to give a free run to his longstanding opponent Denzil Harber, and partly to "straighten him out."[20]

The distinctive position of *World Revolution* thus lies in the fact that its author was already in the process of rejecting Trotskyism, and his ideas were about to evolve towards the position he assumed during the Cannon-Shachtman conflict of 1939 through 1940, and later in his *State Capitalism and World Revolution* of 1950, a political work described by Robin Blackburn as "Anarcho-Bolshevism" (whatever that means).[21]

During the period that James was writing this book, there was a political sub-culture of left-wing groups who vied with each other to pinpoint the degeneration of Bolshevism and Marxism as early in time as possible (Oehlerites, Stammites, Eiffelites, Marlenites, and so forth, in the USA; and in France, *Cahiers Spartacus*, *Que Faire*, and the Union Communiste). It was a natural result of the disillusionment produced among the left at the time by the rise of both Stalinism and Nazism, a pessimistic feeling that there was something deeply wrong with the Marxism they had inherited. Although *World Revolution* is still quite close to the more recognizably "Trotskyist" approach to these questions, it is influenced by this spectrum of ideas, and in effect marks the beginning of C. L. R. James's own gradual evolution in this direction.

A proper assessment of the book's value can only be made in the light of historical experiences, both of the time and of later times. This test of time is the only valid evaluation of any social theory. Like any other book James's is by no means infallible and increased understanding of some of these past events inevitably shows shortcomings. In spite of the views of some modern commentators[22] the subsequent history of the German USPD (Unabhängige Sozialdemokratische Partei Deutschlands) shows that Rosa Luxemburg was not "mistaken" in arguing that the Spartakists should remain inside it.[23] James's description of the foundation of the Comintern (112–13) can no longer be accepted as it stands. While admitting that "the delegates were dissatisfied," and that it was formed "due primarily to Lenin," he comes to the strange conclusion that, at the time, "Lenin had almost been betrayed against his better judgement into a weak and vacillating position."

In light of evidence that has since emerged it now seems clear that the dramatic appearance and speech of Gruber (Steinhardt) was arranged in order to stampede the delegates into reaching the required decision.[24] James's endorsement of the Comintern's verdict upon Paul Levi, because Levi condemned the 1921 "March Action" as a putsch, does this revolutionary less than justice.[25] James's view that Stalin was responsible for holding back the German Communist Party no longer receives uncritical support from historians of the Comintern.[26] There is some evidence that

Trotsky himself came to have doubts about blaming Brandler for any national errors that led to the failure of October 1923 (187).[27] Another myth of vulgar Trotskyism repeated here is that the Troika were responsible for sending the Chinese Communist Party into the Guomindang, that "had Lenin been sitting as Chairman such an entry would never have taken place,"[28] and that Trotsky voted against it from the very start (236–37, 248).[29] Count Stenbock-Fermoy (331), a great-nephew of Prince Kropotkin, wrote to Trotsky to deny he had joined the working-class movement to promote revanchist ideas.[30] James's description of Nin, Maurin, and Andrade as "prominent leaders of the Spanish Revolution" (308) in retrospect would appear overly optimistic.[31] His acceptance of the first Five-Year Plan's production figures (292) appears naive in hindsight, while time has dealt rather harshly with his remark that "if ever the Soviet Union goes down, that is to say back to capitalism, collective ownership has demonstrated how much capitalism retards the possibility of production." Here he was in good company, for not only did most socialists think this but even as late as 1961 Harold Macmillan, a conservative, feared the dynamism of the Soviet economy.

James's view that the leaders of the Soviet Union were, as already noted, carrying through a conscious policy in encouraging the suicidal behavior of the German Communist Party from 1930 through 1933 remains much more problematic. James links the deliberate policy of undermining Social Democracy to the fact that its foreign policy orientation was favorable to the "western" powers (337), whereas, as is well known, the more right-wing elements in German society traditionally have favored an alliance with Russia. This is the view still supported by some historians— admittedly a minority—today.[32]

When we consider the knowledge available at the time, the basic thesis supported by the book stands up surprisingly well. The writings of Dutt, Strachey, and the Webbs, its opponents of the day, could not be reprinted today without courting immediate ridicule. Scarcely half a dozen books of the Left Book Club's huge output during the same period are worth the shelf space in any Socialist library, and generally they pile up in the dustier sections of second hand bookshops where they remain unsold. James's careful documentation stands him in good stead. At one point he notes, "the writer has used an [sic] Mss translation. Many of the most important articles by Lenin, written after 1918, have to be tracked down in obscure publications or translated afresh. The present Soviet regime does not publish them, or, when it does so, truncates them" (132n. 1). Ever since the revelations of Khrushchev's "Secret Speech" at the 20th Party Congress of the Soviet Union in 1956 we are much better informed about these documents.[33] Yet a comparison of James's account of Lenin's last conflict with Stalin and any modern treatment of the same subject, such as those of Moshe Lewin or Marcel Liebman,[34] would not modify the picture presented by James (134–40) in any substantial way. He perceptively defines Trotskyism as a creation of Stalinism (151), and marshals his facts carefully to establish the existence of the massive famine caused by forced collectivization (303), denied by virtually the entire range of left-wing thinkers at the time.

Even some of James's short-term predictions are found to be surprisingly accurate. He notes in 1929 that "the long cold vistas of Siberia opened before Bukharin, Rykov and Tomsky" (296), and a year before the Trial of the Twenty-One, he asks, "What insurance company would risk a penny on Bukharin's life?" (199) Only a month after the appearance of *World Revolution* the events of the first week of May 1937 in Barcelona bore out his contention that "the day is near when the Stalinists will join reactionary governments in shooting revolutionary workers. They cannot avoid it" (389). The first section of the book's introduction is subtitled "The Coming War,"[35] and in it he prophesies that Trotsky "may be murdered in Mexico" (407). Many of the main events that come later in the wartime and post-war periods are sketched out quite adequately—he writes that "the victory of Fascism in Germany would mean inevitably war against the Soviet Union" (320) and that "British capitalism, may despite all its efforts, be drawn into a war against Germany side by side with the Soviet Union" (408); and he accurately foresaw the end of the Comintern:

> Stalin may even liquidate it altogether to assure the bourgeoisie that he will leave them alone, if only they will leave him and his bureaucracy in peace. But he dare not do this while Trotsky guides the Fourth International. (403)

Looking beyond the end of the Second World War James notes

wisely that "the last war brought the partial freedom of Ireland, a loosening of the chains of Egypt and an upheaval in India which has seriously crippled the merciless exploitation of centuries. How long could Britain's grip on India survive another war?" (10). For a brief moment the veil of the future is even drawn aside for China, Korea, and Indo-China: "In China and the Far East, where Britain has so much at stake, capitalism is more unstable than anywhere else in the world" (ibid.).

James's analysis of the Soviet Union is amazingly fresh in view of the events of the last three years. Speaking of the Soviet economy, he comments, "The whole system would stand or fall by the increased productivity of labour. . . . if Lenin returned today, he would not waste a minute on Stalin's propaganda, but would calculate the income and expenditure per head of population and from it grasp at once the social and political character of the regime" (122). Examining the presuppositions behind Lenin's theory of imperialism, he says:

> If capitalism proved to be still progressive, then the Soviet Union was premature and would undoubtedly fail. It was simple Marxism that the new Society could not exist for any length of time unless the old had reached its limits. But the conflict was not a conflict of entities already fixed. Capitalism in decay might still be powerful enough to overthrow the first Socialist State, whence it would gain a longer lease of life. (119–20)

We can only await the confirmation (or otherwise) of the grim prophecy that flows from this statement: "If the Soviet Union goes down, then Socialism receives a blow which will cripple it for a generation" (418–19).

This book dismissed for its "dogmatic" weakness," despite being written fifty-five years ago, still has lessons to teach if read with a fresh and critical spirit. We warmly recommend careful study as we place it in the hands of the public. We are sure, it will get a better reception than when it first appeared.

AL RICHARDSON

Notes

1. *C. L. R. James and British Trotskyism: An Interview*, London, 1987, p. 1. An amusing picture of James's influence upon middle-class opinion

in the ILP at this time can be found in Ethel Mannin, *Comrade, O Comrade*, chap. 10, 133–35.

2. *C. L. R. James and British Trotskyism*, 1. Among the non-Stalinist books that James was able to influence Warburg to publish at this time were, in addition to his own, his translation of Boris Souvarine's *Stalin* (1939), Mary Low and Juan Brea's *Red Spanish Notebook*, recently republished unfortunately without James's original preface, Harold Isaacs's *Tragedy of the Chinese Revolution* (1938), and Albert Weisbord's *Conquest of Power* (1938). Warburg, far more than Gollancz, was open to texts which came from the general left or ILP milieu and among his list at this period were Brockway's *Workers Front* and both *Next Year's War* and *Papacy and Fascism* by F. A. Ridley, as well as the first edition of Orwell's *Homage to Catalonia* which Gollancz had rejected as being too critical of the Communist Party's line.

3. See below, xxvi; cf. *Harry Wicks, 1905–1989: A Memorial*, London, 1989, 3, 8, 14. For examples of the sort of material provided, cf. below, 132n. 1 and 179n. 1.

4. It is advertised in *Fight*, Vol. 1, no. 5, April 1937.

5. Martin Secker and Frederick Warburg, "Letter to the Editor," 30 April 1937, in *Fight*, Vol. 1, no. 7, June 1937.

6. R. F. Andrews (Andrew Rothstein), "Leninism Trotskified," in *Left News*, June 1937, 291–98. Gollancz's own opinion was that "a Trotskyist book falls as obviously outside the scope of the Club's publications as does a Nazi or Fascist book" (*New Leader*, Vol. 21, new series no. 178, 11 June 1937).

7. George Padmore, letter to *Tribune*, 10 September 1937, 13.

8. K. Tilak, *Rise and Fall of the Comintern*, Spark Syndicate, Bombay, December 1947.

9. Paul Buhle, *C. L. R. James: The Artist as Revolutionary*, London, 1988, 51–52. Contrast this with James comment on p. 159, below: "There is a tendency among Trotskyists to exaggerate the economic and social influences at work in the Trotsky-Stalin struggle in 1923." Other examples of Buhle's anti-Trotskyist bias need not detain us here ("A paroxysm of rage at Stalin," "overly subjective, obsessed with details at the expense of the larger picture," "with minor possible exceptions such as Trotskyists in Ceylon, only the activity of James himself forcefully joined anti-imperialism with Trotskyism," and so forth). They have been discussed by Charles van Gelderen in "CLR," *Socialist Outlook*, April 1989.

10. Op. cit., note 9 above, 52.

11. Op. cit., note 1 above, 9.

12. L. D. Trotsky, "On the History of the Left Opposition," April 1939, in *Writings of Leon Trotsky, 1938–39*, New York, 1974, 260–66. Cf. C. L. R. James below, 164–201, 335.

13. J. R. Campbell, in *Controversy*, Vol. 1, no. 8, May 1937, 36.

14. Buhle, op. cit., note 9 above, 45–47. Here, as is evident from his

preface, he has been misled by his English informants, principally Robin Blackburn of *New Left Review*. Even less relevant are references (58) to Christopher Hill, who, in spite of expressing admiration for Trotsky's *History of the Russian Revolution* (*Sunday Times*, 18 August 1985), was busy, at the time, writing *Lenin and the Russian Revolution* that effectively censored Trotsky out of it.

15. The *Que Faire* group was formed in France in 1934 from ex-Stalinists and ex-Trotskyists, such as Kurt Landau, and set out to trace back the Russian Revolution's degeneration to its earliest stages. The group finally united with Social Democracy in 1939.

16. Souvarine talks about the "Kronstadt commune" and "the legitimate character of the rebels' claims" on pp. 276 and 279 of *Stalin*. Trotsky described Souvarine's theory as a "search for an independent line running directly from Marx to himself, bypassing Lenin and Bolshevism," (letter to Victor Serge, 29 April 1936, in *Writings of Leon Trotsky: A Supplement, 1934–40*, New York, 1979, 659), and Souvarine himself as the archetype of a "gangrenous sceptic." James notes Souvarine's "anarchist bias against the dictatorship of the proletariat" (below 140n. 2; cf. also 309).

17. Description of a meeting with C. L. R. James on 10 October 1937 by Ernie Rogers, "Letter to Jimmy Allen" in *The Trotskyist Movement and the Leninist League*, London, 1986, 7.

18. Op. cit., note 17 above; Sam Bornstein and Al Richardson, *Against the Stream*, London, 1986, 256, 287.

19. Op. cit., note 17 above: "There would have to be a struggle in the International League; efforts would have to be made to alter the line of the I[nternational] S[ecretariat]. I told him that this had already been attempted and had been met with Stalinist methods; suppression, hooliganism. He [James] interjected and said that there was nothing we could say against the I.S. with which he could not agree. He knew all about them. . . . He asked Frost (Max Basch), a member of the EC, to provide him with the documents published by Oehler on the question, also the internal bulletin published by the Sec. on the French turn."

20. Sam Bornstein and Al Richardson, *War and the International*, London, 1986, 24.

21. Robin Blackburn, "C. L. R. James" (Obituary), in *The Independent*, 2 June 1989. Cf. the remark made by James about Trotsky's rejection of democratic centralism in 1903 on 49 below: "He has since admitted that he was wrong; too generously, for the question is not so simple." In view of Trotsky's stated opinion about this conflict, the whole discussion that follows this comment (49–53) shows how far James was, already at variance with Trotsky by 1937.

22. Chris Harman, *The Lost Revolution: Germany 1918 to 1923*, London, 1982, 19–20, 88, 95.

23. Cf. Rob Sewell, *Germany: From Revolution to Counter-Revolution*, London, 1988, 33–34; Mike Jones, "The Decline, Disorientation and

Decomposition of a Leadership: The German Communist Party; From Revolutionary Marxism to Centrism," in *Revolutionary History*, Vol. 2, no. 3, 2. Cf. below, 95.

24. Referring to Angelica Balabanoff, *Impressions of Lenin*, Ann Arbour, 1968, 69–70, Walter Kendall concludes that "the whole affair is so dramatic as to suggest stage management" (*The Revolutionary Movement in Britain, 1900–1921*, London, 1969, 226). The case is established beyond all reasonable doubt in his as yet unpublished MS, *World Revolution: The Russian Revolution and the Communist International, 1898–1935*, to which I am greatly indebted.

25. "Mere condemnation of thousands of proletarians who risk their lives against the bourgeoisie has never been tolerated by Marxists," 169 below. Cf. Mike Jones op. cit., note 23 above, 5–7.

26. Pierre Broué, "The Communist International and the German Crisis of 1923," address to the AGM of *Revolutionary History*, 20 May 1989 (as yet unpublished); cf. L. D. Trotsky, op. cit. note 12 above, 260.

27. Cf. Mike Jones, op. cit., note 23, 8–9; He refers to Jacob Walcher's "Notes on Discussions with Trotsky," 17–20 August 1933, published in the *Oeuvres*, Vol. 2. This text recently came to light in the SAP (Sozialistische Arbeiter Partei) archives in Sweden and only became known after the publication of the Pathfinder English edition of the works of Trotsky's last exile. Hopefully an English translation will be published in the near future. For Trotsky's later return to his original opinion, cf. "On the History of the Left Opposition," April 1939, in *Writings of Leon Trotsky, 1938–39*, New York, 1974, 261.

28. On the strategy as a whole cf. Michael Cox's verdict: "The general strategy developed by the Comintern by 1923 and 1924 was unambiguously bourgeois democratic. I can find no suggestion of any serious attempt to pose or even discuss the possibility of proletarian dictatorship, as a solution to the tasks of the anti-imperialist struggle in the colonies. That is, a well developed stages conception of the colonial revolution preceded Stalinism." See "The National and Colonial Question—The First Five Years on the Comintern, 1919–22," in *Searchlight South Africa*, no. 4, February 1990, 38.

29. Trotsky maintained that on various dates he supported the withdrawal of the Chinese Communists from the Guomindang. In a letter written in December 1930 he claimed that he had done so "from the very beginning, that is, from 1923" ("Letter to Max Shachtman, 10 December 1930, in *Leon Trotsky on China*, New York, 1976, 490), but in *My Life* written a year earlier he said that it was "since 1925" (Penguin edition, Harmondsworth, 1975, 552). "As a matter of fact," notes Paola Casciola, "despite these assertions, no documents preceding the spring of 1927 are available in which Trotsky called for a withdrawal of the Chinese Communist Party from the Kuomintang," *Trotsky and the Struggles of the Colonial Peoples*, Centro Pietro Tresso, Foligno, 1990, 11–12.

30. *Cahiers Leon Trotsky*, no. 36, Dec 1968, 51–53.

31. Cf. C. L. R. James, *The Spanish Civil War: The View from the Left*, Socialist Platform, 1992, for rather damning counter evidence.
32. Thomas Wiengartner, *Stalin und der Aufstieg Hitlers*, Berlin, 1970; cf. the references given in A. Westoby, *Communism since World War II*, Brighton, 1981, 410n. 28, especially Robert Black, *Fascism in Germany*, London, 1975, Vol. 2, 749–55, 858–60.
33. Mostly to be found in Vol. 32 of the 1966 English edition of Lenin's *Collected Works*, along with the material in L. Fotieva's *Pages from Lenin's Life*, Moscow, 1960.
34. Moshe Lewin, *Lenin's Last Struggle*, London, 1969; Marcel Liebman, *Leninism under Lenin*, London, 1975, 417–25.
35. Obviously many of these forecasts derive from the common stock of analyses James had at his disposal in the Trotskyist movement. We should remind ourselves that Trotsky, two years before the Second World War broke out, prophesied its outbreak to within a month (Daniel Guérin, "Trotsky and the Second World War," part 2, in *Revolutionary History*, Vol. 3, no. 4, 13), and that other writers acquainted with Trotskyist ideas, such as F. A. Ridley, sketched out the main lines of the coming conflict in such books as *Next Years's War*, which Secker and Warburg published a year before James's book appeared.

Facsimile from pages 45 and 46 of "The Theory and Practice of Leninism," by I. Stalin, price 1/6, C.P.G.B., 1925.

But to overthrow the power of the bourgeoisie and establish that of the proletariat in a single country is still not to assure the complete victory of Socialism. The chief task, the organisation of Socialist production, is still to be accomplished. Can we succeed and secure the definitive victory of Socialism in one country without the combined efforts of the proletarians of several advanced countries? Most certainly not. The efforts of a single country are enough to overthrow the bourgeoisie: this is what the history of our revolution proves. But for the definitive triumph of Socialism, the organisation of Socialist production, the efforts of one country alone are not enough, particularly of an essentially rural country like Russia; the efforts

46 THEORY AND PRACTICE

of the proletarians of several advanced countries are needed. So the victorious revolution in one country has for its essential task to develop and support the revolution in others. So it ought not to be considered as of independent value, but as an auxiliary, a means of hastening the victory of the proletariat in other countries.

Lenin has curtly expressed this thought in saying that the task of the victorious revolution consists in doing the "utmost in one country for the development, support, awakening of the revolution *in other countries*." (Vide *The Proletarian Revolution*.)

Preface

THIS BOOK IS AN INTRODUCTION TO AND SURVEY OF THE revolutionary Socialist movement since the War—the antecedents, foundation and development of the Third International—its collapse as a revolutionary force. The Bolshevik Party, and the Soviet Union which it controls, being the dominating factors in the Third International, are given extensive treatment.

The ideas on which the book are based are the fundamental ideas of Marxism. Since 1923 they have been expounded chiefly by Trotsky and a small band of collaborators. Many who sneered or ignored for years are now uncomfortably aware that inside Russia there is something vaguely called "Trotskyism," which the Soviet authorities, despite the economic successes, discover in the very highest offices in the State and in increasingly wide circles of the population. At the same time in Western Europe, statesmen and publicists, frightened at the steady rise of the revolutionary wave, join with the Stalinist régime in Russia to condemn "Trotskyism." Mr. Winston Churchill, in the *Evening Standard* of October 16th, 1936, unleashes a fierce diatribe against the "Trotskyists," coupled with scarcely veiled approval of the Stalinists, i.e. of the Third International. Governments and national statesmen do not concern themselves with jesuitical differences between interpretations of Marx and Lenin. The whole future of civilization is involved.

The present crisis in world affairs, the growth of Fascism, the Spanish revolution, the inevitable revolution in France, the rôle of Russia yesterday, to-day, and to-morrow, the constant ebb and flow of political parties and movements all over the world, these things must be seen, can only be understood at all, as part of the international revolutionary movement against Capitalism which entered a decisive stage in 1917 with the foundation of the first Workers' State and, two years later, the organization of a revolutionary International. Ruhr invasion; the illness and death of Lenin and the quick victory of Stalin over Trotsky in 1923; Chiang Kai-Shek's northern expedition in 1926, the failure of the

Shanghai Commune and the disastrous adventure of the Canton insurrection; the breakdown of the New Economic policy in 1928, the "liquidation of the kulak," and the capitulation without a blow of the powerful working-class movement of Germany before Hitler; the restoration of private property on the Russian countryside, the Popular Front in France, the murder of Zinoviev and Kamenev, the turning of guns by the Third International on the P.O.U.M. in Spain because it agitates for the Socialist revolution—all these major events of post-war history are one closely-connected whole. Seen in isolation they are a jumble. This book shows their inter-connection.

How much the book owes to the writings of Trotsky, the text can only partially show. But even with that great debt, it could never have been written at all but for the material patiently collected and annotated in France, China, America, Germany and Russia. My task has been chiefly one of selection and co-ordination. Yet in so wide and complicated a survey, differences of opinion and emphasis are bound to arise. Therefore while the book owes so much to others as to justify the use of the term "we," the ultimate responsibility must remain my own.

I have called things and persons by the names I thought most fitted to characterise their political significance. Yet it is as well to remind the reader of the words of Marx: "My standpoint, from which the evolution of the economic formation of society is viewed as a process of natural history, can, less than any other, make the individual responsible for relations whose creature he socially remains, however much he may subjectively raise himself above them."

I would like here to thank Harry Wicks of London and those who, in Canada, and, particularly, South Africa, read the manuscript, pointed out errors, and gave valuable advice.

C. L. R. JAMES

January 17, 1937.
Since the above was written the Radek trial has taken place. To readers of this book, however, any discussion of that or succeeding trials is unnecessary.

C. L. R. J.

World Revolution
1917–1936

WORLD REVOLUTION
1917–1936

INTRODUCTORY

THE COMING WAR

THE THIRD INTERNATIONAL, FORETOLD BY ENGELS OVER A quarter of a century before it was formed, received its immediate impetus from the havoc wrought in the existing forms and organisation of society by the Great War. With the memories of that war still in our minds, we move swiftly and inevitably towards another, more embracing in its scope, infinitely more deadly in its potentiality for destruction, not only of the security and lives of human beings, but (a far more serious thing for the war-makers) of the very basis of the society on which their power and authority depend. Communism is no longer a spectre. There, after nearly twenty years, with all its defects and short-comings, stands the Soviet Union, making concrete in the minds of millions of working men and women the hitherto theoretical conception of a Workers' State. It is not only achievement but inspiration. The working-classes of Germany, of Austria, of Italy and of Hungary, will not bear the strain of the coming war as they bore the strain of the last. Russia in 1917 showed a way out, and Capitalism in those countries knows that it must win and win quickly. The war will begin as a conflict between nation and nation. The end of it will be the beginning of an era of conflict between rulers and ruled, in which all the cruelties and deceptions suffered by the workers in Central Europe, the bitterness and despair accumulated during the past twenty-five years, will find decisive expression in the working-class struggle for power.

The workers in Europe will make new mistakes, but they will not make the mistakes of 1919.

But it is not only in Central Europe where Fascism reigns, that Capitalism realises the mortal risks which it runs in the coming war. Capitalism in Britain, superficially the proudest and most stable of the surviving democracies, is as frightened as the rest. J. L. Garvin, the ablest and most experienced of its publicists, knows that the coming war heralds the end of the British Empire. Baldwin, the British Prime Minister, a man of widely different temperament, skilled in deception, saying little in few words, in the House of Commons and on the public platform daily voices an even deeper fear. The inevitable revolution haunts him. While Mussolini's war-planes were pouring liquid fire on the Abyssinian people, Baldwin unctuously held up his hands in horror. If nations use gas, he informed the British public, then at the end of the next war the common people will rise up in their wrath at wickedness in high places and sweep their governments away. The warning is soundly based, and yet at the same time Baldwin's government, and every other government in Europe, provide their millions of gas-masks for the destruction which each prepares.

And there are things Baldwin knows but of which he dare not speak. The last war brought the partial freedom of Ireland, a loosening of the chains of Egypt, and an upheaval in India which has at last seriously crippled the merciless exploitation of centuries. How long could Britain's grip on India survive another war? A mere threat of war in the autumn of 1935, and Egypt and Palestine flared in revolt. In China and the Far East, where Britain has so much at stake, Capitalism is more unstable than anywhere else in the world.

The failure of the working-class movement in 1918-20 was due chiefly to inexperience and the lack of a revolutionary international. It was in just such another crisis as the one which faces us that the Third International was set up to be the deciding factor, ceaselessly struggling against nationalism in all its forms, patiently pointing out to the national sections of the working-class movement the international unity of the proletariat and the suicidal folly of sectional conflict. Thus, in those rare moments when the national class-struggle reaches a high pitch of intensity and the working-class as a whole instinctively seeks its class allies in other countries against its own capitalists, the theoretical and practical basis would already have been laid, and the International would be ready with policy, programme and organisation. Lenin and Trotsky, who, more than any other men, were responsible for the formation of the Third International, who laid down its guiding principles and shaped the policies of its early years, taught that until the workers of the world could overthrow Capitalism in the great capitalist countries of Europe and Asia great wars between the rival imperialisms were inevitable.[1]

The majority of workers would go to such wars under the pressure of national tradition, the immediate instinct of self-preservation, life-long education, the propaganda of press, pulpit and radio, the shameless lying of their rulers, and the inevitable participation in that deception by trade union leaders and labour politicans. Not until 1935 did the Third International ever openly encourage any illusions about being able to stop war except by revolution. The workers, Lenin taught, would fight. But the memories of the last war, the unmitigated horrors of the new war when it came, the extension of hostilities from the fighting forces to the civil population, would bring early disillusionment and inevitable revolt in one country after another. Bourgeois nationalism and patriotic fervour would reach their highest pitch at the beginning of the war, and the bourgeois State would strike heavily at the international revolutionary movement. But after the first rush of enthusiasm the movement, with its foundations well and truly laid, would become stronger with every succeeding day of the war. The more powerfully it had resisted every aspect of war-preparation before the actual outbreak, the quicker would it be able to take advantage of the reaction, inevitable after the devastation of the civil population. Every section of the

[1] The men who disarmed Germany, took all that they could from her, and then tied the Treaty of Versailles to the League of Nations Covenant, obviously thought much the same.

Third International would struggle for the defeat of its own country. "Turn imperialist war into civil war." The years following 1917 had shown the possibilities of response to this audacious slogan by masses war-weary, maddened by suffering and stimulated by the prospect of peace and a new social order. If the Marxist theory of the class-struggle was the basis of the whole ideological structure of the Third International, the peak of its edifice, the banner which waved over all its teachings, was the repudiation of the first duty laid upon every citizen by the bourgeois State—the duty of national defence. It was subservience to the doctrine of national defence which had ruined the cause of the masses of the people in August, 1914. It was the great gulf between the Second International and the Third, the gulf which could never be bridged.

A bold stand for internationalism at the very beginning of the war would have enormous significance in every country. The knowledge and the evidence that the same policy was, from the outbreak of war, being heroically followed in every country would give increasing courage to the awakening revolutionary spirit of the masses. Conversely any breach in the international front might imperil the success of the whole movement, perhaps delay it for years at a time when every month was an historical period.

The Third International and the Coming War

Yet to-day, with the war long predicted imminent at last, with the great cracks in the imperialist structure widening day by day, with the rapacious Treaty of Versailles and its consequences, the fiasco of disarmament, the imposing assembly and pitiable collapse of the World Economic Conference, all teaching the masses the truth about Capitalism far more ably than the propaganda of the Third International; with the clash of interests over the Abyssinian question stripping to rags the drapery of the League of Nations, and exposing to millions of the most politically backward the hideous lusts and nauseating corruption of what they will be called upon to fight for, at this moment the Third International has refurbished the doctrine of national defence, is ready to fight for tricolour or stars and stripes, and clamours to defend the Union Jack. In France, after the election victory of the Popular Front, the so-called Communists of France sent a special deputation to the French Prime Minister to ask for the strengthening of the French army, that army which for years they have so rightly taught is for use not only against enemies abroad, but against those who do not submit to Capitalist law and order at home. In their propaganda against the Hitler menace they outdo the most fanatical diehards who inveighed against Germany before 1914. In Czechoslovakia it is the same.

But it is not only in countries which have a direct military understanding with the Soviet Union that the Communists shatter the foundations of the building which houses them. British Capitalism at the present moment wavers between an understanding with Germany and a "reform of the League," and a straight alliance with France, the Soviet Union, Czechoslovakia and other small nations, a bloc which could be held up to the light as the League, pure, unadulterated and unreformed. In Britain the Third International seeks the good graces not only of labour leaders but also of Liberals and churchmen, pacifists and cravens, and even for some weeks supported Eden against Baldwin as the protagonist of peace. In Italy the Italian Communist Party calls to its "brothers," the Fascists, to fight for collective security and international peace. In America they summon to the new crusade "farmers' organisations, the Communist Party, Socialist Party, state Farmer-Labour parties, veterans' organisations, working women's organisations, workers' and farmers' co-operatives, workers' fraternal societies, tenants' leagues, anti-war societies, groups of intellectuals, etc. . . . The new mass party of toilers should also strive to include sections of the sprouting Fascist or partly Fascist organisations and tendencies—such as company unions, American Legion posts, and groups of the Coughlin and Long movements, etc."[1]

All the world must fight against Hitler and Japan. The African enslaved by the Kenya settler and French colonist, the starving millions of India whom for nearly twenty

[1] *The Communist*, October, 1935.

years they have called to struggle for their national independence, these also are summoned to fight for the peace-loving democracies against war-making Fascism. In 1914 it was the war against German militarism. To-day it is the war against Fascism. In 1914 it was the war for the independence of small nations and the pledged word of the allied nations. To-day it is the same, except that the pledge is to be sanctified at the altar of Geneva, revised version or unreformed.

To gain scope for this monstrous deception, the Third International does not hesitate to sacrifice every principle which stands in the way. It commits the unspeakable treachery and folly of impeding with all its power the revolutionary movement in France. Unity is the cry, and the sections hammer at the gates of the Second International. The British section makes strenuous efforts to enter the British Labour Party, and pledges itself to obey the constitution of the most reactionary Labour movement in Europe. This at a time when the temper and suspicion of the masses is so great that the leaders of the Second International dare not use even the vapid pre-war phrases of resistance to war, but pledge themselves openly to fight for "international law."

In August, 1914, Lenin was with Zinoviev in a little mountain village in Galicia when he heard that the German Social Democracy, the most powerful and influential section of the Second International, had voted for the German war-credits. He refused to believe the news, said that the copy of *Vorwaerts* was forged. When he received confirmation his first words were: "The Second International is dead." After such a betrayal not its millions of members, its hundreds of parliamentarians, the range and variety of its publications, could make of it an instrument fit to carry out the first wish of the masses who supported it—the wish for international peace. Every succeeding year has confirmed that instantaneous judgment. Léon Blum is one of the greatest jingoes in France. In September, 1935, not even waiting on their more cautious masters, Herbert Morrison, Walter Citrine and the British Social Democracy shouted war at Mussolini. Before Hitler planted the boot that

14

they were bending to kiss on the face of German Social Democracy, Wels had promised the support of the Social Democracy to his foreign policy, that is to say, war to the death against foreign Capitalism and the Soviet Union. And, following in the footsteps of these men whom it has condemned for twenty years, the Third International has announced its capitulation in advance.

How has it fallen so fast and so far? What blindness is it that, at this most critical time, makes it even more short-sighted and more criminal than those Labour leaders who in 1914 thought that they could forget internationalism for the duration of the war and manœuvre with history as at a game of cards. It is superficial to say that it is due to a mistake in judgment, or that it is merely a tactic of the moment. It is ignorance or self-interest which attempts to deny the complete break with a past whose whole history is in the memory of so many living men. The Third International has not arrived where it is to-day by accident. The apparent volte-face is in reality the culmination of a process the first significant date of which can be stated with precision: October, 1924, when Stalin, in defiance of all the teachings of Marx and Lenin, first produced his theory that it was possible to build Socialism in a single country, that country being Soviet Russia. The present policies have resulted from this first conscious concession to nationalism. The opponents of this theory said at the time that, if it was adopted, then it led straight to the liquidation of the Third International as a revolutionary force. But the theory was forced through the International and acted upon, with the results that we see to-day. It is chiefly that process which we propose to trace. Not so much a history of events, as a history of principles, their origin, when and why they were departed from, the necessity for their regeneration. And for us any such study necessarily demands a parallel account of the foundation and development of the Soviet Union. The men who led the Russian Revolution and guided the Soviet State through those early years believed that the fate of the Soviet Union depended, in the last analysis, on the success or failure of the Third International.

The U.S.S.R. Cannot Survive without a Revolutionary International

How far does the fate of the U.S.S.R. depend to-day on the Third International? What has been achieved in Russia? How much of it is permanent, whatever the course of world history during the coming years? On the one hand we have the Seventh Congress of the Communist International celebrating in a resolution, undebated and unanimously voted for, "the final and irrevocable victory of Socialism in the U.S.S.R."[1] Between 1917 and 1923 a resolution of the Communist Party of the Soviet Union or the Communist International aimed at that objective statement of the truth which alone can be the basis of scientific Socialism in thought or action. It could be pointed to with pride as the only political writing in the world which could dare to tell the truth so far as apprehended in a political world compounded of lies and deception, a promise of the Socialist society to come. Those days are over. For suppression, evasion and hard lying the documents of the Soviet Union and the Third International to-day form, along with British colonial propaganda and fascist demagogy, a trilogy which future historians will contemplate with wonder. "The final and irrevocable victory of Socialism" deceives nobody to-day, not even the "Communists" themselves. But the enquirer who turns in despair from this subservient acquiescence in a mendacious absurdity is bewildered by the conflicting judgments in that section of the bourgeoisie which, within the limits of its own security, is not unfavourable to the Socialist State.

In a long leading article devoted to the Soviet Union the *Manchester Guardian* gives a summary of the position to-day based on recent investigations. "The level of life is still desperately low. Housing conditions are primitive. Professor Polanyi's interesting calculations put the nutritive value of the food supply per head as less than in 1913. The average monthly wage is no more than the pre-war wage (Professor Polanyi puts it at 52s. 6d. a month)."[2]

[1] *International Press Correspondence.* September 17, 1935.
[2] 20th February, 1936.

This dismal enumeration is, however, lightened by a hope: "But everywhere there is industrial progress and confidence."[1] In what do these originate? "The change in policy is seen in many fields—in the growth of private property on the collective farms; in the abolition of the rationing system and the reintroduction of marketing and of a uniform value of the rouble; in the encouragement of piecework and the incentive to earn (which the high prices of a freer market stimulate); in the drive for profitability in industrial plants, the increase in managerial powers, and the lessening of the rigidities of 'planning.'"[2] Is it then as the scoffers say, that after nearly twenty years of herculean effort and suffering Socialist Russia is at last discovering what the capitalists knew hundreds of years ago? And, if so, where will all this end? "But whatever problems these changes bring in their train a sceptical world has to admit that collective ownership is surviving, that it has created a new kind of patriotism and new incentives (like the Stakhanovite movement) to labour."[3] What is this new incentive, the Stakhanovite movement? As much pay (and honours) as possible for as much work as possible. Neither more nor less. And to crown this explanation which explains nothing "It may not be the Socialism of the fathers or the prophets, but it works."[4] It is not the Socialism of the prophets, it is not any sort of Socialism, and it does not work in any precise sense of that word. "But whatever problems these changes bring in their train. . . ."[5] That was and is the whole question. What has determined these changes in the past? What will determine them in the future? Where goes the Soviet Union? The answer is to be sought not only inside but outside of Russia, in the fortunes of the revolutionary movement in the East and West, in the rise and fall of the Communist International.

Let us take other commentators. On the surface an entirely different appraisal of Soviet Russia is given us in *Soviet Communism* by Sidney and Beatrice Webb; nearly a thousand

[1][2][3][4] Ibid.
[5] The Zinoviev-Kamenev trial has pulled up complacent bourgeois observers sharply. If war is delayed in Europe we can expect without any hesitation far-reaching economic changes in Russia.

pages, indulgent to the Soviet past, panegyrical of its present, lyrical as to its future, and hailed by the Third International and that recently discovered political phenomenon, the progressive person, as conclusive proof of Socialism triumphant in the Soviet Union. On a casual examination, and then after careful study, the book turns out to be a monument of painstaking research, with gross errors of historical fact, infantile political judgments, and, where evidence is too much for the enthusiasm of the authors, the most unscrupulous juggling.[1]

But both these widely divergent points of view are united on one common basis. They see no connection whatever between the Soviet Union and the Third International. For both of them the future of "collective ownership" is taken for granted; yet both rejoice in the bankruptcy of the Third International. For them the Soviet Union is better off without it. The *Guardian* is always derisive, the Webbs deprecating. The whole consistent body of thought which links the Soviet Union and the Third International, and makes them but component parts of the international workers' movement has no significance for either. The *Manchester Guardian* ignores the issue. The Webbs, in a book of a thousand pages, cannot avoid it, and they resort to one of the most blatant and discreditable evasions that has ever appeared in a book of such scope and pretensions. The prophets and fathers who laid the foundations on which the Soviet Union was built would have abjured such errors as dangerous crimes. The leaders who were responsible for bringing it into being, who, all things considered, foretold the future developments of history with astonishing precision, ceaselessly taught, and those who are alive still teach, the dependence of Russia on the revolutionary International, not only for its external safety, but also for its internal development towards Socialism. "The C.I. will not survive five more years of similar mistakes. But if the Comintern crumbles neither will the U.S.S.R. long survive." That was Trotsky's opinion, written eight years ago.

[1] See Appendix 1, where we give some indication of the most notable errors in this misleading compilation.

How far is that true to-day? The *Manchester Guardian* and the Webbs (typical of many) have no doubts, and their unity on this question is no accident. It is but another manifestation of nationalism, the common vice which is leading the Capitalist world to destruction, and unites Fascists, Conservatives, Liberals, Labourites, the whole of modern bourgeois society, against their common enemy—international Socialism. Nationalism in economics, and therefore nationalism in politics, nationalism in thinking, however bravely those on the left may use internationalist phrases. The radical bourgeois no sooner casts his eye towards international Socialism than he seeks to divide it into its component parts. That is not to be wondered at. It is in the nature of things. What is to be noted, however, is the close relationship which now exists .between this section of Capitalism and the Third International. The International seeks to do in fact what Liberals and Socialists wish it to do in theory, lose its identity in the nationalist state of Capitalism in the hope of building a national Socialism in Russia; it seeks to separate the ultimate destiny of the Soviet Union from the organisation of Socialist revolution in the rest of the world. For us the errors of such a view are fundamental and complete. For us bourgeois nationalism of any sort is incompatible with Socialism. The defence of the U.S.S.R. from hostile capitalist countries cannot be artificially separated from its internal economic and social development. The problem is one.

Every defeat of the Third International in Western Europe has thrown the Soviet Union further from the Socialist road. If the Third International loses its last stronghold, in France, and Fascism conquers in that country, then unless the workers of the world can create another international organisation (that work has already begun), the Workers' State of Soviet Russia is doomed. No major economic or political development in Russia, and few of the minor ones, can be understood, except in relation to the strength of the revolutionary movement in Western Europe, so long dominated by the Third International. But for the defeat of the German proletariat in

1933, the new constitution might never have seen the light. For it is not only a reflection of the alignment of social forces in the Soviet Union, but it is a direct bid for more support in the democracies of the West. The Russians themselves admit it openly. "No honest fighter for Socialism, not even he who honestly fights for no more than elementary democratic rights for the toiling masses can any longer find the least excuse for refusing to co-operate, for refusing to work together with the Communist Party. The fact that the fullest democracy in world history is now being carried out by the Communist Party has finally cut the ground from under the feet of all the enemies of the *proletarian united front*.[1] No one can longer dare to oppose this united front in the name of democracy without exposing himself in the eyes of the masses as in reality an enemy of democracy."[2]

Yet Professor Harold Laski in appraising the constitution[3] either does not see or does not think it necessary to mention one of the most powerful and obvious motives behind this sudden development. Thus nationalism leads to error after error. The Russian Revolution of October, 1917, began as the first stage in the international Socialist revolution, and despite the strangeness and variety of the historical developments of the past years the two remain indivisibly linked. We shall show in detail not only how the revolutionary working-class movement, through the Third International, has influenced the development of the Soviet Union, but how the development of the Soviet Union has in turn exercised a constant influence on the fortunes of the Third International and, through it, on the fate of the whole world. The intelligent observer, still more the commentator, may or may not accept the doctrines of Marx and Engels, of Lenin and Trotsky. But he ignores them at his peril. Without a firm grasp of these he sinks deeper into the mire at every step. There is no understanding the U.S.S.R., its past, present and future, except by the principles of Marxism. That is why the bourgeois from

[1] Italics their own.
[2] *International Press Correspondence*, June 20, 1936, p. 785. See also p. 767. The new constitution appeared in full in this number.
[3] *Manchester Guardian*, June 22, 1936.

1917 to the Zinoviev–Kamenev trial[1] have always been so consistently wrong, and will go on being wrong. Of late so many distortions have been introduced into these doctrines that it is necessary for us to restate them and bear them well in mind; otherwise it will be possible to avoid palpable inconsistency only by taking refuge in transparent and easily demonstrated falsehood.

[1] To many well-informed people the trial and its revelation of wide-spread Trotskyist sympathies in the U.S.S.R. came as a great shock. Yet the Marxists had been predicting just such a frame-up for years and had specifically warned against it as far back as 1929.

Chapter 1

MARXISM

WHAT THEN IS SOCIALISM ACCORDING TO THE PROPHETS? To answer this question we have to look back and not forward, at the origin of Socialism in the scientific sense, placing it in the particular phase of social evolution to which it belongs. For though it is to be attained by the will and energy of men, it will not be attained how and when men please. It is neither pious hope nor moral aspiration but a new form of society which will arise for one reason and one only, the unavoidable decay of the old.

THE FRENCH REVOLUTION AND MARXISM

This emergence of a new society from the old Marx and Engels deduced from wide and profound studies of economics and history, and their standard illustration of it was the emergence of fully-fledged Capitalist society out of the bankruptcy of the feudal régime in France. So much of their work was based on their analysis of the French Revolution, so emphatic were they as to the value of French history for the proper understanding of their ideas, the French revolution of 1789 acquires such historical significance with each succeeding year of post-war history, that we shall give here some idea of this revolution as they saw it in the early forties of last century, a view which has been at last accepted by official French historians of to-day.[1]

For Marx and Engels the basic division of society was into classes, groups of people who were distinguished from other groups by the fact that they earned their living and lived in a common way and therefore had common needs, aspirations and ideas.[2] These classes in the France of 1789 were the

[1] Notably Mathiez.
[2] Is it superfluous to state this to-day? The French Communist Party ummons the whole French "nation" to struggle against "two hundred

22

working masses, the landed aristocracy, the bourgeoisie, the petty-bourgeoisie (peasants in the country, small masters and clerical employees in the towns). The outstanding feature of pre-revolutionary France was the breakdown of peasant economy, the basis of the whole structure. The peasants, still bound by the laws of serfdom, could not secure enough food. France suffered from chronic famine and the increasing dislocation of the finances and administration of the State. Nothing could improve the plight of the millions in the countryside and regenerate the country but the release of the peasantry from the feudal laws. But the State-power in France was held by the monarchy which, though it had deprived the feudal aristocracy of political power, yet did not have, or at least believed that it could not have, any support in the country except from the aristocracy and the land-owning clergy. The State-power, as always, sought to maintain the existing régime, with its anarchic economic conditions in the countryside, and its privileged castes, corporations, and other social and political anachronisms. Within the State, however, had developed in the course of the centuries a new class, the French bourgeoisie. The French bourgeoisie was the richest class in France; its wealth, created in trade and industry, was already greater than that of the aristocracy. The bourgeois had the experience and education which is acquired by those who organise and administer industrial and commercial wealth, and it had power over those large sections of the population whose livelihood was dependent upon them. Great as was their wealth and power they could see possibilities greater still. But for this, their first need was the creation of a free market for the increased distribution of their goods. This free market was hampered on all sides by the feudal organisation of France into tariff-surrounded provinces, the chronic disorder of production in the countryside, the incapacity of the peasant to feed himself, far less to buy, the parasitism of the aristocracy and clergy, whose extortions burdened the peasant and were wasted

families;" such is the Marxism of the most powerful section of the Third International. If it were a question of two hundred families the whole matter could be settled any morning between nine and eleven.

in luxurious and unproductive consumption. The bourgeois wanted to reorganise the State in accordance with the necessities of their industrial and commercial power, in which they justly saw the present, and still more the future, strength of the country. They had a model before them—England, where Cromwell had broken the feudal State-power a century before. In addition, their pride suffered from the insults to their dignity and the restrictions on their social and political activities, which the long tradition of the feudal State-power imposed upon all who were not members of the nobility or the clergy. These were the basic elements of a revolutionary change in society. On the one hand the recurrent break-down in production and the bankruptcy of the State-power; on the other a new class which, growing up within the old society, had, already reached the stage when it was fully able to embark upon the business of freeing the productive forces from the old social and political fetters.

This struggle of economic forces for their full expansion was translated, as always, into a political struggle, the struggle for control of the State-power without which it is quite impossible to transform the organisation of society. It took, as always, a long and bloody revolution to accomplish this necessary change. This struggle against the aristocracy, the bourgeoisie quite genuinely inflated into the doctrines of the rights of man, only to recoil violently when the masses interpreted mankind to mean all men. The great bourgeoisie who began the agitation grew frightened at the revolutionary vigour and energy of the petty-bourgeoisie which they had unwittingly unloosed; they became counter-revolutionary and were swept away by more mobile sections of their own class, driven by the pressure of ever broader and broader groups of people seeking to widen the economic and political formulae of the revolution so as to include themselves. It was the petty-bourgeoisie of the towns and the country who carried the revolution to its conclusion. Nor did they in their turn fail to crush the Paris masses, feeling their way to Communism a century before their time. The peasant having got his land came to a dead stop, and isolated the revolution in the towns. Liberty,

24

equality and fraternity appeared to end in the Napoleonic dictatorship. But by the time Napoleon became Emperor the destruction of feudalism, the main business of the revolution, had been accomplished, and to this day France has never known a single famine. Napoleon instituted a modern system of legislation, which gave the French bourgeoisie full opportunity to develop the resources of the country. The irritating and hampering privileges of the aristocracy and the clergy were swept away. Careers were now open to those who had talent. However much Napoleon might disguise his bureaucracy as princes, dukes and counts, the outworn paraphernalia of the old feudal system, the revolution had accomplished its purpose. Louis XVIII might be restored to the throne by reactionary Europe in 1815, his nobles might mulct the treasury of millions, but the ancien régime was dead. No power on earth could restore it, for it had been replaced by an economic system and a social organisation that were vastly superior to the old. It is in that sense and that sense only that a new society is finally and irrevocably victorious. And whenever a Socialist society is established in the world its armies might conceivably (through act of God) be defeated by hostile powers, but the restoration of Capitalism is impossible.

The Economic Impossibility of a National Socialism

Even before the revolutions of 1848 Marx and Engels had foretold a similar inevitable breakdown in the economic system of Capitalism. They based their prediction on the periodic recurrence of commercial crises, due to the ownership by the bourgeoisie of the means of production. In these crises "The productive forces at the disposal of the community no longer serve to foster bourgeois property relations. Having grown too powerful for these relations, they are hampered thereby; and when they overcome the obstacle, they spread disorder throughout bourgeois society and endanger the very existence of bourgeois property. The bourgeois system is no longer able to cope with the abundance of the wealth it creates. How does the bourgeoisie overcome these crises? On the one hand by the

25

compulsory annihilation of a quantity of the productive forces; on the other, by the conquest of new markets and the more thorough exploitation of old ones. With what results? The results are that the way is paved for more wide-spread and more disastrous crises and that the capacity for averting such crises is lessened."[1]

Bourgeois economists, having sneered at this analysis for over eighty years, have been frantically trying, since 1929, to find some more consoling explanation for the present encircling crisis which has apparently eased its coils for a moment, only (as the bourgeois economists themselves admit) in preparation for a still more merciless grip.

But the breakdown of Capitalism did not mean that Capitalism would shake at the knees and collapse of itself, any more than feudalism collapsed of itself. The economic disorder would be translated, as always, into political struggles and be resolved by the revolutionary victory of a new class.

The other element for the revolution was therefore a new class which, suffering intolerably from the difficulties created by the chaos in production, would be driven to seize the State-power and create the conditions for the new Socialist society, in the same way as the bourgeoisie had taken over the State-power and created the political conditions for the new Capitalist régime. This class Marx and Engels found in the proletariat. And as the bourgeoisie within feudal society had been consolidated and disciplined by the direction and organisation of wealth, in the same way the proletariat, organised in factories by the development of the Capitalist system of production, disciplined by the increasing discipline of large-scale Capitalist organisation, would be forced to combine industrially and ultimately politically by the increasing pressure upon them of the bourgeois system of production protected by the bourgeois State. In this way, and in this way only, could they find themselves fitted to assume the direction of affairs and to initiate the new society. And in the same way as bourgeois assumption of State-power had been caused ultimately by

[1] *The Communist Manifesto.*

26

the breakdown, and resulted in the liquidation, of feudal property relations, so the proletarian assumption of State-power would be caused by and would result in the liquidation of bourgeois property relations. It was here, however, in the liquidation of bourgeois property that Marx and Engels saw the profound difference between all previous revolution-ary changes in society and the change from Capitalism to Socialism. For whereas all previous revolutionary changes had merely substituted one ruling class for another, they claimed for this change that it would ultimately result in the abolition of all classes and the establishment of a society without exploitation over the whole of the world. On this important aspect of Marxist theory a lamentable confusion exists, not only in liberal bourgeois thought (which is not important, except so far as it misleads the workers), but also throughout the working-class movement, a confusion deliberately created by the rulers of the Soviet Union, the ideological leaders of the Third International. An under-standing of this elementary piece of Marxism would riddle the delusion that there is no exploitation of man by man in Russia to-day. For to Marx and Engels the division of society into exploiters and exploited was not due to wicked-ness. "The separation of society into an exploiting and an exploited class, a ruling and an oppressed class, was the necessary consequence of the deficient and restricted develop-ment of production in former times. So long as the total social labour only yields a produce which but slightly exceeds that barely necessary for the existence of all; so long, therefore, as labour engages all or almost all the time of the great majority of the members of society—so long, of necessity, this society is divided into classes. Side by side with the great majority, exclusively bond slaves to labour, arises a class freed from directly productive labour, which looks after the general affairs of society; the direction of labour, State business, law, science, art, etc. It is, therefore, the law of division of labour that lies at the basis of the division into classes. But this does not prevent this division into classes from being carried out by means of violence and robbery, trickery and fraud. It does not prevent the ruling class, once having the upper hand, from consolidating

27

its power at the expense of the working-class, from turning their social leadership into an intensified exploitation of the masses.

"But if, upon this showing, division into classes has a certain historical justification, it has this only for a given period, only under given social conditions. It was based upon the insufficiency of production. It will be swept away by the complete development of modern productive forces. And, in fact, the abolition of classes in society pre-supposes a degree of historical evolution, at which the existence, not simply of this or that particular ruling class, but of any ruling class at all, and, therefore, the existence of class distinction itself has become an obsolete anachronism. It presupposes, therefore, the development of production carried out to a degree at which appropriation of the means of production and of the products, and, with this, of political domination, of the monopoly of culture, and of intellectual leadership by a particular class of society, has become not only superfluous, but economically, politically, intellectually a hindrance to development."[1]

For Marx and Engels, collective ownership did not mean Socialism. Everything depended on the development of the productive forces which this collective ownership would make possible; and even in the world of 1848 the productive forces necessary for such a development were already international. As they wrote in the *Communist Manifesto:* "By the exploitation of the world market, the bourgeoisie has given a cosmopolitan character to production and consumption in every land. To the despair of the reactionaries, it has deprived industry of its national foundation. Of the old-established national industries, some have already been destroyed and others are day by day undergoing destruction. They are dislodged by new industries, whose introduction is becoming a matter of life and death for all civilised nations: by industries which no longer depend upon the homeland for their raw materials, but draw these from the remotest spots; and by industries whose products

[1] *Socialism, Utopian and Scientific.* F. Engels. Chicago, Kerr & Co., 1917, pp. 129–130. This book is an abridgement of the more famous *Anti-Düring.* Does any except the most fanatical "communist" claim that such a state of affairs exists in Russia to-day?

are consumed, not only in the country of manufacture, but the wide world over. Instead of the old wants, satisfied by the products of native industry, new wants appear, wants which can only be satisfied by the products of distant lands and unfamiliar climes. The old local and national self-sufficiency and isolation are replaced by a system of universal intercourse, of all-round interdependence of the nations. . . .

"By rapidly improving the means of production and by enormously facilitating communication, the bourgeoisie drags all the nations, even the most barbarian, into the orbit of civilisation. . . . Moreover, just as it has made the country dependent on the town, so it has made the barbarian and semi-barbarian nations dependent upon the civilised nations, the peasant peoples upon the industrial peoples, the East upon the West." In this atmosphere nationalism could not breathe.

It was the all-round interdependence of Capitalist production which was always the basis of the thought of Marx and Engels. They did not proclaim the international Socialist revolution on the humanitarian principle of the more the merrier. With them it was sheer economic necessity. For ultimately, without the collective ownership of these means of production, it would be impossible to have that abundance of products without which the natural division of society into exploiters and exploited would remain. For thousands of years educated men had solaced themselves with dreams of a Communist society, but the realistic conceptions of scientific Socialism could only arise when the international forces of production had made possible the abundance of commodities. For Marx and Engels, therefore, basing their whole structure on the economic interdependence of the modern world and the consequent political ties, the mere idea of a national Socialism would have been a pernicious absurdity, to be driven out of Socialist ideology with whips and scorpions back into its natural home, the camp of the radical petty-bourgeoisie. "Proletarians of all lands, unite" was no idealistic slogan, but the political expression of economic need. They would not have raised it otherwise.

29

CLASSES NOT INDIVIDUALS

From this economic basis of society and its division into classes, with the Socialist revolution as their aim, they judged all political phenomena, from the future Socialist society to the activities of single individuals. They defined with exactness the rôle of individuals in history. They knew how much the quality of individual genius counts in social struggles, but they knew that in politics an individual is more important for what he represents than for what he is. They would not have been deceived first by Sir John Simon, and then by Sir Samuel Hoare, and then once more by Anthony Eden.[1] They claimed that both social and political types were created by the particular section of society which they served, and the portraits they drew of the typical political figures of their own day are as good a testimony as any of the fundamental soundness of their materialistic conception of history. To us who have known the Russian Mensheviks, as well as Léon Blum, Otto Bauer, Fritz Adler, Walter Citrine, Herbert Morrison, it comes almost as a shock to know that Marx knew and understood them quite well. "But the democrat, because he represents the petty bourgeoisie—a transitional class in which the interests of two classes are simultaneously blunted—arrogates to himself a position of superiority to class conflicts. Democrats admit that they are faced by a privileged class, but they think that they themselves, in conjunction with all the rest of the nation, constitute the 'people.' What they represent, is the right of the people; what interests them, is the popular interest. Consequently, when a struggle is impending, they see no reason for studying the interests and attitudes of the various classes, or for carefully reckoning up the forces at their own disposal. They need merely give the signal, and the people (whose resources are inexhaustible) will fall upon the oppressors. If it should turn out that their interests are inadequate and that their supposed power is impotent, they ascribe their defeat to the activities of pernicious sophists who have spread disunion and have split up the indivisible people into a number of mutually hostile factions; or the army,

[1] In regard to the League of Nations.

they say, was so brutalised and misguided that it could not perceive the pure aims of democracy to be its own true advantage; or the whole plan was wrecked by some error of detail; or, on this occasion, an unforeseen accident ruined the scheme. Whatever happens, the democrat comes forth unspotted after the most shameful defeat, just as he was a blameless innocent before he entered the battle; defeat merely fortifies his conviction of ultimate victory, there is no reason why he and his party should abandon their old outlook, for nothing more is requisite than that circumstances should come to their aid."[1]

Although in their polemical writing Marx and Engels were violently abusive, they did not think that all men were selfish hypocrites, that the petty-bourgeois democrat, for instance, was always trying to enforce his own selfish class interest. He genuinely believed that the special conditions requisite for his own liberation were likewise the conditions requisite for the salvation of modern society. In no other way could society be saved and the class war averted. Nor were we to think that democratic deputies are all shop-keepers[2] or enthusiastic champions of the small shop-keeper class. In culture and by individual status they might be the opposite of members of the shop-keeper class, but intellectually they had failed to transcend the limitations which naturally were imposed upon the petty-bourgeois by the conditions of petty-bourgeois existence. Consequently in the theoretical field they were impelled towards the same aspirations and solutions as those towards which in practical life the petty-bourgeois was impelled by material interest and social position. Even the bourgeois and aristocrat, ruthless and deceitful as they might be, were not crudely and without illusion merely seeking their own material interests. Speaking of the rivalry between capital and landed property which disguised itself as support on the one hand of the House of Orleans and on the other of the House of Bourbon, Marx poses and answers this question: "They

[1] *The Eighteenth Brumaire of Louis Bonaparte*, by Karl Marx.
[2] The Social Democrat to-day calls himself a Socialist and preaches Socialism. But, as we shall see, his Socialism is essentially the adaptation of Socialist ideas to the needs of the petty-bourgeoisie, to whom by the conditions of his life he is far more closely allied than the majority of the workers he claims to represent.

were bound by old memories, personal enmities, hopes and fears, prejudices and illusions, sympathies and antipathies, by convictions and articles of faith and principles? Who denies it? Upon the different forms of property, upon the social conditions of existence, as foundation, there is built a superstructure of diversified and characteristic sentiments, illusions, habits of thought, and outlooks on life in general. The class as a whole creates and shapes them out of its material foundation, and out of the corresponding social relationships. The individual, in whom they arise through tradition and education, may fancy them to be the true determinants, the real origin, of his activities."[1] And of the British Tories in 1832: "Thus the British Tories believed for generations that they were defenders of the monarchy, the Church, and the beauties of the venerable English constitution—until in the day of danger, there was wrung from them the admission that what they really worshipped was land-rent."[1]

Whatever the vagaries of individual persons yet the actions of the class as a whole and those who represented it would be governed ultimately by its material interests.

MARX'S TACTICS, 1850–1936

Marx and Engels were not theoreticians only, but active revolutionists and it was this basic knowledge reinforced by close observation which made them the masters of political tactics that they were. Lenin did not discover—he merely adapted, applied and developed.

The instructions Marx wrote for the revolutionaries in Germany in 1850 retain all their validity to-day, and were the tactical basis of the Third International. In Germany, as in France of 1789, the classes were the feudal aristocracy, the bourgeoisie, the petty-bourgeoisie and the proletariat. The democratic petty-bourgeoisie in those far-off days might be stirred into revolutionary activity, but their chief desire was always to finish with the revolution as soon as they could see a possibility of satisfying the demands of the democracy. They might fight side by side with the

---

[1] *The Eighteenth Brumaire.* This is still an indispensable book for the student of any period of history.

proletariat against the feudal aristocracy, but it was inevitable that sooner or later they would turn and crush the proletariat of whom they were more afraid than of the bourgeoisie.

The workers were, therefore, to be independently organised in groups and centralised under a directorship functioning from the central point of the movement.[1] The quick organisation of provincial connections of the workers' groups was one of the most important points in the strength and development of the workers' party. The workers from the very first hour of their victory must arm and organise themselves. The workers' candidates for the revolutionary assembly were to be put up in opposition to those of the democratic party; even in those localities where there was no prospect of winning, the workers must put up their own candidates in order to preserve their own independence, to calculate their own strength, and to be in a position to bring their own revolutionary attitude and party straightway before the public mind. Above all, the revolutionary workers were to struggle to break the influence of the democracy upon the masses of the workers. They were not to listen to the phrases of the democrats that the democratic party would be split because of the independent action of the workers, and that this would make possible the victory of the reaction. Wherever such phrases were used the final result would be the swindling of the proletariat. Both during the struggle and after it, the workers at every opportunity were to put up their own demands in contradistinction to the demands put forward by the bourgeois democrats. This wisdom remains. It was the neglect of these directives that ruined the Chinese Revolution of yesterday, threatens the Spanish revolution of to-day, and if persisted in will ruin the French Revolution of to-morrow.

But Marx never envisaged the simultaneous victory of the proletariat in every country in the world or in every advanced country. The uneven development of Capitalism in various countries meant inevitably the uneven development of the proletariat, and for this and other historical

[1] Marx made this a firm principle only after noting that the advanced workers in Germany during the revolution of 1848 had insisted on their own independent organizations. As always he generalized from experience.

33

reasons a different correlation of class forces in each country. He therefore detailed to the German proletariat the likely demands of the German petty-bourgeoisie and the demands which the revolutionary party should put up in opposition. In Germany the petty-bourgeois democratic party in 1850 was extremely powerful. The German proletariat might not be able to establish the proletarian State-power. Yet they were to drive the democratic revolution as far forward as possible. And even if they were not able to come to power and carry through their own class interests, yet they had the certainty that such success as they might win would be a signal for the immediate and complete victory of the more highly developed proletariat in France and would be very much helped by it. Proletarians of the world, unite. The German workers, by forming their own party as early as possible and by not permitting themselves to be fooled as to the necessity for the independent organisation of the proletarian party, would have accomplished the greatest part of the final victory. There would be another revolution in Germany, and the revolutionary movement would spread all over Europe. The revolution would continue until all the propertied classes were more or less dispossessed, until the governmental power was acquired by the proletariat and the association of proletarians was achieved, not only in one country, but in all important countries of the world, thus ending the competition of the proletariat in these countries. But, and this is what is most significant for us to-day, even with the State-power in their hands in all the advanced countries of Europe, the proletariat would continue to make revolutionary changes in the economic organisation of society until the most important productive forces were socialised. For it was only in this way that it was possible to attain that immense development of production that would destroy private property as an institution and establish the classless socialist society. "Their battle-cry must always be—the Permanent Revolution."

The history of the last seventy-five years, and particularly the history of the last twenty, has shown, and the prospects of the coming twenty-five years will show, that in comprehensive analysis and constructive thought these two men,

neither yet thirty-five, had made the greatest of all contributions to the theory and practice of human society.
They were fortunate in their age. They owed their insight
to the fact that they lived in Europe just at the time when the
rapid development of Capitalism and its social and political
consequences could be seen more easily than in its more
extended development in England. They had seen in
France the first great batttle of the proletariat against the
bourgeoisie; they had the training and ability to disentangle
the permanent from the transitory, the creative imagination
to plunge boldly into the future, the scientific scrupulousness
and immense capacity for labour which tested every
hypothesis. They were not dreamers but the most sober and
realistic of men. Revolution was the only way, and boldly
and without reservation they advocated the permanent
revolution. But they warned that revolution was not to be
played with. It was "a calculus with very indefinite magni-
tudes the value of which may change every day; the forces
opposed to you have all the advantage of organisation,
discipline, and habitual authority; unless you bring strong
odds against them you are defeated and ruined. Secondly,
the insurrectionary career once entered upon, act with the
greatest determination. . . ."

They were masters of retreat as well as of attack. In
1850, six months after Marx had sent the instructions which
we have detailed above, it became clear that the industrial
crisis was over and a period of prosperity had begun. Marx
said that under these circumstances a real revolution was
unthinkable, and was furiously angry with those who
continued to toy with the idea at such a time. He ordered
a drastic change of tactics; his party settled down to ordinary
constitutional agitation, and he began the long years of
labour on *Das Kapital*. In 1871 he was against the insurrection of the Paris Commune because he thought it would
fail, though he accepted the fact and defended the Commun-
ards. Finally he and Engels, although they maintained their
revolutionary élan and enthusiasm to the end, never
underestimated the colossal difficulties of the Permanent
Revolution. They miscalculated in time, that was all. But
from the first they knew the stupendous task that faced the

revolutionaries. In 1851 Marx wrote that the revolutions of the eighteenth century were child's play compared with the social revolutions which faced the nineteenth century proletariat. He foresaw many many attempts and many many failures. The bourgeois revolutions went quickly from success to success, but they were short-lived. The proletarian revolutions, said Marx, were self-critical. They again and again stopped short in their progress, retraced their steps in order to make a fresh start. They were pitilessly scornful of the half measures, of the weaknesses, the futilities of their preliminary essays. It seemed as if they had overthrown their adversaries only in order that these might draw renewed strength from contact with the earth and return to the battle like giants refreshed. Again and again they shrank back appalled before the vague immensity of their own aims. But at long last they reached the situation whence retreat was impossible and where the circumstances clamoured in chorus—

Hic Rhodus, hic salta![1]

We have seen between 1919 and to-day the hesitations of the workers, the half-measures, the shrinking back before the immensity of the task before them. But the moment approaches when for many of the working-classes in Europe retreat will be impossible, and they will bring Capitalism to the ground, not because Marxists tell them to, but because life offers no other way. And if Marx and Engels in the middle of the nineteenth century were too optimistic over the possibilities of proletarian revolution, they also necessarily envisaged a long period in which proletarian States would wage war against reaction. That period, happily, is not likely to be as protracted as it seemed in 1850; 1918-20 showed the speed with which a revolutionary movement could spread in the conditions of the modern world. To-day the proletariat of Belgium follows the French proletariat almost overnight in a nation-wide strike movement, and Portuguese reaction struggles to dam the overflow from Spain. We may well see, especially after the universal ruin and destruction of the coming war,

[1] *The Eighteenth Brumaire.*

a revolutionary movement which, beginning in one of the great European cities, in the course of a few short months, will sweep the imperialist bourgeoisie out of power, not only in every country in Europe, but in India, China, Egypt and South Africa. With an organised International revolutionary Socialism could face the future without dismay. The task of rebuilding such an international has been begun. It is a race with time. For its original purpose, the emancipation of the proletariat, the Third International, despite the sincerity and devotion of many of the rank-and-file, is already useless. The betrayal on the major question of war could only have been reached by a degeneration which has since been intensified. Tested and amplified by the blood of millions and by the labours of some of the finest of modern minds, the ideas and principles outlined above have almost completely vanished from the theory and practice of the Third International. So far as individuals personify movements, Trotsky personifies the principles of Marxism, Stalin the degradation of the Third International. For years the world believed that Stalin, master of Russia, wielder of greater power than any living man, had triumphed. Trotsky seemed an egoistic exile, employing an embittered energy in futile attacks on a rival successful in the struggle for power. Then suddenly in the summer of 1936 the June strikes in France, the Spanish Revolution, and finally the trial and Trotskyist purge in Russia, showed the undying vigour of revolutionary Socialism and nowhere so much as in Russia where its greatest enemy reigned. The bourgeois world realises day by day that the banner of world revolution has passed from the Third International of Stalin to the Fourth International of Trotsky, and—a gigantic irony—the rulers of the Workers' State and its satellites in the Third International are more eager than the bourgeois to crush the pioneers of the resurgent revolution.

Chapter 2

THE FORERUNNERS OF THE THIRD
INTERNATIONAL

THE FIRST INTERNATIONAL, THE PRECURSOR OF THE THIRD, was formed in 1864. Marx had nothing to do with its actual foundation, but was invited to assist and wrote the original drafts of both the inaugural manifesto and the constitution.

INTERNATIONALISM THE BASIS OF THE FIRST
INTERNATIONAL

So heterogeneous was the composition of the International that Marx could not state with his usual clarity the programme and tactics of the Permanent Revolution. Yet the following contains his essential ideas and was transferred bodily by Lenin to the statutes of the Third International:

"That the economical emancipation of the working classes is therefore the great end to which every political movement ought to be subordinate as a means;

"That all efforts aiming at that great end have hitherto failed from the want of solidarity between the manifold divisions of labour in each country, and from the absence of a fraternal bond of union between the working classes of different countries;

"That the emancipation of labour is neither a local nor a national, but a social problem, embracing all countries in which modern society exists, and depending for its solution on the concurrence, practical and theoretical, of the most advanced countries."

The defeat of the Paris Commune in 1871 was a death-blow to the First International, but it should be noted that one of the immediate causes of its collapse was the conflict between Bakunin, the anarchist, and the strong central control of the General Council, dominated first by Marx

38

and in its last years by Engels. These two devoted themselves with equal interest and energy to whatever national section seemed most important for the movement as a whole. Nationalism of any sort was quite foreign to them. In 1848 the centre of the international working-class movement was for them France, and remained so until 1870. With the defeat of the Paris Commune they saw that the leadership of the working-class struggle had now passed to Germany, which henceforth became the centre of their activities. As in France, after the destruction by the revolution of the provincial restrictions to trade, so the national unity of the German states which resulted from the Franco-Prussian War widened the opportunities of German Capitalism. The reparations tribute extracted from France, the mineral resources of Alsace-Lorraine, were the dynamic forces in this larger arena, and with the growth of German Capitalism followed inevitably the development of the Labour movement in Germany. There was much theoretical confusion in the German party between the years 1870 and 1880, but the party had fought against the Franco-Prussian war in true revolutionary fashion. Chiefly through the untiring efforts of Engels, Marxism in time became the prevailing doctrine of the German Social Democratic Party. The leaders of the German party, Bernstein, Liebknecht, Bebel, Kautsky, were in close and constant touch with Marx and Engels; they taught the irreconcilability of the struggle between classes, and that the State was merely the executive committee of the ruling class, foretold the inevitable collapse of Capitalism, and preached the necessity of the working-class seizing the State-power by armed insurrection. But, there being no immediate prospect of a revolutionary crisis, with the full agreement of Marx and Engels the German party organised itself to wrest immediate concessions from German Capitalism through trade unions and legal political activity. In the course of these struggles the workers would steel themselves for the revolutionary seizure of power.

But despite the recurrent crises the decades that followed the Franco-Prussian War saw a steady expansion of European Capitalism. Revolution seemed more and more remote.

The betterment of working conditions, increases in wages, could be won. There was the immediate struggle for full political rights under the constitution. As the years went by Marx and Engels could see that the prosperity of German Capitalism and the concessions which the organised workers could win from their masters were corrupting sections of the German leadership. They used the Marxian terminology but more and more they were slipping into purely parliamentary methods, and, what was worse, purely parliamentary aims. Universal suffrage and the secret ballot gradually superseded the revolution as the means of working-class emancipation. In 1883 Bismarck's anti-Socialist laws drove the most revolutionary leaders into exile and strengthened the hold of the parliamentarians on the workers. The corruption of the movement by these leaders was so great that Engels seriously considered a split by the revolutionary section. Perhaps if Marx had been alive the split would have taken place. But Marx had died in 1883, and in 1887 Engels was still hopeful, at times even confident, that these tendencies would be counteracted by the "wonderful commonsense" of the German workers who had stood so firm and fought so splendidly against Bismarck's repression. But he was wrong. After his death in 1895 bureaucratic corruption conquered in every important Labour movement in Europe, except the Russian, and there it was defeated only after a hard struggle. Marx and Engels in full vigour could have assisted the opposition to organise itself, given it theoretical clarity and helped it to lay such a basis that it could have rallied the most advanced elements to itself and thus been ready for the next great crisis of Capitalism, the war of 1914. More they could not have done, for the roots of the change lay deep in the economic developments of the time.

THE SECOND INTERNATIONAL REVERTS TO NATIONAL SOCIALISM

The end of the nineteenth and the beginning of the twentieth century saw European Capitalism making a last attempt to solve its difficulties by more intense exploitation of the old markets and a piratical seizure of the hitherto neglected continent of Africa. Capitalist prosperity increased and side by side with the expansion of trade and industry went the growth of the European Labour movement. In all the great European countries, particularly in Britain, the Labour movement became the happy hunting-ground for a rising crowd of Trade Union officials, parliamentarians, municipal counsellors, election agents, organisers, journalists, printers, publishers, a new caste in society which, on the basis of the successful struggle for better wages and more Labour representation in parliament, controlled the organised Labour movement. The growth of imperialism, the spread of trade, the accumulation of super-profits, strengthened their position. It gave them support from below—in a thin stratum of well-paid and privileged workers who had no quarrel with Capitalism. It gave them support from above, in the radical sections of the increasing petty-bourgeoisie of the cities, notably the intelligentsia, itself a product, as an administrative necessity, of the world-wide expansion of Capitalism. The petty-bourgeois intellectuals supplied the new Socialist ideology—the inevitability of gradualism, the commonsense of municipal trading—Socialism without tears. These ideas,[1] perfectly adapted to the petty-bourgeois environment of their authors, permeated through the bureaucracy and its apparatus into the working-class movement. Basing itself, as all ideas except those of revolutionary Socialism are based, upon the inevitable growth of national Capitalism, this Socialism was national in origin and outlook. Such internationalism as it professed was merely a quixotic gesture having no roots in economics and therefore none in politics, doomed to perish at the first breath of the storm. That this decline from Marxism into national Socialism was no accident but an inevitable phase can be seen from the course followed by the Labour movement in Germany after the death of Engels. Even before Engels died he had had fierce quarrels with the leaders of the German Social Democracy for suppressing the revolutionary passages in his last writings. Now with the old man out of the way Bernstein in 1897 began openly to revise

[1] As late as 1926 Bernard Shaw was preaching them in his *Intelligent Woman's Guide to Socialism*.

Marxism. By 1899 he had discarded the theory of the class-struggle and the inevitable breakdown of Capitalism, and substituted instead collaboration with the democratic and progressive bourgeoisie,[1] and the gradual growing-over of Capitalism into Socialism. Kautsky and others of the German party led the rejection of this adulteration, but in a lukewarm fashion that showed how near they already were to Bernstein. 1914 and the years of post-war history were to show that this Revisionism was identical with Fabianism. And it is another remarkable testimony to the influence of economic and social environment on men, even men above the average of intelligence and education, that Sidney Webb of the Oxford tradition and the English civil service and Kautsky, disciple and companion of Marx and Engels, the greatest revolutionaries in history, should have arrived at identical conclusions which were demonstrably false.

Yet Marx's internationalism remained on the lips of the Social Democratic bureaucrats. They organised themselves into the Second International in 1889. But so tenacious were they of their own national independence that it was only in 1900 that they formed a central bureau, and in reality each section always pursued its own policy. In 1904 at the Amsterdam Congress the Second International condemned Revisionism, yet continued to act as if the future of Capitalism were assured and each working class in the fullness of time would win a majority at the polls and institute the Socialist order.[2]

And yet, before their very eyes, the system was showing unmistakable signs of the great fissures into which peer fearsomely all the Capitalist world to-day. Side by side with the superficial prosperity went, as Marx had foretold, the development of Capitalism into monopoly and the enlargement of the scale of competition. The export of capital was industrialising the native populations of foreign countries, and the class-struggle was sharpening steadily all over the world. In the years before the war a series of

---

[1] Despite all the revolutionary trimmings the Popular Front is nothing more.

[2] The Social Democrats of to-day do not believe that. But it is highly probable that most of them did before 1914.

great strikes in Britain presaged the great conflicts of our own day. Over all, as even the Second International stated in its high-sounding but empty resolutions, the increasing rivalry of national Capitalisms was leading steadily to the most gigantic war in history. But all this had no ultimate significance for the parliamentarians and Trade Union bureaucracy, with their eyes glued on seats, increase of wages, the extension of the party press and all the other day-to-day activities of the organisation, which coincided so admirably with their struggles for personal advancement. It was not a question of intellectual ability or moral calibre. There were many J. H. Thomases and Ramsay MacDonalds among them, and few men of this age were personally superior to Jean Jaurès. Yet all went the same road. The leaders of great parties judge history from the necessities of their organisations and not their organisations from the necessities of history.

The disintegration of Capitalism did find some expression in dissenting political groupings within each national section. In Britain, for example, the English Social Democratic Federation, later the British Socialist Party, professed Marx's doctrines. Keir Hardie, of the Independent Labour Party, opposed the Liberal-Labour tendencies of the British working-class leaders, but paid little attention to theory and never stiffened his party with the doctrines of scientific Socialism. Inside the Social Democratic Party of Germany, Karl Liebknecht and Rosa Luxemburg fought the internationalism in phrase and Revisionism in action of Kautsky and Bernstein. But the revolutionary wings were weak. Even in Germany they were held in check by the organisational strength and discipline of the German party. The revolutionary leaders feared the isolation which would follow a split. Few, if any of them, could have foreseen how corrupt the leadership was. In every great European country except one, 1914 found them helpless before the Revisionists.

We have devoted an apparently disproportionate amount of time to these two tendencies in the labour movement— Marxism and Revisionism, international and national Socialism. The disproportion is only apparent. With the

43

ormation of the Third International and the adhesion to it of the revolutionary internationalists, Revisionism became openly and without shame the ruling doctrine of the Second International. But in 1924 Revisionism made its appearance in the Russian Bolshevik Party, for similar reasons to its appearance in the Second International and with the identical results. The Third International and the Russian Bolshevik party is to-day completely revisionist. And yet it was in the Bolshevik Party that unrevised Marxism was kept alive during the years when Revisionism was triumphant all over Europe. The Russian Bolshevik Party gave its stamp to the Third International. The strength of the International was the strength of the Bolshevik Party, but the weakness of that party was the weakness of the International also.

Lenin's Background

But for Tsarist reaction the war would have found only a few sects in possession of Marxism, and the working-class movement, even though it was certain to find its way in the end, might have floundered for years.

Throughout the nineteenth century the Tsarist feudal autocracy had ruled Russia, a Government that even at the end of the nineteenth century was in many respects more backward than the monarchy which the French Revolution had overthrown a hundred years before. Despite the execration of democratic Europe (hypocritical as far as the financiers and rulers were concerned) Tsarism remained, and would continue to remain until the development of the forces of production had created the social and political forces which would overthrow it and take its place. Through the centuries the peasants had tried in vain to rid themselves of the burden of serfdom. The historical development of Europe and Russia had resulted in the weakness of Russian industry, and the corresponding weakness of the towns. The peasantry, from the geographical conditions of its existence and the intellectual backwardness which this entails, the constant differentiation between its members, is unable to create an effective political party of its own, and the agrarian revolution which lacks the

44

political guidance and support of the towns cannot succeed. By 1861 the defeat in the Crimean War and the increasing pressure of the peasantry warned Tsarism of the necessity of ameliorating the conditions in the countryside. But though serfdom was abolished the peasant was cheated in favour of the landlord, with the result that the agrarian situation was merely temporarily relieved, and, as in pre-1789 France, periodical famines undermined the fabric of the Russian State.

Court conspiracies had at critical moments substituted one Tsar for another more suitable to the nobility. The system remained. The intellectuals who sought the overthrow of Tsarism without the backing of a mass movement slipped, as always, into the morass of terrorism. It was European capital, inevitably seeking new markets and as inevitably creating the means of its own destruction, which provided the basis for the revolutionary Marxist party in Russia, and thereby paved the way for the first great breach in the Capitalist system. Into this predominantly feudal country came the surplus of Western capital, constructing modern large-scale industry with its concomitant organisation of the proletariat and impoverishment of the peasantry, drawing Russia into that relentless see-saw of boom and crisis which was already undermining the far more stable Capitalisms of the west.

The soil was fruitful for Marxism. In 1883 was formed the Emancipation of Labour Group, composed of Russian intellectuals in exile with Plekhanov as its leading figure. In 1889 Plekhanov paid a special visit to London to see Engels and to seek his advice on the new developments in Russia. At the inaugural congress of the Second International in 1889 Plekhanov made his famous pronouncement that the revolutionary movement in Russia could triumph only as a revolutionary movement of the working class. "There is not, nor can there be, any other way." Even to the Liberal bourgeoisie in Russia, stifled economically and politically by Tsarism, Marxism came as a revelation. They could see Marx's analysis of Capitalism being enacted before their very eyes. But these gentlemen no sooner touched Marxism than, as is their way, they expelled

from it all that was revolutionary and made it "legal";
the backward workers of Russia should confine themselves
to economic struggle, and in politics support the Liberal
bourgeoisie. This was the theoretical origin of the first
Russian variant of Revisionism—Economism. Between 1890
and 1900 Capitalism in Russia developed at a furious rate.
The production of pig iron increased by 220 per cent, iron
ore by 272 per cent, oil by 179 per cent. The organisation
of industry, being new, was on the largest modern scale,
giving the workers, though proportionately few, enormous
power in action. The number of workers in industry was
1,424,000 in 1890. It was 2,098,000 in 1897. There were
17,000 on strike in 1894, 48,000 in 1895, 67,000 in 1896,
102,000 in 1897, 87,000 in 1898, 130,000 in 1899. In this
period of Capitalist expansion the workers could win
concessions, for it paid the employers to maintain production. But in 1900 the European crisis struck Russia. The
decline in production threw the whole of Russian economy
into disorder, the increase of unemployed killed the strike
movement. Both workmen and the Liberal bourgeoisie
were brought sharply up against the burden that the country
carried in the mediæval Tsarist Government. In 1900,
1901 and 1902 the influence of Economism declined,
the students began to take to the streets in political
demonstrations, and the striking workers joined them. In
November, 1902, at Rostov-on-Don a great economic strike
ended as a political strike, and for days the organised
workers called for the revolutionary overthrow of the
Government. In the middle of 1903 in Baku, Tiflis, Odessa,
all the towns of the Ukraine and Trans-Caucasia, a quarter
of a million workers took part in political strikes which
again demanded the revolutionary overthrow of the Government. Even the bourgeois intellectuals could see the coming
revolution.

Lenin was a genius, but it was this environment which
enabled him to read Marxism and accept it so thoroughly
that he could apply its principles to Russia and the rest
of the world with the confidence and sureness which
made him the greatest political leader in history. Social
Democratic propaganda groups sprang up in the large

towns, at first small circles, then reaching out to make contact with the masses. In 1900 some of them coalesced, and sent Lenin abroad to found a paper.

LENINISM: THE ORGANISATION

By 1903 his ideas were already clear. The revolution was inevitable. The masses would be inexorably driven to take the solution of Russia's problems into their own hands. But in the modern world the successful accomplishment of the revolution was essentially the work of an organisation, a revolutionary political party which would lead the masses. He distinguished three stages in the perspective—the first when insurrection was a theoretical objective, the second when the political party organised the insurrection, and the third when the party issued the call for insurrection. Each of these merged into the other, and their demarcation would depend on historical factors, some of which could be foretold, others recognised, proclaimed and acted upon. It was the party which would do these things. "Give us an organisation of revolutionaries and we will overturn Russia." This was, and remains, his greatest contribution to the practice of Marxism. The party's first duty was to give theoretical direction, to clarify. "No revolutionary theory, no revolutionary practice." Only that party could lead the revolution which was guided by an advanced political theory— Marxism; and for Lenin Marxism embraced every phase of human thought. The ideas of any epoch were the ideas of its ruling class, dominated always by the conception that the existing form of society was permanent. If the revolutionary party did not propagate its own ideas, scientific Socialism, the Marxist interpretation not only of politics but of society, then the ideas of the ruling classes, directed to the maintenance of the existing system, would continue to corrupt the minds of the masses and weaken their will to struggle. Bourgeois ideology was with him no hysterical term of abuse, but a definite obstacle in the way of the revolution, to be hacked away from the working-class movement wherever it appeared. The idea of workers putting faith in the bourgeois conception of a League of Nations would have been intolerable to him.

47

By means of an all-Russian newspaper the party could do more than spread its Marxist analysis of politics and society and give general directions. The very work of disseminating such a paper over the huge country would keep the various members of the party in close touch with the centre, and build up a skeleton organisation in preparation for the revolutionary mass movement. For him the first aim of the masses was to seize the State-power. Between 1900 and 1903 therefore he waged ceaseless war against the Economists. But although the day-to-day economic struggle was always waged with a view to the ultimate political objective, yet the members of his party dug themselves deep into the workers' movements, pointing out the political implications of the struggle between capital and labour, but fighting with the workers for their immediate demands. Lenin spent two years writing a philosophical work against a philosophical deviation from Marxism, but his party was always rooted in the masses, speaking to them in their own language about the things they could understand.

The Second Congress of the Russian Social Democratic Party met in London in 1903. Chiefly owing to Lenin's paper and the intensification of the class-struggle following the crisis, Economism seemed defeated. The majority of the class-conscious workers in Russia were supporters of Lenin's revolutionary wing. Neither Lenin nor any other member of the party had any idea of a split. Yet it came over a matter comparatively simple but which by degrees was seen to be what it really was, another variant within the Russian Labour movement of the opposing tendencies which we have seen at work in Western Europe. Lenin wanted a rigid narrow organisation, with a highly centralised discipline. Far better to lose ten absolutely first-class revolutionaries, rather than allow one chatterbox in. He wanted a strict division of labour inside the party, each member being responsible for a job of work with which he mainly concerned himself. The regulation of the party, he demanded, should be equally harsh. Under the régime of Tsarism formal democracy was impossible. He advocated democratic centralism. The Central

Committee should be freely elected, whenever possible there would be free discussions, but once a decision had been taken it would have to be obeyed blindly. This meant long periods when the Central Committee living abroad would have to take decisions which party members in Russia would have to obey without question. Lenin himself could hardly have been conscious of all that these plans implied; otherwise he would not have been so shocked and grieved at the opposition he met with.[1] But he would not give way, and won by a narrow margin. Thenceforward his group was known as the Bolsheviks (the majority) and the others the Mensheviks (the minority). Trotsky, a young but even then a very brilliant member of the party, went with the minority on this question of organisation. He has since admitted that he was wrong; too generously, for the question is not so simple. The leaders of the Second International, even the revolutionary internationalists, were divided on Lenin's democratic centralism which had split the Russian section. Rosa Luxemburg was against Lenin. It is only on reading the old disputes in the light of to-day that we see the complex gravity of the issues involved. Few in Lenin's party understood them. Stalin and the Stalinists do not understand them to this day.

LENINISM: THE PARTY AND ITS RELATION TO THE MASSES

Lenin saw the party as a small cog putting the great body of the workers into motion. Hence his insistence on the quality of the party.

"The stronger our party organisations, made up of *genuine* social democrats, and the less the waverings and instability *within* the party, the broader and more varied, the richer and more fertile will be the influence of the party on the working-class masses who environ it and whom it leads."[2]

[1] Krupskaya says that the break then and afterwards with old friends severely shook his health.

[2] Half the secret of a revolutionary party is wrapped in those words. Not only the layman but many so-called revolutionaries cannot understand that mere size is not and never has been decisive.

49

Trotsky, believing in a much broader organisation, attacked Lenin with extreme bitterness and sarcasm:

"In order to prepare the working-class for political power, it is necessary to develop and exercise in it the spirit of initiative and the habit of constant and active control over the entire executive personnel of the revolution. This is the great political task pursued by the international social democracy. But for the 'Social Democratic Jacobins,'[1] for the fearless representatives of the system of organisational substitutionalism, the preparation of the class for the government of the country, is supplanted by an organisational technical task, preparation of the apparatus of power. . . .

"The first task sees its main problem in the methods of political education and re-education of the entire, constantly increasing proletariat by the means of drawing them into active political work. The second task reduces everything to the technical selection of disciplined executives into the links of the 'strong and authoritative organisation,' a selection which, for the sake of reducing the work cannot but be carried on by the mechanical elimination of those considered to be unfit: by 'derivations' and 'deprivations' of rights."

Lenin had answered this objection in advance: No political party could educate the whole working class.

"We must not confuse the Party as the vanguard of the working class with the whole class. . . .

"We are the Party of a class, and therefore *almost the whole class* (and in 'time of war' or civil war, absolutely the whole class) must act under the leadership of our Party and must be associated with our Party as intimately as possible. But it would be sheer Manilovism, sheer *Khvotism*,[2] to think that the whole class, or nearly the whole class, can ever under Capitalism attain to the level of class consciousness and activity of its vanguard, its Social Democratic Party."

There can to-day be no argument about the differing points of view. Trotsky was wrong. Yet from this false approach the specific criticisms which he levelled against Lenin's principles as they worked out in practice cannot be dismissed, least of all to-day. He painted a picture of party life since Lenin's insistent advocacy of centralism. "During the last three to four years of intense party frictions, the life of very many committees has consisted of a

[1] A name flung at Lenin in controversy, which he thankfully accepted.
[2] Tailing behind.

50

series of coups d'état in the spirit of our court revolutions of the eighteenth century. Somewhere way up on top somebody is incarcerating, replacing, choking somebody else, somebody proclaims himself something—and as a result, the top of the committee house is adorned by a flag with the inscription, 'Orthodoxy, centralism, political struggle.'" He accused the central apparatus itself of starting a new discussion every month, "the apparatus supplies the topic for it, feeds it by false materials, draws its summary, dispenses justice, postpones congress for a year, and is now preparing a congress from among its own apparatus workers previously appointed, who are to authoritate the people on top to continue this work in the future as well."

Even to-day after forty years of political life, Trotsky's fundamental intellectual integrity remains unshaken. These charges must have had solid foundation. Between 1903 and 1923 the Bolshevik Party did all that a political party could do. Yet it cannot be accidental that the history of the Russian Communist Party and of the whole Communist International from the moment Lenin lay hopelessly ill, up to the unanimous vote on the "final and irrevocable victory" in 1935, is but a series of gigantic variations on Trotsky's reasons for refusing to accept Lenin's methods of organisation. For fourteen years he fought Lenin on this question. For him Lenin's democratic centralism meant that "the organisation of the party substitutes itself for the party, the Central Committee substitutes itself for the organisation, and finally the dictator substitutes himself for the Central Committee." It was "the replacement of the dictatorship of the proletariat by the dictatorship over the proletariat, of the political rule of the class by the organisational rule over the class." While Plekhanov[1] wrote some equally memorable and prophetic words: "The ultimate end of all this will be that everything will revolve around a single man who, ex providentia, will concentrate all the power in himself."

There is more in this than simple wrong and right. No proletarian revolution can succeed without a revolutionary

---

[1] He sided with Lenin at first, then left him.

party of the proletariat. No party can succeed without a strong centralised discipline, an International without centralism is no International at all. But centralism is a dangerous tool for a party which aims at Socialism, and can ruin as well as build. Lenin was a man big enough to forge this weapon fearlessly, use it to the utmost limit and yet realise its limits. He was a dialectician and knew that democratic centralism was very near to democracy at one time and equally near to pure centralism at another. Yet it would be idle to deny that all through his association with the party he dominated it. But he was utterly selfless and devoted, and, lucky in the fact of his unquestioned superiority, at the height of his power he used party discipline for the party, never for himself. He remained always subject to it, prepared at critical times in 1917 to offer his resignation rather than seek to manipulate the party. Yet despite his authority he was more than once the prisoner of the conceptions he had so rigidly instilled. The dangerous centralism of the Soviet régime in Russia was the constant preoccupation of his last years. He could not have been unaware that he had himself contributed to this by countenancing the usurpation of the power of the masses in their Soviets. He had hoped that until the revolution in Western Europe relieved Russia, the party, always the advance guard, would act in defence of the masses against the bureaucracy, mobilise the masses against it. But it was only during his last illness that he saw clearly what was coming, what had already come in the party, that abuse of democratic centralism which Trotsky had always feared in any system which, like Lenin's, so openly glorified central control. From his sick-bed he fought it with a feverish intensity. He failed, and with the development of the bureaucracy the democracy dropped completely out of centralism. From the Russian party it spread to the whole International. Centralism which helped to create the International helped to ruin it.

There is no specific for this problem. It will have to be fought out anew in each party as every emergency presents itself. But that can best be done only when there is a clear understanding of the issues involved. It is perhaps the greatest of the many bows that the revolutionary Ulysses will have to bend.

INTERNATIONAL AND NATIONAL SOCIALISM THE ROOT DIFFERENCE BETWEEN BOLSHEVISM AND MENSHEVISM

Unconsciously the two groups had been fighting the first decisive engagement in a battle of far-reaching significance, over no less a question than whether international Socialism was to be kept alive in Europe elsewhere than in the studies of a few devotees. Engels had not been dead ten years.

That Lenin and the Bolsheviks won was due chiefly to the Tsarist régime in Russia. Liberal thought kept in contact with the Labour movement through the Menshevik party, seeking to turn the workers from revolution to Liberalism. But Tsarism kept so tight a grip on the nation, allowed so little scope for parliamentary manœuvring, that not even the Liberals, far less the opportunist leaders of the Labour movement, could ever identify themselves with the Russian Government. The Russian petty-bourgeois Socialists had no parliamentary prospects because there was no parliament. Trade Unions were prohibited by law and allowed only on sufferance. An office in a Trade Union was a post of danger, not of security. Yet Menshevism proved itself inside two years to be incontestably another form of Revisionism. All sorts of cross-currents, personal and otherwise, had played their part in the dispute of 1903, and continued to do so during the years that followed. But at every serious crisis the masses of the workers followed the Bolsheviks in action, while in ordinary times they could not see the differences between the two groups and were bewildered and discouraged by the bitterness of the factional struggle. Yet it was in the intervals between political crises that Lenin had to fight hardest, keeping the Bolsheviks ideologically clear and organisationally firm against all forms of corruption, open or insidious. Never was any victory of world-historical importance won so much by a single man as was this victory by Lenin. It is the intrigue, corruption and stupidity of fellow-workers in the cause which destroys revolutionary will, and not the repression of the bourgeoisie. Lenin, one of the strongest of men, nearly gave up in 1904, and contemplated going to America to study statistics. The fit of discouragement passed and he remained.[1]

In the second week of the following year, on January 9, Tsarism in defence of law and order shot down thousands of petitioners going to lay their grievances before their ruler. The great masses learnt from Tsarist bullets what the revolutionaries had been preaching for years. The whole Social Democratic Party recognised that the insurrection, the first stage of the revolution, was on the order of the day, but when Lenin, for the Bolsheviks, issued the call for the organisational preparation and the arming of the people, the Menshevik leaders accused him of adventurism, of trying to overthrow the Government by conspiracy, of Blanquism. Did they admit that the revolution was on the way? They did. What then was to be done? Why not call upon the workers to prepare? No. Instead Martinov, one of their leaders, said that the revolution should be "unleashed" not "organised," that instead of seeking to arm the workers, they should be filled with "a burning desire" to arm. Behind these differences in phrasing were different conceptions of the coming revolution which would make all the difference between a possible success and a certain failure. Like their brothers of the Second International to-day, the Mensheviks trembled at the prospect of the armed workers.

In the middle of 1905, under the influence of the coming revolution, the groups held separate conferences, and with the Menshevik resolutions before him Lenin realised clearly for the first time that there was more between Bolsheviks and Mensheviks than the organisational question. "Theoretical differences have grown." The Mensheviks had watered down the whole revolutionary analysis of the insurrection "lest the bourgeoisie desert." Whatever their internationalism in phrase the Mensheviks were looking to their

[1] Souvarine, Stalin's French biographer, says categorically: No Lenin, no Bolshevism. The writer subscribes entirely to that dictum. Those who would oppose this designedly sharp formulation have to produce some evidence in contemporary leaders of Lenin's peculiar quality—that combination of theory and organisation which was Bolshevism. It has not been seen on any scale in Europe since.

own bourgeoisie for help in the revolution. Lenin was looking to the Russian proletariat and beyond them to the proletarian revolution in Europe. It is this belief in the international proletariat which so sharply distinguished Marx and Engels, Lenin and Trotsky, from other leaders of the working-class movement. That is the eternal struggle in the Labour movement, in 1905 against Tsarism, in 1914, in 1935 on behalf of Abyssinia, in 1936 on behalf of Spanish workers and peasants, either to be with and therefore subordinate to your own bourgeoisie, or to be with the international proletariat. It is a struggle which will go on until international Socialism is achieved. Men like Citrine, Bevin and Léon Blum have a contempt for the proletarian movement far greater than many capitalists have. And Stalin has joined them. Stalin to-day is the complete Menshevik, seeking to save Soviet Russia with the help of the French, British and Czechoslovakian bourgeoisie. Trotsky maintains the Leninist position. The new ideological conflict is only another variant of the old.

LENIN'S DEMOCRATIC DICTATORSHIP OF THE PROLETARIAT AND THE PEASANTRY

In those early days of the 1905 revolution there were three views of the coming upheaval, the Bolshevik view of Lenin (for those close to Lenin had no views apart from his own or if they had soon dropped them), the Menshevik view, and Trotsky's theory of the Permanent Revolution.

It was in the shock of the first events of the revolution that Trotsky produced his theory. It was opposed in essentials by Lenin, adopted by him in April, 1917, at a most critical moment in the history of the third revolution, and formed the theoretical foundation of the Soviet Union and the Third International until a few months after the death of Lenin in 1924. Both Lenin and Trotsky, like Marx and Engels in their instructions to the German revolutionaries of 1850, based their analysis on a scrupulous examination of the Russian problem in its relation to the international Socialist revolution.

Peasant Russia in 1905 was a country with some hundred million peasants in the countryside, living under semifeudal conditions. The great landlords who dominated the countryside formed the natural support of the reactionary Tsarist autocracy. In France in 1789 the peasant revolt was successful because the bourgeoisie was also hostile to the existing régime. The French bourgeoisie using (however reluctantly) the leverage of the peasantry to destroy feudalism and create the conditions for the expansion of Capitalist production, give the classical example of the bourgeois-democratic revolution. Such a revolution seemed to be facing Russia at the beginning of the twentieth century. But the Russia of 1905 was vastly dissimilar to the France of 1789.

The more to the East they are, the more treacherous and cowardly are the bourgeoisie. This is a famous Marxist aphorism. With the discovery of America the bourgeoisie of the sea-board countries of Europe so dominated the economy of the State that they were the natural leaders of peasants and people against feudal reaction. In Russia, however, owing to the Tartar invasions which cut off the Eastern trade and ruined the industrial towns, and on the other hand to the long start of Western European industry whose goods flooded Russia and impeded native production, the bourgeoisie remained always helpless before Tsarism. Just as Spanish feudalism used the gold of America to strengthen its position against the Spanish bourgeoisie and ruin the future of the country, so Russian autocracy was able to use the means of repression developed in Western Europe, and later, Western capital, in order to retain its position and thus retard the industrial development of Russia. For the big bourgeoisie of Western Europe, while prating of democracy, quite shamelessly supported Tsarism against the bourgeoisie and lent it money, because State loans were more dependable in their short-sighted view than any other. To this age-old historical weakness of the Russian bourgeoisie was added the rapid development of the Labour movement in the last years of the nineteenth century, so that whereas the peasantry of France and the masses in Paris and the other big towns of France marched against feudalism full of confidence in their bourgeoisie, and could always find some section of the bourgeoisie to lead them when one section

56

deserted, the industrial workers in the Russian towns long before the revolution were already in bitter conflict with their own bourgeoisie, the insoluble conflict of capital and labour.

Lenin, therefore, saw that the Russian bourgeoisie might talk of overthrowing Tsarism (as Liberals will talk of overthrowing Fascism). But as soon as the Liberals saw the workmen in the streets they would see not only the enemies of Tsarism, but their own enemies, and would of necessity rush to compromise with the reaction. Neither could they lead the peasantry. For the bourgeoisie in Russia were dependent, as the industrial bourgeoisie everywhere, upon the banks to which the landlords were heavily indebted. The bourgeoisie could not give the peasants the land without ruining the bourgeois banks. The proletariat therefore would have to lead the peasantry and the petty-bourgeoisie against Tsarism, and accomplish the bourgeois revolution over the heads of the bourgeoisie. Hence the Bolshevik slogans—the eight-hour working day for the proletariat, the confiscation of land for the peasants, and the democratic republic.

This plan of linking the proletarian revolution with the agrarian was, as with so much in the history of the Russian Revolution, Lenin's own; and as with so many of Lenin's ideas, he was developing a thought of Marx during the revolutionary period of 1848–1850, when he suggested that the task in Germany was to link the struggle of the German proletariat with the desire of the serfs to free themselves. In all this Trotsky followed Lenin.

The question on which they split was: what form would the State-power take which would carry through this revolution, and what would happen afterwards? All revolutionaries, indeed all students of history except Social Democrats, know that the transition from one social régime to another is made by a stern dictatorship, which violently destroys the basis of the old order and clears the way for the new. Cromwell's dictatorship had been a dictatorship of the petty-bourgeoisie; Robespierre's dictatorship had been the same. Marx had therefore labelled the dictatorship which would accomplish the transition from Capitalism to Socialism the dictatorship of the proletariat.

57

But for Lenin, as for Trotsky and all the great European Socialists of the time, Socialism for backward Russia was an absurdity. The proletariat could lead the nation against Tsarism and destroy it. But in Russia, overwhelmingly an agrarian country, the productive forces were too backward, the proletariat, the new class which would create Socialism, was too weak in relation to the rest of the country to begin the task of transforming Russian Capitalist society into Socialist with any real prospect of success. Therefore, for Lenin, the dictatorship of the proletariat in the familiar Marxian sense was out of the question. The dictatorship of the proletariat was a Government that would destroy the bourgeois State and maintain power until the abolition of every vestige of Capitalism. But the Russian proletariat had to abolish feudalism and institute a democratic republic. The dictatorship he foresaw was, therefore, a democratic dictatorship. But though the proletariat was to lead, the driving force of the revolution was to come from the peasantry, and the proletariat would have to share the political power with a party representing the peasantry. Hence his final formula of the democratic dictatorship of the proletariat and the peasantry. The relationship between proletarian party and peasant party in this revolutionary Government he did not know, and according to the period at which he was writing he gave a different content to the formula. The Social Revolutionaries, the party which worked among the peasantry and claimed to represent its interests, were an unknown factor. He at one time even considered that it might have such support from the peasantry as would enable it to dominate the proletarian party. Lenin did not know. The most cautious of men, he put forward his formula and observed events to see how things would work out in practice. Whatever form this revolutionary Government took, its work was to give the land to the peasants, clear away Tsarism, crush the reaction, and call a constituent assembly to elect a democratic parliament. He knew the elementary truth, that the nature of the constituent assembly and the coming democratic constitution of Russia depended on the class nature of the revolutionary dictatorship which summoned the assembly and laid down the conditions of election and suffrage. His intention was to drive the democratic constitution as far forward as possible.

His further perspective was a great development of Russian Capitalism under a democratic Russia.[1] It was the revolutionary proletariat of Russia leading the peasantry that would give the craven Liberal bourgeoisie its chance at last. In this republic the proletarian party would for a period occupy the same position that the Communist parties in Western Europe to-day occupied up to 1935, fighting for the Socialist revolution. But the revolution did not end there. The peasantry as a whole would have supported the revolution at the beginning, but as the revolution drove forward, the richer peasants would detach themselves and join with the reaction. The democratic revolution, left to itself, would then most certainly be defeated. Lenin was as clear on this as he was on any point.[2] But the proletariat and the poorer peasantry in Russia had an ally—the proletariat of Europe. He calculated that the first few years of a revolution in Russia led by the proletariat would unloose tremendous upheavals in the shaky structure of European Capitalism. He counted on a Socialist revolution in Western Europe, and stated over and over again that, unless there were such revolutions, even the democratic republic of Russia would collapse. With Socialist revolutions in Europe, however, the Russian proletariat, further strengthened by the Capitalist development in Russia, would be able to achieve the second revolution in Russia—the Russian Socialist revolution. This would institute the dictatorship of the proletariat and set out on the building of Socialism.

TROTSKY'S PERMANENT REVOLUTION

Up to 1904 Trotsky had a similar perspective. Then in 1905 he changed and waged irreconcilable polemic with the Bolsheviks against Lenin's formula of the democratic dictatorship of the proletariat and the peasantry, leading to a bourgeois régime. According to Trotsky's new theory

[1] See for example his *Two Tactics*, which contains a dozen references to this future Capitalist development of Russia after the revolution.
[2] See p. 64.

the Russian proletariat would lead the revolution from the start, but the revolutionary Government would result in the dictatorship of the proletariat and the road to Socialism, or it would collapse. The peasants could not form an effective political party of their own. The moment the proletariat held the power, the proletarian Government would be faced with the opposition of the capitalists. These would immediately decide upon the lock-out because, there being no Socialism, their property was still capitalist property. The proletarian Government, faced with un-employment and the disorganisation of economy, would have no alternative but to take over the factories and run them themselves for the benefit of the workers. This was the Socialist road, and once begun the process could not stop. The proletariat would have to hold the power. The peasantry would support the revolution until the confiscation of the land. But after that, every socialistic step that the proletariat would be compelled to take would send the richer peasantry into the arms of the reaction, so that these allies of the proletariat to-day would be its enemies of to-morrow. So backward Russia was ready for Socialism! Both Bolsheviks and Mensheviks derided him. No. He saw the salvation of the premature dictatorship of the Russian pro-letariat in the Socialist revolution in Europe, which would place the State-power in the hands of the proletariat of one or more of the advanced countries such as Germany, England or France. Like Lenin, his analysis of European Capitalism led him to the belief that the revolution in Russia would serve as a detonator for the revolution in Western Europe. Without that revolution the Russian proletariat was doomed and the reaction would conquer. He did not ask for the slogan of the dictatorship of the proletariat to be raised forthwith. The struggle would begin as a struggle for a bourgeois-demo-cratic revolution, but the logic of the situation in Russia would lead inevitably to the proletariat establishing its own dictatorship and beginning the Socialist reconstruction of Russian economy. So that the revolution was permanent in three ways. First, in the way that what was apparently a revolution for the rights of bourgeois democracy would grow inevitably into the dictatorship of the proletariat.

Secondly, the way in which the dictatorship of the proletariat would be compelled to begin the long transformation of Russian Capitalism into Socialism. Thirdly, the way in which the Russian revolution would lead to proletarian revolution in Europe and the permanent economic revolution in Capitalist society. We shall understand and appreciate the range and profundity of these analyses when we remember that for both this was a perspective covering decades. The Russian Revolution would last years.

The Mensheviks produced a special theory of their own. Marx had said that a new social order appeared only when the old is exhausted. Obviously Capitalism in Russia still had a large capacity for expansion. Therefore they agreed with Lenin that the revolution was a bourgeois revolution, and agreed with him and Trotsky that Russia was not ripe for Socialism. But like the Russian bourgeoisie they saw Russian Capitalism in isolation. They would not see what Marx and Engels had always seen, that Capitalist production was international and therefore was always to be seen as a whole. For these nationalists, therefore, the only ally of the Russian proletariat was the Russian bourgeoisie. Nothing was to be done to frighten it. The workers were not to arm themselves too soon. Instead they should be stimulated with "burning desire." The revolution would be "spontaneously" accomplished somehow. The Social Democratic Party was to take no part in the provisional revolutionary government—this was to be left to the bourgeoisie. The workers' party would supply vigilant criticism. Thus, even when hounded down by tyranny, imprisoned, tortured and executed, driven by the knout of Tsarism to admit the necessity of revolution, with the workers of their own accord challenging the Government in the streets, the Mensheviks, first in theory and afterwards, as we shall see, in practice, had no perspective beyond supporting the Liberal bourgeoisie. They would "urge" the Liberals, they would "bring pressure to bear" on them.

After 1903, as soon as Trotsky realised where the Mensheviks were tending, he disentangled himself from them. But separated from Lenin first by the organisational question and then by his opposition to Lenin's democratic dictatorship of the proletariat and the party, he remained outside both groups. It was one of the fundamental weaknesses of Trotsky as a revolutionary leader that he could produce this masterly theory of the Permanent Revolution, driving ahead so far beyond Lenin, and yet at the same time advocated organisational fusion with the Mensheviks.

Lenin was consumed with rage at the programme which the Mensheviks put before the revolutionary workers. "The revolutionary mood of the proletariat is growing daily and hourly. At such a moment Martinov's views are not only absurd, they are criminal." He proposed that more workers should be brought into the local committees which controlled various sections of the movement. In 1903 his rigid restriction of the party membership was aimed at keeping out the bourgeois intellectuals. Now in 1905 he closed the net against them still tighter. They did not understand discipline, and he knew that the Menshevik ideas which would assuredly lead the revolution to ruinous defeat came from above—from the Liberal bourgeoisie.

LENINISM: THE INTERNATIONAL BASIS

So often to many even of his closest followers did Lenin's ideas at their first utterance seem the product of a disordered brain, so logically on the other hand did they follow from his Marxist outlook, that it is imperative and convenient here to give some example of how he thought. Without this his theorising about Russian revolution and world revolution (and Trotsky's theory of the Permanent Revolution) must seem to be mere raving. A quite casual article, written in 1908 after the failure of the 1905 revolution, will show us how different from those of the bourgeois and the Second Internationalists was his view of politics. He entitles his article "Inflammable Material in World Politics,"[1] but he is really writing about the second Russian Revolution which for him is "inevitable."

"The revolutionary movement in the various states of Europe and Asia has manifested itself so formidably of late that we can discern quite clearly the outlines of a new

[1] P. 297. *Selected Works*, Vol. iv, Martin Lawrence.

and incomparably higher stage in the international struggle of the proletariat."

He begins with Persia. It is nothing unexpected that the Tsar had helped the barbarous rulers of Persia to crush a revolution, but he notes as a phenomenon that the Liberal English bourgeois, irritated by the growth of the Labour movement at home, and frightened by the rise of the revolutionary struggle in India, are more and more frequently revealing how brutal the most civilised European "statesmen" can be in defence of Capitalism. In Turkey the young Turk movement has won only half a victory, but such a half-victory involving concessions given by the old Government under pressure are the direct pledges of new, far more decisive, and acute vicissitudes of civil war, involving broader masses of the people. Civil war includes "inevitably" the victories of the counter-revolution with its debaucheries of enraged reactionaries, and savage punishments meted out by old Governments to rebels. But only down-right pedants and decrepit mummies can grieve over the fact that the nations have entered the painful school of revolution in which the oppressed learn how to conduct a victorious civil war.

There is no end to the violence and plunder which is called British rule in India. Lenin details the oppression and the tyranny, but notes that the Indian masses are beginning to come out into the streets in defence of their native writers and political leaders. "The Indian proletariat too has already matured sufficiently to wage a class conscious and political mass-struggle—and that being the case Anglo-Russian methods in India are played out." Further plunder and terrorism will only harden millions and tens of millions of proletarians in Asia. "The class conscious workers of Europe now have Asiatic comrades and their number will grow by leaps and bounds." There is little information from China, but the transformation of the old Chinese riots into a conscious democratic movement is inevitable. In France, and even in America and England "where there is complete political liberty," and revolutionary and Socialist traditions are lacking, the growth of Socialism and the independent proletarian struggle are plainly

63

visible.[1] "Two hostile camps are slowly but surely increasing their forces, are strengthening their organisations and are separating with increasing sharpness in all fields of public life, as if silently and intently preparing for the impending revolutionary battles." In France and Italy the conflict has reached sudden outbursts of civil war. The international revolutionary movement of the proletariat does not proceed and cannot proceed evenly and in the same form in different countries. The thorough and all-sided utilisation of all possibilities in all spheres of activity comes only as a result of the class-struggle of the workers of various countries. Every individual country has its own weaknesses, theoretical or practical; every country has its own distinctive traits to contribute. But international Socialism has made an enormous stride forward, and in a number of concrete encounters the millions of proletarians are welding themselves together for the decisive struggle against the bourgeoisie—a struggle for which the working-class is immeasurably better prepared than at the time of the Paris Commune, the last great struggle of the proletariat.

It is in relation to this background that he places the "inevitable" second Russian revolution. This "stride forward by the whole of international Socialism together with the sharpening of the revolutionary democratic struggle in Asia, places the Russian revolution in a peculiar and particularly difficult position." The Russian revolution possesses a great international ally both in Europe and in Asia, but "*just because of this*" it possesses "not only a national, not only a Russian, but also an *international* enemy." Reaction against the growing struggle of the proletariat is inevitable in all Capitalist countries, and this reaction unites bourgeois governments of the whole world against any revolution, in Asia and especially in Europe. The opportunists, the Mensheviks, like the Russian intelligentsia, were dreaming of a revolution which would not "scare" the bourgeoisie. "Vain hopes! A philistine Utopia!" Inflammable material is accumulating in the progressive countries, and awakening so rapidly the countries in Asia which yesterday were fast asleep, that the struggle of inter-

[1] The great strikes that preceded the War were still to come.

national bourgeois reaction against each individual national revolution is absolutely inevitable. The Russian proletariat must therefore follow its own path independently and assist the peasantry to destroy feudal reaction; "it must set itself the task of establishing the democratic dictatorship of the proletariat and the peasantry in Russia and bear in mind that its struggle and its victories are indissolubly bound up with the international revolutionary movement. Fewer illusions concerning the liberalism of the counter-revolutionary bourgeoisie (in Russia and the entire world); more attention to the growth of the international revolutionary proletariat!"

That was Lenin. He saw society internationally, not nationally; horizontally, not vertically. In the unruffled confidence of this luminous survey we see into the basic structure of his thought. He could no more wrench the Russian Revolution (or for that matter any other revolution) from its international background than he could wrench the heart out of his body. "Fewer illusions concerning the liberation of the counter-revolutionary bourgeoisie (in Russia and the entire world); more attention to the growth of the international revolutionary proletariat." Who but Lenin, Trotsky and a few others were thinking of the international proletariat as a force in 1908? The war accelerated, it did not create. The international proletariat, despite Fascist victories over so many countries in Europe, is still a powerful force to-day; it could have been used on behalf of Abyssinia, on behalf of Spain, if the will and the means existed to set it in motion. Lenin would have made a pact with France, but never at the cost of the French proletariat. Having to choose, he would have chosen the proletariat. Stalin, his successor, has been congenitally unable to think in this way. Whenever faced with a choice between proletariat and bourgeoisie, he and the bureaucracy whom he represents have always chosen the bourgeoisie, and always paid heavily for that choice.

1905 AND AFTER

The 1905 Revolution failed. But the whole course of the revolution served only to strengthen Lenin's belief in his ideas. A general strike in 1903 had indicated that this was the initial form the revolution would take. The October strike of 1905 began in Moscow, and in a few days had stopped the whole life of the country. Trotsky and one of his collaborators in the theory of the Permanent Revolution took over a small paper, the *Russian Gazette*. In a few days the circulation went from 30,000 to 100,000. Inside a month it was at half a million. To Witte, the Tsarist bureaucrat, the whole people seemed to have gone mad. For Lenin, 1905 was only another proof of the terrific driving power and creative capacity of the masses during a revolution. On the initiative of the Mensheviks the workers formed their Soviets or factory councils, one delegate to every five hundred workers, and Trotsky, the acknowledged leader of 1905, as far as there was one, in time became president of the Petersburg Soviet. Lenin reached Russia late, and as always without him his party blundered. The workers, irrespective of party, rushed to join and support the Soviets. But the Bolshevik leaders, misunderstanding Lenin's insistence on the organisational integrity of the party, wanted to keep the Bolsheviks away from the Soviet as a non-party organisation. It was only after Lenin arrived that the Bolsheviks entered these mass organisations of the workers to influence them. In the onward sweep of the revolution Bolshevik and Menshevik workers insisted that the two fractions should work together. The Menshevik leaders exercised little influence, and Trotsky's policy at the Soviet coincided so closely with Lenin's that the two groups for a time worked harmoniously. When Tsarism, in an attempt to split the anti-Tsarist [1] forces, offered a travesty of a constitution, it was at once gladly accepted by the Liberals. The Mensheviks were ready to trot docilely behind, but the masses of the workers followed the Bolsheviks always. With the defeat of the revolution, however, and the decline of the movement the differences again became acute. At a unity congress in 1907 the Mensheviks had a majority of sixty-two to forty-nine. They raised the cry that the revolt should not have taken place. Lenin ordered a change of tactics from the organi-

[1] To-day read "anti-Fascist."

sation of revolution to ordinary hum-drum everyday constitutional activity. But he poured scorn on the impertinent thesis that the great mass uprising of the Russian people against Tsarism "should not have taken place."

In the international field the revolution showed that the analyses of both Lenin and Trotsky were fundamentally correct. The Russian Revolution, failure though it was, stirred the sleepy Second International; it gave universal suffrage to Austria; it was felt in the Liberal elections of 1906. In those days when revolution at home was, in their opinion, impossible, the Second Internationalists had no objection to revolutions elsewhere. Even Ramsay Mac-Donald was pro-Bolshevik in those days, and insisted that some money for the Russian revolutionaries should be used for active revolution and not for propaganda.[1]

Confident of a second uprising, Lenin called for and set the example of a close study of the revolution to see why it failed, in order to guarantee success next time. The period of the reaction saw a great development of Russian capitalism, and the strengthening of the liberal bourgeoisie. Their influence on the Mensheviks increased. They subsidised the Menshevik papers. A large body of Mensheviks, the Liquidators, sought to liquidate the illegal organisation and the preparation for a new revolution in Russia. They were expelled from the party. Trotsky, still outside both groups, fought for unity, making his last attempt in August, 1912. But Lenin, though anxious for unity, was adamant on his principles, and this time the split was final. The movement began to rise again in 1912, and with its rise it was clear that the majority of the Petersburg workers were following the Bolsheviks. Despite his untiring abuse of Trotsky for seeking unity, Lenin always knew the calibre of the man, and as the movement rose again asked him to write for his paper. Trotsky refused. He edited a paper of his own, and in addition to polemics with Lenin made one important contribution to Marxist theory. In his studies of economics, he discovered that after the failure of a revolution and the demoralisation of the masses, a period

[1] *Lenin on Britain*, Martin Lawrence, p. 109.

of prosperity was needed to strengthen the masses and make them take up the struggle again. As prosperity increased, the masses on the basis of increased wages, successful strikes, etc., grew stronger and more militant. Another economic crisis would then precipitate the new revolution. The theory was to prove its value in the post-war years.

The revolutionary movement gathered strength. In July, 1914, there were barricades in Petersburg. The war dammed the revolution for a time, only to give it greater force three years later. August, 1914, found Bolsheviks and Mensheviks still split, each section claiming to represent the Russian Social Democracy at the Second International. The Bolsheviks had kept alive the theories and practice of Marxism. Thus it happened that when they were needed the European Labour movement did not have to search painfully for them.

Chapter 3

THE WAR AND THE RUSSIAN REVOLUTION

Engels Foretells the Third International

Before the Franco-Prussian War was over Marx had written that a war between France and Germany meant of necessity war between Germany and Russia, unless previously a revolution broke out in Russia. "If they take Alsace-Lorraine, then France with Russia will arm against Germany. It is superfluous to point out the disastrous consequences."

Engels by 1895 could trace the full consequences of this division of Europe, intensified by the development of Capitalism, the ensuing scramble for domination of the continent, which spread, when Europe became too small, to Asia and Africa. It would be a war, he foretold, of positions and varied success on the French frontier, attack and capture of Polish frontiers on the Russian border, and a revolution in Petersburg "which will at once make the gentlemen who are conducting the war see everything in an entirely different light." Between fifteen and twenty million armed men would slaughter one another and lay waste Europe as never before, and this would lead either to the immediate victory of Socialism or leave behind such a heap of ruins that the old Capitalist society would become more impossible than ever before. Socialism might be set back for ten or fifteen years, but would then conquer in a more speedy and thorough fashion. But much as he hoped otherwise, Engels had at last realised the full corruption of the German Social Democracy. A European war would smash it to pieces, and throw back the movement twenty years. But the new party that must inevitably arise in the end from these

69

conditions would in all the countries of Europe be free
from a host of vacillations and pettinesses "which to-day
hem in our movement on every side." Not in Germany
alone but "in all the countries of Europe." It was the
Third International.

Between 1897 and 1912 the Second International at
conference after conference passed resolutions calling for
international action of the working-class against war. A
special conference was called at Basle in 1912 to prepare
for the imminent war danger. All words, and words only.
On August 4th, 1914, the Second International split into
its component parts, each section of the belligerent nations
going with its own bourgeoisie, except the Russian party
(Bolsheviks and a wing of the Mensheviks) and some small
parties in the Balkan countries.

LENIN CALLS FOR THE THIRD INTERNATIONAL
IN SEPTEMBER, 1914

Lenin was in Galicia in August, 1914. He was arrested
on August 8, and released on August 19, as an enemy of
Tsarism. On the 28th he left for Switzerland, reached
Berne on September 5 and on that very day wrote his
first article on the ideological and political collapse of the
old international and the necessity for the new. It is these
things that distinguish the great Marxist from all the
peddling Social Democrats and the blundering Third International of to-day.

The future international, he said, must "realistically and
irrevocably" free itself of the "bourgeois trend in socialism,"
by which he meant collaboration with the national bourgeoisie, instead of reliance on the international proletariat.
By October he was full of confidence. "The proletarian
international has not perished, and will not perish. The
working masses will overcome all obstacles and create a
new International . . . long live a proletarian International
free from opportunism." And later in the same month,
"the Second International has died . . . long live the Third
International."

From that time on he devoted himself to preparing its
theoretical foundation. Look through his works between

70

September, 1914, and March, 1917. Though he was still almost entirely responsible for the direction of his party, his writings on the international situation and in what way the new International must differ from the old overshadow his writings on Russia. He brushes aside the responsibility of individuals and, ranging over the whole Socialist movement in Europe, traces the social basis of the bourgeois trend in Socialism, or as he called it opportunism. He seeks to split the true internationalists from those who have destroyed the international working-class movement by following their own bourgeoisie. He explains that by the collapse of the Second International he means its collapse as a revolutionary force. He appeals for a programme which will call on the workers to build a Marxian international openly and without the opportunists: "Only such a programme showing that we believe in ourselves, that we believe in Marxism, that we declare a life and death struggle against opportunism, would sooner or later secure for us the sympathy of the real proletarian masses." Never was any doctrinaire leader better served by the teeming heterogeneous millions of every country, and he won their support because he believed in them. He could not have got it otherwise.

When the International would be formed neither he nor any one else could say. It was a revolutionary duty to work for it, and the first necessity was a clear programme which would not compromise on a single aspect of Marxian Socialism.

The immediate issue was, however, the war. He formulated his policy without hesitation or equivocation. Startling as it appeared at first, it flowed inevitably from his political background. The workers had no business fighting each other. The enemy was in your own country. Peace, but peace by revolution, by fighting the class-war against your own bourgeoisie, by turning the imperialist war into civil war.[1] The war was not for democracy or any such impudent deception, fit only for Liberals and Social Democrats.

[1] No Lenin, no Bolshevism. What record is there of leading Bolsheviks who adopted this position? Trotsky did not, and opposed Lenin's policy fiercely. Stalin has the lid clamped down on any views he may have expressed. Rakovsky opposed Lenin. Doubtless they were all "against the war," as millions of people are to-day.

Was Tsarist Russia fighting for democracy? It was a war for the redivision of colonies and spheres of influence. Any imperialist peace would therefore be a mockery. To lead the masses to expect a democratic peace, without annexations and with self-determination for nations, was bourgeois lying or petty-bourgeois ignorance and stupidity. Peace, but peace by revolution. The slogan of peace without the call for revolution was a preacher's slogan. When the revolution would come no one could say. Cautious as ever, he said that it might be during this first imperialist war or during the one which would certainly follow it. The task was to work to that end. To refuse to enter the army was a rejection of the struggle. When there was no revolutionary situation and you were given a ballot box— take it. To-morrow when you were given a rifle, it was your business to take this weapon of death and destruction. "Do not turn to the sentimental whiners who are afraid of war. Much has been left in the world that *must* be destroyed by fire and iron for the liberation of the working-class. When the revolutionary situation was at hand these useful weapons were to be used against your own government and your own bourgeoisie." To the objection that the masses were not ready for these ideas he replied with his old conception of the difference between the working-class party and the working-class: "the slogans of the class-conscious vanguard of the workers (revolutionary Socialist democracy) are one thing and the elemental demands of the masses quite another," and, another profound revolutionary maxim: "It is never too early to tell the proletariat the truth about its own condition." History would bring the masses. Meanwhile he sought to unite all who remained true to Marxism to lay the foundations of the new revolutionary international. Without it the unity and cohesion of the working-class struggle against Capitalism was impossible. Not that he sought the universal overthrow of each national Capitalism at the same time. The uneven development of Capitalism, the peculiarities of the class-struggle in each individual country, would bring the conflict to a decisive issue sooner in certain countries than in others. Each national party would have to lead the struggle against its own bourgeoisie. But the national party must be built on the international Marxist foundation, so that the growth of the national party meant the growth of the International.

LENINISM: THE TACTICAL APPROACH TO SYMPATHISERS

But having stated his principles and his programme so that the simplest-minded worker, whether he accepted or rejected them, would at least have no doubts as to their meaning, Lenin set out to seek allies, "however vacillating, however temporary," for his views. And in his approach to those elements in the Second International who were moving, however slowly, to his own position and the position of his party, he showed yet another side of Leninism, its flexibility of tactic without which its programmatical rigidity would have doomed it to a dangerous and perhaps fatal sterility. The Second International, as we have seen, had not been homogeneous in its adherence to its own bourgeoisie. But even in those national organisations which had shepherded the workers to the slaughter, opposition had early shown itself. It ranged from those very close to revolutionary internationalism on the left to pacifists who abjured violence of any sort; behind the banner of anti-war a motley crowd will always march. As the full horror of the war unfolded itself, these began to seek some concrete means of checking the murderous savagery that was being enacted all over the world in the name of civilization.

In January, 1915, a conference of women Socialists met at Berne. Lenin sent his wife and some others to represent the Bolshevik Party. The conference rejected the revolutionary programme of the Bolshevik women (which Lenin had, of course, written) and passed a "miserable pacifist" resolution. Lenin's delegation refused to sign it and withdrew. In September, 1915, came the conference of anti-war Socialists at Zimmerwald, which Lenin attended at the head of the Bolshevik delegation. His resolution condemning the Second International and calling for peace by revolution and civil war was rejected by nineteen votes to twelve, and the Bolshevik delegation signed a compromise resolution.[1] In his paper Lenin openly faced the doubts

[1] It was written by Trotsky.

73

as to whether the Central Committee was right in signing this manifesto, suffering as it did from "lack of consistency and from timidity." He put the case to the Russian workmen that it was. At the conference the Bolsheviks did not hide one iota of their views, slogans nor tactics. Their writings were distributed. "We have broadcasted, are broadcasting and shall broadcast our views with no less energy than our manifesto." After all, the manifesto, with all its shortcomings, was a step forward. "It would be sectarianism to refuse to take this step together with the minority of the German, French, Swedish, Norwegian and Swiss Socialists, when we retain full freedom and a full possibility to intrigue unceasingly and to struggle for more. . . ."

That was the Leninist method; an inflexible rigidity in theory and organisation, but a willingness to combine for specific purposes with any other group once his independence for action and criticism was not tied. Trotsky and Rosa Luxemburg had early called for the new international, but Trotsky refused to accept Lenin's uncompromising demand that each Socialist should fight for the defeat of his own country. He still sought to bring together the various fractions of the party. He talked about peace without annexations. He maintained his theory of the Permanent Revolution. On all these points, particularly the first three, Lenin was violent in his denunciation of Trotsky. Yet he again asked Trotsky to write for his paper. Trotsky again refused.

The Second Internationalists, now violently pro-war, excelled the Capitalists in patriotic wrath against Zimmerwald, but events were steadily flogging waverers towards Lenin's position. In April, 1916, there was another conference at Kienthal. The cruelty and rapacity of the imperialist statesmen were now plain to all who wanted to see, and the Kienthal conference passed a resolution which stated that Socialism was the only way out. It called upon the proletariat to fight, but though it criticised strongly the jingoists of the Second International it hesitated to break with them. Though the conference condemned bourgeois pacifism, it shirked the simple call, "Turn the imperialist war into civil war." But the revolutionary left, under the leadership of Lenin, convinced of the necessity of a break and the formation of a new International, had consolidated itself. The rest was now merely a matter of time. Then suddenly the steady left-ward tendency in the international working-class movement exploded in the Russian revolution. Lenin's tactics at once changed. When he had been in Russia a few weeks, and seven months before October, the Zimmerwaldists proposed another conference. Lenin refused to have anything to do with them, and was in a minority of one in his own party for so doing. As the Bolsheviks without Lenin had failed to understand the necessity of immediately working in the Soviets in 1905, so now they failed to understand that the revolution in Russia had made it necessary to break with the vacillating Zimmerwaldists, that from the higher plane of the Russian Revolution the Bolshevik Party was now dominant, and if it could lead the Russian workers to victory would be able to impose its own terms for the fight against war. His followers did not understand his method then. They do not understand it yet.

In January, 1917, Lenin delivered a lecture on the 1905 revolution to an audience of young Swiss workers. He concluded with what is perhaps the most representative passage in his writings during the war. In it we see the range of his conceptions, the caution and precision with which he expressed them, his passionate convictions and his almost inhuman impersonality.

"Very often we meet West Europeans who argue about the Russian Revolution as if events, relationships and methods of struggle in that backward country have very little resemblance to West European relationships, and, therefore, can hardly have any practical significance.

"There is nothing more erroneous than such an opinion.

"No doubt the forms and occasions for the impending battles in the coming European revolution will differ in many respects from the forms of the Russian revolution.

"Nevertheless, the Russian revolution—precisely because of its proletarian character—in that particular sense of which I have spoken[1]—was the *prologue* to the coming European revolu-

[1] Only in the sense that the proletariat would lead it. The view that this would lead in Russia to the proletarian revolution with a Socialist content, Lenin at this time was still opposing as one of Trotsky's heresies.

75

tion. Undoubtedly the coming revolution can only be a proletarian revolution in the profounder sense of the word; a proletarian, Socialist revolution also in its content. The coming revolution will show to an even greater degree, on the one hand, that only stern battles, only civil wars, can free humanity from the yoke of capital; on the other hand, that only class-conscious proletarians can and will come forth in the rôle of leaders of the vast majority of the exploited.

"The present grave-like stillness in Europe must not deceive us. Europe is charged with revolution. The monstrous horrors of the imperialist war, the suffering caused by the high cost of living, engender everywhere a revolutionary spirit; and the ruling classes, the bourgeoisie with its servitors, the governments, are more and more moving into a blind alley from which they can never extricate themselves without tremendous upheavals.

"Just as in Russia, in 1905, a popular uprising against the Tsarist government commenced under the leadership of the proletariat with the aim of achieving a democratic republic, so, in Europe, the coming years, precisely because of this predatory war, will lead to popular uprisings under the leadership of the proletariat against the power of finance capital, against the big banks, against the Capitalists; and these upheavals cannot end otherwise than with the expropriation of the bourgeoisie, with the victory of Socialism.

"We of the older generation may not live to see the decisive battles of this coming revolution. But I can, I believe, express the strong hope that the youth which is working so splendidly in the Socialist movement of Switzerland, and of the whole world, will be fortunate enough not only to fight, but also to win, in the coming proletarian revolution."[1]

He was only forty-six at the time and in good health. "We of the older generation may not live to see the decisive battles of this coming revolution." He was never rhetorical. Three months after he heard that Tsarism had been overthrown and he prepared for the international proletarian revolution.

LENIN ABANDONS THE DEMOCRATIC DICTATORSHIP

There is no exaggeration here. Lenin in January had seen that, in case of the collapse of Tsarism, the most probable Government would be a Government of Miliukov, the right-

[1] *Lenin's Selected Works*, Martin Lawrence, vol. iii., pp. 18–19. The quotation exactly expresses his limited conception of the Russian revolution even at this time.

wing Liberal, and Kerensky, that most mischievous type, the left-wing Liberal with a Socialist colouring. When the news actually did reach him that such a Government had been formed, there are his letters to tell us exactly what his ideas were. The very first letter, March 16th, written to A. M. Kollontai, says: "*Never again*[1] along the lines of the Second International. . . . Republican propaganda, war against imperialism, revolutionary propaganda, as heretofore, agitation and struggle for an *international*[1] proletarian revolution and for the conquest of power by the 'Soviets of Workers' deputies. . . .'"

On the next day he hammered again at the two cardinal principles of his life—the independence of the party and the international character of the Socialist revolution: "In my opinion our main task is to guard against getting entangled in foolish attempts at 'unity' with the social-patriots (or what is still more dangerous, with the wavering ones, and the Organisation Committee, Trotsky and Co.) and to continue the work of *our own*[2] party in a consistently *international* spirit."[2] Lenin knew his colleagues, knew how easy was the descent into nationalism.

The international revolution would begin with the inevitable second revolution in Russia. The people had not made a revolution to get rid of Tsarism. They wanted land, bread, peace and freedom. But the Miliukov Government was a bourgeois Government. It could not give the peasants the land because that would ruin the banks on whose stability bourgeois life depended; it could not give peace because it was bound by financial ties to the war-making bourgeoisie of Western Europe; it could not give bread because bread could only be got by revolutionary measures against the landlords and capitalists, and these measures a Government of landlords and capitalists would not take; it could not give freedom because it was a Government of the propertied classes and was afraid of the people.

In his first letter Lenin still speaks of a democratic republic. But his mind travelled fast. On March 20th he had not yet left the democratic dictatorship of the

[1] Italics his own.   [2] Italics his own.

77

proletariat and the peasantry. "Our revolution is a bourgeois revolution, therefore the workers must support the bourgeoisie, say the worthless politicians among the *liquidators*. Our revolution is a bourgeois revolution, say we Marxists, therefore the workers must open the eyes of the people to the deceptive practices of the bourgeois politicians, must teach the people not to believe in words, but to depend wholly on their own strength, on their own organisation, on their own unity, and on their own arms."

But during that night he definitely changed his mind (there were hints in the previous letters). In this third of the *Letters from Afar*, March 21st, he writes: "We need revolutionary power, we need (for a certain period of transition) the *State*.

"We need the State but not the kind needed by the bourgeoisie, with organs of power in the form of police, army bureaucracy, distinct from and opposed to the people. All bourgeois revolutions have merely perfected this government apparatus, have merely transferred it from one party to another." In those few words was the end of his long struggle with Trotsky's Permanent Revolution. If the State was to be merely for a period of transition, then it meant that he had thrown over the conception of a period of bourgeois democracy and the development of Russian Capitalism. The transitional Government, during the period when the development of productive forces would gradually make a State unnecessary, could only be the dictatorship of the proletariat. Why had he changed? It was because he was now confident that the Russian Revolution, coming in the middle of the greatest crisis Capitalism had ever known, would most certainly place the proletariat in power in one or more of the advanced countries of Western Europe. Thus the Russian proletariat, reinforced, would be able not only to capture the power but to hold it. Trotsky in America, whither he had been deported from Europe, writing for a Russian emigré paper, was making identical analyses based on the theory he had so pertinaciously maintained against all comers for twelve years.

78

THE WORKERS GIVE THE POWER TO THE MENSHEVIKS

We shall go in some detail into the course of the Russian Revolution. As Lenin told the delegates to the Second Congress of the International, the great theses which were laid down during those early congresses were but the heritage of Marx and Engels enriched by the revolutionary experiences of the Bolshevik party, particularly in 1905 and 1917.

Under the strain of the imperialist war, Russia, the weakest Capitalist State, had cracked first. As usual the cracks had begun from above. Not only were the Liberal bourgeoisie hostile to the incompetence of Tsarism, but Tsarism, owing to the crisis, was itself split, and one section had murdered Rasputin, the guiding star of the other. But all the ruling classes feared the proletariat of Petersburg, Moscow and the revolutionary towns in the south. The Liberal bourgeoisie were willing to criticise Tsarism but dreaded the consequences of overturning it. Thus they merely made their own overthrow the more certain and complete. In March the workers, led chiefly by unknown Bolsheviks who had been through 1905, had read the Bolshevik daily paper and Lenin's writings, came out into the streets, and with the infallible instinct of masses in revolution set themselves to win over the soldiers. By standing their ground before the charges of the Tsarist police and the Cossacks they showed the revolutionary elements in the army that this was not a demonstration but a struggle for power, which they could join with the hope of ridding themselves of the intolerable burden of the war and the whole system of Tsarist reaction, which pressed more heavily on the soldiers than on the civilian masses. The revolution triumphed and the workers and soldiers, remembering 1905, immediately elected a council of representatives of the factories and of the soldiers—the Soviets. The workers, in gratitude for the help of the army, gave a great number of deputies to the soldiers, and these, politically inexperienced, elected chiefly Mensheviks and Social Revolutionaries, members of that party which had long claimed to represent the interests of the peasants. An Executive Committee consisting chiefly of Mensheviks and Social Revolutionaries was elected.

THE MENSHEVIKS GIVE THE POWER TO THE BOURGEOISIE

The Menshevik view of the place of the bourgeoisie in the Russian Revolution we know. The Social Revolutionaries shared it, Mensheviks and Social Revolutionaries being determined believers in democracy. So that with the proletariat and the soldiers behind them, with the whole force of the Russian people in their hands, the Executive Committee of the Soviet, some of them men who had suffered hard labour under Tsarism and had shown conspicuous personal bravery and courage, could do no better than seek out a committee of the Tsarist Duma and offer the Government to a group of landlords and industrialists, who were quaking with fear at their helplessness before the revolution. All that these democrats asked in return was freedom to make propaganda. By this means they would "urge" the Government and "bring pressure to bear" upon it.

The revolutionary workers, especially those of the Vyborg district, the proletarian centre of Petersburg, were bitterly angry when they heard what had been done. So hostile were the workers to the propertied classes that they refused to allow any member of the Soviet to participate in the Government. Kerensky, from his reputation as a radical lawyer, had been elected a member of the Soviet, but broke Soviet discipline to gain the highest ambition of this kind of politician—a place in a bourgeois Government.

STALIN AND OTHER BOLSHEVIKS FOLLOW THE MENSHEVIKS

All this was astonishing enough. But the history of the Social Democracy since the war shows that this cowardice is organic. What was far more astonishing, and is of enormous significance for the history of the Third International, is that the acknowledged leaders of Lenin's party, men who after his death were to play a dominating part in shaping the policy of the Soviet Union and of the International, took up an almost identical position with the Menshevik Executive Committee. What Lenin meant to Bolshevism, unpalatable as this may be to some Marxists, is proved by the fact that not a single Bolshevik leader, in a party trained to lead the workers, could give the correct lead until Lenin came. Stalin and Kamenev, coming to Petrograd from Siberian prisons, voted for the manifesto which promised the support of the Russian Revolution to the Entente. Misusing Lenin's doctrines of control from the centre, in the manner which had always kept Trotsky hostile to it, they exercised their authority as members of the Central Committee, removed Molotov and Shliapnikov, the editors of *Pravda*, the Bolshevik daily paper, and took over the direction themselves. *Pravda* despite sentimentality and confusion had been vaguely following Lenin's instructions to refuse any support to the Capitalist Provisional Government. The revolution had merely put another Capitalist Government into power; the revolutionary Social Democracy would seek to overthrow it. Stalin and Kamenev therefore did not have the responsibility of finding a policy. It was there already. But they reversed Lenin's policy, and under their direction *Pravda* promised to support the Provisional Government in so far as it carried out the policy of the Executive Committee of the Soviet, composed for the most part of Lenin's lifelong political enemies, who no sooner had the power than they ran to give it to the bourgeoisie. Lenin's years of insistence on the international nature of the revolution, his long struggle against the Mensheviks as being penetrated by bourgeois ideas leading inevitably to nationalism and subservience to the bourgeoisie, all had passed them by. The international proletariat for Stalin then, as to-day, was not a living reality, but a shadowy abstraction. It proves once more that a purely intellectual conviction of international revolution is a rare thing among men, that Lenin was Lenin precisely because of this conviction, and that without him there would not have been in March 1917 that combination of organisation and Marxism which led the Russian workers to victory.

But what is so difficult for intellectuals to understand is the natural instinct of revolutionary workers. In the course of class-struggle against their employers they accumulate such hostility that at moments when the struggle reaches open warfare, the support of their own bourgeoisie is impossible and they turn instinctively to internationalism. It is this instinctive internationalism to which theoretical Marxism must give organisation and direction. To the Menshevism of Stalin and Kamenev the Petersburg workers reacted violently. They demanded the expulsion of Kamenev and Stalin from the party. The committee of the Petrograd Bolsheviks protested to the Bureau of the Central Committee of the party. The former editors were reinstated with the new-comers as associate editors.[1]

Lenin, caged in Geneva, raged furiously at this betrayal. What would have happened if he had never been able to leave there? Despite his political backwardness Stalin, as future events were to show, was, after Lenin, the most powerful personality in the Bolshevik party. He retreated after the rebuff administered by the Petrograd workers; but at the session of March 29 of the party conference Stalin urged support of the Provisional Government. "In so far as the Provisional Government consolidates the advance of the revolution, to that extent we support it; but to the extent that the Provisional Government is counter-revolutionary, support of it is inadmissible." He recommended at that same session support of the Kraskojarsk Resolution, which called for support of the Provisional Government in so far as it carried out the wishes of the people. The revolution was a month old. Stalin and Kamenev were still hankering after the Miliukov Government. Tseretelli, one of the Menshevik leaders of the Soviet, made a proposal of unity to the Bolsheviks. Stalin was in favour. "We ought to accept. It is necessary to make precise proposals as to the lines on which we can unite. Unity is possible along the lines of Zimmerwald-Kienthal." Molotov expressed doubts. Stalin silenced him. For Stalin the gulf which separated Lenin's view of the future development of the revolution and the Menshevik view was of no significance whatever. "There is no need to run to meet or to forestall disagreements. Without disagreements, there is no party life. In the bosom of the

[1] Shliapnikov, *The Year* 1917, Vol. ii, 1925. This whole period is dealt with comprehensively and with the necessary references in No. 46-47, Jan.-Feb., 1933, of *La Lutte de Classes*, the French Trotskyist monthly.

party we shall overcome the minor disagreements."[1] He had then been a member of the party some fifteen years. The fierce implacable Bolshevik, the revolutionary of the school of Lenin, the man of steel, all this is pure myth. Stalin is implacable, but against rivals in the party. From 1917 to the present day, whenever faced with a choice between the international proletariat and the bourgeoisie, the test of the revolutionary leader, he has always chosen the bourgeoisie. Nor was he alone; a majority of the old Bolsheviks was with him. They defended this reversion to Menshevism by sticking to Lenin's old formula of the democratic dictatorship of the proletariat and peasantry. The revolution was a bourgeois-democratic one, and could go no further. Any step beyond would lead to the dictatorship of the proletariat, which was the Permanent Revolution of Trotsky.

The result of this was an immense confusion in the Bolshevik Party. The Mensheviks, at first frightened of Lenin's insistence that the necessity to overturn your own Government still remained, now rejoiced openly at this new commonsense and unexpected moderation in the Bolsheviks. In the more backward provinces Bolsheviks and Mensheviks drew closer together. At the very end of March, as we have seen, at their All-Russian Conference, the Bolsheviks voted for a resolution supporting the Provisional Government.

No Lenin, no Bolshevism

Lenin arriving in Petrograd in early April recognised quite clearly that not only the deputies in the Soviets and the petty-bourgeoisie, but the rank and file of the masses shared the illusions of those whom the revolution had lifted to power. They had to be won for the international Socialist revolution. For the time being it was enough to consolidate his own party. He was confident that he could win the Bolshevik workers of Petrograd and through them bring to heel "those old Bolsheviks who already more than once have played a sad rôle in the history of our party by

[1] March Conference of the Party. Session of April 1, p. 32. See *La Lutte de Classes*, Ibid., p. 31.

stupidly repeating a formula learnt by heart instead of studying afresh the new actual situation." He knew them well. Zinoviev had worked closely with him for years, and from August, 1914, had assisted in all his writings on the War, but he was no sooner in Petrograd than he edged over to Stalin, Kamenev, Kalinin and the others. But as later years were to prove they were no match for Stalin, far less for Lenin. When Lenin put forward his policy, the majority of political Petrograd, from the members of his Central Committee to the British Ambassador, thought him quite literally mad. But in one month the party had adopted his policy. He redrafted the programme, and to emphasize the break with everything Menshevik he proposed to change the name of the party from the Russian Social Democratic Party to the Communist Party of Russia.

LENINISM: THE ART OF INSURRECTION

The revolutionary situation had arrived and he now had his party ready, organised and disciplined, the fruit of his long struggle from 1903. Marxists believe in the predominant rôle of the objective forces of history, and for that very reason are best able to appreciate the progressive or retarding influence of human personality. For the moment it is sufficient to state our belief that without Lenin there would have been no October revolution, and another Tsar might have sat in the Kremlin.

Lenin fought for the slogan, "All power to the Soviet," of which his own party was but 13 per cent. He knew the Mensheviks too well to think that they would ever do anything else except "urge" and "bring pressure to bear" on the Provisional Government. But, if the Bolsheviks knew that, the masses did not know it, and merely to tell them was not sufficient: they would have to see it for themselves. Therefore, "All power to the Soviet," and let the leaders expose themselves. For the time being, "patiently explain, in simple language." Among all the millions of Russia the Bolshevik Party in March was only 25,000 strong;[1] in the Putilov works of 30,000 men, the heart of the Russian Revolution, there were only thirty Bolsheviks. But they

[1] One account says only 12,000.

had at their head a master in the art of insurrection, and the discipline and cohesion of the party he had built up was such that from him through his party to the Russian people radiated all the wisdom and knowledge and insight which he had learnt from his masters and developed in his profound studies of history and of revolution. But the process was not one-sided. From his party, rooted in the factories, the Trade Unions, wherever there were groups of workers, came back to him the moods of the masses and the stages they had reached in understanding the real development of events. In April he proposed a demonstration—to test the feeling and temper of revolutionary Petrograd. It showed him that the moment was not yet. The masses still trusted in the leaders of the Soviet, and the power of the Soviet rested on the masses. He therefore repudiated the very thought of insurrection, for no workers' party could preach insurrection against revolutionary workers. When a working woman helped him on with his coat and said laughingly that, if he were Lenin, she would help to murder him, he pondered long and deeply over this manifestation of working-class feeling. Near the end of April some of the Bolsheviks raised the slogan of "Down with the Provisional Government." Lenin checked them sternly. The masses were not ready yet to take action on such a slogan, and if advanced it might lead to adventurism and the disorganisation of the more advanced workers. And day by day, as he knew it would, the Provisional Government exposed itself and the temper of the people rose. It would not take steps to give the land, it would not stop the war but organised an offensive "in defence of the revolution." The Capitalist Government would not take the drastic measures against Capitalism necessary to feed the population. Instead the capitalists profiteered, prices soared, strikes spread, the capitalists replied with the lock-out and sabotaged whatever feeble measures the Government proposed for the improvement of the situation. Under the pressure of the masses and its incapacity to solve the problems of the day, the Provisional Government began to break, and strengthened itself by bringing in members of the Executive Committee of the

85

Soviet. Thus Kerensky, ready to go on with the war and not prepared to touch property, and therefore acceptable (for the time being) to the bourgeoisie, full of revolutionary phrases and therefore acceptable to the awakening but as yet politically unconscious masses, was of necessity forced to higher and higher power. Another source of confusion for the Provisional Government and the Second Internationalists of the Soviet was the national question. Second Internationalists of all sorts combine an indefatigable capacity for passing resolutions on the self-determination of nations with a readiness to support their own bourgeoisie in keeping in subjection Indians, Egyptians, Africans, Irish, Palestinian Arabs, Chinese and Moors. The self-determination of these Socialists is limited very strictly by the needs of their own Capitalism. Tsarism held in subjection parts of Poland, Finland, Georgia and numerous other subject nationalities. Lenin had maintained as a general principle the rights of all small nations to self-determination, even to the extent of splitting away from the Tsarist empire. The March revolution proclaimed liberty; the subject nationalities interpreted this liberty to mean liberty to govern themselves as they pleased. The Provisional Government, representing Russian Capitalism with powerful interests in all these countries, understood this liberty to be strictly subordinated to the Russian imperialism which had changed its name but not its nature. Between Finland, Georgia, etc., and the Provisional Government violent conflicts arose. The leaders of the Soviet, just like their counterparts in Western Europe, gave national freedom in words but in deeds supported the Government. The Bolsheviks supported the demands of the subject nationalities, fought for them and gained the interest and support of the nationalist masses.

By July the workers and soldiers and sailors, maddened by the continuance of the war that they had made a revolution to stop, and the incapacity of the Government to substantiate the promises of the revolution, marched to the Executive Committee and demanded "Down with the minister Capitalists!" They were ready to seize power that day. Lenin and the Bolsheviks knew that they could hold Petrograd, but that the country as a whole was not yet ripe. Yet the masses were on the streets and ready for action. The party, as a party, must put itself at the head of the demonstration, but only in order to prevent the workers making the mistake of seizing power too soon. There was a serious clash, there was shooting, and the movement swung backwards. "Now they will shoot us down one by one," said Lenin, "This is the right time for them." But decayed classes cannot produce men and parties able to act in such a situation. Yet Kerensky's Government, with Mensheviks and Social Revolutionaries in it, opened an attack on the Bolsheviks. The Bolshevik Press was smashed, Lenin and Zinoviev had to fly for their lives, Trotsky and other leading revolutionaries were put into gaol, and reactionary gangs beat up and murdered Bolsheviks in the streets. For the moment the situation seemed almost hopeless. The Executive Committee was triumphant at the apparent rout of the Bolsheviks. But before he was arrested Trotsky had noticed hopeful signs in the canteen at Smolny, the Soviet headquarters. "The canteen was in charge of a soldier named Grafov. When the baiting of the Bolsheviks was at its worst, when Lenin was declared a German spy and had to hide in a hut, I noticed that Grafov would slip me a hotter glass of tea or a sandwich better than the rest, trying meanwhile not to look at me. He obviously sympathised with the Bolsheviks but had to keep it from his superiors. I began to look about me more attentively. Grafov was not the only one: the whole lower staff of the Smolny—porters, messengers, watchmen—were unmistakably with the Bolsheviks." Lenin and Trotsky had their eyes fastened on the masses; Tseretelli, Dan and Cheidze had theirs fixed on the bourgeoisie. It is the difference between the proletarian revolutionary and the bourgeois intellectual, between Marxism and Revisionism, between the Workers' Front and the Popular Front, between Trotskyism and Stalinism.

Nothing now could change the situation but an insurrection. Lenin, not certain of gaining a majority of Bolsheviks in the Soviet, therefore changed the slogan: "All power to the factory committees." There the influence of the Executive Committee would be less. But at this point counter-revolution appeared. Property, taking advantage of the reaction against the July days and the inevitable confusion of a Government half-Liberal, half-Socialist, was about to make its last desperate effort under the Cossack General Kornilov. Kerensky, bestriding the bourgeoisie and the proletariat like a paper-colossus, intrigued with Kornilov, but the negotiations breaking down at the last minute he turned to the Soviet, and it is here that we have the crowning stroke of Lenin's strategic genius, the classical example of the policy of the United Front.

LENINISM: THE CLASSICAL EXAMPLE OF THE UNITED FRONT

The Executive Committee of the Soviet were represented in the Government which was persecuting his party. Lenin dared not come out of hiding. Yet he called on his party to form joint committees of action with the Menshevik Soviet and fight side by side with them and with Kerensky against the counter-revolution. The letter in which he outlined the tactic shows his capacity for manœuvring without compromising his own position, his care that the masses should understand. In tactical skill as well as world-wide strategy his hand was equally sure.

"*Even now*, we must not support the revolution of Kerensky. It would be a failure of principle. How then, it will be said, must Kornilov not be fought?—Certainly, yes. But between fighting Kornilov and supporting Kerensky there is a difference. . . .

"We wage and shall continue to wage war on Kornilov, but we do not support Kerensky; we unveil his feebleness. There there is a difference. That difference is subtle enough, but most essential, and it must not be forgotten.

"In what, then, does our change of tactics following on the Kornilov rising consist?

"In this: that we modify the form of our struggle against Kerensky. Without diminishing the least bit in the world our hostility, without withdrawing a single one of the words we have pronounced against him, without renouncing our intention to beat him, we declare that consideration must be given to the circumstances of the moment, that we shall not concern ourselves at the present with overthrowing Kerensky, that we shall now conduct the struggle against him in another way by emphasising to the people (and it is the people who are engaged in fighting Kornilov) the *weakness* and *vacillations* of Kerensky. That we were already doing previously. But now it is this which comes to the forefront of our plan of campaign, and therein lies the change.

"Another change: at this moment we place equally in the forefront of our plan of campaign the reinforcing of our agitation for what might be called 'partial demands.' Arrest Miliukov, we say to Kerensky; arm the Petrograd workers; bring the troops from Krondstadt, from Viborg and from Helsingfors to Petrograd; dissolve the Duma; arrest Rodzianko; legalise the handing over of the big estates to the peasants, establish working-class control of cereals and manufactured products, etc. And it is not only to Kerensky that we should put these claims; it is not so much to Kerensky as to the workers, soldiers and peasants who have been carried away by the struggle against Kornilov. They must be carried further, they must be encouraged to demand the arrest of the generals and officers who side with Kornilov; we must insist that they immediately claim the land for the peasants, and we must suggest to them the necessity of arresting Rodzianko and Miliukov, of dissolving the Imperial Duma, of closing down the *Rech* and other bourgeois newspapers and bringing them before the courts. It is particularly the Left Social-Revolutionaries who must be pushed in this direction.

"It would be erroneous to believe that we are turning away from our principal objective; the conquest of power by the proletariat. We have, on the contrary, got considerably nearer to it, but *indirectly*, by a flanking movement. We must at the very same moment agitate against Kerensky—but let the agitation be indirect rather than direct—but insisting on an active war against Kornilov. Only the active development of that war can lead us to power, but of that we must speak as little as possible in our agitation (we keep it well in mind that even to-morrow events may compel us to take power, and that then we shall not let it go). In my opinion, these points should be communicated in a letter (a private one) to our agitators, to our propagandists, training groups and schools, and to the members of the Party in general. . . . "

And we have an unforgettable picture of Krupskaya supervising the duplication of these letters, scrupulous over every comma, so that the Bolshevik agitators might be able to put Lenin's precise ideas clearly before the eager masses and weld them for the revolution.

Trotsky walked straight from prison to the Committee of the Soviet which had helped to put him there, in order to organise the defence of Petrograd. Kornilov's force disappeared. Lenin, still in hiding, again offered to support the leaders of the Soviet if they would take the power from the Provisional Government. Lenin had early called for the arming and drilling of the workers, but still he hoped that these leaders would take the power without bloodshed, which they could easily have done. But they would not. Lacking Lenin's faith in the international proletariat, they feared isolation and could only urge the Liberal bourgeoisie to do something while they warned the Bolsheviks against violence. Ramsay MacDonald during the General Strike testified as to his faith in the ancient British constitution. Tseretelli, even before Russia had a constitution, was prepared to abide by it. Ex-Prime Minister and ex-convict, the political type is the same. Only historical materialism, which sees these men as the product of their social environment, can charitably explain them.

The Kornilov episode, however, had made the masses see clearly what the Bolshevik party had preached so steadily and so patiently. The Bolsheviks gained a majority in the Soviets at last. Again the slogan was changed: All power to the Bolshevik Soviet. Lenin, studying carefully the situation all over Russia, judged that the moment was near. He called on the Central Committee to organise the actual insurrection. But the Central Committee, now that the moment was approaching, for which so much labour and thought had been expended and so much suffering heroically borne, wavered. Zinoviev and Kamenev were openly against, Kalinin said yes, "but in a year's time." Lenin, still in hiding, threatened to resign and to appeal for insurrection over the heads of the Central Committee to the masses. He knew that the temper of the masses for an insurrection lasts over a period of weeks at most, sometimes only for a few days, after which it ebbs away. And he knew also that there was no question of a democratic republic for Russia. For once the spirit of the people, wearied by deception and disappointment, had subsided, the counter-revolution would grow stronger day by day, and end in the destruction of the revolution. The chance, if any, of a bourgeois-democratic republic (and that could only have been temporary) had been thrown away by the leaders of the Soviet when they handed the power to the Provisional Government. But many members of the Central Committee could not see this. Zinoviev and Kamenev carried their resistance into the open, writing against the insurrection in a non-Bolshevik paper. Zinoviev wrote against it in *Pravda* of October 20. This article was accompanied by an editorial note which stated solidarity with Zinoviev and Kamenev. Sokolnikov, one of the editors, stated that he had no part in it. The other editor was Stalin. The Central Committee was thrown into confusion. Kamenev resigned; he and Zinoviev were forbidden to carry on agitation against the policy of the Central Committee. Stalin opposed this and offered his resignation from the editorial board. The Central Committee at that critical time refused to accept it. What would these men do when Lenin died, if they acted like this when he was merely in hiding?

But Trotsky, now a member of the party, other leading revolutionaries, and the bulk of the party and the Petrograd masses were unreservedly for the revolution and ready to follow. Lenin had his way. The insurrection achieved an almost bloodless victory in Petrograd; there was fighting later in Moscow and other regions in Russia, but on the first night of the insurrection, power was in Bolshevik hands. The next night Lenin broadcast a decree informing the peasants that all land was now the property of the State and to seize it and divide it among themselves pending legislation. And when, a few days later, the Commander-in-Chief of the army refused to obey his orders to make overtures for peace, he ordered the soldiers to shoot or bayonet their officers and fraternise with the Germans.

MARXISM: THE RÔLE OF THE INDIVIDUAL

It may seem here that we have given too much prominence to Lenin. The foundation and maintenance of Bolshevism, the theoretical preparation for the Third International, the October revolution, we have made them centre around him. In all of them he was the driving force, theoretician and organiser. The October revolution is the beginning of twenty years of such tense history as no age has seen. Now Lenin, it is true, did not make the October revolution. We have pointed out and emphasised heavily enough the inevitability in history which enabled Marx and Engels to foresee the first world war, the revolution in Petersburg, the death of the Second International, the inevitable rise of a Third International. So far Historical Materialism. It was within those limits that the most gifted of individuals had to work. But Trotsky, who played so great a part in the revolution, has stated categorically: "You know better than I that had Lenin failed to reach Petrograd in April, 1917, there would have been no October revolution."[1] In addition to the fact of the revolution it might have been a failure or a success. Lenin ensured its success. Trotsky was capable of both the strategy and tactics. Could he have brought the party with him? It is doubtful. And without October the Third International might have taken many years to come. It might have taken a very different form. That the International came so quickly and in the way it did was due to the work of Lenin. He could not have done it without the party, but it was he who made the party. When he was in hiding, Trotsky led the Bolshevik Party, not only with immense vigour and executive skill, but with a brilliance of appeal and personality which not even Lenin could have equalled. As we have seen, his analysis of perspectives was more correct than Lenin's. But though the actual revolution brought them together, Lenin to Trotsky on the theoretical appraisement, and Trotsky to Lenin on the organisational question (he joined the party in July), yet without Lenin it is, to say the least, extremely doubtful what road the Bolshevik Party would have ultimately taken after the March revolution. It is not only the road the party has taken since Lenin died which encourages us to think the worst, it is what they did even while he was there to watch them. In this short chronicle Stalin appears only as making grave mistakes. A chronicle ten times as large would have little else to add. Except that he delivered a report at the

[1] In a letter to Preobrajensky. See *New International*, April, 1936, p. 61.

Sixth Congress when most of the other leaders were in hiding or out of Petrograd, it is difficult to find in chronicles of the time any trace of his share in the October revolution.[1] Not only were they incapable themselves; they could not recognise capability in other men. When Trotsky arrived in Petersburg in May, and was still outside the Bolshevik Party, Lenin, now having no quarrel with Trotsky over the Permanent Revolution, and remembering Trotsky's work in 1905, proposed to the Central Committee that Trotsky should be made the editor of *Pravda*. The Central Committee refused. To Lenin's urgent plea they replied with his own arguments against organisational unity—a unity they had been quite prepared to forget on the far greater question of the international revolution. They were many of them men of ability and character. Lenin's superiority, the breadth of his spirit, his knowledge of men, his tolerance, enabled him to use them all. But who knows how far the judgment of his colleagues by so clear-sighted a man was responsible for his tenacious advocacy of central control? It is when we watch the rôle in 1917 of those who became dominant after Lenin's death that we can see the germs of the future failures and ultimate collapse of the Third International. The absence of Lenin, different social relations in Russia, would bring out and fortify, not in new men, but in these reputed internationalists, those Menshevik tendencies which after fourteen years of preparatory work had to be crushed by Lenin, almost single-handed, in the very heat of the long-awaited revolution.

[1] The curious reader is invited to get a selection of histories of the revolution (except those published in Russia since about 1927) and look up Stalin's name in the index.

Chapter 4

THE FAILURE OF THE WORLD REVOLUTION AND
THE FOUNDATION OF THE INTERNATIONAL

IT WOULD TAKE US TOO FAR TO TELL IN ANY DETAIL
the history of the revolutionary movements in Europe
after the war. Yet we shall have to consider the
movement in Germany and to some extent in Austria
to see how far Lenin's expectation of international
revolution was justified, how far his conception of
the political party as necessary to the revolution was
proved valid. It was to Germany that he looked most
anxiously.

The obvious leaders of a revolution in Germany were
Karl Liebknecht, and Rosa Luxemburg. If we confine
ourselves here chiefly to pointing out their errors, it is simply
because in the historical period which is approaching we
have to bear in mind what caused the failure of such
splendid intellectual gifts and revolutionary fervour. Their
virtues we know, nothing that could be written here would
exalt them further. Nor do we imply any reproach. We to-
day who can point out where they failed know that what is
so clear to-day, after twenty years of revolution and the works
of Lenin and Trotsky, could not possibly have been as clear
in 1919 and before. Yet it must be remembered that Lenin,
who before 1914 had several sharp controversies with Rosa
Luxemburg, nevertheless saw the Sahara that separated
her and Liebknecht from the opportunist leaders of their
party. In 1914, at the meeting of the Social Democratic
Party which decided to vote for the war-credits, Liebknecht
fought for three days and was defeated by seventy-
eight votes to fourteen. He tried to convince the other
thirteen to vote with him against the credits. Such

a vote at the beginning would have exercised a powerful influence. They refused, and Liebknecht followed them. It is in crises like these that the individual quality of men tells.

Rosa Luxemburg, immediately after the treachery of the Social Democratic Party, proposed to issue an anti-war manifesto which should be signed by a number, however small, of leaders known to the workers. At once some of the left fell away. She called a small meeting at her house. Only seven came, and of these Clara Zetkin, Franz Mehring and herself alone were willing to sign.

Liebknecht did not yet see the necessity of a clean break, and to issue the leaflet without him was to make the workers ask why the name of the most widely-known of their militant leaders was not there. They decided to wait. Is it necessary to state that Lenin would have issued the manifesto alone, and set about building an organisation to spread his ideas? It is in this way that individual men make history. It was only in December that Liebknecht recognised his error and decided to vote against the war-credits. That month Lenin had a personal report on the situation in Germany. His first question was whether Liebknecht had made a clean break with the opportunists. He had not. But even his solitary vote and declaration had raised enthusiasm in the party and among the left section of the workers. He and Rosa Luxemburg began to issue illegal literature under the pseudonym of Spartacus. The Government mobilised Liebknecht in a labour battalion, but had to move him from place to place because wherever he went the soldiers gathered round him in crowds. The ground was fertile but the seed had been lacking.

Late in 1915 another group finally split off from the German party and voted against the war-credits. Its leaders were Kautsky and Bernstein, whose return to Marxism consisted in their being now "against the war," but nothing more. Later the Spartacists although they knew Kautsky and Bernstein and the vacillating centrist nature of these Independent Social Democrats, entered the new party, a mistake that was to have disastrous consequences.

For months Liebknecht had preached the negative "Peace with no annexations." It was only nearing Zimmerwald that he approached Lenin's initial position that to lead the workers to expect a peace with no annexations except by overthrowing imperialism was hypocrisy or ignorance. By Zimmerwald Liebknecht had reached "Not civil peace but civil war"—"The main enemy is in your own country," and sent a letter embodying his views to that conference.

To Zimmerwald Rosa Luxemburg also sent theses calling for the new International. She differed widely from Lenin on many points of organisation,[1] she opposed the harshness of his democratic centralism, with very clear ideas as to the necessity of democracy and the participation of the masses in the Government. Rejected much too unceremoniously by Marxists because of Lenin's criticisms, time has proved that her views foresaw only too well the dangers of excessive centralism and the glorification of the idea of dictatorship, but she was with him on the necessity for centralised control of the new International. On this question the Spartacists and the Independent Social Democratic group split sharply at Zimmerwald. Ledebour, the representative of the Independents, wanted, as centrists always do, an International in which each section could do exactly as it pleased, in other words, no International at all. Lenin pressed the Spartacists to break with these new allies. Rosa Luxemburg refused. She could not see the necessity of establishing a clear position and organisation of her own so that all could see what the Spartacists stood for, on this basis establishing contacts with all who were moving towards her position, and working for those sudden turns in the moods of the masses that the war was bound to bring.

The movement of the masses towards revolution was taking place day by day. A down-with-the-war meeting summoned by Liebknecht in May, 1916, brought 10,000 workmen into the streets of Berlin, and sympathetic

---

[1] Rosa Luxemburg has recently fallen into disfavour with Stalin and the Stalinists. It is to her credit. A study of her life and work is badly needed in England.

demonstrations in many big towns in Germany. Liebknecht and Rosa Luxemburg were arrested and imprisoned. They continued their underground work, but the movement naturally suffered.

THE GERMAN SOCIAL DEMOCRATIC LEADERS STAB THE GERMAN REVOLUTION IN THE BACK

The revolution which came in Berlin on November 9, 1918, is still thought by many to have been nothing more than a spontaneous explosion of anti-war feeling. The bourgeois publicists, as usual, go out of their way to prove that every revolution always aims at everything else except socialising bourgeois property. The German Revolution was anti-war but it was much more than that.

There are periods in history when the events of a few hours or a few weeks exercise an overwhelming influence on the history of a continent for years to come. Such a period were the few weeks that followed November 9 and also, of even more importance, the few weeks that preceded that day. Lenin was ten thousand times right in the expectation that the Russian Revolution would unloose Socialist revolutions in Western Europe. The revolutionary workers of Berlin had prepared an uprising in October, 1918. They, comprising chiefly those key workers in any capitalist society, the workers in heavy industry, had been stirred by October, had organised a shop steward movement, and were aiming at a Socialist republic. But Lenin was more right than he knew when he had insisted on the necessity for a revolutionary party. He thought that the European revolutions might succeed without one. It was, on the whole, a justifiable assumption. What neither Lenin, nor for that matter, any man could have foreseen, was the incredible treachery of the Social Democratic leadership. With Capitalism defenceless they stepped into the breach on its behalf. But for them all Europe would have been Socialist to-day.

First Ebert, Scheidemann and others joined the Kaiser's Government at a time when, if they had stood firmly against any entanglement with a war that at least was none of their making, the Government would have fallen.

97

No one but these leaders of the workers could have deceived the workers. And they did it voluntarily. The Independent Social Democrats, with Kautsky and Bernstein on the right almost indistinguishable from Ebert and Schiedemann, and Ledebour on the left near to Rosa Luxemburg and Karl Liebknecht, represented such a diversity of aims and views (it is always thus in a party without tight organisation and a clear programme) that they lacked all capacity for cohesive action, the life of a revolutionary party. Liebknecht and Rosa Luxemburg had delayed too long, and it was to this centrist party that the shop stewards perforce looked for revolutionary leadership. Even led as it was, this revolution, definitely prepared with definite aims, could not have failed to succeed, so rotten was the Government of the Kaiser. Who among the soldiers or sailors would have fought for it? These shop stewards after the revolution were powerful enough to seize the Executive Committee of the Greater Berlin Soldiers' and Workmen's Councils. They had wide support all over Germany. The masses would infallibly have followed them. The masses, without whose partial support and goodwill a revolution is impossible, do not revolt for Socialism or for Communism. They revolt against intolerable conditions or for some concrete issue, as the peasantry for land or against a war or to stop Fascism. In Lenin's phrase, a revolution is made on the slogans of the day. The masses will follow whoever has the will and courage to lead the revolt and bring it to a successful conclusion; they will accept a programme and support it so long as the political actions of the leaders are progressive and in harmony with their general aspirations. The Socialist measures which the shop stewards planned would have been backed by the demand for Socialisation which was so widespread in Germany in 1919. The possessing classes were powerless. There was the question of Entente intervention. We shall deal with that later. It is sufficient to say here that a revolution which waits to be guaranteed from hostile capitalist interference will never take place.

But as history would have it, this revolution, aiming at a Soviet Republic in Germany, was accidentally forestalled by the mutiny at Kiel. And this mutiny, already very different in aim from the other, was safely side-tracked by the Social Democrats. The Social Democrats to-day try to say that they acted as they did in Germany after November, 1918, because the people were merely anti-war and did not want Socialism. They lie. Ebert had seen the revolution coming. He could have put himself at the head of it and declared for Socialism. But he feared the Socialist revolution. He therefore conspired with Prince Max of Baden, and these two prepared in advance a policy which would switch the revolutionary fervour of the masses into harmless channels—a kind of Popular Front manœuvre. When the mutiny broke out at Kiel, Ebert, primed for treachery, went down to interview the sailors. Skilfully putting himself at the head of the mutiny he and his circle appeared to the great millions as leaders of the very revolution they had been preparing to stab in the dark. Now that it had broken out they directed it into purely political channels, against the Kaiser, and succeeded ultimately in strangling it.

There was no revolutionary political party in Germany known throughout the length and breadth of the country. It was not until December 30, 1918, that the Spartacists split at last with the Independent Social Democrats. At their conference in January, the nearest approach to a revolutionary party, they had less than a hundred delegates. It had proved impossible to build an organisation during the heat of the conflict, and in addition to this organic weakness, at every crisis the two on whom so much depended acted in exactly the opposite way to which Lenin acted in similar crises. They had no control over the party, for the party had not yet learnt their value by individual experience. They had had no time to educate their followers in the very elements of Marxism. Not only the objective situation, but Lenin's authority and prestige, had enabled him to swing the party very quickly round to his own views in 1917. Lenin would have fought for independence, but also for a common agreement with the obvious revolutionary force in Berlin—the shop stewards' union. He would have taken what terms he could and trusted to events to bring them to his side. But the anarchist tendencies of the Spartacists frightened the shop stewards and the necessary alliance between them and the Spartacists did not take place. Liebknecht was against taking part in the elections. Rosa Luxemburg was in favour. The party decided against, 62 votes to 23. The leaders of the shop stewards were definitely in favour of revolution, but not of adventurism, and we recall here again Lenin's admonitions to his party and the workers in April against the premature slogan of "Down with the Provisional Government." On the one hand is Lenin, master of tactics and able to carry them out through his organisation, relatively small but powerful in its cohesion. On the other we see two highly gifted revolutionaries, able, honest and fearless, widely-known and respected, but unable to make headway against the tendencies of every type which surrounded them. They lacked the organised party and the training and experience which the buiding of the party would have given to them as well as to the members.

Berlin at the Mercy of the Spartacists

The Social Democrats who formed the Revolutionary Government were, as always, afraid of the people, and looked instinctively to the bourgeoisie. In the inevitable clashes of that uncertain time they compromised themselves so completely with the discredited German generals that on December 6, not a month yet after November 9, one of these actually attempted a counter-revolution with the aim of putting Ebert at the head of the Government. The counter-revolution so soon after the revolution startled Germany. It was the opportunity that a revolutionary party expects, foretells and prepares to seize, though few could have foreseen that so-called Socialists would turn counter-revolutionary so quickly. There was a mass swing of opinion against Ebert, and on January 5 the crisis came to a head over the dismissal of a left-wing Independent, Eichorn, the Berlin Chief of Police. For the moment Independents, Spartacists and shop stewards formed a bloc and called the workers into the streets.

The response was magnificent. There were arms to be

had and trained fighters in thousands among the workers. On January 6, the next day, a hundred thousand revolutionary workers again filled the streets of Berlin. But even then none of the three groups of leaders knew its own mind. Some were thinking only of a demonstration, others of revolution. Fighting began without any preconceived plans. In this action the Spartacist group was as bewildered as the other two. And yet despite all this confusion they could have held, and very nearly did possess themselves of, the power that day.[1]

The Government fled for refuge to a private house, and the Chancellor's palace, the seat of government, was open to the revolution. Usually it is only by desperate mass fighting and barricades that a section of the army, refusing to shoot its own people any more, massacres its officers and comes over to the side of revolution, giving point and edge to the weight of the masses. In this action, even before the fighting, the soldiers, sailors and police in Berlin were neutral. But the revolutionaries, lacking all organisation and leadership, instead of installing themselves in the traditional seat of power and making themselves a Government in the eyes of the masses, directed their main attention to seizing newspaper offices of rival political parties. Not many revolutions could have recovered from such an error. For the German Revolution, deflected from the start, the mistake was fatal. Yet even when the movement had begun to disintegrate the Government dared not remain in Berlin and had to move to the suburbs. And to crush the revolution Noske had to go to the German junkers, who joyfully took the opportunity of destroying the extreme left.

It can be urged that a party and leaders of Lenin's type only arise on a background vastly different from that of pre-war Germany. That can be freely granted, but the argument should not be allowed to stifle the consideration of all other possibilities. We have seen that without Lenin much the same charge in all probability would have been

[1] This is admitted even by G. P. Gooch, a Liberal historian, and Liberal historians as a rule only countenance revolutions when they are successful and at least 150 years old. See his chapter on the revolution in his book, *Germany*. See also F. Lee Benn's *Europe since 1914*, 1930, p. 308: "If they had had determined leaders with clearly defined aims, they might have seized the city; but these they lacked."

made against similar indecision and inexperience in the Russian Bolshevik Party. We have seen Stalin, Zinoviev, and Kamenev, in 1917. We shall see them again. The lessons of history are there to be learnt by all men. The Russian Revolution of 1905, the causes of its failure, Lenin's views about organising revolution, all were the subject of heated discussion by Rosa Luxemburg and the left-wing of the German Social Democracy. Kautsky, destined to prove himself one of the most reactionary of Social Democrats, had been Lenin's master, and quoted by him as such for years until he ratted in 1914. Marx and Engels had worked out a complete armoury of tactics nearly seventy years before. In the years before 1916, when revolution seemed dead in Ireland, James Connolly had studied the history of every revolutionary movement in Europe, preparing for the moment to overthrow British Imperialism in Ireland. The discipline and organisation of his Irish Citizen Army was in its own way quite comparable to that of the Bolshevik Party. We need pursue the subject no further except to state the last and greatest of the mistakes that Karl Liebknecht and Rosa Luxemburg made. When the revolution was finally crushed they could have escaped, but remained and were murdered, the murderers being openly incited by the official Social Democratic paper *Vorwaerts*. It was the greatest mistake of all. Liebknecht was not thoroughly a Marxist, and he had defects of character which might have impeded his development. But for Lenin, Rosa Luxemburg was an eagle, and Lenin did not throw bouquets. 1919 would have been to them, certainly to her, what 1905 had been to Lenin. And, equally important, being head and shoulders above all in the Third International except Lenin and Trotsky, they and they alone could have prevented the corruption from Moscow of the German party leadership which began during Lenin's last illness and ended in the ruin of 1933.

THE SOCIAL DEMOCRATIC LEADERS STIFLE THE AUSTRIAN REVOLUTION

It was the Social Democratic leadership that killed the European revolution in 1919. To prove this finally we shall let one of these, the Austrian Otto Bauer, speak for himself.

Before the war the Austrian Social Democrats had a great reputation for Marxist learning. Like their English counterparts of to-day they were advocates of freedom, independence of nations, and all that is included in Socialism, but collaborated willingly with the suppression of the subject peoples by the Austrian monarchy. They invented a special theory wherein the economic and political oppression of subject nationalities was compensated for by unity of culture (or its independence—which it was is not important). Czechs, Serbs, Slovenes and Slovaks were as necessary to Austro-Hungarian Capitalism as Indians, Egyptians and Africans to British Capitalism. Like their counterparts in Britain, these servants of the bourgeoisie acquiesced in any action of their masters which allowed them to bargain with employers about wages and make speeches in parliament urging the Government and bringing pressure to bear. Every day when the Emperor Francis Joseph read their paper, *Wiener Arbeiterzeitung*, he used to say, "They reason very sensibly, but what do they want of me?"

When war broke out Austrian Social Democracy unreservedly placed its influence on the masses at the disposal of the military authorities. They were men of war until the mood of the working-classes began to change. After the February revolution in Russia "the revolutionary ferment made itself felt more and more in the ranks of German-Austrian workers." The Austrian Social Democracy felt that if a revolution was on the way they had better take charge of it. But they did not yet know how things would develop. So they played both sides. "If we wanted to address the masses openly, we had to remain within the limits of censorship; we could not speak openly of revolution, we had to speak of it in some such terms as the complete 'victory of democracy,' 'convocation of the Constituent Assembly'; we could not openly bring forward the slogan of the disintegration of Austria, but had to use such expressions as 'there can be common government for all those who agree to it of their own free will.'"[1] Thus one of the leaders of these despicable time-servers. Otto Bauer had been a war-prisoner in Russia, and was released by the February revolution. Of the Russian Revolution he wrote in 1920: "For the first time the proletariat has assumed power in a great state. . . . The Capitalist world is trembling. . . . With the help of cannon and howitzer . . . the international bourgeoisie makes war on the proletarian revolution. But all this makes the hearts of the proletarians of all countries beat in unison with the heart of the Russian proletariat."[2] His own heart, however, beat with the heart of Austrian Capitalism. The proletarian dictatorship in Russia was possible, he argued, owing to the numbers and backwardness of the peasantry. For Europe there was no possibility of any such thing. In 1920 he propounded a new brand of Revisionism tinged with Guild Socialism by which, peacefully and by parliament, the proletariat would establish Socialism. Meanwhile, immediately after the war, Otto Bauer, Fritz Adler and the other leaders set themselves with might and main to prop the collapsing bourgeoisie of Austria. When Germany was on the verge of defeat, eleven days before Poland was declared an independent State, ten days before the Czech National Assembly put forward its demand for a Czech Republic, Austrian Social Democracy, seeing that the oppressed nationalities could not possibly be held in subjection any longer, declared boldly for the national independence of all the German regions in Austria. This Bauer called "a revolutionary act." When the Emperor Charles had informed William II that he would make a separate peace and a truce within twenty-four hours, and after Croatia, Slovakia, Dalmatia and Serbia had been amalgamated into an independent State, with the whole Austrian structure crumbling to ruins, the Austrian Social Democracy then called for a revolution, Social Democratic brand. "On the battlefields of the Balkans and of Venice the revolution smashed the iron mechanism which hindered its development. In the meantime we in the rear could

[1] *The Austrian Revolution of* 1918, by Otto Bauer. See *The Communist International*, No. 16.
[2] *Bolshevism or Social-Democracy?* by Otto Bauer. See *The Communist International*, No. 16.

make revolution without using violence."[1] Meanwhile, day after day, the soldiers and enormous crowds of workmen demonstrated in Vienna. The workers were ready to seize the power. "Every newspaper brought news of the struggle of the Spartacists in Germany, every speech gave information of the glorious Russian Revolution, which by one stroke had put an end to all exploitation. The masses who had recently witnessed the downfall of a strong empire had no suspicion of the strength of the Capitalist Entente. They imagined that revolution would spread like wildfire through the victorious countries. 'A dictatorship of the proletariat!'—'All power to the Soviets!'—nothing else was heard in the streets." The peasants were ready. "Peasants had also returned home from the trenches full of hatred for war and militarism, for the bureaucracy and for the plutocracy. They too welcomed the freedom which had been won; they welcomed the republic and the downfall of militarism. They rejoiced at the fact that local organs which were formerly under the administration of the representatives of the king-emperor were now under the administration of representatives of the peasantry. Together with the proletariat they imagined that the political revolution must needs bring with it a revolution with respect to property ownership." Without the party, without organisation, despite all the treachery to the cause of the Social Democrats, the revolutionary tide was flowing strongly; the German Social Democracy and the Austrian Social Democracy had the fate of European Capitalism in their hands. But the Austrian Social Democracy did not look to the masses. They had their eyes fixed on the bourgeoisie, on the Entente leaders and President Wilson. No one except these leaders could have checked the revolution, and like Ebert they had proclaimed their revolution "without violence" only to place themselves in a position where they could kill the mass movement. Bauer bursts with pride as he explains this. "The Social Democrats alone could put a stop to the stormy demonstration by means of negotiation and remonstrances. The Social Democracy alone could negotiate

[1] *The Austrian Problem of* 1918, by Otto Bauer. See *The Communist International*, No. 16. All other quotations are from the same source.

with the unemployed, could manage the People's army, could restrain the masses from revolutionary adventures which might have been conducive to revolution. How deeply the bourgeois social order had been affected was best shown by the fact that bourgeois governments without participation of Social Democrats had become an impossible proposition." This was the world revolution that Engels had written about and Lenin was counting on. Come it did. Austrian Soviets developed. Bauer and his Socialist friends crushed them. Next door the Hungarian Soviet Republic begged for arms. They refused. But they arrested the Austrian Communist leaders and when a mass demonstration of Communists marched to the House of Detention to free the imprisoned leaders, these servants of the bourgeoisie shot them down. "The bourgeoisie could not have shown any resistance either in Vienna or in the industrial regions of Lower Austria; the police would have been quite powerless." There is no need to continue with the miserable record. They were afraid of France with whom they sought to curry favour, they were afraid of famine, they were afraid of starting Socialism with a ruined economy. They were afraid of everything except fighting tooth and nail to preserve that system of property which they had sworn to destroy. The people trusted them because they believed that they really meant the things they had said so often and so long. Germany, Austria, Hungary and Russia, each proletarian dictatorship stretching out its hand to the other, and sending out a united call to the workers of the world for support. The Entente would have been powerless. After November, 1918, Lenin in a public speech offered the German Revolution a million Red soldiers and all the resources of Russia if the Entente should interfere with it. Ebert's reply was to send German soldiers to the Baltic to do a little Social Democratic imperialism against what was Russian territory. All history was there to tell them, Russia was soon to show, that war-weary and tired as the masses were, under a strong and inspiring leadership, in the hope of a new society, they would fight again and endure threefold the very privations that had driven them in the first place to revolt. The Austro-Marxists stuck to Capitalism. Lenin and Trotsky had watched and waited and prepared all the years for the world revolution, knowing by 1919 that without it another Imperialist war would cripple civilization and kill millions, could see the new Socialist order striving to be born all over Europe, and a thin scum of bureaucrats with the ear of the masses holding up the historical process and throwing humanity a generation back. And what have they got for it? To-day in all Central Europe a dreadful tyranny reigns. The state that Lenin founded, isolated, is in deadly peril from the very forces they helped to maintain. In exile, their parties broken to pieces, living on sufferance (or on money saved and carefully put away) they continue to spread their pernicious doctrines and encourage Blum, Attlee, and those whose turn has not yet come, in the same dangerous folly and treachery which has ruined them. "Whatever happens the democrat comes forth unspotted from the most shameful defeat, just as he was a blameless innocent before he entered the battle; defeat merely fortifies his conviction of ultimate victory; there is no reason why he and his party should abandon their old outlook, for nothing more is requisite than that circumstance should come to their aid." Noske, Scheidemann, Adler, Bauer, Léon Blum, Attlee, Morrison, Bevin, Citrine, Lansbury. Marx knew.them a hundred years ago. When the international working-class movement knows them the road to victory is clear.

The International Proletariat

The Hungarian Soviet failed; so did the Bavarian. This is not a complete history but a thesis, and their failure can be studied elsewhere. It was the German and the Austrian Revolution that would have saved them. Lenin's expectations seemed to have failed. But only on the surface. Lenin and Trotsky and the Bolshevik Party, Trotsky and the organisation of the Red Army, the heroism of the workers, the determination of the peasants to fight for the land, these things alone did not save Russia. Without them Soviet Russia would have collapsed. It was the international proletariat which was the decisive factor, and in a way that is not too clearly realised even up to the present time. It is not only what it did but what its masters feared it might do. Capitalism tried its hardest to crush the Workers' State, but could not find the forces to do so. Of Europe in February and March, 1919, Louis Fischer says: "The whole continent seemed on the brink of a social upheaval that threatened to sweep all governments into the ashbin of history,"[1] and he gives the evidence of the capitalist statesmen themselves. For Sir Henry Wilson, the soldier, the main problem was "getting our troops out of Europe and Russia, and concentrating all our strength in our coming storm centres, viz England, Ireland, Egypt, India."

Lloyd George had almost as little doubt of the imminence of world revolution as Lenin had. "If a military enterprise were started against the Bolsheviki, that would make England Bolshevist, and there would be a Soviet in London." "We are sitting on the top of a mine which may go up at any minute," wrote Sir Henry Wilson. And again at a Cabinet meeting in London: "I emphasized the urgency of the situation, pointing out that unless we carried our proposals we should lose not only our armies of the Rhine, but our garrisons at home, in Ireland, Gibraltar, Malta, India, etc., and that even now we dare not give an unpopular order to the troops and discipline was a thing of the past." The Council of Ten in Paris reported officially for January 21, 1919: "Bolshevism was spreading. It had invaded the Baltic provinces and Poland, and that very morning they received very bad news regarding its spread to Budapest and Vienna. Italy, also, was in danger. The danger was probably greater there than in France. If Bolshevism, after spreading in Germany, were to traverse Austria and Hungary and so reach Italy, Europe would be faced with a great danger. Therefore something must be done against Bolshevism." Twenty years before Engels had written just that, but Marxism was not taught in European universities any more than it is taught to-day. But history goes on just the same.

They had to do something against Bolshevism. But they

[1] Louis Fischer, *The Soviets in World Affairs*, 1930. Vol. I, Chap. IV.

could do little. The armies they sent mutinied. The Russian counter-revolution they supported was defeated on front after front. When they tried to support Poland as a last hope, Czechoslovak workmen stopped trains, searched them for munitions and, when they found them, refused to let the trains proceed. The workers in Danzig harbour refused to load munition ships which lay idle for days; the workers of Britain organised Councils of Action and threatened the British Government with revolution if British Capitalism did not cease its support of Poland against Russia. The man whom H. G. Wells had the impertinence to call "the dreamer in the Kremlin " had learnt in the works of Marx and Engels that the international working-class movement was a living reality, had based his calculations fearlessly upon it, and had not been disappointed.

THE INTERNATIONAL IS FOUNDED

The vast stage of history at its most dramatic moments is full of large-scale comedy. The war was no sooner over than the leaders of the Second International set about with undiminished ardour to become international once more. They passed international resolutions for peace, quarrelled about war-guilt, and sent a memorandum and a deputation to Clemenceau, Lloyd George and Wilson, giving their idea of a just peace. British delegations took their part in resolutions demanding self-determination for small nations, what time British imperialism rained bullets on Indians, Egyptians and Irish to prove to them the benefits of British rule. But now, to their former stock-in-trade, they soon added something else—a shrill faith in democracy. First a conference at Berne in February, 1919, and preliminary conferences of a Permanent Commission at Amsterdam in April and Lucerne in August, prepared for a General Congress in Geneva on February 2, 1920. But despite these antics and the old flow of words all was not the same as before. The international Socialist revolution had begun, Soviet Russia was visible proof, and opposition to these Social Democratic futilities was strong, even among the participants at these preliminary conferences; great bodies of the workers were indifferent or hostile to these men without principle passing resolutions which meant nothing and ready at every turn to shoot down workers on behalf of Capitalism. In March, 1919, the Third International was founded and so strong was the response that it nearly destroyed the Second.

That the Third International was formed at that time was due primarily to Lenin. And the circumstances of its formation is yet another example of his grasp of revolutionary processes, his insistence that the business of leaders is to lead, to show the way, and then fight to carry the masses. After Kienthal the left-wing of the Second International, under the influence of the Russian Revolution, had attempted to hold an anti-war conference at Stockholm. By this time they had powerful support among the workers of their own countries. Inside the ranks of the Second International, the movement for peace defied the efforts even of governments and was silenced by the only forces able to do it—the Social Democratic leaders themselves. The Stockholm Conference failed. In September the Zimmerwaldists held a small conference of their own and decided on the formation of a new international. But the second revolution in Russia made this decision a dead letter. German imperialism at the Treaty of Brest-Litovsk in March, 1918, dismembered Russia, only to be treated in like manner when their English and French rivals got their chance at them. Then came the war of intervention and the invasion by the counter-revolution, financed by allied capital, armed with allied arms. The new Workers' State was blockaded and the Soviet armies suffered defeat after defeat late in 1918 and early in 1919. It was in the midst of this crisis that Lenin decided to call immediately for the new International. He, Tchitcherin, Sirola, (of Finland) and Fineberg, a member of the British Socialist Party, met one night in January, 1919, in the Tsar's large bedroom in the Kremlin to discuss Lenin's proposals. It was in one sense almost like the old meetings in holes and corners of the emigré days. The huge room was lighted by a single lamp, for electricity was precious in Russia in those days. The meeting was almost informal; Fineberg had been asked to come only that morning. Russia was attacked within and without. In Europe the world revolution was being sabotaged by the Social Democratic leaders. The revolutionary workers were in confusion, being continually misled and deceived by the men who stood at the head of their outworn organisations. Lenin proposed the immediate formation of a new revolutionary International with a Marxist programme of its own which would make a decisive break with the Second International. The plan was agreed to and the manifesto and invitation broadcast by radio, Trotsky signing instead of Lenin for the Central Committee of the Russian Communist Party. The Congress was fixed to take place on February 15, but had to be postponed to March. Passports were refused, delegates were arrested, some lost their lives, and in the circumstances of the blockade very few were able to enter Russia. Furthermore, the democracy which the Second Internationalists were asserting so vigorously in speeches and resolutions did not extend to invitations for a revolutionary conference, and there was little information in Europe, and that inexact, as to the aims and scope of the conference. The only delegates from abroad were Eberlein, representing the Spartacists, Rutgers, representing the American League of Propaganda, and representatives from Sweden, Norway, Austria and some of the smaller countries. The other foreign parties were represented by persons already staying in Moscow. The most important question was whether the congress was an inaugural congress or only a preliminary conference for the purpose of discussing the ultimate formation of an international. And here Rosa Luxemburg nearly prevented the decisive step. She got the invitation at the beginning of January, 1919. As neither she nor Karl Liebknecht were able to leave Berlin at that moment, she proposed to Eberlein that he should go, and discussed with him what line he should take. She told him that even if there were only a few delegates the Bolsheviks would most certainly propose the immediate formation of the International. She, however, thought that it should be definitely founded, but only when Communist parties would have arisen out of the revolutionary movement of the masses, which was growing in nearly every European country. In particular it would be necessary to choose the moment for founding the International in such a manner as to accelerate the detachment of the revolutionary masses from the German Independent Party. She asked Eberlein to press for the point of view that this February conference should be a preparatory conference. A commission should be created composed of the representatives of the different countries, and the foundation congress should take place between April and June. Three days later Rosa Luxemburg and Karl Liebknecht were murdered. But the Spartacists endorsed her point of view, and Eberlein and Levine set out with an imperative mandate. Levine was arrested before they got out of Germany, but Eberlein reached Moscow.

He had an interview with Lenin and told him the views of Rosa Luxemburg and the Spartacus Central Committee. Lenin and Rosa Luxemburg knew each other well, for Lenin said he was not surprised at what she thought and had foreseen this attitude. Her arguments, however, had only a certain tactical value. The International must be formed *immediately*. The revolutionary movement, the influence of the Russian Revolution on the advanced section of the proletariat, the recognition by great numbers of working men that the Second International was bankrupt, and above all the historic necessity of directing and co-ordinating the revolutionary actions of the proletariat, demanded it imperiously. But Eberlein was rigidly mandated, in 1918–1919 everything revolved around Germany; so that when Eberlein put his position before the fifty-seven delegates there was consternation. Only a few weeks earlier Karl Liebknecht and Rosa Luxemburg had been killed. Even as the conference was going on Noske and the Social Democrats were using the old German army officers and shooting down the revolutionary workers. Yet Eberlein maintained this hesitant attitude as the final word of his party. Doubt and distrust seized the delegates. Could the German Revolution ever succeed if this was their spirit? Yet even Lenin and the Bolshevik delegation accepted Eberlein's proposal, such was their respect for the German party, and for the first forty-eight hours the conference sat as a preliminary conference. But the delegates were dissatisfied. They felt that the decision was wrong, and on the evening of the second day Gruber, the Vienna delegate, cleared the air; "He was an agitator of the masses, full of talent. Electrified still more before his departure from Vienna by the deadly struggle of the few cadres of Austrian Communists against the social-traitors, clericalism, the bourgeoisie and militarism, Gruber with his colleague struggled for seventeen days against a thousand dangers to arrive at Moscow. They had travelled on locomotives and on tenders, on springs and on cattle wagons, they had tramped, had got by trickery through the front lines of Petlioura and Polish bands. See them finally in Red Moscow. Gruber hardly takes time to wash and runs to the Kremlin to be the sooner among his comrades, to help raise the standard of a new, a third International, truly revolutionary. Here among the delegates he speaks to them, describing in flaming words the struggle, the enthusiasm, the devotion of the Austrian comrades. What magnificent speaking! It is impossible to give any account of it. Moved as one was by it, it seemed that he gave forth magnetic waves, communicating to his listeners his boundless enthusiasm, his audacity, his faith in our movement. I had many opportunities later in Moscow to hear Steingart,[1] but never have I heard anything comparable to this first speech."[2]

The speech was followed by the formal proposition to found the new international. With the German five votes abstaining, the congress unanimously decided to found it at once. Lenin had almost been betrayed against his better judgment into a weak and vacillating position.

THE SECOND COMMUNIST MANIFESTO

The congress issued a manifesto signed by Rakovsky,[3] Lenin, Zinoviev, Trotsky and Fritz Platten.

". . . The national State, which gave such a mighty impulse to Capitalist development, has become too restricted for the continued development of the productive forces. . . .

[1] For obvious reasons revolutionaries have different names.

[2] B. Rheinstein, *Sur la voie du Ler Congres de L'I.C. Dix Années de lutte pour la Révolution Mondiale*, Bureaux d'Editions, Paris, 1929.

[3] Of the four Russians Lenin is dead, Zinoviev murdered by Stalin, Trotsky driven into exile by Stalin. Rakovsky, after years of exile, has "recanted," and after the Zinoviev-Kamenev trial, wrote (or signed) a denunciation of Trotskyism, in which he called Trotsky Fascist, unclean fellow, etc.

"The only means of securing the possibility of a free existence for the small nations is by a proletarian revolution which releases all the productive forces in every country from the tight grip of the national States, unites the nations in the close economic co-operation based on a joint social economic plan, and grants to the smallest and weakest nation the possibility of developing its national culture independently and freely without detriment to the united and centralised economy of Europe and of the whole world. . . .

"The last war, which was certainly a war for the sake of the colonies, was also a war that was waged with the help of the colonies' populations on a scale never before known. Indians, Negroes, Arabs, Madagascans, all fought in the European contingent—and for what? For their right to remain in the future the slaves of England and France. . . .

"The liberation of the colonies will only be feasible in conjunction with the liberation of the working classes in the mother countries. Not until the workmen of England and France have overthrown Lloyd George and Clemenceau will the workmen and peasants, not only in Annam, Algiers, and Bengal, but also in Persia and Armenia, have a chance of an independent existence. In the more highly developed colonies the fight is already proceeding not merely under the banner of national liberation, but with a social character quite openly expressed. If Capitalistic Europe forces the most backward parts of the world into the whirlpool of capital, Socialist Europe will come to the aid of the liberated colonies with its technique, its organisations, and its spiritual influence, to facilitate the transition to a methodically organised Socialist establishment. . . .

"The outcry by the bourgeois world against civil war and the Red Terror is the most abominable hypocrisy ever noted in the history of political fighting. . . .

"Civil war is forced on the working classes by their mortal enemy. The working classes must return blow for blow, unless they would prove faithless to themselves and their future, which is also the future of all mankind. The Communist parties never try by artificial means to encourage civil war, but exert themselves, as far as possible, to shorten the duration of it, and, if it does become an imperative necessity, they endeavour to keep down the number of victims, and, above all, to secure victory for the proletariat. . . .

"Fully conscious of the world-historical character of their undertaking, the enlightened workmen, as the first step in organising the Socialist movement, aimed at an international union.

"In repudiating the vacillation, mendacity, and superficiality of the Socialist parties, we—the united Communists of the

Third International—feel ourselves to be the direct successors of a long series of generations, heroic champions and martyrs, from Baboeuf to Karl Liebknecht and Rosa Luxemburg.

"Even though the First International foresaw the coming development and inserted a wedge, and though the Second International collected and organised millions of proletarians, still it is the Third International that stands for the open action of the masses and for revolutionary operations.

"Socialist criticism has thoroughly stamped the bourgeois world-order. It is the duty of the International Communist Party to overthrow that order, and to establish instead the system of Socialist order.

"We appeal to Labour men and women in all countries to join us under the Communist banner, under which the first great victories already have been won.

"Proletarians in all lands! Unite to fight against imperialist barbarity, against monarchy, against the privileged classes, against the bourgeois State and bourgeois property, against all kinds and forms of social and national oppression.

"Join us, proletarians in every country—flock to the banner of the workmen's councils, and fight the revolutionary fight for the power and dictatorship of the proletariat!"

As is proper with the initial statement of a Marxist political organisation, the manifesto stands to-day, after nearly twenty years, far more valuable than when it was written. The analysis of Capitalism has been proved correct over and over again since 1919. Millions all over the world are far more ready for the call to-day, more will be to-morrow, even than in 1919. Yet to repeat those words to-day is Trotskyism. Men are imprisoned, tortured and shot in Russia for doing so, and outside Russia reviled without ceasing by the agents of the Third International. For this manifesto, and all that it means, the Third Internationalists have substituted as tattered and torn a collection of outworn political rags as can be found in the footnotes of any old Liberal school-book. A strong, free, and happy France; merry England; the Popular Front, with progressive individuals and right-thinking persons; and, despite the stench from the corpse of Abyssinia, the League of Nations and Collective Security. They dare not publish to-day the old documents of the International and for years have suppressed them, for many years it should be noted, and not since 1935.

But the men who wrote and signed and the men who voted for that manifesto meant it, and some of them are in exile to-day still fighting for the principles it maintains. At that first conference Trotsky, describing the Red Army, which he had organised and which was fighting on thousands of miles of front, told the delegates: "And I can assure you that the Communist workmen who form the true foundation of the army conduct themselves not only as the army for protection of the Socialist Soviet Republic, but also as the Red Army of the Third International. . . .

"And if to-day we do not even think of invading East Prussia—on the contrary we would be very much obliged if Messrs. Ebert and Scheidemann leave us in peace—it is yet true, that when the moment comes in which our brothers of the West will call to us for help we shall reply: Here we are, during this period we have learnt to handle arms, we are ready to struggle and to die for the cause of the world revolution!" And not only the leaders but the people of Russia were animated by the same spirit.

Through Moscow itself ran a fire of enthusiasm. Ever since October the idea of the Third International had caught on. Orators of various countries, ex-prisoners of war, spoke at crowded Moscow meetings about the Third International. The revolutionary workmen gave the name to clubs and organisations. Leaders and proletariat were convinced that the Soviet Union was merely the beginning of what the Third International and the international proletariat would conclude; and further that the existence of Russia as a Workers' State depended upon the international proletariat led by the Third International.

As the news of the new International penetrated into Europe it was seen how right Lenin was in opposing Rosa Luxemburg's idea of waiting. Millions rallied to the call, and many of the leaders of the Second International, fighting hard to avoid contact with the Third, had for the time being to abjure association with the Second. The Geneva Conference of the Second Internationalists, already put off from January to July, was a complete failure. Of the great countries in Europe only the German and the British were represented, and in addition to their urgings and pressures, resolutions about international peace and national self-determination, they added violent denunciations of the Bolsheviks as violators of their precious democracy. Henceforth that was their slogan. How tightly they hold on to it. It is not quite straightforward dishonesty, nor rhetoric, nor habit, nor ignorance, though there are solid elements of all these in it. The basis of it all is self-preservation, and when that is at stake men do not reason. Bourgeois parliamentary democracy was that form of political organisation which had brought the Social Democrats into being and on which they flourish. They can find a place in neither Fascism nor Communism. They are therefore democrats and will remain democrats, though the world fall to ruins around them.

Chapter 5

LENIN AND SOCIALISM

THOUGH BEFORE VERY LONG THE SOVIET UNION WAS TO be the only Workers' State in the world, the international Socialist revolution had begun. As time passed and the isolation of the Soviet Union became clear, it might have been thought that the dictatorship of the proletariat in Russia enforced by the situation inside the country was premature. Difficult and dangerous as was its position, liable to collapse at any time, yet the Soviet Union fitted into the basis of Lenin's first consideration, the economic condition of world Capitalism. He had during the war worked it out very carefully in his little book, *Imperialism, the Last Stage of Capitalism*, one of his most important theoretical works.

THE SOVIET UNION HISTORICALLY JUSTIFIABLE

In it he traces the inevitable development of Capitalism into huge monopolies, the dominant and decisive feature of world economy to-day. These monopolies gradually control the whole economic and financial life of the great Capitalist countries. It is a characteristic of Capitalism to separate the ownership of capital from its application to production, financial capital from industrial, the rentier who lives on his income from the entrepreneur and those who share in the management of capital. Imperialism is that highest stage of Capitalism in which this separation reaches vast proportions. Capital and finance tend to greater and greater amalgamation. The supremacy of finance capital over all other forms means the rule of the investor and of the financial oligarchy on a national scale, and on the international, the crystallisation of a small number of financially powerful States out of the general body. In the old type of Capitalism, that of free competition, the export of goods was the most typical feature. In the modern Capitalism of monopolies the typical feature is the export of capital. The surplus of capital is not put aside to raise the standard of living of the masses; this would mean a decrease of profits. The surplus capital is used to increase profits by the export of capital abroad to backward countries where capital is scarce, wages low, land and raw materials cheap. In proportion as the surplus of capital in each country increases, the competition between the monopolies for more colonies and greater spheres of influence increases. Finance capital has to divide up the world, not from original sin, but because the concentration of capital makes this method of getting profit a necessity. New imperialisms like Japan and America emerge. The competition between imperialism and imperialism goes on peacefully at first, first by industrial and commercial and then by political negotiation; this competition becomes more acute and ends in war, war being only a continuation of politics by other means. By 1914 the world had been divided up. Nothing was now possible but a redivision, and that redivision could take place only according to the strength of the competing imperialisms. Capitalism had reached its limit. Henceforth it would be imperialist war after imperialist war, until the destruction and slaughter or the economic chaos and social misery which would inevitably follow such wars would drive the international proletariat section by section to overthrow Capitalism and build international Socialism. The waste of armaments, the colossal destruction involved in unavoidable imperialist wars, the evils these brought in their train, were the unmistakable signs of the breakdown of the old system and the necessity for the new. As always the change would be accomplished by violent revolution, this time on an international scale. As Lenin was to say later, the new era which was opening was the era of imperialist wars and proletarian revolution.

The Soviet Union, viewed as a beginning, was therefore historically justifiable. If Capitalism proved to be still progressive, then the Soviet Union was premature and would undoubtedly fail. It was simple Marxism that the new Society could not exist for any length of time unless the old had reached its limits. But the conflict was not a conflict of entities already fixed. Capitalism in decay might be still powerful enough to overthrow the first Socialist State, whence it would gain a longer lease of life. Or the Soviet State might so establish itself and organise the international proletariat as to strike great blows at Capitalism. All this would depend on the opportunities that the development of history presented and the use men made of them.

LENINISM: THE THEORY OF THE STATE

Yet in the struggle for survival, the weakness and isolation of the workers' State might well seem insuperable barriers to Socialism. It was not only defence against imperialist countries; it was a question of the internal economy of the country. Lenin at first hoped for at least one advanced Capitalist economy to become Socialist. As he had reminded his readers in one of his early articles during the war: "It is impossible to pass from Capitalism to Socialism without breaking national frameworks, as it was impossible to pass from Feudalism to Capitalism without adopting the idea of a nation." During 1917, 1918 and 1919 he did confidently expect the revolution in Western Europe, particularly in Germany. While he was in hiding during the summer and autumn of 1917 he, as usual, was very methodically clearing his mind (and the minds of his followers) about the immediate future in his book, *The State and Revolution*. It was under this expectation that he had made the notes before the March revolution, and there is a reference to them in one of the early *Letters from Afar*. So that while in January he contemplated the possibility of not seeing the revolution in his lifetime, he was getting everything ready in case it came.

Whereas formerly his writing had been directed towards the achievement of a successful insurrection, now he is concerned with what will happen after—the forming of the dictatorship of the proletariat. Marx and Engels had always considered this problem from the point of view, that this task would be begun by the proletariat of one of the advanced countries, and it is from this basis that Lenin, expecting his revolution in one or more advanced countries besides Russia, prepares his notes. It is characteristic that the final draft of the book, though written while he was preparing for the Russian Revolution, devotes seven chapters to advanced countries. Only in the last two chapters did he intend to deal with Russia, and events prevented him.

An advanced country meant a country highly industrialised, and therefore with a proletariat urban and agricultural, but chiefly urban, which, with the petty-bourgeoisie closest to it, constituted a majority of society. A majority was necessary because it was this class, working through its representatives, which had to remould society. The first thing was to smash the bourgeois State machinery. On the experience of the Paris Commune Marx had seen that the proletariat could not use the bourgeois State as a means of introducing Socialism. Its main purpose, however disguised, however modified by the organised force of the working-class, was to keep the working poor in subjection. Its army, police and prisons, were mainly for the protection of the rich against the poor. As we have seen Lenin recognised that in England there was complete political liberty, but this was only on the surface. In reality democracy was democracy for the small minority, the rich. When the rich had been dispossessed a new type of State was wanted—a State which, being a State, would be the instrument of class-domination, the executive committee of the ruling-class, only this time the ruling-class would be the working-class. The content of this rule by the workers would vary as the rule of the rich varies from democratic Switzerland to Fascist Germany. The form of the new State, however, Lenin saw in the Soviet of workers' and peasants' deputies. The absence of wealthy property owners would make for real political equality among the proletariat, a real majority of the people. There would be among them real freedom of the Press, and an intimate control over their political representatives. There was to be no army set up against the people, the people would be armed in a national militia. The first business of this new State organisation was to dispossess the rich, and suppress their inevitable attempts at restoration. But he stated many times that this was essentially a subordinate task. Socialism did not aim at substituting the rule of the poor for the rich, justified as this might be on the score of a majority. The real task of the dictatorship of the proletariat was to increase production and create such abundance that first the petty-bourgeoisie would be drawn, on the basis of their own experience, to support the proletariat, and by a series of economic transformations extending over many years ultimately the new system would be so obviously superior to the old that there would be no danger of a restoration to a system of society based upon the private ownership of the means of production. The whole system would stand or fall by the increased productivity of labour. "This expropriation of the means of production will make a gigantic development of the productive forces *possible*. And seeing how incredibly, even now, Capitalism *retards* this development, how much progress could be made even on the basis of modern technique at the level it has reached, we have a right to say, with the fullest confidence, that the expropriation of the capitalists will inevitably result in a gigantic development of the productive forces of human society." If Lenin returned to-day, he would not waste a minute on Stalin's propaganda, but would calculate the income and expenditure per head of the population and from it grasp at once the social and political character of the régime.

Neither Marx nor Engels, Lenin nor Trotsky, cultivated any illusions as to the difficulties of the task. They looked forward with supreme confidence to the gradual change of human society and the whole psychology of mankind, but very strictly in relationship to the development of the forces of production. It will have been noted that in the passage quoted above Lenin underlined the word possible.

As Marx carefully explained (and Lenin quoted it with emphasis) this mere seizure of the property of the bourgeoisie and the maintenance of the State-power did not mean Socialism. Bourgeois ideas of right were not entirely abolished, but "only in part, only in proportion to the economic transformation so far attained, i.e. only in respect of the means of production. 'Bourgeois right' recognises them as the private property of separate individuals. Socialism converts them into common property. To that extent, and to that extent alone, does bourgeois right disappear." It was a fundamental postulate of Marx that, whatever the political system, the law and justice of no society can rise higher than the technical level of production.

There was, however, another aspect of this development of production to which too little attention has been paid—the part the workers were to play in it. The great value of the Soviet form of State was not only the nearness of government to the masses, but the opportunity it gave them to enter into the main business of any society—production. Ultimately the standard of education, of fitness for the complicated duties of citizenship, rested on the level of production. As Lenin wrote later, the discipline of slave-society was the whip, the discipline of capitalist society was hunger. "The Communist organisation of labour—to which Socialism is the first step—is based upon the free and conscious discipline of the workers themselves who have thrown off the yoke of landlords and Capitalists." The creative capacity of the masses—he believed in it as no other leader of the workers ever did. That creative capacity had hitherto been seen only in revolution. The Soviet system based on the masses in the factories was to organise this creativeness not only for purpose of government but also for production, linking the two closer and closer together until ultimately the all-embracing nature of production by the whole of society rendered the State superfluous. Thus the inherent development of the productive forces which was "*possible*" under collective ownership would be immensely stimulated by the direct participation of workers in the business of accounting and control. The higher the productivity of labour, the greater would be the leisure, the education, the capacity for service of the worker, and his emancipation from bureaucracy, leading in turn to a still greater productivity of labour and increasing opportunities. It was from this interaction, the development of the productive forces and the continually increasing active participation and capacity for participation in that work by the millions, that would be evolved the Socialist society. "The narrow horizon of bourgeois rights " which compels one to calculate, with the hardheartedness of a Shylock, whether he has not worked half an hour more than another, whether he is not getting less pay than another—this narrow horizon will then be left behind. There will then be no need for any exact calculation by society of the quantity of products to be distributed to each of its members. Each would take freely ' according to his needs.'

It was under those conditions with every member of society doing his share of work, with war and its huge unproductive expenditure abolished by the international character of production, with society reconstructed on the basis of such abundance as to minimize and abolish the competition for goods which breeds struggle, it was under such conditions only, that the State, the instrument of class-domination, in this case of working class domination, would gradually become superfluous and wither away. There would not be any one class to oppress another, for classes would have been abolished. People would behave decently and the few abnormalities (for the most part the product of a grossly unequal society) could be dealt with by society without any apparatus of prisons and police, but by the mere good sense and general will of the community, as they were dealt with in the only known form of classless society, primitive Communism.

When would this take place? "We do not and cannot know," words which Lenin very frequently used. It was not going to come smoothly. The very name Permanent Revolution implies the constant recurrence of great social and political upheavals. But Marxists did not make the world. They found it as it is. And their policy was the only policy because based on the decisive factor, the inescapable development of production. Meanwhile the greatest enemy to the development of the productive forces was Capitalism. And when Capitalism was conquered and the economic revolution began, the greatest enemy to the creative capacity of the masses was bureaucracy. And yet as we have seen, in the most advanced stages of capitalist society, owing to the fact that production barely exceeded the minimum requirements of the whole population, some such administrative group was inevitable. Lenin was quite aware of this, but writing in August, 1917, and having the world revolution in mind he was confident.

The Dangerous Isolation of the Workers' State

By 1920, however, it was clear that support from an advanced proletarian State in Europe was not coming for some time, and a task which would have strained the energies of the most advanced proletariat in the world had now to be faced by one of the most backward with an economy that was almost in ruins. The Russian proletariat was too weak to accomplish the building of Socialism. It was a small minority of the population, between two and three million workers and their families, so that what would have been in Germany the rule of a majority meant the political domination of a minority in Russia. There was no help for this, neither then nor for many years to come. The capacity to lead the nation in every sphere, the discipline that Lenin counted on so much "was not born of good intentions." It sprang "from the material conditions of great Capitalist production and from these alone. Without these conditions it is inconceivable. The power destined to turn these conditions to account is an historical class created, organised, trained and hardened by Capitalism." Under the best of conditions this was a small and backward class in Russia. And in 1920 the proletariat was at its last gasp. Output was only 18 per cent of the pre-war level, the output of pig-iron was 2.5 per cent. Then in 1921, to add to the destruction caused by the war, the two revolutions, the allied blockade, the civil war, came one of the most terrible famines in the whole history of Russia. It is in the weakness of the proletariat and these terrible conditions that we have to look for the disappointment that the workings of the Soviet system brought to Lenin and other Bolsheviks. The Capitalist world outside sneered, the Social Democrats thundered at the absence of democracy even among the workers in Russia. Even inside Russia a section of the Communist Party at the Eleventh Congress brought forward a resolution reminding the party that "according to the law the Trade Unions participate in all the local and central organs of industrial management." Lenin, who saw it far more clearly than they, rebuked them with grave words: "We know that Capitalist production has been built up by decades with the assistance of every advanced country in the world. Have we fallen back into infancy to think that at the time of the greatest need and impoverishment of the country in which the workers constitute a minority, in a country with the proletarian vanguard worn out and bled white, and with a mass of peasants, we will be able to complete this process so quickly . . . a year or two of rest from starvation, a year or two of regular supply of fuel so that the factories should work, and we will get a hundred times more support from the working class and no one among its ranks doubts or can doubt this. At present we do not get this support, not because we do not want it . . . but we know that the need is desperate, that we have hunger and poverty everywhere and this constantly leads to passiveness. Let us not fear to call an evil and a calamity by their real names. That is what prevents the use of energy among the masses." But the lack of energy among the masses meant the increase of bureaucracy.

Bureaucratic control from above by the party was not wholly due to the necessity of holding the power. It was to some degree forced upon it. Lenin applied the only antidote: a rigid, an almost fanatical honesty before the masses, of which the quoted extract is an example from hundreds. Not only the party but the proletariat, small and dispirited as it was, had to be kept aware of the real dangers of the State and the necessary measures of guarding against them. And the greatest danger to Socialist Russia was Capitalism, not only outside, but the seeds of it inside—the peasantry. It is still the danger to-day, with the peasant disguised as collective farmer.

The peasant had fought for his land, he had fought against the Tsarist régime side by side with the Bolsheviks, he had submitted to the premature Socialism known as War Communism, forced on the cautious Lenin by the pressure of war. But the moment the civil war was over and the land was safe, the peasant first of all refused to produce and then revolted. Democratic dictatorship of the proletariat and peasantry, or Permanent Revolution, Lenin and Trotsky had all through the years long foreseen these troubles. In 1920 Trotsky, whose work took him about the country, had observed that the economy of the country could stand the forced requisition no longer and had proposed the first outlines of the New Economic Policy. The Central Committee rejected the proposal.[1] Now Lenin abolished the system of requisition, allowed the peasant to pay a tax in kind and by degrees gave him the right to trade. And with the restoration of the right to trade Capitalism was on its way again. Lenin knew that, until the revolution in the west, there had to be an alliance between proletariat and peasantry, but he had no illusions whatever as to the nature of the conflict between these two classes. In April, 1920, a year before the N.E.P. and while the system of War Communism was still in being, he let the Russians know what to expect. The peasants would be grateful for the emancipation given them by the workers, "but on the other hand under the conditions of commodity production the peasants remain owners, property holders; every instance of the sale of bread in the open market, every sack of flour or other food carried from place to place by private traders, every speculative deal means the restitution of commodity production and therefore the restitution of Capitalism. The overthrow of Capitalism involved and brought about the emancipation of the peasantry, but against this overthrow there was the petty bourgeoisie—in old Russia undoubtedly a large class. The peasantry remain private owners as far as their production

[1] This was the origin of Trotsky's insistence on organizing the Trade Unions as organs of the State. If War Communism continued, he foresaw collapse unless the unions were knit tightly into the fabric of the Soviet State. The moment Lenin agreed to N.E.P., Trotsky accepted Lenin's Trade Union policy.

is concerned, and are establishing new capitalistic relations. These are the principal features of our economic position, and it is this that gives rise to those absurd speeches emanating from men who fail to understand the real position; speeches on liberty, equality and democracy. We are conducting a class struggle and our aim is to abolish classess; so long as there still exist two classes, those of peasants and workers, socialism cannot be realised, and an irreconcilable struggle goes on incessantly."

If this was so in 1920 under War Communism, the N.E.P., which established free trading, would intensify the danger in geometrical progression. But Lenin was not afraid of it—at first. The Socialist proletariat held the great industries, the transport system, the banks. And in the struggle between the development of peasant Capitalism and the development of Socialist industry, the party representing the proletariat had the enormous advantage of controlling the State-power. State-power cannot permanently defeat economic development but it can exercise an immense influence, and the Russian proletariat had absolute control, perhaps too much, Lenin warned. The Soviet constitution gave one Soviet representative to 25,000 workers, but one to 125,000 peasants, thus ensuring the dominance of the proletariat. With energy, economy and flexibility industry could be improved, the balance could be held, and the standard of life raised until help came from the revolution in the West. Everything, until the revolution in the West.

But while so many know of the change, of equal importance for the building of Socialism was the method of the change.

In the spring of 1921, Lenin proposed the N.E.P. and called it by its name—a retreat. In October he weighed up the question and stated that it was necessary to retreat still further, passing from the first concessions to the creation of purchases, of sales, and of monetary circulation regulated by the State. "To conceal from oneself, from the working-class, from the masses, that in the economic domain, in the Spring of 1921 and at present, too, in the Spring-Winter of 1921–22, we are still continuing to retreat, is to condemn ourselves to complete unconsciousness, is to be devoid of the courage to face the situation squarely. Under such conditions, work and struggle would be impossible." How many in Western Europe can understand these words? Certainly those who gloss over Stalin's monumental falsifications do not understand the elements of Leninism.

On March 6, 1922, he said that he hoped the retreat was completed and that the party congress would be able to say so officially in the name of the party. The congress presented the resolution and every party member, every worker in the State, every peasant knew the exact position and could take his share in the measures that the party advocated for the progress of the country. With the enormous responsibility which lay on the party exercising the dictatorship of the proletariat, it had to keep itself clean like a sword. Speaking of the retreat in 1921, Lenin said: "It is not the defeat which is so dangerous as the fear of admitting one's defeat, the fear of drawing from it all the conclusions. . . . Our strength in the past was, as it will remain in the future, that we can take the heaviest defeats into account with perfect coolness, learning from their experience what must be modified in our activity. That is why it is necessary to speak candidly. This is vital and important not alone for the purpose of theoretical correctness, but also from the practical point of view. We cannot learn to solve the problems of to-day by new methods if yesterday's experience has not made us open our eyes in order to see wherein the old methods were at fault." He viewed every aspect of the new State in the same sternly critical way. At first he defended the Soviet régime, but when as time passed he began to see its shortcomings, he exposed them to the masses. No severer or more consistent criticisms of Soviet Government were made by any Social Democrat. He said over and over again that it was bad, that there was a thin surface of democracy above, but that below it was the same old Tsarist bureaucracy over again. He pointed out the reasons, the ignorance and backwardness of Russia, far behind the Capitalist countries. Even in Lenin's time, the Soviets were being deprived of power by the party and the bureaucracy. Lenin preached ceaselessly of the main reason—the backwardness of the people. There could not be democracy, far less Socialism, in such a country, and without democracy there could be no Socialism. The Russians had first to learn, secondly to learn, and thirdly to learn, not proletarian art and proletarian culture and such like nonsense on which he poured a contemptuous scorn, but simply to read and write. The Communist Party reflected this backwardness and added to its incompetence an arrogance which he continually denounced before the masses. For him this Communist arrogance was the chief danger, next came corruption and thirdly the ignorance of the people. The internal remedy was increase of production. No sentimentality was to stand in the way of this. He advocated dismissal from high posts of Communists who had suffered years of imprisonment under Tsarism for the revolution, and the substitution for them of competent bourgeois. He pointed out the Communist lack of culture in comparison with the bourgeoisie, the necessity to use these bourgeois, at high salaries (the secret police would deal with them if they were in any way disloyal), to help the Soviet State until it had trained its own Communist personnel.

He could see the bureaucracy and the corruption growing around him. The party would have to fight them. No party member could draw more than 270 roubles, the pay of the skilled workmen. Thus he strove to keep the self-seekers out of the party. And by precept and example he showed the party the Socialist way, facing the truth fearlessly before the masses and encouraging them to feel that the State was theirs. His great error—and he saw it too late—was to have taken too lightly that filching of their power from the people in the Soviets. Yet the underlying remedy for all this, the pressing necessity for every aspect of life in the Soviet Union, was the restoration of Soviet economy. Under his direction the party set itself to this task. But while he did so and called on the country to bend all its energies to this work, he lost no opportunity of telling the party and the workers and peasants that not only the external safety but the internal development of the State towards Socialism depended in the last analysis upon the international proletariat. From every conceivable angle, with unwavering insistence he never let them forget it.

LENINISM: THE IMPOSSIBILITY OF SOCIALISM IN A SINGLE COUNTRY

At first his emphasis was on the impossibility of the two systems, Capitalism and Socialism, existing side by side.

In March, 1918, he told the Seventh All-Russian Congress of Soviets: "International Imperialism . . . could in no case and under no conditions live side by side with the Soviet Republic." And a year later, at the Eighth Congress, "We live not in a State but in a system of States, and the existence of the Soviet Republic side by side with imperialist States for an extended period is unthinkable."

The danger, however, was not only external but internal. "In a number of writings, in all our speeches and in our Press, we have emphasised the fact that this is now the position in Russia, that in Russia we have a minority of industrial workers and a vast majority of small agriculturalists. In such a country a social revolution can be definitely successful only under two conditions. The first condition is that it be supported by a modern social revolution in one of the several advanced countries. The other condition is an agreement between the proletariat which is exercising its dictatorship, or which holds the power of the State in its hands, and the majority of the peasant population.

"We know that only an agreement with the peasantry can save the Socialist revolution in Russia until such time as the revolution takes place in other countries." [1]

When the revolution was seen to be further away than had been expected he shifted the argument to the international character of modern production. Socialist or Capitalist, Russia was tied to world economy. At the Eighth Congress of the Soviets in December, 1920, he told the delegates: "Whilst our Soviet Russia remains a solitary suburb of the whole Capitalist world, during that time to think of our complete economic independence

[1] V. I. Lenin, "The Food Tax," a speech delivered to the Tenth Congress of the Russian C.P. on March 15, 1921.

and the disappearance of all danger would be an utterly ridiculous fantastry and utopianism." And not only was Russia tied to world production, but the collective system in isolated backward Russia was at a disadvantage against even Capitalist anarchy on an international scale. For the time being the Russian State could keep out foreign goods and protect backward Russian industry by the rigid control of everything exported or imported, the monopoly of foreign trade. But this was an unnatural device. The ultimate test of a new civilisation was the higher productivity of labour in comparison with the old. "We are confronted with a test which is being prepared by the Russian and international market, to which we are subordinate, with which we are bound up, from which we cannot break away. This is a serious test for here they may beat us both economically and politically."

And in the last article he ever wrote: "Shall we succeed in maintaining ourselves with our petty peasant production, with our ruined condition, until the Capitalist countries of Western Europe complete their development to Socialism? Such is the question which faces us at this moment. We are not civilised enough to pass directly to Socialism though we have the political premises for it." [1] We could quote dozens more of the same type. Why was he so insistent? It was because he knew that ideas are not a force until they are seized upon by the masses, and knew the difficulty of maintaining the international Socialist conception and the pitfalls that awaited any deviation from it. While he lived he held the party there, and the Russian proletariat followed faithfully. [2] But in July, 1922, Lenin fell ill and was away from work until October. When he came back he

[1] "Better Less but Better," *Pravda*, April 4, 1923. The writer has used an MSS. translation. Many of the most important articles by Lenin, written after 1918, have to be tracked down in obscure publications or translated afresh. The present Soviet régime dare not publish them or, when it does so, truncates them.

[2] In face of the mass of evidence quoted above it is clear that as a rule when Lenin said Socialism he meant that highly developed form of society based on a productivity of labour far beyond Capitalism, and impossible in the isolated economy of Soviet Russia. To-day, however, Stalin claims the final victory of Socialism. Having to explain away the gross inequalities existing under this Socialism, he propounds that by Socialism Lenin meant collective ownership and planned economy only. The thesis is the usual

noted in a draft for a speech: "There is no evil without good. I have been sitting quiet for half-a-year and looking on 'from the side-lines.'" What he had seen was not only the degeneration of the Soviet system, but also the degeneration of the party. And if that were not checked then the dictatorship of the proletariat was in grave peril. From his sick-bed he set himself to fight it—the last and, without a doubt, what would have proved the greatest battle of his life. The next two or three years were critical for the Soviet Union and remain the most difficult years on which to form a judgment.

THE DICTATORSHIP OF THE PROLETARIAT

No more vicious mistake in Socialist theory can be made than the too prevalent habit of using the term dictatorship of the proletariat as synonymous with the personal dictatorship of a Lenin or worse still of a Stalin. Mussolini's régime in Italy, the democracy in the Scandinavian countries, are equally the dictatorship of the burgeoisie.

The dictatorship of the proletariat is a formula whose evaluation depends at a given time in a given country upon the relationship between the classes on a national and international scale. We have seen the national and international reasons for the harsh form it of necessity assumed in Russia between 1918 and 1922. The dictatorship of the proletariat in Russia, Germany and France, all Socialist at the same time, would result, if by any conceivable chance a Capitalist Britain should survive for any length of time, in such Fascist tyranny in Britain that not only the working-class but all except the Fascists themselves and a few of the very biggest bourgeois would have less freedom than the meanest street-sweeper in the emancipated States. The political

---

Stalinist falsification, and Stalin himself, as can be seen from the photograph reproduced after the Preface, used the word for years in precisely the sense that Lenin so often used it. But it should be noted that Marx and Engels and Lenin did use the words Socialism and Communism interchangeably, at other times making a distinction between Communism as the highest stage of Socialism. For an able study on the use of the words at different times by Marx, Engels and Lenin see *The Socialist Standard*, August, 1936. For the most plausible version of the Stalinist falsification, see *The Theory and Practice of Socialism*, by John Strachey, p. 113.

content of the dictatorship in any particular country rests on the rate and successes of the economic transition to Socialism, which in turn depends upon the natural and industrial resources of the Socialist country, its relationship abroad with other countries, Socialist or Capitalist—in fact the whole international background against which any political form in any European or other highly developed State must be judged to-day. While ultimately it is the economic situation and the class-relationship resting on this which is the deciding factor, yet the State-power exercises a powerful influence. The regulator of all these relationships in a Socialist State is the Communist Party which controls the State-power and, in close association with the representatives of the international proletariat, governs the country in the interests of international Socialism. Until the abolition of classes a Communist Party must function. It is composed of the ablest and most trustworthy elements of the working-class movement in each country, some Marxist intellectuals, but the majority workers from the bench, in order to keep the party in the closest contact with the working-class through which, not from inherent virtue but from its rôle in production, the regeneration of society is to be attained. Though the party will in the last analysis reflect the general stage of development of the country, yet its leadership can, as Lenin's case proves so conclusively, rise to heights of character and insight which will help to maintain the party at a high level and accomplish tasks of world-wide importance; or it can, as within a few months of Lenin's illness, drag the party down until it is nothing but the docile instrument of a degrading tyranny. The precise relationship between dominating individuals and social forces, always a difficult thing to determine, is exceptionally important here. For the moment it is enough to say that we do not accept the view that the degeneration of the Bolshevik Pary was inevitable.

THE PARTY IN POWER

In the years before October, 1917, Lenin's insistence on the discipline necessary for illegal work and armed insurrection, then the ruin of the war, the civil war and military intervention, the temporary failure of the world revolution, the relative weakness of the Russian proletariat, had driven the Communist Party of Russia steadily along the path of becoming almost a military organisation ruled from above. Yet in the most desperate times of the civil war Lenin had insisted on maintaining what we can see to-day to have been an astonishing freedom of discussion. He dominated, but only by his personal authority. Immediately the civil war was over he initiated a resolution calling for party democracy, or as it was euphemistically called workers' democracy. He knew that it was necessary to curtail the freedom he had promised in Russia, to hold on at all costs for the sake of the international revolution. Yet the party had to remain a free instrument; with the enormous power that it wielded ossification would be a disaster. How far could there be full and continued freedom in the party if there was restricted political freedom in the working-class as a whole? This was the danger of which Rosa Luxemburg was always aware in her struggle for a full democracy against Lenin's centralism. Lenin in his resolution stated that with the same energy and decisiveness with which the party had militarised itself it should now set to work to have free democracy within itself. But in 1921 came the rebellion at Kronstadt and all the troubles that led to the N.E.P. For a moment the situation was more dangerous than ever before, and for the first time in nearly twenty years Lenin had to forbid fractions or organised groups in the party. The resolution on democracy within the party remained in abeyance. Now after his return from his illness he was appalled to find that the party was being corrupted from above as well as from below.

The head of the bureaucratic fungus was Stalin, now General Secretary of the party, Commissar for Nationalities, and Commissar of the Workers' & Peasants' Inspection. He dominated the party machine. In the vast, backward and unsettled country, party members and officials of the Soviet State had great power, and by a system of appointing from above, unparalleled even in the harshest times of the civil war, he had built up in the organisational apparatus of the party a powerful support for himself. He was also in close relationship with Djerzhinsky, the head of the all-powerful secret police. Lenin's authority was no sooner impaired by illness than he found himself in constant conflict with Stalin.

The monopoly of foreign trade was the only safeguard of the Soviet State against the higher productive system of Capitalism. To this day Russian production is so backward that if goods from Germany, Britain or the U.S.A. were allowed in, they would ruin Russian economy. Yet as soon as Lenin was away Stalin, Zinoviev and Kamenev, as incompetent in economics as in organising insurrection, introduced important exceptions into this monopoly. Trotsky opposed them unsuccessfully. Lenin, as always when he found himself in difficulties, turned to Trotsky, and asked him to defend the position at the party conference in April. Trotsky did so and it was established that the monopoly of foreign trade is "one of the pillars of the Socialist dictatorship in the circumstances of capitalist encirclement," the phrasing being a clear indication that in those days no one in the Soviet Union dreamt of surpassing capitalist productivity of labour while the workers' State was surrounded by world Capitalism.

On December 25, Lenin wrote the famous Testament [1] in which he characterises Stalin. "Comrade Stalin, having become General Secretary, has concentrated an enormous power in his hands; and I am not sure that he always knows how to use it with sufficient caution." Then came the Georgian affair and Lenin's swift realisation that the party, if it were to save itself, must get rid of Stalin. Stalin and Djerzhinsky had been entrusted with the mission of smoothing out the difficulties which were being experienced in the admission of the smaller republics to the U.S.S.R. Stalin, sent to Georgia, had behaved with such brutality as to call forth the strongest censure from Lenin. Ordjoni- kidze (to-day Commissar of Heavy Industry and one of

---

[1] There are references to it by Stalin himself in the *International Press Corres- pondence* of November 17, 1927, and in *The Truth about Trotsky*, by R. F. Andrews, London, 1934, p. 68.

the chief supporters of the Stalinist régime) had continued Stalin's policy in Georgia and had even struck a Georgian comrade. "We live in a sea of illegality" was one of the first letters the sick Lenin had written to the Politbureau, and now he could see where the chief danger was coming from. He demanded that Ordjonikidze should be expelled from the party for two years. That such a thing could happen showed "to what a morass we have fallen." He asked that the persecuted subject nationalities should be protected from the Diejimordes (tyrants and brutes). The tyrants and brutes were Stalin and Djerzhinsky. To the Georgians he wrote: "I am working for you with all my heart" . . . and while, for the time being careful in public statements, in his private correspondence he showed the anger and distrust he felt for the coarse, ignorant, and immoral Georgian . . . "Internationalism from the side of the oppressing, or so-called great nations (although they are great only in their violations), must consist in observing not only a formal equality, but an equality which would destroy upon their side that inequality which is created factually in real life. The hastiness and administrative impulsiveness of Stalin played a fatal rôle here, and also his spite against the notorious "social-chauvinism"; spite in general plays the worst possible rôle in politics. It behoves us to hold Stalin and Djerzhinsky politically responsible for this genuine great Russian nationalistic campaign."[1] He wrote these letters in the last days of December, and on January 4 he added a note to the Testament, more restrained in tone but unmistakable in intent. "Postscript: Stalin is too rude, and this fault, entirely supportable in relations among us Communists, becomes insupportable in the office of General Secretary. Therefore I propose to the comrades to find a way to remove Stalin from that position and appoint yet another man who in all respects differs from Stalin only in superiority

[1] Cp. *The Theory and Practice of Socialism*, by John Strachey, p. 430. "The way in which the Soviet Union has known how to reconcile the claims for cultural, educational and administrative economy made by the subject peoples of the Tsarist Empire, without sacrificing any of its essential strength and unity, has been one of its greatest triumphs. This work has been, above all, inspired by Stalin." Stalin, claiming to hate social-chauvinism i.e. excessive nationalism, was as harsh to the nationalities as any Great Russian.

—namely, more patient, more loyal, more polite and more attentive to comrades, less capricious, etc." Once again he turned to Trotsky. Enclosing all his notes he wrote: "That affair (the Georgian affair) is now under investigation at the hands of Stalin and Djerzhinsky. I cannot rely upon their impartiality, indeed just the contrary. If you would agree to undertake its defence, I could be at rest."

LENIN STRUGGLES TO DESTROY STALIN

The last three months of his working life Lenin spent in a vain attempt to reorganise the party machinery for the fight against Stalin and bureaucratic corruption. He began as always from below. On December 26 he recommended that the Central Control Committee should consist chiefly of workers in close touch with the masses and not those who have had a long period of Soviet employment "because these workers have already acquired certain traditions and prejudices which are just the ones we want to struggle against." And having decided that Stalin should go, he in January took the struggle into the open but still with caution. The Government represented "to a very large degree a survival of the past. . . . It has only been slightly painted up on top and in all the other respects it represents the most typically old of our old government machinery." The party must concentrate its best forces and, as it did in the period of the most dangerous times of the civil war, find new forces "where our dictatorship had its deepest roots." The reference to the civil war showed how seriously he estimated the position and knew what so few Communists know, that the greater the danger the greater the necessity of mobilising the great masses of the people. It was the personal power of the brutal and disloyal General Secretary which had to be curbed first. Lenin therefore proposed to elect between 75 and 100 new members of the Central Control Committee from among the workers and peasants, who should be given full rights as members of the Central Committee. The Workers' and Peasants' Inspection (the organisation Stalin controlled) should be reduced and the two bodies fused. In all these arrangements there is as far as we can see to-day only one serious error. He gave his authority to the idea of fusing the party with the State-apparatus. Even with the party as it might have been this plan was dangerous, and we have little doubt that with the increasing growth of the Soviet bureaucracy Lenin would have changed his mind about this, as he so frequently did about many things. But all this meant the end of Stalin's use of his position to bribe people to support him. Stalin, already disgraced as Commissar of Nationalities, attempted to use his chief political argument—suppression of the article. One of Stalin's confederates, Kuibyshev, proposed that a special copy of *Pravda* should be printed and shown to Lenin to pacify him. Trotsky opposed this so vigorously that Stalin had to give way and the article appeared in *Pravda* of January 25. Lenin then decided to destroy Stalin and showed how serious he considered the position by taking the struggle into the open.

In his last and perhaps the very finest article he ever wrote [1] he combined a profound warning of the necessity of getting the very best elements and training them carefully for government with a series of bitter attacks on Stalin's Workers' and Peasants' Inspection. "The People's Commissariat of Inspection does not enjoy even a shadow of authority at present. It is well known that there are no institutions working worse than our Commissariat of Inspection and that under the modern conditions there is nothing to expect from this Commissariat." And, "Why indeed form a Commissariat that will work without any efficiency, so that it will not arouse any confidence and the work will not enjoy the least prestige?" and, "Our new Commissariat of Inspection will leave behind the quality which the French call pruderie, that is ridiculous affectation, of trying to look important, which plays very much into the hands of our bureaucracy, both in the Soviets and in the party. It should be said parenthetically that we have a bureaucracy not only in the Soviet institutions but in the party institutions as well." And then, as was his habit, almost abruptly, he concluded the article by a long dissertation relating the matter in hand to the international

[1] "Better Less, but Better."

139

Socialist revolution, ending with the quotation we have given above.[1]

"Vladimir Ilyich is preparing a bomb against Stalin at the Congress," wrote Lenin's secretary. He wrote a letter, his last, breaking off all comradely relations with Stalin. But he was seized by another attack and he could not speak at the congress. His last strength had been spent in a vain endeavour to drive from the high councils and confidence of the party the man who concentrated in himself all the evil tendencies that Lenin feared for the future. In those few critical and uncertain months that Lenin lay ill Stalin and his clique used their only weapon—the consolidation of their personal hold by the intensive bureaucratisation of the party apparatus. It was in the beginning nothing else but a struggle for power. [2] Even before Lenin died in January, 1924, power was in the hands of Stalin, whom Lenin feared most, and Zinoviev and Kamenev, whom in his Testament he had told the party never to trust. These three, the Troika, ruled Russia, and ruling Russia controlled the Communist International. We have seen how in March, 1917, Stalin and Kamenev had switched the Bolshevik Party on to a road that would have imperilled the Russian Revolution, which had been served only by the timely appearance of Lenin. We shall see them acting in the identical way when faced with the German Revolution in October.

But in October, 1923, Lenin lay on his bed, dying, and, though neither he nor anyone else knew it, the defeat of the German Revolution in that month heralded the death of international Socialism in his party, its creed of twenty-five years.

[1] Page 26
[2] The best short treatment of this last period of Lenin's life can be found in *The Suppressed Testament of Lenin*, by Leon Trotsky, Pioneer Publishers, New York. See also *Since Lenin Died*, by Max Eastman, London, 1925, a well-documented survey; and *Staline*, by Boris Souvarine, Paris, 1935, Chapter VII, a book with an anarchist bias against the dictatorship of the proletariat but irreproachably documented, very fair, and full of insight.

Chapter 6

STALIN AND SOCIALISM

IN THE TESTAMENT, LENIN, AS SUPERIOR TO HIS CON-
temporaries in grasp of men as of politics, had warned the
party of a probable split between Trotsky and Stalin.
It was, he said, a trifle, but "a trifle as may acquire a
decisive significance." Lenin believed in historical materialism but he did not underestimate the significance of
individuals, and the full immensity of the consequences are
visible to-day.

Yet, as Lenin, quite obviously, saw, the immediate origin
of the danger was personal. Lenin did not say so in so many
words. The Testament is very carefully phrased, but all
through the civil war there had been clashes between
Trotsky and Stalin. Stalin, with Zinoviev and Kamenev,
who supported him at first, hated Trotsky, but Stalin
hated him with a hatred which saw in him the chief obstacle
to his power; Zinoviev and Kamenev Stalin knew he could
manage. Zinoviev on his part feared Trotsky, but feared
Stalin also. He had the idea of balancing one against the
other. But he went with Stalin for the time being. What
manner of man was this who was so soon to usurp Lenin's
position and attempt to play Lenin's part? No man of
this generation, few men of any other, could have done
this adequately.

LENIN

Lenin, first and foremost, knew political economy as few
professors in a university did. He was absolute master
of political theory and practice. He knew the international
working-class movement of the great countries of Europe,
not only their history theoretically interpreted by historical
materialism, but from years of personal experience in

Britain, France, Germany and Switzerland.[1] He spoke almost faultless German and wrote the language like a second tongue. He was at home in French and English and could read other European languages with ease. Intellectual honesty was with him a fanatical passion, and to his basic conception of allying the highest results of theoretical and practical knowledge in the party to the instinctive movements of millions, honesty before the party and before the masses was for him essential. The range and honesty of his intellect, his power of will, the singular selflessness and devotion of his personal character, added to a great knowledge and understanding of men, enabled him to use all types of intellect and character in a way that helped to lift the Bolshevik party between 1917 and 1923 to the full height of the stupendous rôle it was called upon to fulfil. No body of men ever did so much, and how small most of them really were we can realise only by looking at what they became the moment their master left them. Lenin made them what they were. He was sly and manœuvred as all who have to manage men must manœuvre. But through all the disagreements of those years which often reached breaking-point he never calumniated, exiled, imprisoned or murdered any leaders of his party. He was bitter in denunciation, often unfair, but never personally malicious. He was merciless to political enemies, but he called them enemies, and proclaimed aloud that if they opposed the Soviet régime he would shoot them and keep on shooting them. But Trotsky tells how careful he was of the health of his colleagues; hard as he was it is easy to feel in his speeches, on occasions when the party was being torn by disputes, a man of strong emotions and sensitiveness to human personality. In his private life he set an unassuming example of personal incorruptibility and austere living. No man could ever fill his place, but it was not impossible that someone able and willing to act in his tradition could have carried on where he left off, and all knew that Trotsky was best fitted for that difficult post. Lenin had designated him as such in the Testament. But

[1] No finer volume on the realities of English politics and history exists than his occasional articles collected in the volume *Lenin on Britain*.

the irony, the cruellest tragedy of the post-war world is, that without a break the leadership of the over-centralised and politically dominant Bolshevik party passed from one of the highest representatives of European culture to another who, in every respect except singlemindedness of purpose, was the very antithesis of his predecessor.

STALIN

Stalin's personal character is not the dominating factor of Soviet history since 1924. Far greater forces have been at work. But if Lenin's individual gifts were on the side of progress to Socialism, Stalin touched only to corrupt. Of political economy he was, and to a great extent is, quite ignorant; in Marxism he and his henchmen are to-day capable of errors that a raw Social Democrat would not be guilty of. These things will be proved in their place. For the moment it is sufficient to give some significant incidents in his early history.

In January, 1928, Verechtschaks, one of his early companions, gave in the Paris newspaper, *Dui*, some recollections of Stalin in prison.[1] Their authenticity will not be denied by the Stalinists, for in *Pravda* of February 2, 1928, and December 20, 1929, Demian Biedny, a Stalinist scribbler, quoted such scraps as reflected credit on the beloved leader. He did not quote the following. One day a young Georgian was badly beaten by his brother-prisoners in the Benlov prison as a provocateur, a charge which turned out to be false. Later it was discovered that the rumour came from Stalin. On another occasion an ex-Bolshevik knifed and killed a worker whom he did not know but whom he believed to be a spy. The murderer confessed afterwards that Koba (as Stalin was then called) had incited him. At the end of 1901 Koba suddenly left Tiflis. The Georgian Social-Democratic magazine, *Brdzolis Khma* (Echo of Struggle) tells us why. Stalin, by means of slander and intrigue, had attempted to undermine the position of the leader of the organisation. After he had been warned many times he spread still more vicious slander and was unanimously expelled from the Tiflis organisation. This

[1] See the early chapters of *Stalin*, by Souvarine.

143

story is told not to blacken his character or cast him for the part of villain. It is of importance because he remains to-day what he was then, only where in early days he went round whispering and writing letters, from 1924 onwards he had all the resources of a great country at his disposal. The moment Lenin was incapacitated Stalin began to stamp the image of his corrupt and limited personality on the Bolshevik party. There is no inevitability in this. He was one kind of man and Lenin was another. The trial of Zinoviev, Kamenev and the others is no surprise to those who know the history of the Bolshevik party since Stalin has had power in his hands.

One final characteristic will also explain his supreme unfitness for authority in the Socialist State. In 1911 he wrote a letter giving his opinion on the struggle Lenin was waging against those who wished to liquidate the revolution and against Trotsky still striving for an impossible unity. "We have heard about the tempest in the tea-cup, the bloc of Lenin-Plekhanov on the one hand, and Trotsky-Martov-Bogdanov on the other. As far as I know the workers incline toward the former. In general, however, they mistrust the emigrés. Why should they bother themselves about them; as far as we are concerned, everyone who has the interest of the movement at heart does his own work. The rest will follow of itself. That is, in my opinion, the best."[1]

He neither knew nor cared. There are other instances of his national limitedness, his sneers at the emigrés, his contempt for theory. The Leninism which he has preached so assiduously since 1924 means nothing to him. With the veneer of an Oxford education in England, or a personal fortune in France and America, he would have been an ideal Prime Minister or President. An army of personal advisers and a traditional system would have given him scope for his powers of organisation, and intrigue and ruthless will. He could never have built a mass movement but as a second or successor to a Hitler or a Mussolini he could have found perhaps the best scope for his extraordinary abilities. As guide to a State based on

[1] *Zaria Vostoka*, December 23, 1925. See *La Lutte de Classes*, January-February, 1933.

the principles of scientific Socialism and formulator of the policies of the Third International, it is impossible to imagine any person more unsuitable. But it is these very qualities and defects that made the bureaucracy instinctively side with him against Trotsky in the struggle that followed.

He was without reputation and had reached where he was by rigidly siding with Lenin on nearly every occasion. In 1905 and October, 1917, he had done little. He had no personal appeal whatever. Nor had Zinoviev and Kamenev. All knew the part they had played not only before October but immediately after, when they had urged a coalition with the Mensheviks and had resigned from the Central Committee on account of their disapproval of the uncompromising policy of Lenin and Trotsky. Lenin had broadcast it to the whole population of Russia. Zinoviev was known to be a coward; his unoriginality earned him the nickname of Lenin's gramophone. Despite a certain popularity, neither he nor Kamenev could rival either Stalin or Trotsky.

Trotsky

Trotsky, on the other hand, was, even while Lenin lived, the most brilliant figure in Russia. As far as the strategy of October was concerned, Lenin's had been the guiding hand, but while he was in hiding Trotsky had been the leading figure before the masses in Petrograd. He was the "Man of October." His organisation of the Red Army had given him not only an international reputation but a vast popularity among the peasants. As Commissar for War, travelling from front to front, he had become personally known to and beloved by millions. He was the greatest orator in Europe, and at congresses of the International delivered the chief address in Russian, German and French, and would then, as War Commissar, review the Red Army for the delegates. His pamphlets appealed equally to professors and peasants. Most important of all, he was Lenin's right hand, acknowledged by all as his successor. His personal weakness was imperiousness and a certain inability to function easily with men his equal in status but obviously inferior in quality. He lacked Lenin's comprehensive good-nature and homeliness. His very brilliance and audacity in action carried with it a compensating incapacity for that personal manœuvring at which so many lesser men excel. His great weakness, incapacity in party organisation, did not impede him so long as he was a member of Lenin's great organisation. While Lenin lived he smoothed over all difficulties, and Lenin and Trotsky were two names indissolubly linked together. Stalin, jealous, small-minded but ambitious, lurked in the background and schemed and plotted. He found kindred spirits in Zinoviev and Kamenev. About priority Lenin and Trotsky never quarrelled. After the October revolution, Lenin proposed Trotsky as Chairman of the Council of Commissars. Trotsky saw that the suggestion was preposterous and insisted on Lenin taking his rightful place. They were concerned with policy not with place. But some old Bolsheviks hated this outsider who after opposing their master for years had suddenly walked in and ousted them from the position they thought theirs by right. But to the great masses Trotsky, even when Lenin was incapacitated, had still the prestige of his gifts and achievements and the magic of his close association with Lenin.

THE TROÏKA DESTROY THE PARTY

Trotsky was not only beloved by the masses, but was popular in the rank-and-file of the party. What had Zinoviev, Kamenev or Stalin ever done to make anyone except their own immediate followers enthusiastic over them? But the three had the party apparatus and the party funds in their hands. Djerzhinsky, who had shared with Stalin Lenin's castigation on the national question, was close to them, and they won over Bucharin in control of the party press. Stalin is supreme in his management of men. The emergency of civil war, blockade and famine, the forcible requisitioning from the peasants in the civil war, the fatigue and passivity of the masses, all these had given power to the party apparatus. Officials in the party were increasingly appointed from above. All over the vast, almost roadless, countryside Soviet officials and party officers held almost unlimited power, subject only to the central authority. While Lenin and Trotsky were immersed in economics, politics and the international revolution, Stalin worked for power.[1] He had had a narrow escape from Lenin. But after Lenin's final incapacitation he bureaucratised the party more and more, Zinoviev, Kamenev and Bucharin helping. What must not be forgotten is that this struggle went on in a narrow circle, so small had the governing group become, even under Lenin. The masses played little part, and Trotsky either could not or dared not bring the masses into it, as Lenin would infallibly have done sooner rather than later. Dissatisfaction began to grow; the party youth resented this tyranny as youth will. Then in September, 1923, with the economic situation critical, two secret societies were discovered in the Bolshevik Party. Measures were instantly taken to suppress them, but such formations were obviously the result of the bureaucratic régime which Lenin had recently attacked so openly and so pointedly. Trotsky brought the struggle into the open. He and many other members demanded that the old resolution on Workers' Democracy be implemented. On October 8, he wrote to the Central Committee pointing out that the apparatus had been bureaucratised by the method of selection instead of election, that the party was now in a dangerous condition and might be taken unawares by a crisis of exceptional severity. He had tried for a year and a half inside the Central Committee, but there had been no improvement, and he felt it his duty to bring the matter to the notice of the party. The reply was typical of that boorishness which has more and more distinguished Soviet politics the more Stalin's influence has increased. The Central Committee said that Trotsky's attacks on the Communist Party, which had continued for "several years," and his "determination to disturb the party," were due to the fact that he wanted the Central Committee to place him and Comrade Kalegaev at the head of industrial life. He was striving for unlimited powers in industry and military affairs and had "categorically declined

[1] Zinoviev and Kamenev have exposed it all. What was not so clear in 1927, when Trotsky was expelled from the Soviet Union, is clear to-day when one by one Stalin has destroyed every member of the old Central Committee.

147

the position of substitute for Lenin. That evidently he considers is beneath his dignity. He conducts himself according to the formula 'All or nothing.'" Years have not abstracted anything from the coarse personalities of this Government reply to a political accusation by a man who still occupied the position in the Socialist State that Trotsky occupied: the degradation of political life before the party and the masses had begun. But opinion in the party was in those days too strong for Stalin and his clique, and they were finally compelled to pass a resolution binding them to institute workers' democracy. The resolution was unanimously carried. But the three could not put it into operation, for it was the absence of democracy that gave them their power. Now that Lenin was away, a democratic régime, and Trotsky's authority and moral and intellectual superiority, would automatically place him at the head of the party. Somehow they had to destroy him. Stalin has no principles of any kind, political or otherwise, but Zinoviev and Kamenev lent themselves to this intrigue not only out of personal enmity, but because they feared all that Trotsky stood for. Trotsky wanted to push on with the industrialisation of the country. Zinoviev, notoriously a coward, feared to upset the equilibrium of Soviet economy. Trotsky wanted to utilise the bourgeois technicians as Lenin had always advocated. Stalin opposed this. It was on a similar question, the utilization of Tsarist officers, that he had intrigued against Trotsky during the civil war, and had been snubbed and suppressed by Lenin. Trotsky was the centre of the intellectuals of the party, of Marxist learning and analysis with its insistence on the necessity of going forward— the permanent reconstruction of the economic basis of society. Where Zinoviev and Kamenev from temperament stood for caution, Stalin, as his speeches during the next four years proved, undoubtedly did believe (if he ever gave any serious thought to the matter) that if one maintained the Soviet power Socialism would come somehow.[1] For these various reasons the three were united in their desire

[1] As far back as December, 1923, Trotsky had pointed out the immense political dangers lurking behind party bureaucracy. See *The New International*, January, 1935, p. 16.

to destroy Trotsky. What Zinoviev and Kamenev did not see was that behind them in this quarrel the party bureaucracy would inevitably range itself; behind the party bureaucracy was the State bureaucracy, and behind these were the capitalist elements in the Soviet Union. There is an observation by Lenin in one of his last articles which shows that he was always aware of the unstable nature of the class-relations in the country and feared a split for the very reason that the classes would seize the divisions to align themselves. But neither Zinoviev nor Kamenev nor anyone else could have foreseen the lengths to which Stalin would go in allying himself with reaction in order to destroy Trotsky and the international revolution for which he stood, and in which they, with all their faults, believed. For the time being they worked to destroy Trotsky.

The resolution had pinned them down. A few days after they got their opportunity. Flushed with his paper victory, Trotsky had written a letter to his own party local with the intention of elucidating the significance of workers' democracy. Without a shadow of malice or personal references he analysed the dangers which beset the party: "Destroying self-activity, bureaucratism thereby prevents a raising of the general level of the party. And that is its chief fault. To the extent that the most experienced comrades, and those distinguished by service inevitably enter into the apparatus, to that extent the bureaucratism of the apparatus has its heaviest consequences on the intellectual-political growth of the young generation of the party. This explains the fact that the youth—the most reliable barometer of the party—react the most sharply of all against party bureaucratism.

"It would be wrong to think, however, that the excess of apparatus-methods in deciding party questions, leaves no trace on the older generation, which incarnates the political experience of the party and its revolutionary traditions. No, the danger is great also on this side. It is needless to speak of the enormous significance—not only on a Russian, but on an international scale—of the older generation of our party; that is generally known and generally acknowledged. But it would be a crude mistake to estimate that significance as *a self-sufficient fact. Only a continual interaction of the older and younger generation within the frame of party democracy* can preserve the Old Guard as a revolutionary factor. Otherwise the old may ossify, and unnoticed by themselves become the most finished expression of the bureaucratism of the apparatus."[1]

Still pursuing a theoretical analysis he showed how the leaders of the Second International had degenerated from revolutionary Marxism into Revisionism, and the responsibility which the seniors bore: "we ourselves, the 'old men,' while naturally playing the role of leaders, should recognise the danger, state it openly, and guard against it by fighting against bureaucratism." On this recurrent question, the interaction of the old and the young, no more valuable advice has ever been given to any political party. Stalin, Kamenev and Zinoviev read the document and did not object to its publication in the party press. Kamenev spoke about it without enthusiasm, certainly without hostility.[2] But the very quality of the letter was a sign-post of their approaching eclipse, and suddenly they decided to use it against Trotsky. They accused him of setting the youth against the Old Guard. Stalin began in Moscow. "Whence this attempt to uncrown the Old Guard and demagogishly tickle the youth, so as to open and widen the little rift between these fundamental troops of our party? To whom is all this useful, if you have in view the interests of the party, its unity, its solidarity, and not an attempt to weaken its unity for the benefit of an opposition?" Zinoviev in Leningrad called it an attack on the "direct disciples of Lenin" and the Leningrad Soviet of which he was President passed a condemnatory motion by 3,000 votes to seven with five abstaining. Bucharin followed in the party press. "However, Bolshevism has never contrasted the party with the apparatus. That would be, from the Bolshevik point of view, absolute ignorance, for there is no party without its apparatus. . . ." The "direct disciples of Lenin," "Bolshevism, that is to say Leninism." That was the cue. They

[1] This and other relevant documents are given in full in appendices to Eastman's *Since Lenin Died.* See also *Le Cours Nouveau*, by L. Trotsky, Paris, 1925.

[2] *Since Lenin Died.* Fully documented with the important references easily verifiable in a file of *Pravda.*

had to break the name Trotsky from its inseparable association with the revered name, Lenin. They therefore posed as Leninists, as the heirs and guardians of the true tradition against Trotsky's perversions. That and that only was the origin of Stalin's Trotskyism. They had begun by calling Trotsky a left Communist. But now they quickly shifted over and called him Menshevik. For in order to prove that Trotskyism had always been opposed to Leninism they dug down into past history and raked up the old quarrels between Lenin and Trotsky. Now these quarrels had been on two main points, one the organisational question, on which Trotsky had been wrong. But the second was the Theory of the Permanent Revolution, and this embodied the whole theoretical basis of the Soviet Union and the Communist International. But Zinoviev and Kamenev followed Stalin and performed prodigies of casuistry. Incapable of even the most primitive theoretical analysis, Stalin, in his simple-minded way, elaborated upon the ideas they put forward. But the management of the campaign of slander, the scope it assumed, its success, these were the contributions of Stalin. His gifts were useless in a revolution. In a period of calm and an internal struggle for power in the apparatus Trotsky was out-generalled from first to last. What is important is not that Trotsky was beaten, but that he was beaten so quickly.

The Troïka Create Trotskyism[1]

Lenin died in January, 1924, and then followed a campaign on an unprecedented scale which vilified Trotskyism and Trotsky, and prepared the way for removing his supporters. Paul Scheffer,[2] Max Eastman,[3] Louis Fischer [4] and Walter Duranty,[5] the last two firm supporters of the

[1] Trotskyism has never been admitted as a label by the supporters of the views which are associated with the name of Trotsky. The Stalinists insist upon it in their attempts to prove Trotskyism something opposed to Leninism. The so-called Trotskyists are officially known as Bolshevik-Leninists. For a book of this kind, however, Bolshevik-Leninist would, for many reasons, have been confusing, and for convenience a wilderness of quotation marks around the oft-repeated Trotskyism and Trotskyists has been omitted.

[2] *Seven Years in Soviet Russia*, p. 143.
[3] *Since Lenin Died.*
[4] *The American Nation*, May 2, 1934.
[5] *I Write as I Please*, 1935, p. 218.

Stalinist régime, have testified to the nature of this campaign, its baselessness, its dishonesty. No evidence is more valuable than that of Louis Fischer, wholly devoted to the Stalinist régime. In the *New York Nation* of May 2, 1934, he tells how Stalin rewrote "Soviet history, so that Trotsky's rôle either disappears or becomes besmirched"; how propaganda excited hate against him, "not only in the party and youth but among the general population which once revered him"; how his supporters had to undergo years of "well-nigh intolerable physical, mental and moral suffering." Lenin's eyes used to blaze at any hint of political power used for personal ends. How is this better than bourgeois parliamentarism, he would ask. Here was the whole power of the State being used to destroy the finest and ablest servants of the revolution. Political reason for this baseness and disloyalty there was at the beginning none. Few of the cynical bourgeois who relate these facts, however, seem to have understood one of its most important aspects for any Socialist who understands the part the masses must play in the building of Socialism—the degradation of political life and the political thinking of a country already backward. What Lenin in the face of enormous odds had striven for as the only counter to the dictatorship, the political education of the masses, hoping to bring them more and more into control of production, and political activity and understanding as the country developed, all that Stalin, and he is the individual responsible, no sooner in power, began to destroy on a scale that has no parallel in history. To account for this in 1923 purely by the class-relationships in the country is to make a geometrical theorem of the materialist conception of history. The process then begun has continued. In the early days—there are still fools who say it—Trotsky was compared with Danton. He was an individualist unable to work with a party. But during the years the full force of Stalin's dictatorship has been used to prove to the Soviet workers that Trotsky, Zinoviev, Kamenev, Rakovsky, Rykov, Tomsky, Bucharin, all their leaders, have at one time or another been guilty of counter-revolution and have plotted to restore Capitalism in the

Soviet Union. Stalin alone has been good, faithful and true. To the Webbs and other bourgeois philistines, corrupted to the marrow by bourgeois politics, this is merely worth a footnote whereby they show exactly what they mean by Socialism. Whatever the future of the Soviet Union, it will be many, many years before political life recovers from this corruption injected from above. Given the defeat of the world-revolution degradation was inevitable. But that it took this particular form, and so early, is due to the evil personality of its chief representative.

"Trotsky has always been in the sphere of political questions a mere revolutionary *dilettante*." So read a sentence from a pamphlet published by the Leningrad Soviet under Zinoviev. And in addition to personal abuse of the fish-wife·variety, every sentence that Trotsky had ever written against Lenin or Lenin against Trotsky was raked out and published in unlimited editions. Lenin in his controversies with Trotsky had stated somewhere that Trotsky underestimated the peasantry. The Soviet Union was suddenly overwhelmed with pamphlets, articles and speeches proving that Trotsky underestimated the peasantry. The three conspirators had in their hands the party organisation, the party funds, the party Press, —every means of monopolising publicity. Dzherzhinsky and the secret police, the strong centralised control and tradition of discipline, did the rest. Many party members, old Bolsheviks, were bewildered by the charges. But in the confusion their old habits of loyalty to the party induced them to side with the ruling group against Trotsky, who was unceasingly made to appear as someone striving to break party discipline. Discipline, orthodoxy, centralism. This, said Stalin, was Leninism, and used the tradition to cover his aims. All who supported Trotsky and had any influence were dismissed from their posts, the more distinguished sent as ambassadors to foreign countries, others less in the public eye sent to remote parts, the students were dismissed from universities in thousands, and the G.P.U. was active against these new "class-enemies," meaning Trotsky's followers. The intellectuals, who were able to investigate all the trumpery about

Trotskyism, were driven out of the party. The party conference in May was managed with equal ruthlessness and cunning. Krupskaya had given the Troika the Testament to read at the conference. The Central Committee decided that it should not be read but discussed only with the most important party members. The fetish of party unity, party discipline, ceaselessly hammered by Stalin, Zinoviev and Kamenev, stifled criticism.

Lenin had asked that more workers should be introduced into the party. In January Stalin's secretariat selected 100,000 workers all over the country, in May 100,000 more.[1] All were given votes, all voted against Trotskyism.

Trotsky was ill and remained silent. Soon his friends dared not speak, for it might mean banishment to Siberia. Unemployment was rife, and the rank-and-file who would not see and acknowledge the difference between Stalin's Leninism and Trotskyism stood in fear of losing their jobs.

In October came the climax. Trotsky published his articles and speeches of 1917 with a preface on "The Lessons of October," in which, comparing those who opposed Lenin in October, 1917, with the leaders in October, 1923, in Germany, he laid the blame for the failure at the door of the pusillanimous and incompetent German Central Committee. October, 1917, was above all what Zinoviev, Kamenev and Stalin could not have any discussion upon. The book was unofficially suppressed. But the campaign against Trotskyism reached fantastic heights. A flood of articles and pamphlets against Trotskyism was let loose on the Russian public. Electric lights at night advertised "Replies to Trotsky," what Lenin had said about Trotsky, what Trotsky had said about Lenin. Friendly critics have blamed Trotsky for his continued silence. It was not only illness, a stubborn pride, a respect for the dignity of the Soviet State. Under the influence of his profound studies of history he seems for a time to have accepted with too much fatalism this emergence of bureaucratic corruption in a period of revolutionary ebb.

[1] *I Write as I Please*, by Walter Duranty, p. 201.

A persecution so cruel, in the name of the Socialist revolution for which they had cheerfully risked life and liberty, broke the spirit of many who would have been unshakable against the counter-revolution. Suicide among the party members became so common that a special investigation had to be made and a report sent to the Central Committee with recommendations to check it.[1] Lenin was not yet dead one year. Who that knows his record can believe that had he lived such a state of affairs could possibly have existed at that time? In September, 1924, Trotsky's secretary, expelled from the party, committed suicide.

THE BUREAUCRACY CONQUERS

The split to begin with might appear to be a trifle but it was to have a decisive significance. A political struggle of this kind cannot be isolated from its national and international environment. It took four years to drive Trotsky and those who followed him out of the party. The traditions of Leninism were too strongly rooted. Stalin and his faction by their attacks on Trotsky and Trotskyism were driven further and further from Leninism—the theory and practice of the international Socialist revolution. Trotsky's special contribution to Marxism, the Permanent Revolution, was their special target. But they could not rely on argument and they destroyed physically the Left wing of the party, strengthening thereby the Right. The defence of bureaucratism against workers' democracy caused the Troïka to lean still further on the bureaucracy. The proletariat, exhausted by the herculean efforts between 1917 and 1924, had received a crushing blow with the defeat of the German proletariat. The world revolution and all the hopes of 1917 seemed dead. It was bewildered and confused by the sheer weight of the attacks on Trotsky, the man who, more than all others, it associated with October and the defeat of the European counter-revolution. The party bureaucracy had a clear field. Supporting it was the bureaucracy in the country which knew without being told where its interests lay. It knew Lenin's views, that Trotsky held them, and that if Trotsky and the Opposition

[1] *Pravda*, October 9, 1924.

gained power it would mean a cleansing of the party, a cleansing of the governing bureaucracy in the manner Lenin had suggested, and a vigilant watch on all bureaucratism. Stalin steadily fused the party and the bureaucracy until to-day they are indistinguishable. And supporting the party bureaucracy and the bureaucracy in the Soviet Government were the new class of kulaks in the country and the traders in the towns. Under the New Economic Policy Soviet economy was recovering, but creating inevitably a new capitalist class. Outside, in Europe, Capitalism, fed temporarily by American loans, was stabilizing itself on the ruins of the German Revolution and was re-inforcing the growth of reaction in the Soviet Union. The proletariat outside Russia was moving away from revolution to reformism. From much muddle-headed chatter about the imminent revolution Stalin and Zinoviev were compelled to see that Capitalism was strengthening itself. Using revolutionary phraseology, but in reality from then and for the next three years the ally of kulak and nepman, against Trotsky and the internationalists, the Soviet bureaucracy crystallised its development and clarified its aims in a new theory that struck at the very basis of all Marxist thinking, the theory that Socialism could be built unaided in a single country. When Zinoviev and Kamenev, under pressure from the proletariat of Leningrad and Moscow, recoiled from this theory and its consequences and started to struggle against Stalin, they were helpless. The same methods and machinery which they had helped to build for use against Trotsky and Trotskyism were more than efficient for use against Zinovievism. Kamenev was sent abroad, Zinoviev's followers were weeded out, he was dismissed from his positions and Bucharin set up in his place.

STALIN: MARXIST

Stalin produced his new theory in the autumn of 1924. In the face of elementary Marxism and the whole history of the party Stalin declared that since 1915 (later he made it 1905) Lenin, in opposition to Trotsky and Trotskyism, had always preached that Socialism could be built in a single country. In April of that year (1924) in his own

book, *Problems of Leninism*,[1] he had written that the organisation of Socialist production in the Soviet Union was
impossible. For that the assistance of several of the most
advanced countries was needed. In October he published
a new edition of the book in which the passage was changed
to exactly the opposite.

Marx and Engels, said Stalin, had not known that
Socialism could be built in a single country because they
did not know the law of the unequal development of
Capitalism—one of the first laws learnt by the student of
economics, Marxist or otherwise, during the past hundred
years.

Lenin had at times spoken of the building of Socialism
in the Soviet Union. That, after all, was the ultimate aim,
and every time he said Socialism he could not have been
expected to say "the international revolution." His works
were diligently scoured. Yet so precise was Lenin's phrasing that in all the thousands of letters and articles that he
wrote the Stalinists could find surprisingly little that was
of use to them. An article in 1915 was discovered in which,
writing of Western Europe and arguing against Trotsky's
theory of Permanent Revolution, he had postulated the
organisation of Socialist production in a single country.
He was writing not of Russia at all and he was arguing
against the idea of each working-class waiting to act until
all the others were ready. That no hint of national Socialism
was in his mind is proved not only by his writings before
1915 but by scores and scores of passages in his writings
down to the last paragraph of the very last article he ever
wrote. The passage was torn from its context. In 1923, in
an article on Co-operation discussing the political premises
for Socialism, he said: "Have we not all the means requisite
for the establishment of a fully socialised Socialist society?
Of course we have not yet established a Socialist society,
but we have all the means requisite for its establishment."
That was enough for Stalin. In April, 1925, the new theory
was made party policy. Men held up their hands and
voted for this as the policy of Lenin. To do otherwise was
Trotskyism and already, in the Russia of 1925, party

[1] A facsimile from the English edition is given on page xxiv.

members could see the immediate consequences of Trotskyism much more vividly than the remote results of Stalin's
perversions. They voted.

Zinoviev and Kamenev refused to accept what Zinoviev
could in those days call Stalin's "opportunist nonsense."
Stalin attacked Zinoviev in his clumsy blundering attempts
at polemic. It is impossible to build Socialism in a single
country? "If so, is it worth while to fight for victory over
the Capitalist elements in our own economic life? Is it
not a natural sequence of Comrade Zinovieff's views, to
contend that such a victory is impossible? *Surrender to the
Capitalist elements of our economic life*[1]—such is the logical
outcome of Comrade Zinovieff's arguments."[2] He in-
dulged in a logical retrospect. "The only puzzle is, why
we seized power in October (November), 1917, unless we
intended to establish Socialism! *We ought not to have seized
power in October*,[1] 1917—such is the conclusion to which
Comrade Zinovieff's train of argument leads us."[3] But
after this elephantine casuistry he fell back on his strength:
"I declare, further, that, as regards the fundamental
problem of the victory of Socialism, Comrade Zinovieff has
taken a line which is opposed to the plain decisions of the
Party, as expressed in the resolution 'Concerning the Tasks
of the Communist International and the Communist Party
of Russia in conjunction with the Enlarged Executive
Committee (the Plenum) of the Communist International'
—a resolution adopted at the Fourteenth Party Conference."[4] He used the party machine to create a majority
for anything, however absurd, however false, and on that
basis he expelled, imprisoned, banished and shot.

To such docility had he bludgeoned the party by April,
1925, that Trotsky and Zinoviev and Kamenev found
little support in their opposition. In little more than six
months international Socialism, the whole basis of Leninism, had been dragged out of the ideological armoury by
Comrade Stalin, Comrade Lenin's best friend and helper.
We must guard against thinking that Stalin himself had
made any great change. Neither before 1917 nor after

[1] His italics. [2] *Leninism*, by Joseph Stalin, Vol. I, p. 58.
[3] *Leninism*, by Joseph Stalin, Vol. I. p, 60. [4] *Leninism*, Vol. I, p. 60.

has Leninism meant anything to him. When a young comrade wrote personally to him saying that he had looked through Lenin's works and failed to find any reference to the victory of Socialism in a single country, Stalin, in a public report to the party officials in Moscow, replied: "He'll find them some day!"[1] To many people all this argument about Socialism in a single country is only tedious nonsense. There could be no greater mistake. It signified the defeat of Trotsky, that is to say of Lenin's international Socialism; and the crude violence of the falsification is evidence of the profound changes of which this theory was the outcome and still more the forerunner. The thing to be noted is the extraordinary mastery and speed with which Stalin manoeuvred the party to the new position. With his infallible political insight Lenin, at the beginning of 1923, had pointed his finger at the danger spot. Remove Stalin. As Souvarine[2] has so justly pointed out there was a possibility then that the party, having recovered from the civil war and the famine, could, under Leninist leadership, have regenerated itself and moved forward on the Socialist road, adapting itself flexibly to the economic circumstances. Between the rising strength of the bureaucracy and the proletarian masses, the party was balancing during 1923. It was the illness and death of Lenin on the one hand, and on the other the superiority of Stalin to Trotsky in a struggle of this kind, that so quickly and decisively turned the scale in favour of the bureaucracy.

THE RÔLE OF THE INDIVIDUAL

It is convenient here to point out the enormous tragedy for the whole movement of the illness and premature death of Lenin. The growth of the bureaucracy was inevitable. There were bitter struggles ahead. But with Lenin alive the incredible degeneration of the Bolshevik party between April, 1923, and October, 1924, is unthinkable. To gain control and introduce his theories, Stalin had to destroy the party. There is a tendency among Trotskyists to exaggerate the economic and social influences at work in the Trotsky-Stalin struggle in 1923. By October, 1923,

[1] *Leninism*, Vol. I, p. 244.   [2] *Staline*, p. 318.

Trotsky was beaten. Even under Lenin so much power had been concentrated in the upper circles of the party that Stalin could win by his superior gifts of manœuvre and intrigue. He could never have defeated Lenin in that way. Quite early in 1923 Lenin knew the dangerous range of Stalin's influence, but he could have broken him and intended to do so. And Stalin would have disappeared alone. Zinoviev and Kamenev were never persons to go down fighting for anybody or anything, least of all a Stalin attacked by a Lenin.

Lenin and Trotsky were solid in this matter, and what they said went, not from tyranny but from intellectual power and strength of character. Like attracts like, and they had the best men in the party with them. Whatever the power of the party bureaucracy in 1923, and even of the bureaucracy in the country, Lenin and Trotsky were the ones whom the Red Army, and the masses of Russia, workers and peasants alike, loved and trusted with a blind faith. Such jealousy of Trotsky as existed was in the old clique, not among the rank-and-file of the party. And even the old clique acknowledged the superiority not only of Lenin but of Trotsky. In January, 1924, Zinoviev, speaking at the special conference which pretended to investigate the causes of the German failure, paid an involuntary tribute to the very Trotsky whom his Soviet was calling a revolutionary dilettante. The campaign against Trotskyism, of which Zinoviev was one of the chief authors, had been raging for three months. "On the question of the tempo we erred. There is some consolation in that Lenin and Trotsky sometimes erred on this point."

The more one reads Lenin's last writings the more one sees how clearly he saw the danger. An unanswered question is, why Trotsky never used the army, which was devoted to him. He did not realise early enough the deep menace of Stalin. He thought first of the unity of the party, he did not want to appear anxious to step into Lenin's shoes. Instead of mobilising his considerable support to do what Lenin had said, and remove Stalin, Trotsky tried to collaborate with Stalin.

To understand a problem is to be half-way on the road to solution. Lenin saw it to the end and it is our belief that he would have gone to the masses, using the people, in the army and in the Soviets, against the bureaucracy. Circumstances were driving him to repair another error —too great a concentration of power in the summits of the party. Whenever he was in difficulties he looked below, and his head was already turned that way. He had dominated his party for twenty years. In April, 1923, despite Stalin's intrigues, he was still unquestioned master of it with even Stalin mortally afraid of him, of even an article by him. Without the world revolution the bureaucracy was bound to grow. But to think that with Lenin alive and well, with Trotsky head of the Red Army, and the thousands of old Bolsheviks in the party who followed Lenin and Trotsky, but in reality Lenin, to think that Stalin, or any other bureaucrat for that matter, could have slipped into the power without years of struggle, without even the final resort to force, is to show a complete misconception of what Lenin started out to do and did, when he wrote that with an organisation Russia could be overturned.

Lenin was not only Lenin. He was Lenin plus the Bolshevik party, still intact despite the inroads made upon it, with enormous reserves of strength in the masses of the people. To explain all, as too many do, by economic and social forces, is grossly to simplify a complex problem. Let us not forget that those who were the antithesis of Lenin from the first found their most potent weapon in using his name. They at least had no illusions about what Lenin, his party and his tradition, meant to the majority of the Russian people. The very strength of his leadership was its weakness, for when he went the party, built around him, almost instinctively clung to the centre he had dominated, but which, without him, was already heading for reaction.[1]

[1] Marxism badly needs a careful study of this period. Trotsky's account of it in his autobiography suffers from an over-emphasis on the economic and social forces at work. Lenin's Testament, one of the key documents to the understanding of historical materialism holds a perfect balance. He states early in it that there are two classes in Russia between whom harmony

If anything will emerge from this book, it is not only the strength of principles but the power of leadership. The first helps the second. The party of international Socialism rose with Lenin and died with him. This is not to deny Marxism. Lenin would have fought the bureaucracy, would have striven to keep the party clean, and used the party and the masses unceasingly against the bureaucracy, would have conquered it with the help of the world revolution, would certainly have kept it in check for years. But nobody else could. And yet Marxism, while giving full value to the rôle of remarkable individuals in history—and Stalin, in his own corrupt way is one of the most remarkable men in modern history—yet offers the only conclusive logical explanation of the events we have just outlined. For the working-class movements in Western Europe had begun on an international revolutionary basis in the First International, had each raised, through its own weakness against Capitalism, a bureaucracy. These bureaucracies, with criminal short-sightedness, had gradually succumbed to surrounding circumstances, become penetrated with bourgeois ideas, crushed the revolutionary elements, and then decided each to build Socialism peacefully in its own country, had revised its

---

must be maintained or the Soviet régime would collapse. It is against this solid background that he then considers the personal characteristics of the Central Committee. Selecting Trotsky and Stalin as the dominant personalities, he asks for the removal of Stalin. It seems that he thought, with Stalin out of the way, the Central Committee would regroup itself around Trotsky and, with a larger membership, be linked closer to party and masses. What he seemed most afraid of was an even split, behind the two halves of which a conflict might develop which would imperil the whole State. It is doubtful if he ever dreamt of the possibility that within six months Trotsky would be practically isolated in the Central Committee. On p. 414 of his autobiography Trotsky tells us what he said to Kamenev about this time. "I am against removing Stalin, and expelling Ordzhonikidze, and displacing Dzerzhinsky from the commissariat of transport. But," he goes on to say, "I do agree with Lenin in substance." The contradiction between word and deed was fatal. Still more revealing are his words on Stalin to Kamenev, "Let him not overreach himself. There should be no more intrigues but honest co-operation." That is Trotsky's own confession, and if that is the way he approached this initial struggle he had lost before he had begun We to-day can see that clearly. But it is of profound importance to understand that whereas Lenin, sensitive to the rôle of strong personalities in the flux and reflux of social forces, realised the danger of Stalin and the necessity of his removal, Trotsky, with all his gifts, did not, even after Lenin had urgently pointed it out to him.

theories to suit, and by the logic of events had deserted internationalism at the great crisis of 1914. In the same way the bureaucracy in Russia having gained a victory over the powerful international revolutionary tradition and sections in the Workers' State, succumbed to its weakness against the temporary stabilisation of capital which began in 1924, deserted internationalism for national Socialism, and using its influence on the world working-class movement, is preparing it for a still more colossal betrayal than that of 1914. That is the way that history works. So for historical materialism.

But the national Socialists might have won in 1917. If Lenin had not reached Petrograd in April, 1917, international Socialism would probably have lost, despite the work of the previous thirty years. Lenin was out of it in 1923, and international Socialism had lost this time almost before the battle had begun. We deny emphatically that so complete a defeat at such a time was "inevitable," and shall have no difficulty in pointing out the immediately ruinous influence which Stalin exercised on the Communist International.

Chapter 7

STALIN KILLS THE 1923 REVOLUTION

THE GERMAN REVOLUTION WAS FOR YEARS THE MOST urgent and important for the Communist International. In the war Germany lost over one and a quarter million men killed and four and a quarter million wounded. The allied bourgeoisie blockaded Germany for nine months after the war so that a million children died; (meanwhile they called on God and man to witness how the wicked Bolsheviks were shooting thousands of good Russian bourgeois). Germany lost 100,000 horses, 175,000 cattle, 220,000 sheep, 20,000 goats and 250,000 poultry. The allied capitalists deprived her of all her colonies and twelve per cent of her European territory, ten per cent of her population, seventy-four per cent of her iron industry, sixty-eight per cent of her zinc industry, twenty-five per cent of her coal industry and eighty per cent of her mercantile fleet. In addition they saddled her with a debt which was unpayable. From August, 1914, Lenin had preached openly that there could be no democratic peace except by revolution. Now the advanced Liberals, the advanced Social-Democrats, the advanced churchmen, all the war-mongers on behalf of democracy, raised their lamentations over the peace. But their urging and protests being of no avail, they said never again, and forthwith proceeded to confuse the great masses of the people with a ceaseless babbling about democracy.

Lenin had warned them from August, 1914, to cease their nonsense about a democratic peace. He was equally simple and equally clear about the fate of democracy in the post-war world. Speaking as far back as April, 1918, before the Soviets, Lenin gave the theoretical prognosis of the future history of Europe. For any country passing

164

through a difficult transition or the desperate disorganisation caused by a horrible war, democracy and all other middle courses were advanced by the bourgeoisie in order to deceive the people, or through stupidity by "the petty-bourgeois democrats prattling of a united democracy, of the dictatorship of democracy, of a single democratic front[1] and similar nonsense. Those who have not learned even from the course of the Russian revolution of 1917-1918 that middle courses are impossible, must be given up as hopeless." Have the democrats learned? As we write, the revolution in Spain is fighting for its life, and not only from the democratic press (they are incurable) but also from the press of the Third International, the clamour for a democratic Spain fills the air. And yet the whole history of Europe since the war, and of Germany in particular, shows that for Capitalism in crisis no middle course is possible and that the banner of democracy serves one purpose and one purpose only—to blind the masses to the inevitable onslaught of Capitalist reaction.

THE SOCIAL DEMOCRACY RULES

Ebert, Noske, Scheidemann and the Social Democrats remained in power in Germany, and when the German proletariat and petty-bourgeoisie realised that the Social Democratic Party intended to do nothing to change the social system they lost interest in the revolution. The premature insurrection of the Spartacists had deprived the revolutionary proletariat of vigorous leadership. The Independent Social Democratic Party, a typical centrist party, opposed Ebert and Noske in speeches and resolutions, but gave no lead. A dangerous unrest developed in the country, just the kind of situation in which the forces of reaction can take advantage of the lassitude and disillusionment of the workers, shatter their vanguard, and by their very decision, win over those wavering elements of the petty-bourgeoisie and even some of the proletariat to the temporary support of a reactionary régime. The old ruling-class of Germany planned attempt after attempt, but was so thoroughly discredited that it could not succeed and would

[1] A Popular Front.

have been completely crippled had the labour leaders not leaned on it against Socialism and the revolutionary workers. Whenever the old ruling-class fell prostrate after an attempt at counter-revolution the Social Democrats hastened to its rescue and propped it up again. The Social Democrats allowed the Reichswehr to develop great power and encouraged various illegal military organisations, like the Black Reichswehr. They gave huge pensions to the Kaiser and the old royal familes, they subsidised German industrialists and the large landowners, who used the money to finance the counter-revolution. The more adventurous of the counter-revolutionaries formed secret societies and regularly murdered anyone who seemed dangerous to their future plans, from workers and Socialist deputies and editors to Rathenau, author of the Russo-German Entente. Courts in which the old ruling-class still dominated let these criminals off with light sentences or did not punish them at all. Many of these judges have been rewarded to-day by the Hitler Government.

As the Social Democratic Government disgraced itself before the only class which would fight for it—the workers, General Kapp on March 13, 1920, marched on Berlin, aided by some of these same counter-revolutionary military organisations with which the Social Democrats had made war against the Bolsheviks in the Baltic States and on the Communists at home. Despite all the votes they could point to, the Ebert-Scheidemann Government again proved powerless, and fled from the capital. Kapp seized Berlin. In Bavaria the army officers pushed out the Social Democratic Government, and waited. The army was divided, and waited. It was the masses who rose all over Germany and, by taking power in Rhineland-Westphalia and fighting the counter-revolutionary troops elsewhere, broke the Kapp counter-revolution. Kapp retired on March 18. The Ebert-Scheidemann Government returned to Berlin, and failing to form a coalition with the Independents turned again to the capitalists and the German generals. A Government was formed with Herman Muller as Chancellor and regiments which had stood neutral while the workers had fought for the republic, and even Kapp battalions, were sent against those workers in the Ruhr whose successful uprising had been mainly responsible for Kapp's defeat. Severing, the Social Democrat, induced these workers to surrender their arms, and as soon as they had done so the Kapp battalions massacred them. Social Democratic leaders and workers who seemed dangerous were murdered with or without court-martial. On the other hand, the leaders of the Kapp revolt were given light sentences, most of which were never served. One of them, Ehrhardt, received his full pension; another, Lutterwitz, received an annual pension of 12,000 marks.

The indignation of the workers forced a split in the centrist leadership of the Independent Social Democrats. A minority went back to the Social Democratic Party, while the majority at last joined the old Spartacist organisation and formed the Communist Party of Germany.[1] Lacking in experience but determined, this new party, standing by the principles of the Third International, could constitute a serious danger to the State in times of crisis. In the mining district of Mansfield the proletariat was powerful and maintained its hostility to the increasing reaction of the new Coalition Government. Horsing, a Social Democrat, was sent down to Mansfield with a police detachment to destroy the movement. His slogan was, "The first day shall be a bloody one." The German Communist Party put itself at the head of the fighting, and under the influence of Zinoviev and Bucharin led the Mansfield workers to a crushing defeat. Zinoviev, President of the Communist International, always unstable and lacking the patience so characteristic of the great revolutionaries, had been disappointed by the failures of the workers since November, 1918, and had developed a new theory, the theory of the offensive—desperate attack by the Communist Party and the vanguard, by this means to electrify the great masses. The Mansfield action was fought under this theory. On March 17, the Communist Party press was peaceful. The next day, without that wide preparation for revolution among the organised workers without which revolution becomes an anarchistic adventure, the Communist Party press summoned the proletariat all

[1] Another revolutionary party, the German Workers' Party with syndicalist tendencies, had been formed but did not consolidate itself.

over Germany to the general insurrection against Capitalism. The Mansfield workers, instead of fighting defensive battles against Horsing, opened an offensive with the hope of kindling a nation-wide insurrection. They failed. To these fighters the Ebert Government distributed 2,500 years of imprisonment. A reward of 100,000 marks (eight years value of the pension paid to Lutterwitz), was offered for the capture of Max Hoelz, leader in the fighting, and Weiss, the Social Democratic assistant chief-of-police in Berlin, offered 50,000 marks for evidence that might help to convict him. Hoelz finally received a sentence of life imprisonment and served eight years. Thus the Social Democratic leaders, enjoying their new-found camaraderie with Junkers and big capital, protected them on behalf of democracy and crushed the militant proletariat. The counter-revolution bided its time.

It was under the influence of these events that the Third Congress met at Moscow in June, 1921.

THE THIRD CONGRESS

It is fashionable[1] to-day to say that the Bolsheviks in 1921, seeing the possibility of the Soviet Union surviving for some time at least in a hostile capitalist world, changed the tactics of the International from world revolution, as embodied in the documents of the Second Congress in 1920, towards its present line of propaganda for the defence of the Soviet Union. There is no foundation whatever for that view. Communist tactics must be, and, until the death of Lenin were, based strictly on an analysis of the objective economic and political situation. The Third Congress realised that Capitalism had to some degree recovered from the shock of 1919. But Trotsky, the undeviating protagonist of the theory of Permanent Revolution, made the report to the Third Congress and insisted that, despite the possibility of a temporary recovery, the danger and instability of the system were proved now to every worker, and the perspective of world revolution still remained. The recent experiences of the masses had altered the pre-war relationship of class-forces. The development of Capitalism was

[1]See Arthur Rosenberg, *The History of Bolshevism.*

not a matter of trade figures and prices, but was conditioned by the struggle between the bourgeoisie and the proletariat which, since 1917, had reached and would by the very instability of Capitalism be maintained at a pitch far higher than before the war. The boom, such as it was, was temporary. In accordance with his pre-war theory, prosperity would only strengthen the masses for another decisive clash. Tactics would have to be changed, but the world revolution was only temporarily postponed.

After a heated debate he carried the conference with him. On the question of specific tactics, however, there was almost a split, and it needed all the prestige and authority of Lenin and Trotsky to swing the congress their way.

The March rising had been condemned by Paul Levi, hitherto leader of the German party, and he had been expelled. Mere condemnation of thousands of proletarians who risk their lives against the bourgeoisie has never been tolerated by Marxists. But the Russian Bolsheviks in true Marxist fashion made the action the subject of an exhaustive analysis, and Lenin and Trotsky condemned the theory of the offensive. The German party should, of course, have put itself at the head of the rising under any circumstances. It should have told the workers clearly that if Horsing invaded Central Germany it would stand by them, but that if they allowed themselves to be drawn they would be defeated.

The German representatives, however, stood by the theory of Zinoviev and Bucharin, and Lenin had to speak very harshly against them. "Some people say that we were victorious in Russia though we formed a small party, but those who say this betray their utter ignorance of the Russian Revolution and of how revolutions are prepared." And Trotsky was equally uncompromising; "We must say frankly and clearly that the philosophy and tactics of the offensive is a great menace and any application of it in the future will be a crime."

Under such pressure the congress reluctantly gave way. The new slogan—To the masses—was adopted, though it was not until December, 1922, that the final thesis on the United Front designed to give the Communist Party a preponderating influence among the majority of the workers was adopted. Lenin fought stubbornly for the word "majority," for without the sympathy at least of the majority of workers, there can be no successful proletarian revolution.

THE TACTIC OF THE UNITED FRONT

We have hitherto avoided discussion of tactics in the abstract. But it is necessary to understand thoroughly the tactic of the United Front, which is fundamental to any understanding of the history of Communist revolutions after 1921. Misunderstanding of it was at the root of the failure in Germany in 1923, in China in 1925–27, and, most catastrophic of all, in Germany in 1929–1933. It is being shamefully abused to-day. Yet it remains a basic tactic for any revolutionary Socialist Party. Without a thorough realisation of all its dangers, the party that attempts it will be lost in a swamp of opportunism. On the other hand, without it there can be no success.

It is based on the fact that except at moments of very high tension in national affairs, moments which though long in preparation are of comparatively short duration, a Communist Party is likely to be a definite minority among the organised workers. Most of these are in the Trade Unions, where they struggle for the maintenance or improvement of wages and working conditions. These Trade Unions are the basis of Social Democracy, and the workers, for instance on the outbreak of war, succumb to Social Democratic leadership, their war to end war, neutrality of Belgium, independence of Abyssinia, collective security or whatever capitalist ballyhoo these Social Democratic leaders may be using at the moment. A Communist Party knows that a revolutionary crisis will inevitably approach, but the revolutionary crisis is itself conditioned by the militancy of the masses whom the reformist leaders do everything to deceive, mislead and, when necessary, crush ruthlessly. Hence the slogan, "To the masses." The masses can be reached by worker Communists entering the Trade Unions, Co-operative Societies, sports' organisations, etc., of the workers, and struggling for influence there. But there must be a political approach also. They can form secret groups, fractions as they are called, inside the Social Democratic parties and with discretion propagate Communist ideas there. But this is not sufficient to perform the main task, opening the eyes of the workers to the real nature of the Social Democratic leaders. Party must approach party, and a Communist Party constantly offers the United Front to the Social Democratic parties for purposes of struggle. Obviously to offer a Social Democrat the United Front for the purpose of overthrowing Capitalism is an absurdity. The Social Democratic worker is Social Democratic precisely because he does not believe in revolution. He has seen it fail so often, he dislikes bloodshed, or more simply because the great majority of mankind decide on revolution only after they have tried every other possible way out of their difficulties. But the Social Democratic worker will struggle for an eight-hour day, he will, under certain circumstances, join in a determined struggle against war, if the Capitalists begin an assault on living standards he will resist. While the Communist rank-and-file are assiduously urging the struggle for these or similar measures in the rank-and-file of the Social Democratic workers "from below," the official Communist Party offers the United Front "above" to the Social Democratic leaders. These offers must be unremittingly made at every opportunity which presents itself. The Communist knows that these gentlemen will not carry the fight any distance, very often will not fight at all. He knows that and says so openly. But the Social Democratic worker does not know it. The pathetic faith the average worker has in the leaders of the organisations he has created is one of the chief supports of the capitalist system. By constantly offering the United Front for measures that the Social Democratic Party worker is willing to fight for, not as a revolutionary but merely as a worker, the Communist Party hopes to expose to the workers, before the actual crisis approaches, that the Social Democratic leaders, having to make a choice, will always choose the bourgeoisie. If the Social Democratic Party were homogeneous, its leaders could afford to neglect these appeals, while continuing to assure the workers that everything can be left in their hands. But as capitalist pressure increases, as the State machine becomes more oppressive, the more militant of the Social Democratic workers begin to press on their leaders for action of some sort. These are compelled to stop mouthing phrases and act, or face the loss of large sections of their party and the distrust of others. The Communist Party offers a definite programme of struggle for definite ends. It knows that once a struggle does begin, the revolutionary party inevitably takes the lead. [1]

All the negotiations are made openly and in the light of day before the workers, so that all the responsibility for refusals or broken agreements can be laid at the proper door. The United Front is not for all times. The Social Democratic worker must sense some nation-wide danger to his class before he can be stirred. But persistently carried on during a period of growing crisis, the tactic of the United Front can result in a vast strengthening of the influence of the Communist Party over the millions of workers who might not join the Communist Party en masse, but mentally compare its energy and its activity in the face of danger, with the rhetorical passivity of their own leaders. At the moment of crisis, decisive action over the heads of the Social Democratic leaders will bring enough of the masses to make the revolution. Action is the final pillar of the bridge. Millions of people are never moved to revolution by propaganda alone.

Obviously the tactic of the United Front has great dangers. Few men are like Lenin, and before him, Marx, able to pass from the most furious onslaught on Capitalism to ordinary humdrum, everyday constitutional action a few months later. Few parties have the discipline to respond with the least amount of loss to such leadership. A Communist Party not homogeneous enough might lose its revolutionary identity in the effort for the United Front, especially over a comparatively quiescent period where active struggle is impossible. In such periods, with Communist leaders who have Social Democratic tendencies,

[1] The United Front can, of course, be offered for a minor struggle as a small strike. Co-operation here is easier and often does take place with good results.

especially in Communist parties which have sprung out of Social Democratic parties, the clear line of demarcation that must always exist between the two parties becomes blurred, with fatal results when the time for action comes. A party might still be fiddling about with the Social Democratic leaders at a time when it has already won influence over a majority of the workers and should pass to action, before its influence over the majority, always temporary under Capitalism, evaporates. The party must be able to take united action with Social Democrats and yet remain an independent organisation with an independent banner. A most rigorous principle of the Leninist United Front, therefore, is that never under any circumstances must the right of criticism be abrogated. A joint struggle for the eight-hour day, even if agreed upon and carried out, must not prevent a Communist Party from attacking a Social Democratic Party for supporting, let us say, the despatch of British troops to crush a national movement in China. Yet the revolutionary must exercise discretion. Lenin's letter about the method of attack against Kerensky in the face of Kornilov shows that his granite intransigence was quite compatible with knowing when not to say certain things though in the very heat of revolution.

In December, 1921, the theses on the United Front were finally agreed upon, and in the Fourth Congress, held in November, 1922, they were amplified by a careful consideration of how far entry of a Communist Party into a workers' government could be contemplated. It was decided that a Liberal Labour government such as was likely to be formed in Britain in the near future (the MacDonald government came in 1924) was a capitalist government. A Social Democratic government, such as the German Ebert government, was the same. Communists could under no circumstances take part in these governments but should ruthlessly expose them. Under certain conditions, however, Communists, for the sake of proving to the workers the futility of such governments, might support them. There might, however, be a workers' and peasants' government in such countries as the Balkans or Czecho-Slovakia; or a workers' government determined to struggle against Capitalism. Communists might enter such a government, but only for the purpose of carrying the struggle further. For such governments did not constitute the dictatorship of the proletariat. They might serve, however, as a starting-point for the completion of the dictatorship, though this would depend on the results of struggle.[1]

The theses met with opposition. Certain parties, like the French, were hostile to operating them. But after the March Congress of 1921 a large majority of the German party set itself with a will to win the majority of the German proletariat by the new tactic. As was inevitable some sections of the leadership went so far in their rapprochement towards the Social Democrats that there was violent opposition within the party, and in Berlin, Hamburg and the Ruhr Basin a minority opposition of the left arose under the leadership of Ruth Fischer and Maslov. Brandler was the dominating figure of the right and at the Leipzig Congress in January he was made chairman of the party. In this January, national and international events with startling suddenness put a revolution in Germany on the order of the day.

THE RUHR CRISIS

The Social Democratic leaders, useful only so long as they had some mass support, were by now merely encumbrances to the capitalists. By January, 1923, they were thrown out of the Coalition Government and Cuno, managing director of the Hamburg-American Steamship Line, became the head of a purely capitalist government. He had to put a stop to the inflation by which the middle classes and the masses were being steadily ruined, and to mitigate the intolerable burden of debt to the allies which lay on the German workers. On the German workers, for if Germany paid she had to export. This meant selling goods at cheaper prices than the goods of other countries, and the profits of German capitalists could be made only at the cost of less wages and longer hours. Yet Germany

[1] Experience, chiefly in China, has shown that this was a mistake and that Communists should never associate themselves with any government except one based on Soviets or other workers' organisations.

could not pay and French Capitalism, hoping to break up the German State altogether, established Germany's default and sent an army into the Ruhr in January, 1923. Clara Zetkin, in a speech of welcome at the Leipzig Conference, pointed out the possible consequences of the Ruhr invasion. But neither the party nor the International took any decisive attitude nor put forward any decisive resolution on the possibilities of revolution created by this unprecedented situation. It was the first of a series of colossal blunders.

The invasion necessarily threw a heavy strain on the economic and political system of Germany, but the German capitalists, month after month, showed exactly what the word patriotism means in such mouths. They decided on passive resistance to the attempts of the French to collect coal by force. But nothing, not even the love of the dear country on behalf of which they had helped to devastate the world for four years, ever stands in the way of profits. Says Arthur Rosenberg: "The so-called passive resistance of Germany in the year 1923 is a fable."[1] While the German workers were at first willing to make any sacrifice, the German industrialists, on the specious plea that coal was needed for the inhabitants and for industries, carried on as much production as they could, thus breaking the back of the national resistance. They negotiated with French heavy industry for combining French and German Capitalism against labour. The State had advanced these industrialists money with which to buy securities for the purchase of cheap coal. They accumulated large stocks of raw material and then manipulated the most terrible inflation in history so as to pay back what they had borrowed in worthless currency. The mark at par was 20–40 to the pound. In January, 1923, it was 33,500; by June, 1923, it was 344,500. Prices soared. In inflation wages will follow, but usually at a rate so far behind the rise in prices that the working-class, as always, suffers. But in this crisis the German bourgeoisie set itself to keep wages as low as possible. The Government officials were given increases, but wherever Government officials sat with

[1] *History of the German Republic.*

workers and employers to regulate wages the Government representative sided with the employer to put as much of the national burden as possible upon the workers. The industrialists, the great landowners, made fabulous profits. With costs what they were, German capitalists were able to sell abroad and undercut the foreign competitors. The savings of the middle classes vanished, and the working-class was reduced to a depth of deprivation and misery beyond anything they had suffered during the war. The workers in the Ruhr district took matters into their own hands with mass strikes, organised a militia, disarmed the Fascist bands, fixed prices in the local markets, punished profiteers, and in fact exercised political power in large areas. Capitalism will always forget national rivalries in the face of danger to capitalist property, and Dr. Lutterbeck, the representative of the German Government, asked General Degoutte for French help to crush the rising in the Ruhr. The fatherland lie, for which the German working-class had sacrificed itself in the war, was once more exposed.

Yet the majority of the Central Committee of the Communist Party of Germany, and Stalin, Zinoviev and Kamenev in Moscow were blind to what was happening around them. The Troika was immersed in their campaign against Trotsky. Brandler and the majority of the Central Committee were busy working for the United Front under the slogan of a Workers' Government. On June 12 the enlarged Executive of the Communist International opened in Moscow and held sessions until June 24. Preparations for the coming German revolution had no place on the agenda. Instead the chief discussion was about the Workers' Government which was to be formed by the United Front of Social Democrats and Communists. Zinoviev, always opportunist, said that it was a pseudonym for the dictatorship of the proletariat, and was severely attacked for it, because Brandler and the others knew quite well that it was nothing of the kind. In those days Lenin's tradition was still strong enough to prevent any such deception of the masses, though it could not prevent confusion among the advanced workers.

By July 30 the mark was five million to the pound, and the German proletariat, fifteen millions in the towns, seven millions in the country, had turned towards the Communist Party. The German Communist Party called for a demonstration on July 29, Anti-Fascist day. Cuno prohibited the demonstration. The left-wing of the Communist Party demanded "the conquest of the streets." Brandler and his majority called the demonstration off—a criminal mistake as the whole of Germany was able to see before a fortnight. On July 29, 250,000 workers assembled at the meetings of the Communist Party in Berlin, expecting the party to act. The Communist Party did nothing. Cuno declared a state of siege; the workers refused to obey. They seized motor-trucks and drove out into the country to the peasants to get supplies of food which was running short. The Communist Party seemed paralysed; Moscow gave no lead. Then in the second week of August the mass movement boiled over and a general strike brought down the Cuno Government. Had the Communist Party challenged the Government on Anti-Fascist day, a fortnight before, they could not have failed, and whatever its ultimate fate the German Revolution would have begun. From July 30 to August 31 the mark went from five million to the pound to forty-seven million.

Not since 1918 had there been such a revolutionary situation in any European country, and it is not likely that there will be one so favourable (at least in peace-time) for many years to come. For in addition to the hunger and the revolutionary indignation of the masses, the middle-classes, deprived of every half-penny and reduced to destitution, with the treachery and dishonesty of the capitalists clear to all, had no reason to support far less fight for the existing régime. There was the Reichswehr, but an army is composed more of men than of officers. No profound upheaval such as was imminent in Germany of 1923 could fail to have its effect on the army, and the idea that an army of 100,000 men could hold down a mass uprising of millions, in an industrial country like Germany where the workers control the life of the community, is a bogey with which to frighten children. What army could hold down the millions of workers in the hundreds of German towns? How could the Reichswehr distribute itself in the face of a general strike of railwaymen? What could 50,000 men do in Berlin if half a million workers came into the streets? When the masses in an industrial country move under the leadership of a resolute party they will be invincible. Catalonia is visible proof, and there was no party there in any way comparable to the German party of 1923. The republican police were sympathetic; the German workers were trained to the use of arms. But, outweighing all these things and yet giving them their true significance for an insurrection, was the fact that the German Communist Party had the majority of the German proletariat behind it even before it took decisive action.

THE REVOLUTIONARY SITUATION OF 1923

The evidence for this is overwhelming. Rosenberg quotes one of the rare elections held during this period, at Strelitz, where in 1920 the Social Democrats had received 25,000 votes and the Independents 2,000. In July, 1923, the Social Democrats polled 12,000 votes and the Communist Party 11,000. He notes also that voting at the Berlin metal workers' union in July gave 54,000 votes to the Communists and 22,000 to the Social Democrats. The Social Democratic Party was falling to pieces. On July 29 a conference of Left-wing deputies demanded an end of coalition with the bourgeoisie and co-operation with the Communist Party, evidence of the mass pressure from the Social Democratic workers. The State printing workers in Berlin demanded the formation of a new editorial staff for *Vorwaerts*, the Social Democratic paper, and a Socialist Government to seize property values and dissolve the Reichswehr. But there is no need to draw deductions. Brandler, who (under orders from Moscow) led the retreat and had every reason not to exaggerate the forces at his disposal, stated at the meeting of the E.C.C.I.[1] held to discuss the German events: "There were signs of a rising revolutionary movement. We had temporarily the majority of the workers behind us, and in the situation believed that under favourable circumstances we

[1] The Executive Committee of the Communist International.

could proceed immediately to the attack," an estimate which was endorsed by every member of the German party present.[1] But the leadership of the Communist Party of Germany was as helpless after the Cuno strike as before it. Brandler, faithful to his misunderstanding of the United Front, could not see that when at last Social Democratic workers turn to a Communist Party it is for action, and negotiations then with Social Democratic leaders, however "left," will gain nothing and may lose everything. He continued with his agitation for a Workers' Government, a dangerous slogan always, and now trebly so since Zinoviev's mischievous pronouncement a few weeks before. And now, to add to the weakness and vacillation, and destroy completely whatever chances the German Communist Party might have had to brace itself and rise to the level of events, Stalin in Moscow, the same man in 1923 as in 1917, set himself to hold the German proletariat back.

STALIN SAYS NO

The Executive Committee of the International had remained quite unmoved by events in Germany, and it was the Cuno strike which brought the heads of the German Communist Party and the Comintern out of the sand. We have an account of this period by one of them, "In June," says Kuusinen, "the situation in Germany was still such that no person of any common sense could have thought of regarding the organisation of armed insurrection as the next task. . . . At the beginning of August an abrupt change took place in Germany. The general situation became revolutionary. Of this we have proof in the mighty mass movement leading to the overthrow of the Cuno Government."[2] As if a general situation can just become revolutionary in a few days. And then again in typically contradictory Stalinist fashion he places all

[1] The author has in his possession the report of this conference, "The Lessons of the German Events," a secret document published by the Communist International in 1924. It was circulated to members of the various national committees only, and with good reason. The treachery and corruption of the Comintern are visible on every page, especially in the light of the revelations made afterwards by Brandler and Zinoviev. Brandler made many mistakes, but the worst of them were forced upon him.

[2] *The Errors of Trotskyism.* A symposium, published by the C.P.G.B., 1925, p. 345.

the blame on the local leadership: "Had the German C.P. foreseen this movement, it should have entered courageously into the struggle in July, and have taken over the initiative and leadership of the movement." But after the fall of the Cuno Government the Executive Committee belatedly bestirred itself. Zinoviev, with all his timidity and weakness of character, was a revolutionary, trained in the school of Lenin, and in three days he had his first draft on the immediate tasks in Germany prepared. "The crisis is approaching. Enormous interests are at stake. The moment is coming nearer and nearer in which we shall need courage, courage, and again courage." The leadership of the German party was weak, but there were to be four months before them. There were still possibilities of an attempt at struggle. But here entered Stalin, with his characteristic policy of 1917, an organic distrust in the proletarian revolution, a distrust which was to make him before long the supreme representative of the workers' bureaucracy with its bureaucratic determination never to risk its own position in defence or support of any proletarian revolution. In this month of August where Lenin, as in 1905 and 1917, would have been calling for the party to organise the revolution, Stalin wrote a letter to Zinoviev and Bucharin:

"Should the Communists (at a given stage) strive to seize power without the Social Democrats, are they mature enough for that? That, in my opinion, is the question. When we seized power, we had in Russia such reserves as (a) peace, (b) the land to the peasants, (c) the support of the great majority of the working class, (d) the sympathy of the peasantry. The German Communists at this moment have nothing of the sort. Of course, they have the Soviet nation as their neighbour, which we did not have, but what can we offer them at the present moment? If to-day in Germany the power, so to speak, falls, and the Communists seize hold of it, they will fall with a crash. That in the 'best' case. And at the worst, they will be smashed to pieces and thrown back. The whole thing is not that Brandler wants to 'educate the masses,' but that the bourgeoisie plus the Right Social Democrats will surely transform the lessons—the demonstration—into a general battle (at this moment all the chances are on their side) and exterminate them. Of course, the Fascists are not asleep, but it is to our interest that they attack first: that will rally the whole working class around the Communists (Germany is not Bulgaria).

Besides, according to all information the Fascists are weak in Germany. In my opinion the Germans must be curbed and not spurred on."[1]

That is the voice of Citrine, Otto Bauer, and Léon Blum, and that is the real Stalin. "If to-day in Germany, the power, so to speak, falls, and the Communists seize hold of it, they will fall with a crash. That in the 'best' case." 1917, 1923, 1925-1927 in China, 1930-1933 in Germany, we have always that distrust of the revolutionary proletariat which makes Stalin the banner-bearer of national Socialism. As an old Bolshevik the masses and the party thought him to be a disciple of Lenin. The bureaucracy rallied round this super-bureaucrat early. It is thus that the German revolution was side-tracked.

Stalin, master of the apparatus, imposed his view, and after that one thing only was certain, that the German revolution would never be led to victory by the Communist International.

With the collapse of the Cuno Government German Capitalism faced disaster. Once more nothing could have saved it but the Social Democracy, and these sycophants who can never lead anything except expeditions against colonials and their own followers, rushed to the rescue. Stresemann, the capitalist, formed a Coalition Government, putting the Social Democrats in the most dangerous positions, Home Affairs and Justice, where they would be responsible for the shooting down of revolting workers, and Finance, where they would be responsible for any further fluctuations of the mark.

The new Government was to stabilise the mark and tax the rich. But between August and October the inflation continued, with increasing misery, destitution and the exasperation of the population. The German proletariat waited for the Third International and the Third International waited for the German proletariat.

The pressure of events had had its effect even on the Social Democratic leadership, driving some of them far to the Left. First in Thuringia in March, and then in Saxony in September, the Left Social Democrats had formed Social

[1] P. 322, *The Third International after Lenin*, by L. Trotsky. Pioneer Publishers, New York. The letter was read by Zinoviev at the Plenum of the Central Committee and Central Control Commission in 1927 and noted in the official record of the Plenum.

Democratic governments dependent on Communist support. Stresemann in Berlin wanted to strike at them, but they were legally elected governments, and fearing the workers he dared not make any move. But a revolutionary situation does not stand still. If the Left do not act the Right will. The weeks passed, the revolutionary party did nothing, and reaction, gaining courage, took the offensive. In Bavaria the counter-revolutionaries, hostile to Social Democracy, declared a Right-wing dictatorship. Stresemann in Berlin, ostensibly acting against them, gave full power to the Reichswehr to restore the authority of the Central Government and placed Germany under martial law. At once the capitalists challenged Hilferding with his stable mark and taxation of the rich. To this they added a demand for the abolition of the eight-hour day. Hilferding was thrown out and the Stresemann Government assumed dictatorial powers over economic affairs.

The revolution, says Marx, needs sometimes the whip of the counter-revolution. Here was a heaven-sent opportunity for the Communist Party. The preparation for revolution could be made under the legitimate slogan of the defence of the legal rights of the workers.

Trotsky, in Moscow, was already out of the secret councils of the leaders, and Stalin's part in checking the revolution became known only later when Zinoviev and Kamenev broke with him and exposed the origins of the struggle against Trotskyism. But the incompetence of the German Communist Party for its tasks could be seen by any trained revolutionary. In September Trotsky warned the Central Committee of the German party's "fatalism, sleepy-headedness, etc." He was ridiculed. Claiming that the German revolutionary situation was now fully mature, he asked that a date should be fixed provisionally (subject to sudden changes in the general situation) some eight or ten weeks ahead, and that the party should concentrate all its energies on organising the masses for the revolution. The Stalin-ridden International turned the proposal down.[1]

[1] See the *Labour Monthly*, January, 1924, where Trotsky, though not actually mentioning the German Revolution, argued that a date could and should have been fixed. To-day, strangely enough, the Stalinists all agree that there was a revolutionary situation in Germany in 1923. Brandler, they say, ruined it.

The "November mood "[1] was over the German people. "Remmele has related how the masses remained in the streets the whole night, how they confiscated luxurious automobiles, and what the temper of the women was. Comrades, this, for us, was far more important than the volumes of the theses we wrote. We must have this mass sense. The picture that Remmele described, that Koenig has given, and Thaelmann has often drawn, that was the most important thing in Germany. On October 25 it was not in Leipzig but it was in Germany. Were you the megaphone of this mood?

"The masses were acting spontaneously, but members of the Central Committee, like Heckert, were not acting spontaneously. If he is a leader, he must be able to sense what is in the masses. . . ."[2]

Thus after the defeat Zinoviev apostrophised Brandler and Heckert. But Brandler, Right-winger as he was, was an honest revolutionary. Seeing that the revolution was at hand he went to Moscow in September asking for in-. structions and assistance.[3] For days he went from office to office, but the leaders of the world revolution evaded him and he could not get an interview. At last, at the very end of September, he had a meeting at which Stalin and Zinoviev were present. They gave him the extraordinary instruction to enter the Social Democratic Government in Saxony and form a Workers' Government. Brandler refused. He knew that to do that would be the death of the revolution. They told him that the entry was for the purpose of arming the proletariat and so preparing for the insurrection. He replied that if this was the aim, before the entry there should be intensive preparation both in Saxony and the rest of Germany. Without that, the entry into a Social Democratic Government would be a sign of a retreat, and not of preparation for revolution. Stalin insisted on immediate entry, and under the Bolshevik tradition of

[1] Of 1918.

[2] *Lessons of the German Events*, p. 47. If any of these references are inaccurate or false, doubtless the Stalinists will expose them.

[3] Brandler went to Moscow convinced and optimistic. "Comrade Brandler succumbed to fantastic revolutionary visions. The seizure of power now appeared to him as an easy and certain matter." Thus Kuusinen in the *Errors of Trotskyism*, p. 348.

discipline which Stalin knew so well how to abuse, Brandler gave way, making, as he has since confessed, the greatest mistake of his life. But Stalin (as always working secretly) was taking no chances. Against Brandler's wishes,[1] Zinoviev, as President of the Executive Committee, sent a telegram to the Communist headquarters in Saxony ordering them to enter the Government at once. To ensure that Brandler would not take any individual action, he himself was instructed to enter the Government also. Every avenue of escape was blocked. At the investigation meeting in January, Zinoviev, reading this notorious telegram, read that entry was to be made only on condition that Zeigner and the Social Democratic ministers were prepared to arm fifty to sixty thousand men. But it is doubtful if this condition was sent in the telegram. For when Zinoviev read this passage, Pieck said that the party was not informed of this condition,[2] and Pieck was a member of the Central Committee. Brandler and his colleagues entered the Government.[3] They could not arm sixty, far less sixty thousand men. Some days later the arrangements with the Thuringian Social Democratic Government were also completed. And all that happened afterwards was bluff.

The plan of campaign of the Executive Committee was that the proletariat should rise in Saxony and thus create a barrier between the counter-revolution in the North and Bavaria in the South. At the same time the party was to carry out a national mobilisation of the masses. But between October 8 and October 21 there was not only no arming of the proletariat, there was no national mobilisation, there was no wide-spread preparation for insurrection. The arming of the proletariat for a revolution, the technical preparation, is by far the most insignificant part of insurrection. Given the temper of the masses, the correct political preparation, and the decisive leadership, the actual arming

[1] *Lessons of the German Events*, p. 38.
[2] *Lessons of the German Events*, p. 38.
[3] The writer is reliably informed by a very close associate of Brandler that his only activity at meetings of the cabinet was to relieve his stomachic perturbations in a manner that was highly disturbing not only to the physical comfort but to the polite sensibilities of the Social Democratic ministers. This unpleasant anecdote is related here only on account of its political significance.

will never be an insuperable nor even a grave difficulty. But of this political preparation there was none. Instead, in every Communist centre a few hundred comrades had been armed and were waiting a signal which was to be given according to the result of a conference at Chemnitz. This was conspiracy, not revolution. Rosenberg, who was a member of the German Communist Party and later on the Executive, suggests that the strategy behind the Communist leadership was that if a revolution broke out they would lead it, but if it didn't they would seek to stave off reaction by means of coalition with the Left Social Democrats. It is a characteristic Stalinist manœuvre, and every movement of the Communist Party during the weeks which succeeded Stalin's letter bears out its truth.

On October 21 the conference at Chemnitz took place. Brandler, whose cabinet activities during the previous fortnight we have noted, proposed a general strike and armed insurrection. The Social Democratic members of the cabinet refused, whereupon Brandler called off the revolution. Through a misunderstanding, and as if to give adequate proof of how miserably the German Communist Party had conducted its agitation, Thaelmann began in Hamburg. The episode conforms Rosenberg. That revolutionary city (Hitler fears a visit to it even to-day) was seething. On October 21 a Trade Union conference of all the ship-yard workers had demanded a general strike in order to prevent the Reichswehr units near Hamburg being sent to crush the Saxon Government. The Communist Party in Hamburg restrained them. Yet two days later, at five in the morning, three hundred Communists attacked twenty police-stations and began the German Revolution. No more than three hundred fighters when the membership of the Communist Party alone in Hamburg was two thousand. Since October, 1917, the masses in the countries where there is a strong Communist Party have learnt to look to it for revolutionary leadership, and instead of each of these two thousand being in his factory or union calling on thousands after weeks of preparation, the Hamburg proletariat saw with amazement one Communist in every six engaged on what was no more than a criminal adventure.

Misguided as they were these few score fought with astonishing bravery. By half-past five they had captured nearly all the police stations they had attacked and had possessed themselves of precious arms and ammunition. But the rising petered out and left the situation worse than before.

Immediately after the Hamburg fiasco Radek arrived in Saxony from Moscow at the head of a Russian delegation, and found the same situation there as had been made so plain in Hamburg. Insurrection under those circumstances was madness. The party had missed its opportunity and must recognise its defeat. What was to be feared now was the panic of the masses and their flight from the Communist Party. To make the party once more the rallying centre of the masses so as to be able to resume the fight at a later stage, Radek counselled partial struggles (demonstrations, political strikes, etc.). But the spirit of the party was broken. For three months they had let the grass grow under their feet. The rank and file knew that had the party prepared for concentrated action and taken it the masses would have followed them. Even while the comedy in the Saxon parliament was being played out the Social Democratic Party was falling apart in Berlin. A motion in favour of coalition with the bourgeoisie found so little support that it could not be put to the conference. The proposal to dismiss the staff of *Vorwaerts* was carried by 219 votes to 215. This and similar decisions were deferred to the next meeting and again carried, and delegates are always to the right of the rank and file. The correspondent of the *Observer* estimated that of the rank and file eighty per cent were no longer following the old Social Democratic leaders. The United Front tactic and the objective situation had prepared the ground. Action only was needed, and after August action could have been undertaken after eight or ten weeks of ardent preparation in the mass organisations of the workers. But Stalin did not want himself and his bureaucracy to be disturbed by any German Revolution and had seen to it that there should be no such action. Radek tried to organise demonstrations, but from Berlin, where were concentrated the foremost battalions of the German working-class movement, came the news that the bitterness and disappointment of the party members were so great that the party could not rally the masses, not even to a demonstration. And once more as the impotence of the Left became plain the counter-revolution took the offensive. Stresemann destroyed the Social Democratic Governments of Saxony and Thuringia without a hand being raised in their defence. Hitler tried his first coup in Bavaria and failed, but the Right-wing in Bavaria remained in power, and Hitler and Ludendorff escaped almost scot free. The terror, however, was loosed on the German workers. The Communist Party was made illegal; 9,000 workers were put on trial. "Prison suicides" and "shot while trying to escape" multiplied. And after the political defeat came the cutting of wages and the loss of the eight-hour day, one of the few conquests of the 1918 revolution. The German workers had turned from the Second International to the Third and had gained nothing from it—not even the satisfaction and the experience of a struggle. That part of the lesson many of them were to remember. But though it was clear to some few observers at the time,[1] the German workers did not know, it is only to-day the workers of Europe are beginning to see, that the Russian bureaucracy under Stalin has wanted only to be left in peace, and will risk every working-class movement in Europe going down to defeat rather than face the complications of a proletarian revolution.

THE SIGNIFICANCE OF 1923

The failure of the German revolution clinched the victory of Stalin in Russia. It strengthened the development of the bureaucracy towards the nationalism to be proclaimed a year later in Stalin's monstrous theory. The world revolution does not come on a plate. It has to be fought for. But the consequences of failure are almost automatic.

It is impossible to minimise the importance of the German defeat. To-day, Trotskyists and Stalinists (all except Brandler and his followers) agree that the finest of post-war revolutionary situations was missed in 1923. The roots of the failure were in Moscow, not in Berlin, and in Moscow in more senses than one.

[1] See *After Lenin*, by Michael Farbman, 1924.

We have been careful to point out Lenin's rôle in October, 1917, and the rôle he would have played in Moscow had he been vigorous in October, 1923. Trotsky has made a valuable admission in his recent book, *La Révolution Trahie*,[1] where he states that if Lenin had lived, the advance of the bureaucracy would have been slower "at least in the early years." The significance of this for us is of far more importance outside of Russia than in. If Brandler had met in Moscow, not Stalin, the advance-guard of Revisionism, but revolutionary Socialism incarnate in Lenin, there would have been a revolution in Germany in 1923. A defeat might have been the result. But a defeat in 1923 would have been the surest preparation for the new upsurge a decade or so later. The inaction of 1923 hung heavily over pre-Hitlerite Germany. There are accidents in history. Cleopatra's nose might have been shorter, and a stray bullet might have killed General Bonaparte. The broad outlines of history would have remained unchanged. But we who live to-day in a period where a revolutionary defeat or victory affects in the most literal sense the lives of half the world's inhabitants, cannot afford to be too philosophical about the reasons which made for success or failure. Leninism is the only solution to the problems of the modern world. It might have saved us another world-war on the scale of the one which approaches. But there was too much need of Lenin in both the planning and the execution of Leninism.

There is another aspect closely linked to the first. Neither Danton, Marat nor Robespierre were as individuals essential to the success of the French Revolution. The Jacobin club was an unconscious growth. Cromwell did not ever seem to know where exactly he was going but dealt with the circumstances as they came. The moment we reach the Bolshevik Party and the Communist International, however, we have organisations, based on historical science, created and trained for the purpose of entering and consciously influencing the objective processes of history. At first sight the rôle of individual genius should be lessened. Instead, in the only success such organisations can boast,

[1] Page 112

it assumes an almost terrifying importance. And it is not difficult to see why, especially after a close study of 1917– 1936. Bolshevism is a double-edged weapon. The very emphasis on party and leadership throws an enormous responsibility on party and leadership. But the reading of history and the passing of resolutions is one thing. The capacity to build, to advance, to retreat, to seize the correct moment, to translate theory into practice, not only to see a correct line of action, but to be able to persuade colleagues to act on it with the necessary speed and cohesion, these things require at the centre men of unusual stature. Respect for a theory, valuable as it is, can be a dead weight, which when backed by the force of an organisation can ruin a revolutionary situation. Lenin's democratic dictatorship of the proletariat and the peasantry, as interpreted by Stalin and the old Bolsheviks, nearly prevented October. The Petrograd workers knew better. Over and over again we shall see this instinctive superiority during revolution of the advanced workers to the learned blindness and conservatism of the organisation. Men who can use theory and organisation, and not be used by them, are rare.

Bolshevism is a two-edged weapon in another sense, the emphasis on the centralism of the International. Brandler running around in Moscow asking what to do is a.pitiable and warning figure. No revolution can ever be led to victory by such leaders. Under Stalin as far back as 1923 this subservience was a trap. But even under Lenin it was a danger. The successful leadership of a revolutionary party, collective or individual, is a work of creative genius. The long succession of failures should teach us that. Centralism can assist and guide, it cannot create that leadership. But it can, by the mere weight of the organisation, stunt and kill it. We shall see how the dependence on the centre created a body of leaders who looked always to Moscow and were incapable of independent appraisal and action. The revolutionary movement, in a period of unceasing revolution, has thrown up no great figures. Lenin and Trotsky, Liebknecht and Luxemburg all developed in another period. The heavy hand of Stalin, the need for bureaucratic control in Russia, had its full influence on the International. But the seeds of the trouble were always there. Lenin saw it, warned ceaselessly against it. Even to Trotsky, his destined successor, he administered an admonition in his Testament as being "far too much attracted to the purely administrative side of affairs," that is to say control from above, leading consciously or unconsciously to the suppressing of individual initiative. Democratic centralism demands at the centre men not only of exceptional ability but breadth of vision, far-reaching wisdom and immense patience. Here again Leninism depended too much on Lenin. Small pillars cannot sustain the vast structure of the world revolution.

We must bear these things in mind as essential to a just understanding of Lenin's basic conceptions. If we do not, we leave the door open to those who consider the successive failures as evidence of the Utopian wish—fulfilment of Leninism and point to Stalinist Russia as an "inevitable" development of history. Such fatalism has no place in Marxism. Nor is a just recognition of the rôle of gifted individuals in the historical process as exemplified by recent history a concession to defeatism. To all except the busy-bodies who spend their off-hours running round and round in the revolutionary movement it should mean an increased consciousness of responsibility, the necessity for training and selflessness to measure up to the demands. The disintegration of Capitalism has brought and will continue to bring the masses thus far. But the decisive action, and it is the decisive action which matters, rests and will always rest with a few men who see the historical process as a whole, have the organising skill and determination to solidify the growing dissatisfaction of the masses into a party, and at the given moment consciously make history as history was made in 1917.

THE EBB MISTAKEN FOR THE FLOW

After the failure of the revolution in Germany the first task of the International was to examine with scrupulous honesty the causes of the defeat. It is a commonplace that the 1905 defeat in Russia was, in Lenin's phrase, the dress-rehearsal for 1917. Trotsky tells us that in the fateful months before October he went ahead with the utmost confidence, reaping the fruit of 1905 and the intense study of that experience. But neither the International nor the German Communist Party ever knew the truth about 1923. Stalin and Zinoviev could not let them know it. Here again, therefore, they were driven to use their power over the organisation to stifle criticism. Stalin drew liberally from his bottomless armoury of slander and intrigue. The Polish section which had its own views on the German defeat was abused as factional. One of its members was appointed to work on a commission dealing with German events. Zinoviev did not invite him to the sittings. A meeting of the Executive Committee was held in Moscow in January to draw the lessons of the German defeat. There Zinoviev placed all the blame on Brandler for not being able to arm the workers when he entered the Saxon Government. No attempt was made to plumb the enormous significance of the greatest defeat the International had yet sustained. But certain unmistakable revelations were made at the meeting. The report was never made public, and to ensure that Brandler should not inform the German Party as a whole of what had happened, and how it had happened, a resolution was passed forbidding him and his close associate Thalheimer from returning to Germany. Thus in the party discussion and elections that took place in Germany in 1924 the Right was not represented, the causes of the defeat were never analysed, and the Left leadership, Ruth Fischer and Maslow, supporters of Zinoviev, assumed the direction of the party. These new appointments were significant. For here appeared for the first time in the International a feature which has ever since distinguished it, and has cost the international proletariat thousands of valuable lives— the Stalinist congenital incapacity to understand not only when a revolutionary situation has come but also when it has gone. The revolution was dead in Germany. It would be years before it rose again. The new orientation therefore was to recognise this openly, fall back on the defensive and do years of patient spade-work in preparation for the new upsurge. But by an obvious compensatory requirement for his propaganda (we shall see it again and again) Stalin, now that the opportunity had passed, was vociferous in his call for the revolution.[1] Zinoviev his mouthpiece of these days demanded that the German workers prepare for it. He prophesied the spring or the summer. On January 21 the International issued a manifesto: "The work of arming the workers and of technically preparing for the decisive struggle must be carried on with tenacity." On March 26, 1924, the Executive Committee of the International wrote to the German party: "The mistake in the evaluation of the tempo of events made in October, 1923, caused the party great difficulties. Nevertheless, it is only an episode. The fundamental estimate remains the same as before."

Trotsky and his followers, now known as the Opposition, took the view that the revolutionary crisis in Europe had passed, that owing to the shameful defeat of the German proletariat European Capitalism had entered upon a period of stabilisation, and that the political basis for the future tactics of the Communist Parties should be based on such a reading of the situation. For some months Trotskyism (how strange this sounds to-day) was labelled as a "deviation of the Right" and the Trotskyists as "liquidationists" of the revolution. Trotsky refused to acquiesce in Brandler being made the scapegoat, and was immediately identified with Brandler. The Fifth Congress met in 1924, and Zinoviev and Bucharin, leaders in the attack against Trotskyism, dominated the congress.

The German Communist Party though for some months an illegal party had polled 3,600,000 votes in the May elections, against six millions by the Social Democrats (it is easy to guess what their power had been in the revolutionary crisis between August and the turn-tail defeat in October). In Britain there was a Labour Government, in France Herriot ruled at the head of the Coalition of the Left. This and other things, said Zinoviev, "showed the enormous progress of the class-struggle and the imminence of final victory." Radek, who was the chief spokesman for the Opposition, was abused as a "defeatist" and "reformist," and the Executive Committee finally passed a resolution

[1] It is possible that whatever Zinoviev and the others said and thought, Stalin himself never believed that any revolutionary situation was near in Germany.

which stated that by its brilliant victories in the recent elections, the C.P. of Germany had shown that "its revolutionary force is greater than ever before. The electoral victories in France and Czechoslovakia similarly showed the decisive growth of the influence of Communism on the masses."

For nearly a year Communist Parties all over the world, working on this directive, compromised themselves before the workers, and by their adventurism and needless violence weakened themselves and strengthened the growth of the Social Democracy. The most tragic expression of this exaggeration came in Esthonia where at 5.15 a.m. on December 1, 1924, 227 Communists started a revolution, and by 9 o'clock were completely defeated, doing untold harm to their own party and the idea of proletarian revolution all over the world.

Trotsky took little part in the Fifth Congress, but though his views were repudiated, his personal prestige was still strong inside and outside Russia, and he was elected a member of the Executive Committee. It was, though not in all respects, the last real congress of the International. No other met for four years, and by that time with the growth of bureaucratic power in Russia and the corrupting personal influence of Stalin, Lenin's centralism became merely a cloak for bureaucratic tyranny backed by the power of the purse and the prestige of the first Socialist State. The most powerful weapon of the Stalinist International became slander. That could not defeat the bourgeoisie, but it could help to destroy anyone who refused to submit to the bureaucracy. The change had begun, as so many things in Russia, from the moment Lenin fell ill, and those three whom he feared took the opportunity of consolidating their power. This is a very simple thing to prove. At that very secret session of the Executive which obscured the important question it was designed to clarify, the Polish delegation presented a long protest against the corrupting influence of Stalin's methods in the International. It was not only the German defeat itself but the abuse and discrediting of all who disagreed with the pronouncements of Stalin's henchmen.

"The second point, which is of more international significance, but which is directly bound up with the fate of the
German party, is the danger arising out of the crisis to
the authority both of the Communist International and of the
German Communist Party.

"Since the time that Lenin, the greatest and most authoritative leader of the world revolutionary proletariat, ceased to take
part in the leadership of the Communist International, and
since the time that the authority of Trotsky, one of the recognised leaders of the world proletariat, was placed in doubt by
the Russian Central Committee, the danger has arisen that
the authority of the leadership of the Communist International
may be destroyed.

"It is therefore our common duty not only to devote all
our energies to maintaining the authority of the Executive
Committee and of its Presidium, but also to avoid every step
that may make this task difficult.

"Under these circumstances we regard the charge of opportunism levelled against Radek, a leader who has performed
great services for the Communist International, not only as
unjustified, but also as in the highest degree harmful to the
authority of all the leaders of the Communist International.
We can see no ground for such a charge; for however important
the question is as to who was victorious in Germany in October,
it is clear that no side was guilty of drawing opportunist tactical
conclusions. The differences of opinion that have arisen on the
German question between some of the best known leaders of
the Communist International are such as are inevitable in a
live revolutionary party, particularly when the party is in so
difficult a situation. Such differences of opinion have arisen
in the past within the leadership of the Executive Committee
without giving rise to mutual accusations of opportunism.

"We refuse to see in this the seed of tendencies foreign to
Communism."...[1]

Everything is there, the authority of Lenin and Trotsky
until Lenin fell ill, the violent personal abuse of Trotsky
by the Russian Central Committee under Stalin, their
ignorance or carelessness of the consequences, their habit
of hiding their own mistakes and deceptions by pouring
abuse on those who had urged the correct course, the
absence of all these things in the days when Lenin still had
authority and Stalin, "tyrant and brute," was building
up his power silently but dared not show his hand openly.
The International was not blind to all these things, but the

[1] *The Lessons of the German Events*, p. 61.

fate of the International was sealed with the victory of Stalinism over Trotskyism. The movement is one, must be seen as one, and cannot be understood otherwise.

STALINISM: THEORY AND PRACTICE

Expecting a world revolution Zinoviev and Stalin looked for insurgent masses and not finding any invented them. They formed a Peasants' International, which they informed the faithful contained several millions of members. In America they founded a Farmer-Labour party. At the Fifth Congress Kolarov reported: "In the United States the small farmers have founded a Farmer-Labour party which is becoming ever more radical, drawing closer to the Communists and becoming permeated with the idea of the creation of a workers' and peasants' Government in the United States." Zinoviev reported that several million farmers in America were being pushed by the agrarian crisis towards the side of the working class "all at once."

The Peasants' International, the millions of middle-west Communist farmers, are dead to-day; as dead as Social Fascism and as the Popular Front will be to-morrow. It is the inevitable fate of all the Stalinist violations of Marxist theory. But the Peasants' International and its kindred silliness died quicker than most, for they had lived only in the corrupt imagination of a few powerful bureaucrats. Yet they played their part in the demoralisation and ultimate destruction of the International. In August, 1924, Trotsky, attacking obliquely, had delivered a characteristic analysis of the rôle which America was now to play in the regeneration of Europe to be followed by the inevitable crisis in America, its repercussions in Europe, and the development of new revolutionary situations. Before the mastery of Marxism, the oratorical brilliance, all the glamour surrounding the man of October and the hero of the Red Army, the attacks on Trotsky and Trotskyism faded. Students and intellectuals seized hold of the document, and Lenin's natural successor was once more revealed.

195

Stalin owed it to his prestige to reply, and took upon himself the rôle of theoretician on international affairs, a subject which in Lenin's time he would not have dared to touch, for he had neither theoretical knowledge nor practical experience. In September came his article, by reflex action attacking Trotskyism, that is to say whatever Trotsky was saying at the moment. "Secondly, it is not a fact that the decisive struggles have taken place already, and that the proletariat has been defeated in these struggles and that the bourgeois power has, in view of this, been confirmed. There have been no decisive struggles yet, because there were no Bolshevist mass parties who were fit to lead the proletariat to dictatorship. Without such parties, under conditions of imperialism, decisive struggles for the dictatorship are impossible. The decisive struggles in the West are still to come. There have only been the first serious attacks, which were beaten back by the bourgeoisie, a first serious trial of strength, which proved that the proletariat is not yet strong enough to defeat the bourgeoisie, and that the bourgeoisie no longer possesses the strength to defeat decisively the proletariat. And just because the bourgeoisie no longer has enough power to force the proletariat to its knees, it was compelled to give up the frontal attack, to enter upon byeways and compromises, to take refuge in 'Pacifism.' "[1]

He published this article in September, but by October he had decided to accept stabilisation. The imminent revolution had hastily to be dropped. Stabilisation was declared, and Stalin produced his most distinctive personal contribution to Marxism—Socialism in a single country. In that month also came Trotsky's "Lessons of October." Stalin could see to it in Russia that this poisonous piece of Trotskyism got its deserts. There his control was absolute. But it is important for us to see how in addition to internal intrigue and corruption he prepared for his victories in the International.

---

[1] *International Press Correspondence*, October 9, 1924.

The Communist International publishes a weekly journal, the *International Press Correspondence*, in numerous languages, including English. It deals with all aspects of Communism inside and outside Russia, and in it are published all the important official documents of the Russian Party and the International.[1]

Trotsky's book appeared in October, and the English edition of *International Press Correspondence* of November 18, 1924, published a special number devoted to one long article—"How One should not Write the History of October." On January 5 appeared another special number containing an article by O. W. Kuusinen "A Misleading Description of the German October"; and two others: "Comrades Brandler and Thalheimer on Comrade Trotsky's attack," and "The German Trotskyists and Comrade Trotsky's attitude." On January 20 came yet another special number with an article by Bucharin: "A New Revelation as to Soviet Economics, or How the Workers' and Peasants' Bloc can be Destroyed. (A Discussion on the Economic Substantiation of Trotskyism.)" This number contained a resolution by the Central Committee of the Communist Youth in Germany which stated that Trotsky's book was merely an attempt to raise questions already decided by the Thirteenth Party Conference of the Communist Party of Russia and the Fifth Congress of the International. Trotsky, they said, was at his old game of violating party discipline. On January 22, 1925 appeared an ordinary number in which was printed the decision of the Central Committee of the Communist Party of Russia on the "attitude" of Comrade Trotsky, and a statement that Trotsky was completely isolated in Russia and in the whole Communist International (including Britain) except in Norway and France. On January 23 appeared another special number, "October and Comrade Trotsky's Theory of Permanent Revolution," by

---

[1] It is in its files, lying though they are since Lenin's death, that one can read the history of the Soviet Union and the Third International, and not in the constant refurbishing and falsification of Stalin and his bureaucracy at home and abroad, and the faithful transcriptions of these by Sidney and Beatrice Webb, Maurice Dobb, Romain Rolland, and all the other Friends of the Soviet Union.

Stalin himself; also an article aimed at Trotskyism, "The New Discussion," by Rykov; "The Lessons of October and the Communist Party of Bulgaria," by V. Kolarov; "Was Lenin Really the Leader of the Proletariat and of the Revolution?" by Kamenev; "The Lessons of October," by N. Krupskaya. On January 29 another special number —"The Ideological Principles of Trotskyism," by Bela Kun; "The Theory of Comrade Trotsky and the Practice of our Revolution," by G. Sokolnikov; "How the Revolution Took Up Arms," by S. Gussyev, an attack on Trotsky's mistakes as leader of the Red Army, with details of the Communists he had shot. On February 7, 1925, another special number—"Trotsky's Letter to the Plenum of the Central Committee, and the Resolution of the Plenum condemning Trotsky"; an article, "Concerning the Theory of Permanent Revolution," by N. Bucharin. Then at last, on February 26, 1925, came Cinderella—a special number containing, "The Lessons of October," by L. D. Trotsky. Two months later the Executive Committee met in Russia, condemned Trotskyism, and adopted Stalin's new thesis that Socialism could be built in a single country. Against this typical example of Stalin's methods the rank and file party members, both inside and outside Russia, some of the bureaucrats themselves, were helpless. The curious thing was that the thesis propounded by Trotsky in the "Lessons of October," that pusillanimous leadership in Germany killed the uprising, is orthodox doctrine to-day. His condemnation of Zinoviev and Kamenev for their shortcomings in 1917 was soon to be one of Stalin's main themes. But whereas Trotsky at the time believed that they and not Stalin were responsible for the treacherous policy in Germany of 1923, and linked the two episodes together as concrete evidence of a political tendency, Stalin merely abused both of them in order to discredit them personally. Zinoviev was in fact, by April, 1925, already in disgrace, and Bucharin represented Stalin at the joint session of the International and the Executive of the C.P.S.U. which condemned Trotskyism. At the end of the debate Bucharin thanked the delegates for their adhesion to Leninism against Trotskyism, and told them how the victory had been won. "Comrades, in this discussion, in this struggle, we naturally did not only take organisational steps. We mobilised all the intellectual forces of our Party. We have created quite a new literature on the subject, and as a result of these two discussions we can say that our Party has risen a stage higher. . . . We do not want to maintain that our Party is now 100 per cent Bolshevist. But in these two discussions, we won brilliant Bolshevist victories. We overcame Trotskyism ideologically; we isolated the opposition leaders, and only then did we take various organisational measures. We know what measures we took and what decisions the Party Central Committee arrived at concerning Comrade Trotsky's last move. Comrade Trotsky was removed from the War Commissariat. . . ."[1]

Before many years Bucharin, and later nearly every single one of those who had helped Stalin to destroy Trotsky, were to have some personal experience of ideological victories followed by organisational measures. The leaders, Zinoviev and Kamenev, were to pay with their reputations and their lives. The toll is not yet finished What insurance company would risk a penny on Bucharin's life? But all this was yet to come. Meanwhile on the basis of his ideological preparation Stalin struck at his opponents in the International. The stabilisation was officially recognised and the Lefts went. Fischer and Maslow were expelled, and replaced by Thaelmann and Neumann. In Poland the group led by Domsky were replaced by the Varsky-Kostreva group; Treint and Girault in France were removed, then expelled and replaced by Doriot, Barbé and Thorez. Never has such power been wielded by any man in modern history, never has it been used more viciously and with such immediate consequences. Stalin's dominating personality, his will to power, were reinforced by his empiricism, his ignorance, his cunning, which he and so many others have mistaken for intelligence. Nearly all who had sheepishly followed Lenin were ultimately to follow Stalin. Trotsky alone of the old

[1] *Bolshevising the Communist International.* Published for the Communist International by the C.P.G.B. P. 96.

Central Committee was to maintain the opposition to Stalinism. These men, Zinoviev, Bucharin, Tomsky, aided Stalin in the destruction of what they had always admitted in words to be fundamentals, but did not think to be worth a struggle. Little over a decade afterwards most of them stood in the dock, conscious that one half of the work to which they had given their lives was now destroyed, and the other half, the Socialist structure in the Soviet Union, unutterably degraded and imperilled. Conscious victims of their own moral and intellectual weakness, yet they were so humiliated and so defeated that they were compelled to sue for their lives by a still further betrayal, a further condemnation of Trotskyism, a still more abject abasement before the author of their destruction.

The Stalinist régime has become intellectually so degenerate that it has lost the capacity of making even reasonably intelligent propaganda. While Stalin used Zinoviev and Kamenev against Trotskyism, he of course decried the importance of the disagreements in 1917. Lenin while pointing out in the Testament their political weaknesses expressly warned that their behaviour in 1917 should not be used against them. Stalin, however, could not miss the opportunity of personal slander, and when Zinoviev and Kamenev turned against them he dragged up this old failure and wallowed in it. Trotsky's *History of the Russian Revolution* being so brilliantly received, the Stalinists hastened to produce replies. One of them was a collection of Stalin's articles and speeches, called the *October Revolution*, published by Martin Lawrence. The material covers the period between 1924 and 1928. On page 70 appears the following, delivered on November 19, 1924: "From the minutes it is clear that the opponents of an immediate uprising—Comrades Kamenev and Zinoviev— entered the organ of the political leadership of the uprising on a par with the advocates of the uprising. There was no question, nor could there be any question, of a split." But on page 165 we read, delivered on December 3, 1927: "You know that Kamenev and Zinoviev went to the uprising only when shown the rod. Lenin drove them with a rod threatening to expel them from the Party (*laughter, applause*) and they were constrained to drag their feet to the uprising (*laughter, applause*)."

Stalin's contradictions do not concern us. He can get away with them in Russia. What is so extraordinary is that his supporters in this country have got away with crudenesses such as these—they are legion—among highly progressive persons in Western Europe. The signs are, however, that the Stalinists are approaching the end of their boom period.

Chapter 8

THE KULAK AND THE BRITISH GENERAL COUNCIL

THE THEORY OF SOCIALISM IN A SINGLE COUNTRY WAS THE final triumph of the bureaucracy. For if Russia could build Socialism by herself, then for Russian Socialists the world revolution was a matter not of necessity but of gratuitous benevolence, and gratuitous benevolence has no force in the calculations of governments, Capitalist or Socialist. Henceforth the main business of the Communist International would be not revolution but "the defence of the U.S.S.R." The future development of the Soviet Union was not of necessity, but only incidentally a threat to world Capitalism. Thus the kulak and the nepman inside Russia, the world bourgeoisie outside, had gained an important victory over Marxian Socialism. It has taken years for the full implications of the theory to be seen by the world at large, but Trotsky and the Opposition knew from the first moment what it meant and where it would lead, and from October, 1924, it has been the main dividing line between two irreconcilable camps.

STALIN FIGHTS INDUSTRIALISATION

One would have thought, however, that at least the adoption of this theory carried with it a determination to concentrate on the internal development of Russia. Ask any well-informed Friend of the Soviet Union to-day the origin of Trotskyism *v.* Stalinism, and smoothly will flow from his lips "Stalin wished to industrialise Russia, while Trotsky wished to spread revolution abroad." While the truth is that for four years Trotsky and the Left Opposition fought for the industrialisation of Russia on an extensive scale of planned economy, while Stalin and the bureaucracy stood woodenly in the way and sent thousands of the "super-industrialists" to gaol and exile in Siberia. Neither is it correct to say that the kulak question and the collectivisation of the peasantry was the central question of internal policy at issue between Trotsky and Stalin. Such a presentation of the question is like so much of current thinking about the Soviet Union, completely false, and is due to the fact that the Stalinists try to hide their long struggle against industrialisation. The kulak question was always subsidiary to the industrialisation of Russia, could in the last analysis be solved, even temporarily, only by industrialisation. For Marx and Engels, Lenin and Trotsky, for all Marxists, the very idea of Socialism pre-supposed, in Lenin's phrase, "the enormous development of the means of production," that is to say industrialisation. Russia was a backward country precisely because of the smallness of its industry as compared with agriculture. In April, 1923, at the Fourth Congress of the Party, Trotskyism being as yet undiscovered, Trotsky presented some theses to the party on industry.[1] They were accepted unanimously, and but for Lenin's illness and the consequences, would certainly have been energetically carried out.

The theses laid down that the continuation of the dictatorship of the proletariat depended ultimately neither on the State-apparatus, nor the army, nor the education of the working-class by the party, Trade Unions, etc. All this would "prove as if built on sand" except on the basis of a continually expanding industry. "Only the development of industry creates the unshakable basis for the dictatorship of the proletariat." In Soviet economy agriculture, and agriculture on a very low technical level, was of primary importance. This was a weakness, and only in proportion as industry and particularly heavy industry was restored and developed would it be possible to alter the relative significance of agriculture and industry, and shift the centre of gravity from the former to the latter. "How long the period of the predominant importance of peasant economy in the economic system of our federation will

[1] Printed in full in the *Labour Monthly*, July and August, 1923.

last will depend not only upon our internal economic progress, which in view of the general conditions mentioned above can be but very gradual, but also upon the process of development taking place beyond the boundaries of Russia, i.e. before all upon the way the revolution in the West and in the East will proceed. The overthrow of the bourgeoisie in any one of the most advanced capitalist countries would very quickly make its impress upon the whole tempo of our economic development, as it would at once multiply the material and technical resources for socialist construction. While never losing sight of this international perspective, our Party must at the same time never for a moment forget or omit to keep in mind the predominant importance of peasant economy, when it is estimating the consequences of any step it is on the point of taking."

So far the theses merely stated the fundamental premises of the Permanent Revolution. Trotsky has never wavered in his belief that the revolution in Western Europe, and that alone, can save Russia. But revolution was more immediately the business of the International. For the Russian people industrialisation came first. "Without for a single moment forgetting its permanent revolutionary educational problems, the Party must clearly realise that at the present constructive-economic period of the revolution its most fundamental work lies in guiding economic activity in the basic points of the Soviet process of construction."

Where was the capital to be got? Britain had plundered colonies all through the centuries, Tsarist Russia had attempted the same but had chiefly borrowed Western capital. Soviet Russia had abjured the first method, and in 1923 had little prospect of using the second, besides which it could be used only sparingly or Russia would become a colonial country again. Some of the capital would have to come from an agricultural surplus, but it was equally important for the State industry not to lag behind agriculture, for otherwise "private industry would be created on the basis of the latter, and this private industry would in the long run swallow up or absorb state industry.

"Only such industry can prove victorious which renders more than it swallows up." Trotsky recognised to the full the importance of encouraging peasant production, with its inevitable growth of the kulak. But he was alive to the danger.

If industry could not give the peasant sufficient goods, then peasant produce would remain on the countryside, engendering hoarding, speculation and an accelerated growth of the private capitalist, with a relative weakening of the proletariat. Hence industrialisation was not something good to have, but an absolute necessity for the dictatorship of the proletariat. Yet the agricultural surplus could not be expected to supply too much capital, for if the peasant were plundered for the benefit of industry, he would lose his faith in the guidance of the proletariat, the alliance would be broken and, from his preponderant weight in the community, he would threaten the stability of the whole structure. Trotsky's solution—he based it on a study of the writings of Engels and their development by Lenin—drew from the very nature of collective ownership and the Soviet system. To begin with, the administration of the Soviet State could be far cheaper than that of the Capitalist State with its top-heavy and highly-paid bureaucracy. Rigid economy here would supply capital for increase of production. Vast sums, squandered by the rich in idle luxury, would swell the amount available for capital expenditure. Standardisation in industrial construction, which had given Germany and America such immense advantage over the rest of the world, could be exploited to the full in a Socialist State. The national control of banks, etc. prevented the waste and chaos and disorder which were typical of every capitalist state. The monopoly of foreign trade gave great scope for attacking foreign markets, and bargaining for such foreign products as were most necessary for improving the economy of the Soviet State. All these advantages could best be exploited under a single economic authority for the whole country, the State-plan for industry. The great danger of such a plan in any country but particularly in backward Russia was bureaucracy. The corrective for bureaucratic rigidity was the regulation of constant comparison with the international market on the one hand, and on the other the vigorous intervention of the masses in the processes of production, accounting and control, the party as always acting as guide and mediator.

The idea of the state-plan was peculiarly Trotsky's. It appears in the book, *A Short History of the Russian Revolution*, written after October during spare hours at Brest-Litovsk while he was daily expecting the European Revolution, and this proves once more if proof were needed the place which economic construction occupies in the theory of the Permanent Revolution.[1] Even Lenin, though as every Marxist a believer in planned economy, had opposed the idea of the single state-plan at first, but in December, 1922, three months before he finally ceased work, he said that he had examined the question and found that there was a good idea there.

STALIN CONDEMNS PLANNING

The theses were unanimously adopted at the party conference in the Spring of 1923 at which Lenin had hoped to speak. But Lenin never worked again. And the rôle of individuals at once assumes an importance difficult to exaggerate. For as soon as Lenin was out of the way, Stalin, Zinoviev and Kamenev, and when the latter two were thrown over, Stalin and Bucharin opposed the theses on principle, and to advocate industrialisation and planning became one of the most heinous crimes of Trotskyism. To Trotsky, pressing for the theses to be implemented, Stalin as early as April, 1924 replied with a prodigious sneer: "Who has not had experience of the fatal disease of 'revolutionary' planning, of 'revolutionary' projects which are concocted in the blind belief that a decree can change everything, can bring order out of chaos? Erenburg, in his tale Uskomchel (The Fully-Fledged Communist) gives us an admirable portrait of a bolshevik overtaken by this kind of sickness. The hero has set himself to produce the ideal man. He is absorbed in his work. Unfortunately

[1] *The History of the Russian Revolution to Brest-Litovsk*, by L. Trotsky, 1919. "Only an exact inventory of the resources of the country; only a national universal plan of organisation of production; only a prudent and economical distribution of all products can save the country." P. 149.

the creature is a complete failure. The story is, of course, an extravaganza; nevertheless it is a very shrewd take-off. But no one has ridiculed this unwholesome faith in paper decrees and plans more effectively than Lenin."[1] Stalin, skilled in intrigue and not yet sure of himself, named no names. Zinoviev less discreet came out more openly: "It seems to me, comrades, that the obstinate persistence in clinging to a beautiful plan is intrinsically nothing else than a considerable concession to the old-fashioned view that a good plan is a universal remedy, the last word in wisdom. Trotsky's standpoint has greatly impressed many students. 'The Central Committee has no plan, and we really must have a plan!' is the cry we hear to-day from a certain section of the students. The reconstruction of economics in a country like Russia is indeed the most difficult problem of our revolution. . . . We want to have transport affairs managed by Dzerzhinsky; economics by Rykov; finance by Sokolnikov; Trotsky, on the other hand, wants to carry out everything with the aid of a 'state plan.'" And when Bucharin took Zinoviev's place as chief theoretician for Stalin he, at the joint meeting of the Executive Committee of the Communist International which adopted the theory of Socialism in a single country, put planning in its place. "Comrade Trotsky asserted that the cause of the crisis was to be sought in the fact that there was no plan in industry. The only way of saving the situation was to increase the elements of planned economic life by a drastic concentration of industry, by various administrative measures in the sphere of the organisation of industry, etc. All the opposition comrades shared this point of view. The important thing with them, therefore, was the question of the economic plan. Comrade Trotsky also expressed the same thought as follows. He said: We have now the dictatorship of our Commissariat for Finance, but the Commissariat for Finance often does not give enough money to industry. That was the expression of anarchy and absence of plan in the conduct of industry. Everything else must be considered of secondary importance. Comrade Trotsky and the opposition adopted

[1] *Leninism*, Vol. I, p. 175.

a similar attitude towards the question of prices and the monetary reform. For them they were secondary, and of subordinate importance. The central point was economic planning.[1]

"Our Party Central Committee had an entirely different view of the situation. Its opinion was that we were faced with two important problems: the problem of monetary reform and the problem of lower prices, a prices policy which was bound up with the reduction of the cartel profits of our trusts and syndicates. Of course, planned economy is better than anarchic economy. Our aim is to get closer to planned economy; we prefer planned economy to anarchy in economy. Planned economy is the approach to Socialism.

"But in the situation which then existed all talk of planned economy was empty words, unless the monetary reform could be carried out. . . ."[2] For through all the difficulties of prices, the various "scissors" crises, i.e. the wide discrepancy between the products of the peasant and the value of the industrial goods he received, Trotsky and the Opposition claimed that the only solution was the intensive industrialisation of Russia under a planned economy. Soviet industry was making a rapid recovery. But the Opposition pointed out that this could not last and in any case was not enough. The lag in industry was preparing not only economic but grave political difficulties. Stalin replied that the peasant did not want any plan, what he wanted was a little rain.

STALIN AS ECONOMIST

What was the reason for this persistent hostility to the industrialisation of Russia? One reason was that during 1923 there had been a temporary crisis in which industrial goods could not find a peasant market. For years after

[1] Cp. *The Theory and Practice of Socialism*, by John Strachey, p. 432. "The proposals of Trotsky and his followers amounted, for all their extremely revolutionary terminology, either to a surrender to anti-working class forces in the Soviet Union, or to a fore-doomed and profoundly un-Marxist *sortie* upon the capitalist world."

Stalinist lies and falsification have spread a miasma over the intellectual life of Europe and America. Few escape it. The same pen that wrote the above piece of fiction wrote that admirable book, *The Coming Struggle for Power*.

[2] *Bolshevising the Communist International*, C.P.G.B., 1925, p. 91.

Stalin seemed afraid that the same thing might happen again. But for the obstinacy of those years there is only one explanation. The reader who throws to one side all that the Webbs and the other worshippers have to say about Stalin and makes one careful reading of the first volume of *Leninism* by Stalin will easily be able to supply the answer—it was ignorance, pure and simple, a phenomenal ignorance, incredible at first but as it fully displays itself throwing a great light on all the subsequent history of the Soviet Union and the Communist International. It was as if Hitler were suddenly called upon to do Dr. Schacht's job. What collective ownership implied, the possibilities (and the limits) of industrialisation, the conflict between the proletariat and peasantry, Stalin understood none of these things. The industrial restoration was taking place on the basis of heavy machinery, and capital goods inherited from the bourgeois state. This process was already reaching its limit. Soon would come the question of capital for repairs, replacing wear and tear, and adding to the stock. Stalin's contribution to this problem was very simple. They had no capital, and they could not get any, so they would have to do without. Only his own words can do justice to his ideas. In his address to the Fourteenth Conference in May, 1925, he made as always a preliminary obeisance to Socialist construction. But this preamble over he outlined the prospects of the future: "(a) In the first place, Soviet Russia remains a predominantly agricultural country. The products of agriculture greatly exceed the products of industry. The most important fact about our industry is that its production is already approximating to that of pre-war days, and that the further development of industry presupposes a new technical basis, namely the provision of new machinery and the building of new factories. This is an extremely difficult task. If we are to pass from a policy of making the best possible use of our existing industries to a policy of establishing a new industrial system upon a new technical foundation, upon the building of new factories, we shall require a large quantity of capital. Since, however, there is a great lack of capital in this country, we have good reason to expect that in the future the growth of our industry will not proceed so rapidly as it has in the past. It is otherwise with agriculture. No one can say that all the existing possibilities of our agriculture have as yet been exhausted. In contrast with industry, our agriculture can advance rapidly on the basis of the existing technique. A mere raising of the cultural level of the peasants, the teaching of them to read and write, even such a simple measure as the proper cleansing of the seed they use, would suffice to increase the gross production of our agriculture by from ten to fifteen per cent. You can easily calculate what this would mean for the whole country. These possibilities already exist for our agriculture. That is why the further development of our agriculture does not encounter such technical difficulties as are encountered in the matter of the development of our industry. That is why the disproportion between the balance of manufacturing industry and the balance of agriculture will continue to increase in the next few years, seeing that our agriculture has a number of potentialities which have not yet been fully turned to account, but will be turned to account in the near future.''[1]

Of the staggering percentages of progress, the vitality of collective ownership, and his wild exaggerations of the very solid successes which were to come later, he was at this time and for years after quite oblivious, calmly contemplated a check in the progress of industry and an increase in agriculture by teaching peasants to read and write and clean seed "on the basis of the existing technique." The connection between industry and agriculture did not exist for him. Collectivization was a vision in the dim distance. His peculiar mind then proceeded on various occasions to expound from this an entirely original theory of economics —one in which he denied altogether the importance of new capital.[2]

[1] *Leninism,* Vol. I, p. 395.
[2] Some who hold the views expounded in this book shy at the word ignorance. They prefer empiricism—they say that Stalin was merely giving expression to the tendencies of all bureaucracies to go with the stream and avoid action. That is a dangerous fatalism. We must remember that Trotsky's theses were unanimously adopted in April, 1923. Stalin opposed them because, as his words so clearly prove, he had not the faintest idea of how necessary they

Not a month after the congress he gave a series of answers to questions by students at Sverdloff University. One question was: In the absence of aid from abroad, shall we be able to supply and to increase the capital necessary for carrying on our large-scale industry?

Stalin began as usual, by saying that the Soviet State would exercise the most rigid economy and make the greatest sacrifice in order to become a powerful industrial State, etc. Stalin always began that way. So much for Leninism. Then he told Russia's university students party policy economics. "Certain comrades are prone to confound the question of the 'reintegration and enlargement of the basic capital requisite for the running of our large-scale industry,' with the question of upbuilding a Socialist economic order in U.S.S.R. Is such an identification possible? No, certainly not. Why? Because the former question is far narrower in scope than the latter. Because the question of increasing the primary capital utilised for the running of large-scale industry is no more than part of our national economy, and the industrial part at that; whereas the question of the upbuilding of a Socialist economy touches the whole of our economic life, that is to say, this question includes both manufacturing industry and agriculture."[1]

He seemed vaguely aware that something was wrong and was at pains to repeat his points over and over again. The building of Socialism, he said, included the co-ordination of both manufacturing industry and agriculture, "whereas the question of the expansion of industrial capital hardly touches this problem at all."[2]

One stands astounded at this naïve relegation of basic capital for heavy industry as something apart from the construction of Socialism and "far narrower in scope than the latter." Stalin did not know that without the development of heavy industry not even Socialism, but the

---

were. To believe that if he had initiated some sort of campaign for industrialization the bureaucracy would have opposed it, seems baseless. What he thought is clear from the extracts which follow. Trotsky attributes this hesitation definitely to fear lest industrialization repeat the selling crisis of late 1923. It was a conscious choice—based on false premises.

[1] *Leninism*, Vol. I, p. 331.   [2] *Leninism*, Vol. I, p. 332.

very existence of any State, even a Capitalist State, was threatened. His conception often expressed, was that industry (lagging behind a little) and agriculture would grow side by side, agriculture improving in a few years by ten to fifteen per cent (that would just have brought it to pre-war standard), and thus Socialism would come. "A Socialist society," he said, "is a fellowship, a productive and consumptive co-operative, formed jointly by the workers engaged in industry and agriculture."[1] That there might be no possibility of misunderstanding what he meant he stated again in unequivocal terms: "That is why the question of the re-equipment of our factories and the expansion of our industrial capital should not be confused with the question of Socialist construction."[2]

Was it possible to build Socialism? he asked. "This is not only possible but necessary and inevitable. We are already building up Socialism. . . ."

What profundities were hidden in this incredible stupidity his admirers may be able to explain; they have had a long and strenuous training in such explanations. The fact remains that this was the mentality that Trotsky and the Opposition were fighting against. There is no doubt that for years Stalin very genuinely held these views on the unimportance of basic capital. He changed them radically only in 1928 when he had brought the Soviet Union to the verge of disaster. Holding them, all he could do was to make them party policy and then use the whole force of the machine against the Left Opposition and its drive for industrialisation. And as a cover to this ruthless repression the party and the country were fed with innumerable quotations from Lenin. "One of the great merits of Leninism is that nothing is left to chance,"[3] said Stalin, and one of his henchmen, Rykov, was equally obtuse: "We are not going to introduce any changes into Leninism." But in defending such policies against the international Marxists Stalin and the party bureaucracy were driven ever further to the right. Blind to the danger, he countered the drive for industrialisation (and on that basis, collecti-

---

[1] *Leninism*, Vol. I, p. 331.   [2] *Leninism*, Vol. I, p. 332.
[3] *Leninism*, Vol. I, p. 335.

visation) with greater and greater concessions to the capitalist elements in the countryside. The kulak was allowed
to lease land and employ hired labour.[1] Kamenev drew
the attention of the party to the increasing growth and
influence of the kulak on the countryside, basing his deductions on the statistics published by the Central Statistical
Board. Instead of an investigation into the kulak question
and an honest attempt to meet the difficulty Stalin could
only think of altering the statistics. Kamenev had shown
in 1924 that seventy-four per cent of the peasant farms were
small, the middle peasants were eighteen per cent and the
kulaks eight per cent. This account had gone forward,
was accepted, and was even printed in the international
Press. In June 1924, the Central Statistical Board issued
a statement which showed that sixty-one per cent of the
marketable grain was held by the rich peasants. Kamenev
sounded the first alarm and the Left Opposition supported
him. The Central Statistical Board produced figures shortly
afterwards by which the kulaks were shown to have only
fifty-two per cent of the grain; and before the congress the
figures were still further reduced to forty-two per cent.
Every further reduction went to prove that the fears of the
Opposition about the kulak danger were unjustified, which
did not prevent Stalin at the conference from ridiculing
the "panic" of the Opposition about the kulak and the
untrustworthy figures of the C.S. Board. As far back as
May, 1925, Stalin ridiculed the warnings of the Opposition
about the kulak danger:

"Those who are panic-stricken at the thought of this
danger, are prone to scream: 'Help, help, the kulak is
coming!' It is strange! We introduced the New Economic
Policy, knowing perfectly well that this involved a reinvigoration of Capitalism, a reinvigoration of the kulaks,
knowing perfectly well that the kulaks would raise their
heads once more. Yet directly the kulaks so much as poke
their noses round the corner, many of the comrades turn

[1] The process did not run in a straight line. Under the pressure of the
Opposition measures were sometimes taken against the kulak. There were
spectacular attacks on profiteers. The economic and financial complexities
were more than usually difficult in a new type of State. The general line,
however, was unmistakable.

pale with fear, and shout: 'Help! Murder! Police!'"[1]
He poured scorn on the idea that Russia was on the road
to anything but Socialism.

Krupskaya urged that after all the N.E.P. was Capitalism,
Capitalism tolerated, but still Capitalism. "Is that a
correct statement?" asked Stalin. "Yes and no. It is
perfectly true that we hold Capitalism in leash, and that
we shall continue to hold it in leash so long as it exists.
But it is absurd to say that N.E.P. is Capitalism. It is
absolutely absurd."[2]

Lenin had said: "The Russia *of the New Economic Policy*
will become a Socialist Russia."[3] He had not said "*Capitalist* Russia will become Socialist."[4] Who failed to understand
that were deviating from Leninism.

Socialised industry was eighty per cent, private industry
was only twenty per cent. "Now, in the year 1925, any
one who speaks of State Capitalism as the dominant form
of economic life in Soviet Russia, is completely misrepre-
senting the Socialist character of our State industry, is
utterly misunderstanding the difference between the past
and the present situation, is—as far as this problem of
State Capitalism is concerned—not thinking dialectically,
but scholastically and metaphysically."[5] In the autumn
of 1926, Zinoviev, Kamenev and Krupskaya joined Trotsky
and formed a bloc to fight the pro-kulak Stalinist régime.
The advanced proletariat of Leningrad under Zinoviev,
and of Moscow under Kamenev, had stirred their leaders.

Stalin was now leaning for theoretical guidance on
Bucharin who produced and developed a theory of the
kulaks growing peacefully into Socialism bit by bit "at
a snail's pace." But Bucharin was merely giving a Marxist
colouring to Stalin's economics, and Stalin has always pre-
ferred to have someone on whom he could, in case of
failure, lay the blame. Stalin discovered a natural community of interest between the proletariat and the peasantry. The days when nothing could save Russia but
collectivisation and the Five Year Plan, the ferocious
conflict that was waged between the Socialist State and

[1] *Leninism*, Vol. I, p. 411.   [2][3][4] *Leninism*, Vol. I, p. 435.
[5] *Leninism*, Vol. I, p. 437.

the peasantry between 1929 and 1933, were far away and the warnings of Trotsky and the Opposition were laughed to scorn by Stalin. In those days the peasant equally with the worker was by nature a Socialist. "Thus we see that, primarily, there is a community of interest between proletariat and peasantry, so far as fundamentals are concerned, for both these classes are equally interested in the triumph of Socialism in our economic life."[1] Nothing less. "But this community of interests is contraposed by an antagonism of interests between the two classes in current affairs. Hence arises a struggle within the alliance, a struggle which is, nevertheless, largely neutralised by the preponderant influence of the community of interests, so that the antagonisms will ultimately pass away. Then the workers and the peasants will no longer be separate classes; they will have become working folk in a classless society. There are ways and means for overcoming these antagonisms. We must maintain and strengthen the alliance between the proletariat and the peasantry, for this is in the best interest of both the allies. Not only do we possess the ways and means, but we have already put them to good use, applying them successfully to the complicated situation created by the introduction of the New Economic Policy, and by the temporary stabilisation of Capitalism."[2]

In 1926 he told the Soviet Congress that he had carried through nine tenths of Socialism in Russia. And whoever opposed these flagrant and dangerous absurdities felt the full weight of the Soviet State apparatus. The party had voted, and to oppose was fractionism, lack of discipline, panic against the kulaks, disbelief in the building of Socialism, underestimation of the peasantry, super-industrialism, all minor variants of the one originating vice— Trotskyism.

To the relative weakness of industry was added a succession of good harvests which increased the weight of the capitalist elements in the country, and on this economic basis the balance of forces was shifting against the proletariat. The antagonisms which by some alchemy Stalin

[1] *Leninism*, Vol. I, p. 311.   [2] *Leninism*, Vol. I, p. 311.

imagined would "ultimately pass away" were hardening. The party bureaucracy, now possessed of great power, was solidly for Stalin. So was the bureaucracy in the country. Bucharin has told us that before N.E.P., there had been 7,365,000 functionaries. With the return to freer trade the number had dropped to about four millions. They were far greater in number than the proletariat of the towns in the days of October. The upper castes were increasingly sceptical about world revolution and quite prepared to build Socialism in a separate country with themselves in the position of chief builders. Further, party and bureaucracy were being steadily fused. Before many years had passed Bucharin was to realise that this fusion, criticism of which he had resented from Trotsky, was a powerful factor in the corruption of the party. Marxism, Leninism, had long been abolished in the party. The highest test for Marxism, to support Stalin's Leninism against Trotskyism, was easy to pass when opposition meant persecution more virulent than any under Tsarism.

Pressing on the bureaucratised party and the Soviet bureaucracy were the kulaks on the country-side, the nepmen in the towns, all of necessity supporters of Stalin against the Opposition. The development of revolution in Western Europe, successes of the proletariat, would have altered the situation immediately by awakening the Russian proletariat and bringing the revolutionary leadership and the revolutionary internationalist wing automatically to the front, but the stabilization of Capitalism pressed heavily on the proletariat. By degrees the rights of the party were filched from it. The yearly party congress was postponed at Stalin's will. The Communist International had met every year from 1919 to 1922. After the congress of 1924 none was held for four years. Socialism in a single country did not need congresses of a revolutionary international.

All through 1926 and 1927 Stalin, and the party under his pressure, zig-zagged now to one side and now to the other but steadily to the Right, striking heavier and heavier blows at the international Socialists, and filling the party with yes-men. Stalin built a clique of his own, Molotov,

Kaganovitch, Kirov, Ordjonikidze, Vorochilov. They were his personal followers. Rykov, Tomsky and Bucharin were strong supporters of this clique, the first two being chief representatives of a right grouping in the party strongly susceptible to kulak influence. And under the influence of this pressure the Capitalist elements in the Soviet Union, and behind them the counter-revolutionary groups, gained influence in the country and penetrated into the very heart of the Soviet apparatus. The Oppositionists, by this time fighting with the full knowledge of the ultimate fate that awaited them, pointed out the dangerous economic situation, the growing influence of nepman, kulak and bureaucrat, the weakening of the proletariat, the Soviets and the party, and the increasing danger of capitalist restoration following on any sudden shock to the country. In reply they were accused of slandering the Soviet system, of lack of faith in Leninism, and treated to the redoubled violence of Stalin. Long before 1927 they were practically excluded from the regular party press, Trotsky and his family were often hard-pressed for the means of existence, and while Stalin carefully refrained from touching the leaders, relentless persecution misrepresented their policies, blackened their reputation and dispersed their followers. Outside in Western Europe the return to Capitalism was freely predicted.

THE ANGLO-RUSSIAN COMMITTEE

Right turn inside Russia meant for the bureaucracy right turn in the International also. Peace with the capitalists inside Russia meant peace with those elements of Capitalism nearest to the workers' State. It was the first stage of the process that is so clearly at work to-day. The Peasants' International with its mythical millions, the Communist middle-west farmers of America, vanished from the speeches and propaganda of the International, the recognition of stabilisation making it unnecessary to seek further peasants to make the proletarian revolution. But of the blunders of this adventurous period one remained—the famous Anglo-Russian Committee, which flowered to maturity in the pro-kulak period and did so much harm to the cause of Communism in England.

Late in November, 1924, a large delegation of British Trade Unionists with A. A. Purcell, the president of the Trades Union Congress at its head, visited Russia, inspected the achievements of the Soviet Government and on returning home issued a glowing report. It was one month after Socialism in a single country had appeared. At the Hull Trades Union Congress in 1925 a Russian delegation, headed by Tomsky, chairman of the Central Council of the Russian Trades Unions, paid a return visit. The result was the Anglo-Russian Committee, officially founded in a protocol signed on May 14, 1925. In this the leaders of both movements undertook to promote international Trade Union unity, to struggle against capitalist reaction, and against the danger of new wars. The Reformist Trade Unions had their international centre at Amsterdam; the Red Trade Unions consisted of various groups chiefly in Germany, France and Czechoslovakia and the Russian Trade Unions. Red (or revolutionary) Trade Unions of diverse origin, had come into prominence during the turbulent post-war period. They were a grievous error, for while the advanced workers must be organised in an independent revolutionary political party, the great majority of workers are never revolutionary except at highly charged periods of short duration. To split their mass industrial organisations is to weaken them. Communists work in them and encourage workers to join them, for the basis of Communism is the organised workers stimulated and led to action by a Communist Party. The greatest enemy to the vigorous action of these unions is as always the higher bureaucracy, in England as in the Workers' State owing its power to the lack of leisure, educational backwardness and hard conditions of living among the workers. In Russia the Bolshevik Party holding the State-power had been designed to combat these dangers. Under Capitalism the workers have no organised defence, either in theory or in practice, except the energy of the revolutionary party. In England the revolutionary party was weak, and the peak of bureaucracy in Britain was the British General Council. No Marxist inside or outside of Russia could have the slightest doubt as to the rôle these gentlemen would play at any critical time. They would work for Trade Union unity provided the Red Trade Unions adopted their yellow policy; they would fight against capitalist reaction only if it was a question of wages and hours of work, where in proportion to the militancy of the masses they might go far and even use some very dangerous words. Their fight against imperialist war is limited very strictly by the necessities of their own imperialism.

Yet, once this were well understood, the Anglo-Russian Committee was a useful manœuvre. The General Council wanted it because, in the mood of the British workers, association with Red Russia gave them a protective colouring of militancy which they needed. The workers were ready to struggle. There was a militant section of Trade Unionists organised in the Minority Movement. The bureaucrats also wanted to use the Committee as a lever for the extension of British trade relations with Russia, which would benefit the British working-class. But the Committee was useful to the revolution because the mere fact of its existence focused the attention of the advanced British workers on Russia. The General Council would have to sign resolutions which the Russians and the British Communist Party could keep constantly before the British workers. At the moment when the General Council deserted its paper-struggle and rushed to the side of its own bourgeoisie, it could be exposed with great effect for the treacherous thing it was. There is no dishonest dealing in this. If the Trade Union leaders would really fight for self-determination of nations, or against imperialist war, as they so often promise to do, none would welcome it more than revolutionaries. But inasmuch as they never do, the only thing is to expose their limitations in the eyes of those who ultimately have to bear the consequences of their treachery.

Stalin and Bucharin, however, Tomsky and Andreyev, the leaders of the Trade Union movement, the whole Stalinist faction, in the full tide of their rightward pro-kulak policy, building Socialism in a single country, transformed the General Council into a very bulwark against

Capitalism. Tomsky (aiming, and with Stalin's consent it is fairly certain, at ultimate fusion and finishing with all this talk about revolution) claimed to see in the Council a revolutionary Left which was opposed to the known reactionaries like Thomas and Clynes: "Those (the British Trade Union leaders) who have entered into the agreement with us are maintaining themselves staunchly against bourgeois lies and slanders and against the former leaders of the English movement, Thomas, Clynes and MacDonald. The leaders of the British Trade Unions, the section that is furthest to the Left—one can say with assurance, the majority—are working harmoniously with us. They give us the assurance of and the occasion for hoping that the English, who are averse to striking quick agreements, who take a long time to think, weigh, discuss and hesitate prior to coming to this or another decision, will strictly fulfil the agreement; and that we shall not have to put to ourselves the question: what will the unity of the world trade union movement give the Russian worker?"[1]

This, after 1914 and Germany and Austria in 1919–20, was madness. The British Trade Union leaders in 1920, with all their millions moving against them, did for a moment become the mouthpiece of the protests against Churchill's support of Poland's war against the Soviet Union. But had the movement gone any further they would infallibly have betrayed it, like Ebert and Bauer; and to teach Russian workers and British workers that Purcell and Hicks would "strictly fulfil" any agreement against imperialism, particularly British imperialism, was to encourage the very illusions which it is the main business of Communists to destroy. Like all Liberals (for it must never be forgotten that that is what Social Democratic leaders are), under pressure from the masses they will swing to the Left. But the more the masses begin to move and so place Capitalism in danger, they, like Mirabeau, the Girondins, and Kerensky, begin an evolution which always lands them in the camp of the counter-revolution.

The Opposition did not oppose the formation or maintenance of the bloc. But they knew it for what it was—a

[1] *Practical Questions of the T.U. Movement*, by Tomsky.

purely tactical manœuvre by both sides. In those years Trotsky, ill and isolated, accused of factionalism in any attempt to oppose the Stalinist interpretations of Leninism, expressed his ideas indirectly. Thus the address on the rôle of the U.S.A. in European stabilisation was a criticism of the false line of the Comintern after the German defeat. *Towards Capitalism or Socialism* was a plea for the industrialisation and the plan. Now he wrote a book, *Whither England*, in which he was at pains to expose with the utmost sharpness the rôle that men like MacDonald and Thomas and the majority of the Trade Union leaders were bound to play in any serious struggle between English capital and English labour. It was directed against the extravagant illusions that Stalin and the other Stalinist Marxists were industriously sowing in the minds of British and Russian workers alike. In his book, Trotsky, looking at the coal situation in Britain and the general state of the class-struggle, predicted a miners' strike leading to a general strike. Not only the Tories but the Labour Press raised their voices in wrath and derision. These things happened in barbarous countries like Russia and Italy, and in Germany where the people were not politically educated, but not in England. Trotsky was writing the preface to the German edition when the British democracy had its first and most convincing proof that Marxism did not stop at the Channel. On May 1, after reiterated declarations that the miners would be supported in demands for no reduction of wages, no lengthening of hours, and a national agreement, the resolution for the General Strike was carried by 3,653,529 votes to 49,911.

THE GENERAL COUNCIL BETRAYS

Future historians will know the General Strike for what it is, a landmark in British history and its most important post-war event.[1] A general strike is not an accident due to incidental causes, workmen misguided by agitators, the stock shibboleths of the Tory Press. It is a major political phenomenon springing ultimately from the profound

[1] The strike is treated here only in relation to the general line of the International.

dislocation of the whole economic and social system. Nothing else can so move millions of men to united action. It is the class-war in its most acute pre-revolutionary stage: the next stage is revolution. The difference was that whereas in Russia and, as we shall see, in China the conflict between the old political régime and the new economic forces is so acute that the insurgent workers can see at once the connection between economics and politics, in Britain it is not yet clear. The political super-structure, though being steadily undermined (the grim grasp on the fiction of National Government and the Sedition Bill are the most notable evidences of this), yet has functioned successfully for so many generations that it maintains its traditional influence. This, skilfully exploited by comparison with dictatorial régimes and Britain's comparative prosperity, continues to give it a hold on the minds of British workers which in no way relates to the actual class-relations in the country. Economics has out-run politics, but that contradictory process cannot continue for ever and, historically speaking, the breaking-point is near. It is a powerful revolutionary party that is needed, and 1926 showed that the country was fully ready for one. For when every allowance is made for the presence or absence of revolutionary tradition it can be taken as certain that when the social contradictions in any country reach the stage where the two main classes face each other in a general strike, there are many thousands waiting for a revolutionary party that knows how to lead them.

The British Communist Party in 1926 was small, but size is not everything, and 1926 should have made it a major factor in British politics. It worked hard before the strike, seeking to prepare the workers, but the struggle for the United Front, combined with the necessity of keeping the workers alert for the inevitable treachery of the General Council, was impossible in this case owing to the whole orientation of the Stalinist policy. Where it should have mobilised and warned the workers against the General Council and its inevitable betrayal, the Anglo-Russian Committee made it support the very forces it was its business to expose. For one long year the party popularised

the dangerous slogan, "All power to the General Council."
It is in this way that parties ruin themselves. The miners'
leaders were prepared to fight, but the General Council,
with Arthur Pugh (now Sir Arthur), Walter Citrine (now Sir
Walter) and J. H. Thomas (not yet, alas, Sir Jimmy), as
the dominating figures, supported by Ramsay MacDonald,
from start to finish cringed and crawled before the capitalists, and with the millions of British workers solidly behind
them, stood on the Prime Minister's doorstep even after
he had slammed the door in their faces, dogged only in
their determination to betray. With all the preparations
it had made, the Government was nearly broken by the
shock, as the Government in any industrial country must
always be before the solidarity of millions of workers. The
British working-class showed all that instinctive capacity
for discipline and spontaneous organisation which every
working-class in the world has always shown and will
always show, to the recurrent surprise of bourgeois ideolo-
gists. Slow to move, the British workers have the qualities
of their defects, and were ready to fight to a finish. The
growing number of strikers, the universal disappointment
and wrath which came from every town and village at the
news of the capitulation, were testimony of the unsuspect-
edly deep channels in which the movement was running,
of the resistance that the masses were braced to make.
A few more days of tension and anything might have
happened. The Prime Minister had given orders to the
troops to fire if necessary. Luckily for British Capitalism
the treachery in the workers' leadership made this order
superfluous. But a British Amritsar on a small scale would
have driven the revolutionary movement years forward;
millions can be made receptive by propaganda, but ultimately the masses must see (and feel) for themselves.

The strike was called off, and immediately the Opposition
demanded a demonstrative break-away by the Russians
from the Anglo-Russian Committee with the whole International and the Communist Party of Britain pointing out
clearly to the British workers the political reasons for the
break and the political conclusions to be drawn from it.
With the millions of British workers disappointed and

bitter, with the treachery of the General Council fresh in their minds, such a break would underline the General Council's betrayal and turn the minds of thousands of the most determined to the British Communist Party and the International. One additional development made the break more than ever opportune. The Russian workers had subscribed thousands of pounds for the support of the strike. The General Council had refused this "damned Russian gold." A break was inevitable. This was the time. The General Council might even break first on the score that the Russians were interfering in British affairs, which would be an avoidance of the political issue. It was necessary to forestall them. It is by seizing and using moments as these to their fullest extent that men make history and double or treble the influence and prestige of their parties. In parliamentary political manœuvrings the bourgeois use it with great skill. Revolutionaries can use it with more effect. Stalin and his minions, however, refused. They were determined to stick to these useless and dangerous allies.

The Revolutionary Social Democracy

In July, 1926, two months after the strike, there was a meeting of the Central Executive Committee of the Russian Communist Party at which Stalin droned away about what the General Council would do in case of war against Russia precisely as if nothing had happened to make him change his opinion of a year before. "If the reactionary English trade unions are willing to enter a bloc with the revolutionary Trade Unions of our country against the counter-revolutionary imperialists of their own country— then why not make this bloc? . . . And so, the Anglo-Russian Committee is the bloc between our Trade Unions and the reactionary Trade Unions of England . . . for the purpose of struggle against imperialist wars in general, and against intervention in particular." And then in a typical sentence: "Comrades Trotsky and Zinoviev should remember this, and remember it well."[1]

[1] *Materials of the Plenum*, p. 71. See *New International*, September–October, 1934.

The General Council did not break at once, and on the request of the Russians for a meeting they sent a telegram accepting. The Stalinists were jubilant. "What will you do," asked Losovsky, "if they (the General Council) do consent; more than that, what will you do if they have already consented? We have received such a cable to-day."

Trotsky: "They have consented that we shield them temporarily by our prestige, now when they are preparing a new betrayal (Disorder, laughter)."

Said Tomsky: "Our little corpse is peering out of one eye . . ." (loud laughter).

"What makes you so certain that your second supposition will materialise?" asked Losovsky.

Trotsky: "This means that for the moment the wiser and the most astute among them have gained the day, and that is why they have not broken as yet" (Disorder).[1]

In the highest councils of the Communist International, seven years after 1919, Trotskyism was being jeered at by Stalin and the ruling group for insisting on the first principle of the International, the inevitable betrayal of Social Democrats on the question of imperialist war.

The Russian Trade Unions did issue a sharp criticism of the General Council's conduct during the strike, when the meeting over which there was so much triumph took place at the end of July in Paris. The General Council protested against the criticism, and refused to discuss the strike, either there or at another meeting of the committee arranged for Berlin at the end of August. Once more the representatives of the General Council refused offers of assistance for the miners on the ground that the Russians were meddling in British affairs. This overbearing attitude and the damning conciliationism of the Stalinists increased the demand of the Opposition in the Soviet Union for the break. They urged also that the British Communist Party should raise a demand for the cessation of the miners' strike or support it only as an attempt to reopen the possibility of another General Strike. As an isolated strike it was certain to be defeated and the defeat would be a triumph for the

[1] Ibid.

policy of the General Council. Political foresight should save the miners from this long-drawn-out struggle, certain to end in grave material loss with no political gain. But the Stalinist policy of tacking behind the General Council for the sake of its assistance in a war of intervention was maintained. In September the British Government refused visas to a fraternal delegation of the Russian Trade Unions to the Bournemouth Congress of the British Trade Unions. Tomsky and Dogadov issued a statement to the congress. Stalinist criticism of the General Council had already reached the stage of "particularly" regretting the refusal of the General Council to accept help for the miners' strike, which was still going on. The General Strike betrayal was camouflaged into "unforgivable tactics." The General Council, realising that it held the whip-hand, treated this with the contempt it deserved, and passed a resolution accusing the Russians of violating "international courtesy" and of "intolerable interference in the domestic affairs of the British Trade Union movement." The Russians swallowed this as they had swallowed the General Council's action on the General Strike and on the miners' strike, and the rebuffs in Paris and Berlin.

Thenceforward Stalin's Leninism and Trotskyism fought round the Anglo-Russian Committee. The Opposition contended that, by maintaining a bloc with these leaders and remaining on the defensive, the International was blinding the eyes of the politically-minded worker instead of opening them, and crippling the British Communist Party. Stalin and Bucharin persisted in the belief that the General Council would help to stop war, particularly a war of intervention against the U.S.S.R., and saw in the attitude of the Opposition only gross factionalism.

By the end of 1926 the Chinese Revolution, supported by the Soviet Union, was approaching its climax. The General Council and British Social Democracy, beyond the usual formal protests, supported British Imperialism in its repression of Chinese nationalism. Yet Stalin maintained this farcical United Front. The losses the Chinese Revolution brought to British Capitalism caused a sharp change of attitude to the Soviet Union on the part of the British Government. In the Spring of 1927 there was a possibility of war. In the Soviet Union the Stalinists professed to believe that an early war of intervention on the part of Britain was inevitable. But as the international situation darkened the tighter these tacticians clung to the Anglo-Russian Committee. In April, 1927, the Committee met again in Berlin. The Opposition wanted the Russians to denounce the General Council for its passivity during the bombardment of Nanking, and to propose immediate action against British intervention in China. Either the General Council would agree or its bluff would be exposed and the militant British workers warned in time. Instead the Russian delegation signed a series of paper resolutions whose only value was to shield the acquiescence of the British Trade Union leaders in the support of their own imperialism. The delegations were in "unanimous accord" and agreed on the principle of "non-interference." Tomsky boasted of the "material understanding" and "the heart to heart relations." A few weeks after Chamberlain raided the Soviet Trade buildings in London and broke off relations with the Soviet Union. Like various Liberals and even some Conservatives the General Council protested. But that was all. If war had actually come, British and Russian workers up to the last minute would have had faith in the Anglo-Russian Committee as a means of combined action, and they would have been led as blindly into the trap and left as helpless as they had been in 1914.

The Anglo-Russian Committee did nothing, neither in the General Strike, nor in the miners' strike, nor in the Nanking bombardment, nor in the Arcos raid, and when Austen Chamberlain broke off relations the General Council, having no further need of the Committee, withdrew from it and left Stalin and Bucharin to bury the remains. Three of the most critical years in the history of British politics had been wasted, and the weak British Communist Party, at a period when it should have extended its influence and consolidated itself, was only further confused and weakened by Stalin's persistence with this barren, sterile and essentially Menshevist manœuvre. It is the great crises of revolutions that test a party. But it is in the interim periods that the party is built.[1] The British Communist Party was to have one more splendid opportunity to establish itself as the interpreter of the political demands of the leftward-moving British workers. It was to fail as signally as it had failed to benefit by the General Strike and the political conditions the strike created, and in both cases the reason was the same—the nationalistic blundering of the central direction in Moscow.

[1] A party might lose membership after a great defeat. But the knowledge that the party had shown the correct road and had increased its influence during the crisis, gives its cadres confidence, sinks into the consciousness of the advanced workers and prepares a broad basis for the future upswing.

Chapter 9

STALIN RUINS THE CHINESE REVOLUTION

EVEN WHILE THE STALINISTS, BY FALSIFICATION AND PHYSICAL repression, were destroying the propagandists of international Socialism, the world revolution which had seemed so remote in October, 1924, stirred itself, and even while the new theory was being made law presented the International with one of its greatest opportunities. We have to pass over how the Stalinists forced the Communist Party of Poland support Pilsudski in the *coup d'état* which put him in power. Purcell and Hicks, Pilsudski and Chiang Kai-Shek were Stalin's allies in this period, and the greatest of these was Chiang Kai-Shek.

CHINA AND IMPERIALISM

China remained comparatively untouched by European civilisation until less than a century ago, but even in those early days Britain was already too small for British Capitalism, and between 1839 and 1860 the British bombarded Chinese ports and massacred the Chinese people to ensure the continuance of the opium traffic, one of the main sources of revenue to British India. Besides the profits of this lucrative trade they extorted millions of pounds as indemnities, seized Hong-Kong and territory on the mainland, and opened Chinese ports to British trade by force. In 1842 the Treaty of Nanking limited the Chinese tariff to 5 per cent. ad valorem, to prevent Chinese industry developing behind a high tariff wall. This they maintained by brute force until 1925 when, under the menace of the revolution, the first small breaches were promised. In the war of 1857 the British Government, again at the point of the bayonet, added to the usual indemnity, seizure of territory, etc., a British Inspector General of Customs.

The steady drain of silver from China for the purchase of opium, the ruin of Chinese handicraft industry, the breakdown of the Manchu government under the blows of the British navy, the corruption of the Chinese official class by the opium smuggling, undermined the foundations of the once great but now outpaced civilisation of China.

In the middle of the century a serious rebellion broke out in the South, held power in the Southern provinces for eleven years, and then failed. The British at Hong-Kong sided with the rebels, and the other powers followed their lead. But as the movement disintegrated the foreign powers, chiefly Britain, deserted it and (after first defeating the Manchu Dynasty and bringing it under its financial control) gave assistance against the rebels. By 1870 there were other rivals to Britain in the field. Russia and France stole large territories, the British seized Burma. China was still a market, and between 1851 and 1855 the excess of imports over exports from China was over £175,000,000. But the late eighties were the crisis years for European Capitalism, when for the export of goods was gradually substituted the export of capital. Africa was for the time being divided, but Africa was not enough. The Chinese people had now to give concessions and accept loans in order to buy iron and steel from Europe. They had no choice in the matter. The British Government on occasion offered them the choice of British loans or British shells.

In 1894 the scramble entered its most dangerous but inevitable phase. Japanese capitalism tried to annex a portion of China, but the annexation clashed with British and other European interests. Russia and France intervened and checked her "in defence of their own interests." Japan was too weak to assert her rights (it is a different story to-day). Yet she got a treaty port and £34½ millions indemnity. To pay this, British and other European banks lent China £48 millions. God spoke to the American President,[1] and in 1892 America seized the Philippine Islands and entered the race. This organised banditry threw an ever-increasing load on the millions of peasants

[1] He (Mackinley) has told us himself. See *Imperialism, the Last Stage of Capitalism*, by Lenin, in the Little Lenin Library. Martin Lawrence, p. 126.

out of whose produce came the taxes to pay these loans. As far back as 1856 Karl Marx, basing himself always on the economic unity of modern Capitalism, had seen that the devastating influences of this unceasing plunder of China would end in revolution, destroy a great market for European Capitalism, and thus precipitate the revolution of the European proletariat. In its essential outlines the analysis is to-day as sound as when it was made. But the rottenness of the Manchu dynasty was propped up by the military and financial support given it by the European governments, and the Chinese native bourgeoisie, mainly commercial, could not provide the forces for the liberation of China. As in Russia, it was the entry of capital, and the consequent creation of a native proletariat organised and disciplined by large-scale production, that was to provide a means for the destruction of foreign capitalist domination in China.

It was this process which Lenin saw so clearly in 1908,[1] the inevitable intensification of the export of capital, and the consequent growth of the international revolution. He based on it his calculations for world revolution, described in his book, *Imperialism*. It is the unshakable foundation of the Permanent Revolution. Small though the Chinese or Indian proletariat might be, as in Russia it would have as allies the hundreds of millions of peasants, sucked dry enough before by Oriental feudalism, but now driven to ruin by the burden which capitalist exploitation placed upon them.

China Stirs

The growing Chinese bourgeoisie, now increased by the export of European capital, found itself hampered by the reactionary Manchu Government.

The first spontaneous uprising of the Chinese masses had been easily canalised into the anti-foreign Boxer rebellion at the end of the nineteenth century. But after that failure the Chinese bourgeoisie saw its main enemy in the Manchu dynasty. The Chinese bourgeoisie planned to build a railway with Chinese capital, Chinese material

[1] See p. 63.

and Chinese labour. European capital stepped between and lent the money to the Chinese Government, and a year later, in 1911, the revolution broke out. Sun Yat-Sen, dreaming of a republic and a regenerated China, was made President. But Yuan Shi-Kai from the North, hitherto a supporter of the Manchus, but with large forces at his disposal, ousted Sun from the position of President. The Chinese Liberal bourgeois who were supporting Sun were afraid he might go too far, and thus, even before 1914, had shown their counter-revolutionary nature. Sun Yat-Sen formed the Kuomintang or People's Party, but once again foreign capital came to the assistance of reaction and made a large loan to Yuan Shi-Kai, who crushed the revolution, first in 1913, again in 1915, and died just as he was about to restore the monarchy. Meanwhile industrialisation of China under both European and native capital steadily increased, with the corresponding growth of native bourgeoisie and proletariat and the increasing misery of the peasantry.

The war accelerated all the processes at work in China. Japanese Capitalism seized the opportunity to enforce exorbitant demands on China. Sun Yat-Sen formed a Revolutionary Government in South China, traditionally the revolutionary section of China in revolt. Despite some manœuvring, his main enemy was now foreign capital which had established itself firmly in large concessions, Shanghai the chief, whence it controlled the economic life of the country and drained its blood away, supported reaction and conducted itself to all Chinese, rich and poor, with studied insolence. Yet the insulted Chinese bourgeois was under the domination of foreign capital, and Sun, though no Communist, by 1923 had realised that Chinese reaction, reinforced by foreign Capitalism, could not succeed without the assistance of workers and peasants. By 1923 China was in political chaos. Each huge province, from ancient times economically autonomous, was under the control of a Tchun or feudal military leader, who concentrated into his hands both civil and military power, taxed the peasants for the upkeep of his private armies, and engaged in ceaseless warfare with other Tchuns. The ablest and most powerful of these exercised some sort of overlordship of subsidiary groups and enjoyed the support of the Capitalist countries whose interests predominated in the particular regions he controlled. Thus in Manchuria Japan supported Chang Tso-Lin, while Britain supported Wu Pei-Fu, chief marauder over many provinces in Northern China, and Sung Chan-Fang in Central China. Sun Yat-Sen's Government in South China, seeking to call a constituent assembly for all China, was constantly attacked by militarists supported by British and Japanese Capitalism. He appealed to America for assistance, but America was interested in the Chinese market, not in the aspirations of the Chinese people, and Sun turned at last to the Soviet Union. Russia stood high in Chinese favour for Lenin had given back all that Tsarist Russia had stolen. In 1923 Sun met Joffe, the Russian representative in Shanghai. The Soviet Union promised him assistance in the struggle to free China from imperialism, and its tool and ally, Chinese militarism. Sun Yat-Sen reorganised his party. He declared that the sole aim of the old members was to get rich and obtain posts as high officials, and that the workers and peasants were the only real forces of revolution. But he did not, in the Bolshevik manner, organise a party based on a single class; whence the ultimate ruin of all he hoped for. His reorganised Kuomintang was still a hotch-potch, a few big capitalists, the nationalist bourgeoisie, the petty-bourgeoisie, and workers and peasants. His programme promised the nine-hour day to one, high tariffs to another, reduction of rents to a third, land from the state for landless peasants and tenant-holders, the right of self-determination for the various nationalities, democracy, all lumped together under the one term—Socialism. A determined revolutionary and undoubtedly a great leader, even at the very end of his life, he was only able to leave to his party a programme that Ramsay MacDonald could have drawn up for him without any difficulty in half-an-hour.

LENIN AND CHINA

But Lenin, too, in 1919 had been devoting himself to the problem of China and the colonial countries of the

East, and in 1920 he presented theses on the Eastern Revolution to the Second Congress of the Third International. Lenin saw the Chinese revolution as part of the international proletarian revolution. Without the continued exploitation of the colonial people Capitalism in Europe would collapse. His practical proposals were, as always, based on the independent proletarian movement, intransigence in programme and organisation, flexibility in the formation of the United Front.

He knew that the workers and peasants alone could liberate China. But he knew that the chief danger to their activity was exactly such a Popular Front type of Government as the Kuomintang, which would end inevitably by betraying. He therefore called for "determined war" against the attempt of all those quasi-Communist revolutionists to cloak the liberation movement in the backward countries with a Communist garb. "The exclusive purpose" of the Communist International in all backward countries was to educate the Communist movements in those countries, however small, to "the consciousness of their specific tasks, i.e. to the tasks of the struggle against the bourgeois democratic tendencies within their respective nationalities." It was by fighting against their own bourgeoisie that the workers and peasants would drive out the imperialists. The Communist International would establish temporary relations and even unions with the revolutionary movements in these countries. But it must never amalgamate with them, "always preserving the independent character of the proletarian movement even though it be still in its embryonic state."

In China the peasant question was far more acute than it had been in Russia before 1917. Consequent on the whole Russian experience, therefore, the most inexperienced Bolshevik could formulate the second step after the organisation of the proletarian party. "Above all, we must strive as far as possible . . . to give the peasant movement a revolutionary character, to organise the peasants and all the exploited classes into the Soviets." Lenin wrote this in 1920. In three years the Chinese proletariat had passed even more rapidly than the Russian proletariat before

1905 to the stage where it was mature for revolution. We have to trace this process in some detail, for early in 1923 it was not only already clear that the Chinese Revolution was on its way, but obvious also that the theory of the Permanent Revolution and Lenin's organisational principles could carry it to success.

The Chinese Proletariat Matures

The post-war crisis, the resumption of industry in the West, hit Chinese industry severely. There had been small strikes in 1912, and the beginning of a Labour and Socialist movement before the war; an attempt had been made to form a Trade Union in Hong-Kong in 1915. But the Chinese workers who had served in the war brought back with them experience of Labour organisation. In September, 1919, the Chinese Returned Labourers' Association was organised in Shanghai to fight for better wages, the right to hold meetings, the right to make public speeches for promoting the welfare of the workers. The more backward the country, the closer the relation between economics and politics.

After the war the Japanese attempted to hold Shantung and in May, 1919, a score of students attacked the residences of pro-Japanese ministers in Peking and were arrested. When the news reached Shanghai, Labour leaders declared a strike which spread rapidly even to the public utilities. In a few days the Peking Government was compelled to remove the offending ministers and release the agitators. In 1920 the Overseas Labour Union appeared in Canton. Hundreds of pre-war publications dealing with Syndicalism, Socialism, Anarchism and all phases of the Labour movement were being published. On May 1, 1920, in Peking, Canton and Shanghai, Chinese workers celebrated the workers' anniversary. On January 12, 1922, the Chinese Seamen's Union of Hong-Kong presented its third petition for an increase in wages, and demanded an answer within twenty-four hours. 1,500 men struck the next day. On February 1st the British Governor of Hong-Kong declared the Chinese Seamen's Union an unlawful assembly. The reply was a sympathetic strike of 50,000, a symbolical general strike, representing every trade in the island. The strike lasted for nearly three months, when the seamen won a wage increase of twenty to thirty per cent. The young Communist Party of China organised in Canton the first Chinese Congress of Trades Unions with 170 delegates. Mediæval Chinese Tchuns and post-war European Capitalism recognised a common enemy. In the autumn of 1922 the British police fired on Chinese workers and killed several of them. In February, 1923, Wu Pei-Fu, the British Tchun, banned a railwaymen's conference. On the 6th a conference took place between the foreign consuls, Wu Pei-Fu's military representatives, and the directors of the Peking-Hankow railway. The next day troops in big railway stations opened fire on the crowds of railwaymen. In Hankow alone sixty were killed. The result was a railway strike of 20,000 men. The workers were ready to resist, but parliamentarians in Peking pressed for an investigation, placatory resolutions were passed, the edge of the workers' attack was blunted, and the strike was called off. At once the repression began; arrests, executions, the closing down of workers' papers, the driving of the Trade Union movement into illegality. Like the Russian workers, the Chinese workers were learning the close connection between economics and politics in a country with a backward or disorganised economy.

It was at this time, in the spring of 1923, that Lenin, writing his last article, spoke with supreme confidence of the coming revolution in the East. China he knew would unloose India. For in addition to the insoluble contradictions of their internal economy, the Russian Revolution had given all these millions a concrete example, more potent than a hundred years of propaganda. But after that spring Lenin never worked again, and at once, in the autumn of 1923 Stalin, Zinoviev and Kamenev in Moscow again revealed their lack of principle and their ingrained opportunism by sending the Chinese Communist Party into the Kuomintang—the first and most criminal error. Trotsky, as so often in those days fighting alone for Lenin's ideas, voted against. Had Lenin been sitting as chairman such an entry could never have taken place. It is in this way that men make history. In that autumn Borodin and other advisers went to Canton and opened a military school at Whampoa to train and organise the Kuomintang army. For the average bourgeois observer such a collaboration was well worth to Stalin even the temporary subordination of the Communist movement. It is here that the wide gulf between Menshevism and Bolshevism opens at once. Always when faced with such a choice Lenin chose the proletarian way. He did under certain circumstances advocate the temporary subordination of a revolutionary organisation, not large enough to be a party, to a centrist organisation; to a Social Democratic, or worse still, a bourgeois organisation, never. The sketch we have given of the Chinese proletariat between 1920 and 1923 shows that to the discerning eye the movement was mature. Stalin, an organic Menshevik and profoundly ignorant of international affairs as well as of Marxism, instinctively chose the other way, and Zinoviev and Kamenev followed. The test lies not in argument but in history.

In January, 1924, the reconstituted Kuomintang held its first meeting in Canton. Sun Yat-Sen agreed to admit the Communists into its ranks. But they entered not as a party, only as individuals, and had to swear to abide by the rules of the Kuomintang. The only conceivable justification for such a step was to consider it as a highly dangerous manœuvre.[1] The Chinese Communists might possibly, under a strong and supple leadership, have worked under cover of the Kuomintang for a certain period of time and then, having spread their influence, left demonstratively on some political issue understandable to the masses, and resumed their organisational and programmatic independence. They could make a temporary agreement for some specific objective even with the Liberal bourgeoisie, tenaciously guarding their independence. No one in 1923 could have foreseen that under Stalin's orders they were going to cling desperately to the Kuomintang for four

[1] Lenin's thesis to the Second Congress should be read in full, in order to understand how clearly he saw the main business of the Chinese proletarian party to be opposition to the bourgeois leadership.

years until hacked off by the swords of Chiang Kai-Shek's soldiers.

For the moment, however, the Communists, taking advantage of their new position, began with energy to help the proletariat in its task of organising itself.

THE REVOLUTION BEGINS

At the beginning of 1925 Feng Yu-Hsiang, a nationalist leader, defeated the pro-British Wu Pei-Fu, drove him out of Peking, and proclaimed his army the army of national liberation. The nationalist movement awoke. In Shanghai some worker delegates, elected to negotiate with the management in a dispute, were dismissed. The other workers protested, and the Anglo-Indian police, being summoned, fired on them, seriously wounding five. The Shanghai workers rose against this brutality. They did not know it at the time, but they were beginning the Chinese Revolution. That is the way a revolution often comes, like a thief in the night, and those who have prepared for it and are waiting for it do not see it, and often only realise that their chance has come when it has passed. The protest movement was fed not only from the immediate arrogance and rapacity of the foreigner. It was the whole history of China which was soon to express itself through this channel. The Chinese workers and peasants had reached one of the breaking-points of their history. Inside and outside the foreign concessions the Chinese workers, men, women and children, suffered from some of the most inhuman conditions of labour that obtained in any part of the globe; twelve hours and more seven days a week, no time for meals, no sanitary conveniences in the older factories, foreign and native, overseers with loaded rifles to keep discipline, and all for a few pence a day. National liberation rested on the solid foundation of millions of workers, seeking a way out of intolerable conditions.

What had been a small dispute about wages and a protest against administrative injustice, became overnight a political weapon for the liberation of China. The four months and a half between May 1 to the middle of September showed like clockwork the class-forces which would struggle for mastery in the coming revolution. "Down with the imperialists," was the slogan of the day. The Chinese Government in Shanghai thought it was dealing with a riot, and demonstrations and meetings were met with the killing and wounding of scores of people. The allies of Chinese reaction, foreign imperialism, of necessity rushed to aid in the repression. On June 4 the allied imperialists, whose gunboats are always in Chinese harbours to protect property and rights and interests, landed a party and occupied the University and other buildings in the city. The Shanghai proletariat replied with the general strike. Nearly a quarter of a million workers came out and paralysed the city, and as the mass force of the Shanghai proletariat showed itself, it drew in its wake (exactly as in France in June, 1936) the petty-bourgeois students, the artisans and the small traders, and, in the special conditions of China as a country struggling for national independence, even some of that treacherous brood, the Liberal Chinese bourgeoisie. A special committee was formed, the Committee of Labour, Education and Commerce, which along with delegates from the Trade Unions had representatives from students' associations, the small shop-keepers and even some of the bourgeoisie. But the Trade Unions predominated and, far more clearly than in Russia, from the very start the Chinese proletariat was leading the nation. All classes seemed to support the strike. But in an industrialised country all classes never make a revolution, and as the strike developed, the necessity for Lenin's life-long principle, the proletarian organisations and party retaining their independence, emerged with startling clearness. After one month the Chinese bourgeoisie, who had never been very ardent, ceased to support the strike. During July and August the petty-bourgeoisie, the intelligentsia, the students, wobblers from the very intermediate position they hold in society, began to weaken: nothing but immediate success and continued vigorous action can ever keep these to the proletarian movement. Aid from the international proletariat would have helped, but only the Third International agitated, collected money, made donations. The Second International, those perpetual preachers of self-determination, did nothing. The International Federation of Trades Unions behaved likewise. The British General Council, at this period consorting with the Russians in the Anglo-Russian Committee, refused even to answer telegrams of appeal from the Chinese Unions. Realising their limitations the Shanghai leaders in good time fell back to the defensive. Some of their most pressing economic demands were satisfied, the strike was called off and the Shanghai workers retired in good order and with a living, vital experience to help them in the future.

But so ripe was China that the Shanghai strike had acted as a detonator. There had been over a hundred sympathetic strikes in various towns, and out of one of these developed the Hong-Kong and Canton strike, demonstrating the fighting power and endurance of the proletariat in the manner that so constantly surprises even the most sanguine revolutionaries.

THE CANTON STRIKE

On June 23 a demonstration of protest against the Shanghai shooting took place in Canton. British police from the Anglo-French concession fired on the demonstration, killing and wounding scores of people. As in Shanghai the Chinese proletariat replied with a general strike, and their comrades in Hong-Kong joined. The Chinese bourgeoisie in Canton rallied to the strikers, and supported them, owing to the long revolutionary tradition in Canton and the much more important fact that the strike was accompanied by a boycott of British goods. From all the Chinese communities in the Philippine Islands, East Indies and America, money poured in. The British tried to prevent Chinese money coming into Canton, but failed; in Hong-Kong they unloosed all the forces of repression to break the strike. The Hong-Kong workers were unshakable. In thousands they began to leave Hong-Kong for Canton. Estimates vary, but one Chinese writer claims that from start to finish about 100,000 Chinese left the island for Canton. There a strike committee was formed. The strikers organised propaganda meetings, study-courses and lectures, they drew up regulations for workers and submitted them to the Canton Kuomintang Government, they confiscated and stored contraband goods which British merchants tried to smuggle in, they captured, tried and imprisoned blacklegs, they organised pickets along the entire frontier of Kwangsi province to keep out British ships and British goods from Hong-Kong. They formed a Workers' Guard which led the picketing, fought against smugglers and fought with the Kuomintang Government against counter-revolutionary Tchuns. The strike ruined British trade with China. Between August and December, 1924, the British ships entering Canton numbered between 160 and 240 each month. For the corresponding period in 1925 the number was between 27 and 2.

British Capitalism lost half-a-million pounds per day. In 1926 the British Empire lost half its trade with China, and three-quarters of its trade with Hong-Kong. After fifteen months the British began to give way and sought to placate the workers, handling recalcitrant Britishers very roughly. No Government can continue to fight against strikers who will not even stay to' be imprisoned or shot at. After one year the strike still continued as powerful as ever, the Communist Party of China playing a leading part, and the spirit of the workers all over China rose steadily. Trades Union membership, in May, 1924, 220,000, reached 540,000 in May, 1925, and in May, 1926, over a million. In Shanghai alone during the 1925 strike it had reached 280,000. And this unprecedentedly rapid industrial organisation of the workers was expressing itself in many strikes that were primarily political, which meant that the workers were looking to solve their industrial difficulties by the social revolution.

The Communist Party, 800 in 1925, by January, 1926, was 30,000, and to this powerful proletarian movement could be added the overwhelming revolutionary force of the starving Chinese peasantry. In Kwangtung, a province typical of the South, seventy-four per cent of the population held nineteen per cent of the land. In Wiush in Central China, 68.9 per cent of the poor peasantry held 14.2 per cent of the land. In Paoting in the North 65.2 per cent held 25.9 per cent of the land. Of the Chinese population, on a rough estimate, sixty-five per cent were driven by the most consistent and powerful revolutionary urge in all historical periods—the hunger of starving peasants for land.

THE PERMANENT REVOLUTION IN CHINA

The fundamental task of the Communist Party was basically the task of the Bolshevik Party in Russia—to link the proletarian movement with the peasant, organising the peasants into Soviets for the forcible seizure of the land. In no other way but on the basis of the proletarian and peasant revolution could China then or now achieve national independence. Sun Yat-Sen had learnt that by hard experience, though he shrank from drawing the full conclusions. He had hoped somehow to bring the revolutionary masses into the struggle led by the nationalist bourgeoisie. The thing is impossible. Now since the great strikes when it was clear that the Chinese proletariat was challenging the bourgeoisie, it was inevitable that at the first opportunity the Chinese bourgeoisie would join with imperialists and militarists and crush the revolution.

The farther East the bourgeoisie the more cruel and treacherous. The powerful French bourgeoisie in 1789 had joined with the counter-revolution, how much less likely was the weak Chinese bourgeoisie, far weaker than the Russian, to ally itself with a proletariat which had shown its power. That was the whole theoretical prognosis of the Bolshevik party, amply confirmed by the course of the Russian Revolution. After 1917 the main strategic line of the Chinese Revolution could only be as follows. The Chinese Revolution would begin as a bourgeois-democratic revolution, but only as an immediate slogan. While the Communist Party of China would not oppose this slogan, it would be aware that for a backward country with an advanced proletariat (we shall see it in Spain), the bourgeois-democratic régime is impossible. The revolution would conquer as the dictatorship of the proletariat, or not at all. The Communist Party had already shown that it knew how to link industrial with political demands.

It had to strive to popularise the ideas of Soviets among the peasantry on the simple slogan—the land for the peasants—and, as the party which urged the seizure of the land, would ultimately have the firm support of the peasantry for its political demands. Guarding its own independence, the Communist Party would boldly raise the slogan of national independence based on the revolutionary demands of the proletariat and the peasantry. If the movement developed (there could have been no doubt of this after the Hong-Kong strike, and in Hupeh in 1926 the peasants were already seizing the land), the anti-imperialist pretence of the Chinese bourgeoisie would be exposed and the Chinese petty-bourgeoisie, the traders, the students, and some of the intellectuals would be swept in the wake of the proletarian movement, and follow the proletariat as leader of the national revolution. A Congress of Soviets would appoint a provisional Revolutionary Government, and call a constituent assembly, arranging the franchise to secure the predominance of the poor. In this assembly the Chinese proletariat, organised in the Communist Party and in the Trade Unions, would occupy a dominating position. According to the strength of the movement and the dangers of the revolution, the dictatorship of the proletariat might be established immediately. But either the bourgeoisie would establish their dictatorship; or conversely the proletariat would establish theirs. It was this strategic line which would guide the Communist Party, already superior in the towns. It would jealously maintain its independence as the party of the proletariat and, if it could draw the hundreds of millions of peasants behind it, it would be the most powerful political force in the country. There was the danger of foreign intervention, but nothing would bind revolutionary China so firmly together as the sight of the Chinese bourgeoisie, but yesterday lovers of their country, attacking China along with the hated imperialists. China could stand a blockade far more easily than Russia. A Soviet China linked to a Soviet Russia, supported by the far-flung Third International, would alter the whole relationship of the capitalist and revolutionary forces in the Far

East. Such a bloc would not only throw British and Japanese economy into the gravest disorder, but would unloose movements in India, Burma, and even Egypt and the Near East which would set the whole structure of Capitalism rocking. The movement might perhaps not develop so powerfully but there was a chance that, at least in a substantial part of China, the revolution might hold power and use it as a base for future extension. At worst it might be totally defeated. The proletariat was ready. But the boldness of its slogans, the strength of its attack would depend on the strength of the peasant movement it could develop.

Even if it failed, as the Russian Revolution of 1905, the Chinese proletariat would have acquired an invaluable experience, the more advanced elements in the peasantry would have had time to recognise with which party their future lay, and the party, with tried and experienced leaders, would be able to prepare for the inevitable return of the revolutionary wave as the Russian party prepared for the new revolution on the basis of 1905. Such is the theory and practice of the Permanent Revolution. Lenin, alive and well in Moscow, would from day to day have analysed the development of events and through the Chinese Communist Party would have made the road clear for the Chinese masses. The Chinese proletariat had, by 1926, shown what it was capable of. Starting in 1929, nearly a hundred million peasants were to show for five heroic years how ready for revolution was the Chinese peasantry. It was not only the objective conditions which were so favourable. The Russian Revolution and the Communist International exercised an enormous subjective influence. The Chinese workers and peasants knew broadly what the Russians had done, and wanted to do the same. They trusted the Chinese Communist Party which they knew to be guided by the now world-famous leaders in Moscow. And yet it was the Communist leadership in Moscow which led the revolution in China to disaster. Step by step Stalin mismanaged it with such incompetence and dishonesty that, one year after the final defeat in December, 1927, the name of the International stank in Shanghai and Canton.

In April, 1927, the party had nearly 60,000 members, including 53.8 per cent workers; by July the percentage of workers in the party was seventy-five. On November 8, 1928, a circular of the Central Committee stated: "The party does not have a single healthy party nucleus among the industrial workers." In 1930 not two per cent. were workers. In 1935 at the Seventh Congress of the Communist International the secretary admitted that they had failed to make progress in organising the industrial workers. The blight that Stalin and Bucharin cast on the Chinese revolution in 1925–27 is still upon it.

STALIN'S TWO-CLASS PARTY

Stalin had had as little to do with international politics as with economics. Now in his important position as Lenin's successor he continued the rôle he had begun in October, 1924, when he prophesied the imminent revolution in Europe. In May, 1925, the month in which the Shanghai strike began, he spoke at the University of the Peoples of the East and expounded his Leninism for the revolutionary movement in the Orient. There he put forward, for such countries as Egypt and China, what is from the Leninist point of view the most singular of all Stalin's conceptions, surpassing even the relegation to the dust-heap of basic capital. He proposed a two-class party, a party of workers and peasants "after the model of the Kuomintang." Not all the red professors in Russia could find him any quotations from Lenin to support this doctrine, and the speech is remarkable as one of the few in the collected volumes which is not interspersed with "Lenin said."

"They will have to transcend the policy of the united nationalist front, and adopt the policy of forming a revolutionary coalition between the workers and the petty bourgeois. This coalition may find expression in the creation of a single party whose membership will be drawn from among the working class and the peasantry, after the model of the Kuomintang. But such a party should be genuinely representative of the two component forces, the communists and the revolutionary petty-bourgeois. This coalition must see to it that the half-heartedness and duplicity of the great bourgeoisie shall be laid bare, and that a resolute attack shall be made upon imperialism.

The formation of such a party, composed, as we have seen, of two distinct elements, is both necessary and expedient, so long as it does not shackle the activities of the Communists, so long as it does not hamper the agitational and propagandist freedom of the Communists, so long as it does not prevent the proletariat from rallying round the Communists, so long as it does not impair the Communist leadership of the revolutionary forces. But the formation of such a party is neither necessary nor expedient unless all these conditions are forthcoming; otherwise the Communist elements would become absorbed into the bourgeois elements and the Communists would lose their position as leaders of the proletarian army."[1]

In that muddled blundering paragraph lay the germ of all the muddles and blunders which were to come. It is difficult to say where he got the idea of a party representing two classes from. It was due most probably to a misunderstanding of the phrase "the revolutionary democratic dictatorship of the proletariat and the peasantry." That there can be only one proletarian or Communist Party, that a peasant may become a member of a Communist Party only by adopting the proletarian policy of the Communist Party, that a peasant party would be a separate entity led by the proletarian party, as the Social Revolutionaries formed a minority party in the Soviet Union between November, 1917 and July, 1918, that to talk about a party "composed, as we have seen, of two distinct elements" in which Communists would not be shackled by peasants, was the very antithesis of all that Lenin had fought for, was in complete opposition to what the Communist International stood for, was, in fact, the most dangerous nonsense, especially in the mouth of the leader of the international proletariat. To point out all this, of course, was Trotskyism.

Given Stalin's obstinacy and the servility of his subordinates, we can see to-day that from that moment the Chinese Revolution was doomed. For Stalin and Bucharin the revolution, according to Leninism, was a bourgeois-democratic revolution against the foreign imperialists, and therefore was to be carried out by the bourgeoisie organised in the Kuomintang and the nationalist army of the Canton

[1] *Leninism*, Vol. I, p. 278.

Government which Borodin was training. The business of the proletariat and the peasantry, therefore, was to do nothing which would impede the bourgeoisie and the Kuomintang in their struggle. Not for nothing had they spent the previous two years abusing the Permanent Revolution and all its teachings as the main vice of Trotskyism. After the imperialists had been driven into the sea by the united nation, by all classes, except the biggest of the bourgeoisie, then the proletariat and peasantry would turn upon the bourgeoisie and conquer. This in 1925, after 1905 and 1917, after over twenty years of reading and expounding Lenin.

THE KUOMINTANG

The two-class party Stalin envisaged on the model of the Kuomintang quickly developed into the four-class party of the Kuomintang.

The Kuomintang, whatever Sun Yat-Sen[1] and his wife might think, was a Government party ruling a large extent of territory in Southern China. By 1925 its membership consisted of about a quarter of a million, big bourgeoisie, factory-owners, petty-bourgeoisie, professional men and petty-traders, landowners, gentry, rich peasants and also, after the reorganisation by Sun Yat-Sen, working men and poor peasants. But the proletariat was being organised in Trade Unions under the leadership of the Communist Party. We have watched its steady growth. And the Kuomintang, as organised, could from its very nature have nothing to do with a revolutionary seizure of land by the poor peasants. There might be a Right Wing and a Left Wing (in January, 1926, there were 168 Lefts to 45 Rights, and 65 Centrists out of 278 delegates), but such a party could never lead a revolutionary proletariat and a revolutionary peasantry. Why should it? Not only in Lenin's thesis at the Second Congress, but also in supplementary theses presented at the Fourth Congress in 1922, the proletarian parties in the colonies had been warned against such parties, and in both sets of theses the Kuomintang had been

[1] He died in March, 1925, and later, as the Chinese bourgeoisie was revealed in its true colours, Madame Sen became a Communist.

247

mentioned by name as one of the specially dangerous. Trotsky therefore continued to demand that the Communist Party leave the Kuomintang. Whatever remote justification there might have been for its being in before, now that the revolution had begun, at all costs it must come out. It might be driven underground for a time. So had been the Bolshevik Party. The rise of the revolution would bring it out again with renewed force. Stalin and Bucharin condemned this as Trotskyism, and bound the Communist Party and the Chinese Revolution to the Kuomintang.

During 1925 the Left Wing of the Kuomintang had been following Sun Yat-Sen's directions, and like good Liberals displayed much sympathy for the workers' movements.[1] They had organised peasant leagues to fight against the Ming Tuans, a sort of Fascist militia on the countryside. But they warned the peasants against the seizure of land. That would come after, duly arranged by law. But even the formation of these peasant leagues had been causing dissatisfaction among the Right elements in the party.

The Executive Committee, however, was Left, and the Executive Committee ruled between congresses. Stalin and Bucharin, through Borodin, supported the Left against the Right, that is to say supported the petty-bourgeois traders and small capitalists against their greater brethren. The Political Bureau of nine members was Left. Wang Chin-Wei (the same who was Prime Minister to Chiang Kai-Shek until a few months ago—a bullet caused his retirement) was head of the party and of the Canton Government. He was absolutely Left, and Borodin, the Russian representative, was high in favour with Wang Chin-Wei. Borodin, with Wang's support, drafted programmes for Kuomintang conferences which sounded revolutionary enough, and the Chinese Communist Party worked and grew within the shelter of the Left Kuomintang. But as the Shanghai strike began and unloosed the hundreds of thousands of striking workers on Canton itself, the Chinese bourgeoisie and landowners grew frightened and

[1] As has been pointed out the Social Democrats do more; they even organise and lead it.

demanded the expulsion of the Communists. The Communists had now either to leave and fight for the revolution according to Lenin, or stay and fight for it according to the Left Kuomintang. Stalin chose the Left Kuomintang, and Borodin organised a plan of campaign to suit.

THE NORTHERN CAMPAIGN

In the North Chang Tso-Lin, the pro-Japanese war-lord, had established a dictatorship in Pekin, and gathered some other military chiefs to oppose the nationalists in the South. Borodin and the Left Wing therefore outlined the national revolution as follows. In the coming spring the nationalist forces in the South under Chiang Kai-Shek would set out from Canton in the extreme South, raise the banner of revolution, conquering anti-nationalist Tchuns, uniting with those who wished a liberated China, and end by defeating Chang Tso-Lin and taking the ancient capital of Pekin. Chiang Kai-Shek was willing to lead this revolution but he did not wish to go marching off to Pekin and leave a Radical Kuomintang Government under the influence of Borodin behind him. Yet his party needed the temporary support of the International. It applied for membership as a sympathising party. The Stalinists agreed, as usual Trotsky alone dissenting. To the two plenums of the Executive Committee held in February and again in November, Chiang sent fraternal delegates. He and Stalin exchanged portraits. But on March 20, 1926, while Borodin was out of Canton, Chiang Kai-Shek coalesced with the Right Kuomintang, staged a coup d'état, seized power and forced Wang Chin-Wei, and other Radical members of the Kuomintang, to fly from the country. He had acted too early. He had control of the army, but the nationalist movement was too weak as yet to progress without mass support. There was a sharp reaction against Chiang, and in May Left and Right Wing were reconciled. But Chiang Kai-Shek became head of the party in place of Wang Chin-Wei, and at the May plenum in 1926 he laid down harsh terms. The Communist Party was pledged not to criticise the anti-class struggle doctrines of Sun Yat-Sen. It was compelled to give a list of its members in the Kuomintang to Chiang

249

Kai-Shek (so that he could put his hands on them when he wanted them). It was forbidden to allow its members to become heads of any party or government department. In all important committees its members were limited to one. Members of the Kuomintang were forbidden to join the Communist Party. Borodin, under Stalin's orders, agreed to all these conditions. In return Chiang Kai-Shek expelled some of the members of the Right Wing. (They went to Nanking to await him there.) Thus at the moment when the revolution needed the leadership of the Communist Party Stalin tied it hand and foot. Marxism apart, Chiang Kai-Shek stood revealed. Stalin, however, follows his policies to the end and never gives away to Trotskyism. The news of this coup d'état would have reinforced Trotsky's insistence that the Communist Party leave the Kuomintang at once. Stalin proved his own policy correct by his favourite method of argument. He suppressed the news. When news of the coup d'état eventually leaked out, the *International Press Correspondence* of April 8, 1926, called it a "lying report." In the May 6 issue of the same journal Voitinsky, one of the Russian delegation under Borodin, called it "an invention of the imperialists." Thus encouraged, Chiang made all strikes in Canton illegal, Borodin agreeing.

With his rear tolerably safe from revolution, Chiang set out in July to the North, ostensibly to fight the militarists. He carried with him printing presses and a huge propaganda apparatus, developed and run by Communists, who put forward Chiang's slogans. Believing him to be the leader of the revolution, the masses rushed to his support and the anti-nationalist armies crumbled. As he gained confidence Chiang suppressed Trade Unions, the peasant leagues and the Communists. His support fell away. He recalled the Communists, who came willingly, again did propaganda for him, using the prestige of the October Revolution and the Soviet State in the service of Chiang Kai-Shek, the leader of the revolution. Where the Bolsheviks in Russia had called for Soviets and the confiscation of the land, the Communists now agitated for better working conditions and a twenty per cent reduction in rent. That was all Chiang would allow them to do. Chiang resumed his triumphant progress. By September the Yangtze valley was in his hands, and Stalin and Bucharin and the Internationalist Press were delirious with joy. By October his army had captured the important triple town of Hankow, Wuchang and Hanyang, known as Wuhan. The Kuomintang Government was moved from Canton to Wuhan, and before it left Canton it called off unconditionally the Hong-Kong—Canton strike. This had lasted with undiminished vigour for sixteen months and in all its aspects it is the greatest strike in history. In Canton also the Kuomintang provincial Left Wing was replaced by the Right, the famous workers' guard was disarmed, revolutionary workers were arrested, workers were forbidden to agitate among the peasantry, anti-English demonstrations were prohibited, and the gentry or small landowners in the villages encouraged. The Communist Party leadership submitted to everything. And as the news of all this leaked through to Russia, in Moscow the internal struggle between Stalin's Leninism and Trotskyism was now extended to Stalin's Kuomintang policy.

REVOLUTION FOR RENT REDUCTION

In July, 1926, Radek, a member of the Opposition, rector of Sun Yat-Sen University in Moscow, wrote to the Politbureau of the C.P.S.U. and asked for answers to a series of questions so that he might bring his lectures into harmony with the policy of the International in China. The questions were awkward. What was the attitude of the party to the military dictatorship of Chiang Kai-Shek initiated after the coup d'état of March, 1926, and supported by Borodin? What work was the Kuomintang doing among the peasantry? A manifesto had been issued by the Central Committee of the Chinese party, part of which ran: "We must carry on a minimum of class struggle, and when the policy of the Communist Party is designated as Bolshevik, it is not a matter of Bolshevism but of Bolshevism in the interests of the whole nation." Did Stalin approve of this as Leninism?

Radek received no reply. He wrote a second letter in July. There was no reply. He wrote again in September. Still no reply. Stalin and Bucharin dared not as yet say openly that they were responsible for the instructions to the Communist Party of China to do nothing which would accelerate any conflict with Chiang Kai-Shek. But in November, 1926, after the Seventh Plenum of the E.C.C.I. (at which a fraternal delegate from Chiang Kai-Shek took part), the Executive issued a manifesto. Stalin had proposed a two-class party; Martynov, one of his henchmen, made the Kuomintang into a three-class party. Now this manifesto defined the revolutionary movement as a bloc of four classes, comedy in the mouths of Liberal bourgeois seeking to deceive the masses, but a shameful crime coming from Lenin's International not three years after his death.

"The proletariat is forming a bloc with the peasantry (which is actively taking up the struggle for its interests), with the petty urban bourgeoisie and a section of the capitalist bourgeoisie. This combination of forces found its political expression in corresponding groups in the Kuomintang and in the Canton Government. Now the movement is at the beginning of the third stage on the eve of a new class combination. In this stage the driving forces of the movement will be a bloc of still more revolutionary nature—of the proletariat, peasantry and urban petty bourgeoisie, to the exclusion of a large section of the big Capitalist bourgeoisie. This does not mean that the whole bourgeoisie as a class will be excluded from the arena of the struggle for national emancipation, for besides the petty and middle bourgeoisie, even certain strata of the big bourgeoisie may, for a certain period, continue to march with the revolution. . . ."

What pen wrote this we cannot say. But there can be no mistake about the originator of these ideas. It was the same who called the struggle between Lenin and Trotsky a storm in a tea-cup, and urged support of the Provisional Government in 1917.

On the future Chinese Government Stalin had travelled far since the two-class party.

"The structure of the revolutionary State will be determined by its class basis. It will not be a purely bourgeois democratic State. The State will represent the democratic dictatorship of the proletariat, peasantry and other exploited classes. It will be a revolutionary anti-imperialist government of transition to non-capitalist (Socialist) development. . . ."

All of which meant that the Kuomintang would govern henceforth.

Boldly the manifesto came out for the agrarian revolution:

"The national Government of Canton will not be able to retain power, the revolution will not advance towards the complete victory over foreign imperialism and native reaction, unless national liberation is identified with agrarian revolution. . . ."

This sounded grand enough, but it was only one of the flourishes which Stalin habitually uses as a preface to the blackest reaction. The next paragraph was many flights lower:

"While recognising that the Communist Party of China should advance the demand for the nationalisation of the land as its fundamental plank in the agrarian programme of the proletariat, it is necessary at the present time, however, to differentiate in agrarian tactics in accordance with the peculiar economic and political conditions prevailing in the various districts in Chinese territory. . . ."

This meant simply that the views on property of Chiang Kai-Shek and the Kuomintang leaders of the revolution were to be respected. What, therefore, was the revolutionary programme? It had to be a programme that Borodin and Chiang could carry out peacefully together.

"The Communist Party of China and the Kuomintang must immediately carry out the following measures in order to bring over the peasantry to the side of the revolution."

And the first of a long list of demands was:

(a) To reduce rents to the minimum.

Stalin and Bucharin were asking the peasants of China to make a revolution in order "to reduce rents to the minimum."

Not once was the word Soviet mentioned, and the manifesto took good care to exclude every possibility of the organisation of one. "The apparatus of the National Revolutionary Government provides a very effective way to reach the peasantry. The Communist Party must use this way." The Kuomintang therefore was to make the peasant revolution.

Chiang had severely limited the participation of the Communists in the organisation of the Kuomintang. Stalin and Bucharin, having hidden this from the International, with their tongues in their cheeks proceeded as follows:

"In the newly liberated provinces State apparatuses of the type of the Canton Government will be set up. The task of the Communists and their revolutionary allies is to penetrate into the apparatus of the new Government to give practical expression to the agrarian programme of national revolution. This will be done by using the State apparatus for the confiscation of land, reduction of taxes, investment of real power in the peasant committees, thus carrying on progressive measures of reform on the basis of a revolutionary programme. . . ."

They then dealt the now traditional blow at Trotskyism:

"In view of this and many other equally important reasons, the point of view that the Communist Party must leave the Kuomintang is incorrect. . . ."

The manifesto showed that they knew quite well the nature of the Kuomintang Government in Canton: "Since its foundation the real power of the Canton Government has been in the hands of the Right Wing Kuomintang (five out of the six commissars belong to the Right Wing) . . ." But they called on the Communists to enter this Government to assist the revolutionary Left Wing against the right. As if four revolutionary classes were not enough they envisaged five.

"The Communist Party of China must strive to develop the Kuomintang into a real Party of the People—a solid revolutionary bloc of the proletariat, peasantry, the urban petty bourgeoisie and the other oppressed and exploited classes which must carry on a decisive struggle against imperialism and its agents. . . ."

Stalin and Bucharin might talk about bourgeois-democratic revolution and the democratic dictatorship of proletariat and peasantry and the remaining classes which made up the five, but the Kuomintang Canton Government with five Right-wingers out of its six commissars was quite good enough for them.

"The Canton Government is a revolutionary State primarily owing to its anti-imperialistic character. . . ."

The industrial programme of the revolution was to be:

" (a) Nationalisation of railways and waterways.
(b) Confiscation of large enterprises, mines and banks having the character of foreign concessions.
(c) Nationalisation of land to be realised by successive radical reform measures enforced by the revolutionary State."[1]

For twelve years before 1917 the Bolsheviks had tirelessly preached the simple slogans, the democratic republic, the eight-hour day, the land for the peasants. Yet with the Chinese proletariat already in action and millions of hungry peasants ready to fight, this was the programme and policy imposed on them with all the authority of the October Revolution and the Communist International. This cruelly deceptive and dangerous document went to Borodin and the Communist Party of China, through them to demoralise the ardent but trusting Chinese masses and lead scores of thousands into the death-trap of the Kuomintang.

THE REVOLUTION CHAINED

But it was all that Borodin and the Communist Party could do to hold back the Chinese masses. By January, 1927, the membership of the C.P. was nearly 60,000; the Young Communist League of China was 35,000, and the organised workers, 230,000 in 1923, were now 2,800,000, a greater number than in the Russia of October, 1917. However much Stalin might wish to hold them down in order not to displease Chiang Kai-Shek, the masses in Canton and Wuhan could feel on their backs the blows of reaction. In the Southern provinces by March, 1927, ten million peasants had been organised in the peasant leagues. In Hupeh the peasants were already seizing the land on a large scale. Furthermore, Chiang Kai-Shek's treachery,

[1] The manifesto appears in full in *The Communist*, March, 1927.

made so clear in March, was now becoming open to the masses. In the early months of 1927 he was carrying on negotiations with the Japanese and the pro-Japanese reactionary war-lords; and the Communist Party knew it. The nearer he got to Shanghai the more he threw off the thin mask. Since December he had been in open conflict with Borodin, Galen and other Communists. But their only strength lay in the mass movement, and this they had, by Stalin's manifesto, to subordinate to the Kuomintang.

Suddenly the masses broke away. On January 3 the workers and petty-bourgeoisie of Hankow were holding a meeting near the British concession. The British authorities got into conflict with them and the masses spontaneously occupied the concession, organised a workers' guard and maintained control. The revolution in the South flared up again, and so powerful a wave of nationalist sentiment flowed through the country that even the Japanese supporter, Chang So-Lin in Pekin, found it politic to speak of the return of the concessions. Chiang Kai-Shek, now at Nanking, then as to-day a stronghold of reaction, afraid of the militant workers in the South, demanded that the Government seat should be transferred to Nanking. But the Left Kuomintang, between whom and Chiang there had always been almost open hostility, insisted that according to a resolution passed in Canton the Government should remain at Wuhan. For weeks there existed practically two Kuomintang Governments, two central committees, two political bureaux. Chiang, not yet ready to come out openly against the International, praised Trotskyism because the Trotskyists were demanding the withdrawal of the party from the Kuomintang.[1] In the Russian delegation three young Communists (all anti-Trotskyists), Nassonov, Fokine and Albrecht, were chafing at the suicidal policy of Borodin. The bold action of the Chinese proletariat at Hankow had given Borodin an opportunity. The Left Kuomintang rallied round him and stiffened its resistance to Chiang Kai-Shek. But Borodin, shackled by Stalin, did not know what to do. To the masses holding Hankow neither Borodin nor the

[1] Stalin's representatives in Shanghai stated explicitly Chiang's treacherous reason for so doing.

Chinese party gave any directives. Instead they rebuked the workers who had formed the guard and were keeping order in Hankow.

Nassonov, Fokine and Albrecht urged Borodin to leave Shanghai and go to Wuhan to rally the Left Kuomintang, initiate a broad mass campaign on the rising militancy of the masses, explain that the quarrel over the Government seat was not personal but political, and demand openly from Chiang Kai-Shek a clear and distinct political declaration. Borodin stuck to Stalin's manifesto.

Chiang took the offensive, and he and the bourgeois and imperialist press brought the struggle against Borodin into the open. On February 21 Chiang delivered a pogrom speech against the party, and the conflict could no longer be hidden. Borodin and the party remained silent before the bewildered masses. Urged to unloose the peasant movement against Chiang, they declared that the peasants did not want land.

THE REVOLUTION MURDERED

In Shanghai the revolutionary proletariat, roused to fever-heat by the victories and approach of Chiang Kai-Shek, the leader of the revolution, received the news that Chiang had defeated Sun Chang-Fang, the reactionary feudal general who dominated Shanghai and the surrounding area. The joy of the workers broke out on February 18 into a spontaneous general strike in which 300,000 workers joined. A section of the petty-bourgeoisie shut up their shops and joined in the strike, the fleet came over to the side of the workers and the strike developed into an armed uprising. A detachment of Sun Chang-Fang's troops in the city broke under the strain. Some began to loot and pillage, others wanted to join the nationalist revolution. But the Chinese Central Committee, which did not expect the strike, deliberated as to whether the rising should take place or not, even while it was taking place. No directives were issued. The slogans were "Down with Sun Chang-Fang," and "Hail the Northern Expedition," "Hail Chiang Kai-Shek." Not one anti-imperialist slogan was issued in Shanghai, the centre of foreign imperialism in China. The movement collapsed.

257

Nassonov, Fokine and Albrecht, seeing the revolution being destroyed by those who were supposed to lead it, sent to Moscow a long and bitter complaint against the leadership of Borodin and the leaders of the Chinese Communist Party.

"The slogan of the democratic national assembly, which we had advanced shortly before the strike, was conceived of as a new means of combinations at the top, and was not launched among the masses. As a result, we let slip an exceptionally favourable historical moment, a rare combination of circumstances, where power lay in the streets but the party did not know how to take it. Worse still, it didn't want to take it; it was afraid to.

"Thus, the Right tendency, which has already contaminated the party for a year, found a crass and consummate expression during the Shanghai events, which can only be compared with the tactics of the German Central Committee in 1923 and of the Mensheviks during the December uprising in 1905. Yet there is a difference. It lies in the fact that in Shanghai the proletariat had considerably more forces and chances on its side and, with an energetic intervention, it could have won Shanghai for the revolution and changed the relationship of forces within the Kuomintang.

"It is not by accident that the leadership of the Chinese Communist Party committed these errors. They flowed from the Right Wing conception of the revolution, the lack of understanding of the mass movement and the complete lack of attention towards it."[1]

But the Right Wing conception of the revolution which had contaminated the party for a year had come from Stalin. Stalin dealt with the protest against his policy in the usual manner. He suppressed the letter, recalled Nassonov in disgrace and banished him to America.

While the Shanghai proletariat fought, Chiang Kai-Shek, but two days march outside the city, would not enter. He waited while the soldiers of the reaction "bled" the workers. (The military governor of Shanghai was later to receive a command in Chiang's army.) Instead Chiang spread terror in the outlying provinces. Nassonov and his

[1] *Problems of the Chinese Revolution*, by L. Trotsky, Pioneer Publishers, New York. The letter is printed as an appendix. Its authenticity cannot be doubted, for Andrews, the British Stalinist, quotes from it (most probably unwittingly) in *Where is Trotsky Going?* by R. F. Andrews, p. 57. *Cp. Problems*, p. 404. See also note on p. 256 of this book.

friends had written their despairing letter on March 17, in the belief that the Shanghai proletariat was crushed for some time to come. But on March 21 the workers of Shanghai again rose spontaneously, and this time drove out the Northern forces. Millions of workers all over the globe have suffered at the hands of the Stalin-dominated International, but none so much as the valiant proletariat of Shanghai. For three weeks they held the city. By this time the masses knew that Chiang Kai-Shek meant mischief, for his army had stood outside the gates for several days while they fought with the reactionaries inside. The majority of the workers wished to close the gates to Chiang and fight him. But Stalin's orders were rigid. Mandalian, a Communist official in Shanghai at the time, has written that the orders to the workers were "not to provoke Chiang" and "in case of extreme necessity to bury their arms,"[1] and Bucharin, in his *Problems of the Chinese Revolution*, has confirmed this. From Chiang's army itself came a warning of the coup that Chiang was preparing. His army was not homogeneous, and contained elements devoted to the revolution. Certain sections of Chiang's army entered the city but took no action. The first division was led by Say-O, who had been promoted from the ranks, and he and his division were in sympathy with the mass movement. Chiang Kai-Shek knew this and hated Say-O. While the main army stood outside the gates of Shanghai, Chiang called Say-O to headquarters, received him coldly and proposed that he leave the city and go to the front. Say-O sought the Central Committee of the Chinese Communist Party and told them that he would not go back to Chiang Kai-Shek because he feared a trap. He was willing to remain in Shanghai and fight with the workers against the counter-revolutionary overthrow which Chiang was preparing. Tchen Diu-Su and the leaders of the Chinese party told him that they knew the overthrow was being prepared, but that they did not want a premature conflict with Chiang Kai-Shek. Say-O therefore led his division out of the city.[2]

[1] *International Press Correspondence.* French edition, March 23, 1927.

[2] This narrative Trotsky, who is our authority here, claims was told to the sixteenth session of the XV Congress of the C.P.S.U., December 11, 1927, by Chitarov, home from China. Stalin had the most damaging passages deleted

But the split in the Kuomintang ranks and the coming treachery of Chiang were now no secret and were openly discussed even in the imperialist press. The Chinese party holding fast to Moscow, reassured the doubting Shanghai workers.

On April 6 Stalin addressed a meeting in Moscow, and the meeting unanimously adopted a resolution condemning Trotskyism and endorsing the line of the Chinese Communist Party:

"This meeting considers the demand that the Communist Party of China leave the Kuomintang to be equivalent to the isolation of the C.P. of China and the proletariat from the national movement for the emancipation of China and further considers this demand to be absolutely false and erroneous."[1]

All over the world the Communist International, drugged by the Stalinist policy and the Stalinist lies, was waiting for the victory of Chiang Kai-Shek. On March 23 the Communist Party of France held a great meeting in Paris at which appeared Cachin, Semard and Monmousseau. They sent a telegram to Chiang Kai-Shek:

"The workers of Paris greet the entry of the revolutionary Chinese army into Shanghai. Fifty-six years after the Paris Commune and ten years after the Russian, the Chinese Commune marks a new stage in the development of the world revolution."

But the Shanghai workers knew that Chiang was a traitor. The British and Americans bombarded Nanking and killed 7,000 Chinese and the imperialists were openly inciting Chiang against the workers. To allay feeling, therefore, Communist Party and Kuomintang issued a joint manifesto in Shanghai on April 6. In all the misleading literature of the Stalinist International this manifesto is perhaps the most criminal.

"The national revolution has reached the last basis of imperialism in China, Shanghai. The counter-revolutionaries both

---

from the minutes and Trotsky quotes the pages, 32 and 33, of the chief omissions. The fanatical obedience of the leadership was due to the prestige of Stalin as representative of the Russian Revolution and the strong backbone of control from above in the International. We shall see it even more strikingly and with more disastrous consequences in Germany, 1930–33.

[1] *International Press Correspondence*, April 14, 1927.

inside and outside China are spreading false reports in order to bring our two parties in opposition to each other. Some say that the Communist Party is preparing to form a Worker's Government, to overthrow the Kuomintang and to recover the concessions by force of arms. Others say that the leaders of the Kuomintang intend to make war on the Communist Party, to suppress the labour unions and to dissolve the workers' defence organisations.

"Now is not the time to discuss the origin of these malicious rumours. The supreme organ of the Kuomintang declared at its last plenary session that it has not the least intention of attacking the Communist Party or of suppressing the labour unions. The military authorities in Shanghai have declared their complete allegiance to the Central Committee of the Kuomintang. If differences of opinion exist they can be amicably settled. The Communist Party is striving to maintain order in the freed territories. It has already completely approved of the tactic of the National Government not to attempt to force a return of the concessions by armed force. The trades council of Shanghai has also declared that it will make no attempt to enter the concession by violence. At the same time it declared that it fully approved of the co-operation between all oppressed classes through the formation of a local government. In face of these facts, there is *no basis whatever for these malicious rumours.*" [1]

On April 12 Chiang Kai-Shek, having concluded his arrangements with the imperialists, launched the terror on the Shanghai workers. Chiang's long-sword detachments marched through the streets, executing workers on the spot; some of the strikers in the Railway Department were thrown into the furnaces of the locomotives. Communist Party, Trades Union movement, all workers' organisations, were smashed to pieces and driven into illegality. The Chinese counter-revolution, backed by imperialism, reigned triumphant in Shanghai, while Stalin and Bucharin in Moscow led the whole Communist International in an ear-piercing howl of treachery.

Shanghai might be lost, but one thing had to be saved— Stalin's prestige against Trotskyism. In the following month at the Eighth Plenum of the E.C.C.I., Stalin exposed the mistakes of the Opposition:

"The Opposition is dissatisfied because the Shanghai workers did not enter into a decisive battle against the imperialists and

[1] *International Press Correspondence*, April 14, 1927.

their myrmidons. But it does not understand that the revolution in China cannot develop at a fast tempo. It does not understand that one cannot take up a decisive struggle under unfavourable conditions. The Opposition does not understand that one cannot take up a decisive struggle under unfavourable conditions. The Opposition does not understand that not to avoid a decisive struggle under unfavourable conditions (when it can be avoided), means to make easier the work of the enemies of the revolution. . . ."

For at the Eighth Plenum Stalin and Bucharin insisted that the Communists should remain within the Kuomintang and should now support the Left Kuomintang and the Wuhan Government as leaders of the revolution. Wang Chin-Wei was substituted for Chiang Kai-Shek. Borodin in China was sending urgent messages to Stalin telling him that the Kuomintang leaders in Wuhan were determined to prevent the growing agrarian revolution even at the cost of a split with Moscow. From Stalin's point of view the only thing was to hold the agrarian revolution in. For him now the Left Kuomintang Government at Wuhan, with two Communists in it and supported by Feng Yu-hsiang, (the Christian general)[1] was now the Revolutionary Government, and its head, Wang Chin-Wei was immediately baptised leader of the Chinese Revolution.

It is at this stage that the personal responsibility of Stalin (and Bucharin) assumes international proportions. They could have changed the policy then. It is true that Stalin had the power he held because he was the ideal representative of the bureaucracy. But a change of policy did not in any way involve the internal position of the bureaucracy. Proof of this is that in a few months the policy was violently changed. But Stalin's stubborn ignorance and political blindness held the revolution down.

Seven years before Lenin had said China was ripe for Soviets. Now, in May, 1927, after two years of revolution, Stalin rejected outright the policy of Soviets for which the Left Opposition pressed. "Now can we say that the situation in Russia from March to July 1917 represents an analogy to the present situation in China? No, this cannot

[1] He made his soldiers sing Methodist hymns every day, and say grace at meals. America, it was stated, backed him.

be said. . . . The history of the workers' Soviets shows that such Soviets can exist and develop further only if favourable premises are given for a direct transition from the bourgeois-democratic revolution to the proletarian revolution. . . ."[1]

Trotsky, though conscious that against the Stalinised International arguments were useless, led the attack of the Left Opposition with undiminished vigour and courage.

"Stalin has again declared himself here against workers' and peasants' Soviets with the argument that the Kuomintang and the Wuhan Government are sufficient means and instruments for the agrarian revolution. Thereby Stalin assumes, and wants the International to assume, the responsibility for the policy of the Kuomintang and the Wuhan Government, as he repeatedly assumed the responsibility for the policy of the former 'National Government' of Chiang Kai-Shek (particularly in his speech of April 5, the stenogram of which has, of course, been kept hidden from the International). . . .

"The agrarian revolution is a serious thing. Politicians of the Wang Chin-Wei type, under difficult conditions, will unite ten times with Chiang Kai-Shek against the workers and peasants. Under such conditions two Communists in a bourgeois Government become impotent hostages, if not a direct mask for the preparation of a new blow against the working masses. We say to the workers of China: The peasants will not carry out the agrarian revolution to the end if they let themselves be led by petty-bourgeois radicals instead of by you, the revolutionary proletarians. Therefore, build up your workers' Soviets, ally them with the peasant Soviets, arm yourselves through the Soviets, shoot the generals who do not recognise the Soviets, shoot the bureaucrats and bourgeois Liberals who will organise uprisings against the Soviets. Only through peasants' and soldiers' Soviets will you win over the majority of Chiang Kai-Shek's soldiers to your side. . . ."[2]

The Plenum adopted a resolution against Trotskyism:

"Comrade Trotsky . . . demanded at the Plenary Session the immediate establishment of the dual power in the form of Soviets and the immediate adoption of a course towards the overthrow of the Left Kuomintang Government. This apparently ultra-Left but in reality opportunist demand is nothing but the repetition of the old Trotskyist position of jumping over the petty bourgeois, peasant stage of the revolution."

[1] *Minutes of the Plenum*, German edition, Hamburg–Berlin, 1928, p. 66 See *Third International after Lenin*, by L. Trotsky, p. 840.
[2] *Problems of the Chinese Revolution*, pp.102 and 103.

Barring a note which said that the line of the C.I. had been quite correct, no accounts of this May Plenum were ever published until a year after, long after the Opposition had been expelled and had made some of the documents public. For even while the Plenum was sitting the generals seized power in the province of Honan, a month later Feng Yu-hsiang allied himself with Chiang Kai-Shek, and before another month Wang Chin-Wei, the new leader of the revolution, and the Wuhan Government had come to terms with Chiang Kai-Shek and put to the sword the workers' movement in Wuhan. Even more bitter than that of the workers of Shanghai was the experience of the peasants in the revolutionary district of Changsha, an important revolutionary centre near to Wuhan. The Kuomintang army in Changsha consisted of only 1,700 soldiers, and the peasants around had armed detachments consisting of 20,000 men. When the peasants heard that the counter-revolutionary generals had started to crush the national movement they gathered round Changsha, preparing to march on the city. But at this point a letter came from the Central Committee of the Chinese Communist Party. Faithful to their instructions from the great revolutionists in Moscow, they told the peasants to avoid conflict and to transfer the matter to the Revolutionary Government in Wuhan. The District Committee ordered the peasants to retreat. Two detachments failed to get the message in time, advanced on Wuhan itself and were there destroyed by the soldiers of Wang Chin-Wei.

CONFUSION IN THE OPPOSITION

The pitiless exposure of the false policy in China only intensified Stalin's attacks against the policy of the Opposition at home, and confusion in the ranks of the Opposition gave Stalin and Bucharin the opportunity to win ideological victories. In the early stages of the Chinese Revolution, Zinoviev, as President of the Communist International, had lent himself to Stalin's Leninism. When the Zinoviev-Trotsky bloc was formed, Trotsky's uncompromising stand for the immediate withdrawal from the Kuomintang which he had maintained since 1923 was voted down by Zinoviev, and Trotsky was compelled for the sake of discipline to moderate his demand for the immediate withdrawal. Stalin and Bucharin knew quite well the differences between Trotsky and Zinoviev, but seized on this divergence and made great play with it agains the Opposition, while Chiang Kai-Shek and Wang Chin-Wei massacred tens of thousands of deluded Chinese workers and peasants. After Wuhan the Trotsky Wing won over the Zinoviev Wing and came out unequivocally for the withdrawal from the Kuomintang. Stalin still refused.

THE EBB MISTAKEN FOR THE FLOW

The proletariat had been totally defeated in Shanghai and Wuhan. The peasant movement, which was to show its force a year later, was still hobbled by the Stalinist policy. As always, this was the time chosen by Stalin to make a sharp turn to the Left. Soviets, inadmissible in May, were in July proclaimed the immediate task. Prestige, however, had to be maintained. The first thing to do was to throw the blame on the leadership in China, which was condemned root and branch. Bucharin did the dirty work and let loose a stream of abuse on them. A new representative was sent to replace Borodin. Telegrams from Moscow called a hasty conference. A new leadership was set up and the course set for mass revolt. The Left Opposition raised a protest at the cruel massacres and disillusionment which would inevitably follow. They were now violently abused as liquidationists. On August 9 a joint session of the Central Committee and of the C.P.S.U. made the following declaration: "The Chinese Revolution is not only not on the ebb, but has entered upon a new higher stage. . . . Not only is the strength of the toiling masses of China not yet exhausted, but it is precisely only now that it is beginning to manifest itself in a new advance of the revolutionary struggle." On this dreadful orientation the defeated revolution was pounded to pieces. Rising after rising, doomed in advance to failure, destroyed some of the finest and bravest of the Chinese revolutionaries. On September 19, after two risings had been crushed, the Kuomintang was abandoned at last. But Moscow still preached the rising of the revolution to a higher stage and inevitable victory.

All in China who opposed this policy were driven ruthlessly out of the party. In Moscow the Left Opposition were jeered at as counter-revolutionary. This was the Leninism that led to the ill-fated Canton insurrection in December, 1927, when, without preparation, without a sign as yet of a mass peasant rising, with thousands of Kuomintang soldiers in and near Canton, the Communist International encouraged the workers to seize the city which they held for two or three days. The insurrection had been timed to coincide with the Fifteenth Congress of the Russian Party, where Stalin was expounding the mistakes of the Opposition. Over seven thousand workers paid with their lives for this last Stalinist adventure. From first to last 100,000 Chinese workers and peasants lost their lives, making the Kuomintang revolution.

Some Communists who escaped from the Canton Commune with other remnants of the revolutionary movement, insurgent peasant-bands and ex-Kuomintang soldiers, raised the countryside in Central China and formed Soviet China. With the proletarian movement dead the Chinese Peasant Soviets were bound to be defeated, but it took Chiang Kai-Shek six years to do it and demonstrated what could have been accomplished in China by a combination of proletariat and peasantry. The remains of the Red Army are now wandering somewhere in North China. While Red China lasted, the Communist International, in writings and speeches, trumpeted. Not so Stalin. With the defeat of the revolution his open rôle as revolutionary strategist came to a final end. In the second volume of his collected speeches there is only one direct reference to the revolution. It is in the best Stalinist vein, and deserves consideration. It is one of those revealing statements which explain so many things in the history of Soviet Russia. "It is said that already a Soviet government has been formed there. If that is true, I think it is nothing to be surprised at. There can be no doubt that only the Soviets can save China from final collapse and beggary."[1] Thus the leader of the inter-

[1] *Leninism*, Vol. II, p. 318.

national proletariat in his political report to the Sixteenth Congress. But not only on revolution in China has he been silent. Never since has he openly taken upon himself the responsibility for the policy of the International. He could send the Opposition to Siberia and pass innumerable resolutions condemning their policy and justifying his own, which would have been successful but for the mistakes of the leadership in China. But nothing could wipe away his responsibility for the hideous failure there, and he would not run that risk again.

What explanation can be given of the policy in China between 1923 and 1927? Bucharin's share in it may be neglected. Stalin has used one after the other of the old Soviet leaders as his mouth-piece and then cast them aside if the policy failed. The policy was his. What lay behind it? Not conscious sabotage.

That was to come later. Stalin spent enormous sums in China. He knew that a successful Chinese Revolution would enormously strengthen Russia in the Far East, the failure would leave Russia in the position she is in to-day, with the Chinese Eastern Railway lost, threatened by both China and Japan. He wanted a Chinese Revolution, but he had no belief in the capacity of the Chinese masses to make one. This man of steel, fierce Bolshevik, etc., is first and foremost a bureaucrat (and is therefore the representative man of the Russian bureaucracy). Like Blum, Citrine, Wels, Leipart, Otto Bauer and the other Mensheviks, he believes in the bourgeoisie far more than he believes in the proletariat. He was prepared in 1917 to support the Russian bourgeoisie rather than depend upon the international proletariat. In 1925–1927, despite all facts and warnings, he stuck to Chiang Kai-Shek and Wang Chin-Wei. The consequences, however, did not lead him to recognise error. It had the opposite result. The bureaucracy now not only in theory but in fact turned its back on the revolution. Henceforward the International had one exclusive purpose—the defence of the U.S.S.R.

Chapter 10

THE PLATFORM AND THE FIVE-YEAR PLAN

IN PREPARATION FOR THE FIFTEENTH PARTY CONFERENCE in December, 1927, the Oppositionists summarised their position in a document known as the Platform.[1] It contained their charges against the Stalinist régime and their proposals for the regeneration of Russia. Such success as the Soviet Union has achieved it owes to working on the principles outlined in the document, as far as this was possible under the Stalinist régime.

The Opposition based its whole approach to the fundamental problems of the Soviet Union in the spirit of fearless facing of the truth before the party and the masses, which we have so insisted upon in this book; and the platform begins with a quotation from Lenin's speech at the last Party Congress he attended, where he told the Russian people quite frankly that under the New Economic Policy the Soviet State was slipping away from Socialist control and he did not know where it was going. Stalin's method, on the other hand, was to use the party and State apparatus to cover up failures and under a false appearance of success suppress criticism. By his incessant lying[1] he confused the

---

[1] It is published in full in *The Real Situation in Russia*, by L. Trotsky, 1928. The extracts published by the C.P.G.B. in its brochure *Where is Trotsky Going?* correspond to the version published by Trotsky after his expulsion from the party.

[2] It is perhaps necessary to explain our criticism of Stalin's lying which has now spread over the whole Soviet régime and the International. When Goebbels says, "Not a hair of any Jew's head has been touched," or Eden says, "I will not be the first British Foreign Secretary to break his word," to criticise these as lies is to waste time and mistake politics for a Sunday School. Under the most perfect Socialist State men will lie and intrigue; but the moment the question is one of a political line, its success or failure before the masses, a revolutionary party, in power or out of power, must not lie. The masses must be organised and led on the basis of truth, mistakes openly admitted. Any other policy ultimately will only confuse them and weaken their greatest asset, their mass-cohesion.

party and the masses and made it difficult to find and follow the correct road.

THE PROLETARIAT WEAKENING

Three hostile forces—the kulak, the nepman and the bureaucrat—had grown at an alarming rate between 1924 and 1927. They were the chief support of the Stalinist régime in its struggle against the Opposition and now endangered the very existence of the Socialist State. The difference between agricultural and industrial prices, between wholesale and retail prices, and the difference between domestic prices and world prices, the contraband goods which came steadily into the Soviet Union, all these were a constant source of private gain, creating capitalists. The rôle of indirect taxes had grown at the expense of the direct by which automatically the tax burden moved from the wealthier to the poorer. The income of the kulak had increased incomparably more than that of the worker. Real wages in 1927 stood on about the same level as in the autumn of 1925, yet the national income had increased; that of kulaks, private capitalist merchants and speculators having increased with enormous rapidity.

To mobilise the forces of the party and the masses against the dangers was neither panic nor pessimism, but the duty of the proletariat in the Socialist State. A certain growth of the kulak, nepman and bureaucrat was unavoidable under the N.E.P. As long as Russia remained a small peasant country there was a more solid basis for Capitalism than for Communism. But the capitalist forces could only be overcome by a steady systematic working-class policy, relying upon the peasant poor in union with the middle peasant, working on the preparation and development of the world proletarian revolution. It was necessary to manœuvre, but under Lenin the manœuvring always remained upon the line of the proletarian revolution. Under him the party always knew why a manœuvre was undertaken, the limits of it, the line beyond which the manœuvre ought not to extend, and the position at which the proletariat should begin to advance again.

Under Stalin in recent years the party was being led

blindly, was weakening and confusing the forces of the proletariat. On many important questions the Anglo-Russian Committee, the Chinese Revolution, the kulak policy, the party and the working-class found out the truth, or a part of the truth, only after the heavy consequences of a false policy had crashed over their heads. The result was that inside the country there was an immoderate growth of those forces which wished to turn the country back to Capitalism, and outside a weakening of the position of the Workers' State in the struggle against world Capitalism. Stalin aimed at destroying the Opposition, to cut off from the party a troop of Bolsheviks who were fighting these disastrous policies—a step openly welcomed by all the enemies of the Soviet Union.

Meanwhile the very existence of Capitalism in the form of the N.E.P., not restrained or corrected by a firm class policy, was preparing further dangers. Twenty-five million small farms constituted the fundamental source of the capitalist tendency in the Soviet Union. The slow pace of industry vastly increased the tempo of class differentiation among the peasants and the political dangers arising from it.

The criterion of success in a Socialist State was the condition of the working-class in the material sphere, elevation of real wages, living conditions, etc.; in the political sphere, the power of the party, Trade Unions, Soviets; and in the sphere of culture, schools, books, newspapers, theatres. In the Soviet Union the swollen and privileged adminstrative apparatus devoured a considerable part of the surplus value. During the period of reconstruction the number of workers and their living conditions had risen. But recently there had been a sharp change. The growth of the proletariat had ceased, and the relative weight of other classes in the community was increasing. The raising of wages was being more and more conditioned upon a demand for an increased intensity of labour. This could ultimately lead only to one conclusion:—that the increase of social wealth due to a developing technique (increased productivity of labour) did not in itself lead to an increase of wages. The official number of registered unemployed in April, 1927, was 1,478,000; the actual number was about two million. The unemployed directly or indirectly burdened the budget of the worker. The growing consumption of alcoholic liquor did the same, so did the rationalisation of production. The five-year plan [1] was calculated to absorb no more than 400,000 steadily employed workers. With the continual influx of workers from the country the number of unemployed by the end of 1931 would have grown to no less than three million men and women.

The deterioration of the Trade Unions, noted at the Fourteenth Conference, had continued. The immense majority of the delegates to the Trades Union Conferences were people entirely dissociated from industry. The dissatisfaction of the worker was being driven underground. "We mustn't be too active—if you want a bite of bread don't talk so much."

In the Trade Unions Communist Party members who were elected should not be removed because of inner-party disagreements, and the absolute independence of the shop committee and local committee from the organs of management should be guaranteed.

"An article should be introduced into the Criminal Code punishing as a serious crime against the State every direct or indirect, overt or concealed persecution of a worker for criticising, for making independent proposals, and for voting."

AGRICULTURE

On the agrarian question, Bucharin, Stalin's chief theoretician at this time, had written that "it is necessary to set free the economic possibilities of the well-off peasant, the economic possibilities of the kulak." These ideas and the attempt to insist on the co-operative plan of Lenin as the means of growing into Socialism without the development of large-scale industry, was the most dangerous symptom in the Soviet Union. In the last analysis it was

[1] A plan had at last been accepted and various versions were submitted for discussion. It was characteristic of the limited vision of the Stalinist régime at this period that this plan, produced late in 1927, accepted over a million unemployed as inevitable.

the lagging of industry that retarded the growth of agriculture and the growth of agricultural commodity production.[1] The kulak was necessary, but the task of the party ought to consist in the all-sided limitation of the efforts of the kulak to exploit. He should not be allowed elective rights in the Soviets; there should be a sharply progressive tax system, and the State should introduce legislation for the defence of hired labour and the regulation of the wages of agricultural workers. The co-operative societies could under no circumstances lead to Socialism unless they worked under the immediate economic and political influence of the Socialist elements. "A much larger sum ought to be appropriated for the creation of Soviet and collective farms. Maximum indulgences must be accorded to the newly organised collective farms and other forms of collectivism. Only a suitable attention to the hired hand, only a course based on the poor peasant and his union with the middle peasant, only a decisive struggle against the kulak, only a course towards class co-operatives and a class-credit system in the country, will make it possible to draw the middle peasant into the work towards Socialist reconstruction of agriculture, State industry and the building of Socialism."

THE STALINIST FIVE-YEAR PLAN

After three years of constant struggle and the ridicule of the Stalinist régime, a five-year plan of development, 1926–27 to 1930–31, had at last been produced by the State Planning Commission. The Platform of the Opposition condemned completely the limited scope of this plan. In it capitalist investments in industry would hardly grow at all from year to year, 1,142 millions in 1927, 1,205

[1] From 1923 to 1927 the opposition had made this the basis of its policy. Yet this is what passes to-day as history: "The Trotskyist Left" of two years ago pointed out the danger, it is true, of the Soviet State resting its flank on the village kulak; but they completely failed to bring forward any constructive solution of the problem; they suggested forced levies on the kulak to finance industrialization; but they did not see the essential unity of the process of industrialization and the agricultural revolution, and they left out of the picture the collectivization of peasant agriculture as the road to Socialism in the U.S.S.R." This comes, not from the pen of Pollitt or the professional apologists. It is written by Maurice Dobb, the Cambridge Economist. *In Soviet Russia* 1930, p. 24.

millions in 1931. In proportion to the general sum invested in the national economy, instead of increasing the investments in heavy industry would fall from 36.4 per cent in the first year to 27.8 in the last. The net investment in industry from the State Budget would fall from 200 millions to 90 millions. "Production is supposed to grow from four to nine per cent each year over the year preceding —the rate of growth in Capitalistic countries during periods of great progress. The gigantic advantages involved in the nationalisation of the land, the means of production, the banks, and the centralised organs of administration —that is, the advantages deriving from the Socialist revolution—find almost no expression in the five-year plan." The individual consumption of goods, already at a very low level, was to grow during the five years only twelve per cent. The consumption of cotton fabrics in 1931 would only be ninety-seven per cent of the pre-war amount, the production of electric energy at the end of the plan would be pitiably small compared to that in the capitalist countries. "The consumption of paper at the end of the five years will be eighty-three per cent of the pre-war amount. All this, fifteen years after October! To bring forward on the anniversary of the October Revolution such a parsimonious, through-and-through pessimistic plan really means that you are working against Socialism."

The Permanent Revolution in Economics

By basing itself on a policy of Socialism in a single country the Stalinist régime had no criterion of progress, no method of regulating the development of the country. The ultimate decision between Socialism and Capitalism would be decided by the relative productivity of labour under each system. Soviet production could not be isolated from world economy. The Socialist economy could defend the monopoly of foreign trade only if it continually approached world economy in the matter of technique, cost of production, quality and price of productions. And this could be done, not by developing a shut-in, self-sufficient economy, but by an all-sided increase of the relative weight in the world system, to be achieved by

273

increasing the tempo of production in the Soviet Union to its utmost. It was necessary to understand the gigantic significance of export, now lagging so dangerously behind the development of industry, to change the policy towards the kulak, which enabled him to undermine Socialist export by the hoarding of raw material, to develop the bonds with world economy by speeding up industrialisation and strengthening the Socialist element: "not to scatter our limited accumulations in the near future, but gradually and with deliberate plan to pass over to a new form of production which will assure us, in the first instance, of a mass output of the most necessary and most available machines; skilfully and thoughtfully to supplement and stimulate our own industry by systematically utilising the achievements of the world capitalist technique."

The theory of Socialism in a separate country—of isolated Socialist development independent of world economy, distorted the whole perspective and prevented a correct regulation of the relations of the Soviet Union with world economy. If this theory were renounced it would mean in a few years "an incomparably more expeditious use of our resources, a swifter industrialisation, a more planful and powerful growth of our own machine construction." It would result in the increase of the number of employed workers and a real lowering of prices, and by this means a genuine strengthening of the Soviet Union in the capitalist environment.

Would not the growth of bonds with world Capitalism involve a danger in case of blockade and war? "The preparation for war demands, of course, the creation of a reserve of the foreign raw materials necessary to us and a prompt establishment of the new industries vitally necessary—as, for instance, the production of aluminium, etc. But the most important thing in case of a prolonged and serious war is to have a national industry developed to the highest degree and capable both of mass production and of swift transformation from one kind of production to another. The recent past has shown how such a highly industrial country as Germany, bound up by a thousand threads with the world market, could discover a gigantic life-power and power of resistance when war and a blockade cut her off at one blow from the entire world.

"If with the incomparable advantages of our social structure we can, during this ' peaceful ' period, utilise the world markets in order to speed up our industrial development, we shall meet blockade or intervention infinitely better prepared and better armed.

"No domestic policy can of itself deliver us from the economic, political and military danger of the capitalist encirclement. The domestic problem is, by strengthening ourselves with a proper class policy, a proper inter-relation of the working-class with the peasant, to move forward as far as possible on the road of socialist construction. The interior resources of the Soviet Union are enormous and make this entirely possible."

Ultimately, however, it was only the world proletarian revolution which would give the Soviet Union the possibility of really creating Socialism, that is, a class-free society based upon the most advanced technique and upon the real equality of all its members in labour and in utilising the products of labour.

Where were the means to be found for this development? By severe taxation of all excess profits, a forced loan from the well-off kulaks of 150 million poods of grain, cutting down the growing expenses of the bureaucratic apparatus. The Stalinist bureaucracy had attempted a régime of economy the year before, which was to yield 300 to 400 million roubles a year. But a bureaucracy could not check bureaucracy. A régime of economy was a class question, and could only be realised by the workers and masses themselves exercising this pressure. The monopoly of foreign trade, foreign credit, concessions, contracts, etc., would provide supplementary income if skilfully used. "It is not true that the slow pace of industrialisation is immediately due to the absence of resources. The means are scanty, but they exist. What is wanted is the right policy."

The five-year plan of the State Planning Commission should be categorically rejected and condemned as basically incompatible with the task of transforming the Russia of the N.E.P. into a Socialist Russia.

THE GROWTH OF THE BUREAUCRACY

In the State apparatus the army of officials had been growing in recent years, the weight of the masses was decreasing. There was a growing penetration of the kulak and the nepman into the Soviets through their influence with the administrative staff. The city Soviets, the fundamental instrument for bringing the workers and the toiling masses into State administration, were losing significance in recent years. There could be no administrative revival of the Soviets. This could be done only by a definite class policy, by a decisive opposition to the new exploiters. The tendency of the Stalinist régime to blind its eyes to this process could best be seen in the theory of Molotov that they could not demand a drawing together of the workers with the State and the State with the workers, because their State was already a workers' State. This was the most malignant imaginable formula of bureaucratism, "sanctioning in advance every conceivable bureaucratic perversion." The struggle did not mean transforming a certain number of workers into officials. The apparatus itself could not deal with this matter. It was necessary for the party to separate itself from the apparatus and mobilise the masses in the old Leninist manner.

THE PERMANENT REVOLUTION: FOREIGN POLICY

The international situation was dangerous. The party should, therefore, bring into the foreground before the masses the problems of international politics, and to carry on a "most intense and all-sided preparation of the Soviet Union for defence in case of war." The Platform condemned the Menshevik policy of Stalin, and detailed all his mistakes on the Chinese question, the concealment of facts and falsification of documents concerning the Chinese revolution, the policy which had first called the Chinese Communist party a model section of the International, and then had attempted to throw all the blame for the failure upon it. At the Seventh Enlarged Plenum of the C.I. on December 7, 1926, Stalin had based the policy of the International upon the expectation of continued stabilisation in world Capitalism—wrongly. The General Strike in England, the Chinese Revolution, the workers' uprising in Vienna, showed that the stabilisation was breaking up and would soon show the falsity and folly of a theory of Socialism in one country. "A general strike in England —and only 5,000 members in the English Communist Party. A workers' insurrection in Vienna, with enough victims for a whole revolution—and only 6,000 members in the Austrian Communist Party! A military uprising of the worker-peasant masses in China—and the Central Committee of the Chinese Communist Party turns out to be a mere appendix to the Kuomintang. These are the facts which support and prolong the 'stabilisation' of Capitalism. Our greatest problem is to help the Communist parties to raise themselves to the height of the gigantic demands which the present epoch makes upon them. But this assumes, in the first place, a correct understanding of the character of the world situation on the part of the Communist International itself."

War was an imminent danger: "We are bound to try to 'buy ourselves off' from war, if that shall be possible. But just for that purpose we must be strong and united, unwaveringly defend the tactics of the world revolution, and re-enforce the International. Only thus have we a serious chance of gaining a really long postponement of the war without paying a price that would undermine the foundations of our power, and at the same time, in case war proves inevitable, of gaining the support of the international proletariat and winning."

"We must consistently, systematically, and stubbornly wage the struggle for peace. We must postpone the war, 'buy ourselves off from the war threat.' Everything possible and permissible must be done to this end. . . . At the same time we must get ready for war immediately, not folding our hands for one instant."

There should be "an all-sided preparation of our entire economy, budget, etc., for the event of war."

FOR THE LENINIST PARTY

But all this could not be done without the regeneration of the Communist Party. In the last year and a half the

277

party had lost some 80,000 members, industrial workers, and in return since the Fourteenth Congress in 1925, 100,000 peasants had been admitted into it. Bureaucratism in the party could best be seen by the following quotation. "We have members of the party who still inadequately understand the party itself, just what it is. They think that the party arises from the local—the local is the first brick, then comes the Rayon Committee, and so on, higher and higher, until you arrive at the Central Committee. That is not right. Our party must be looked at from the top down. And this view must be adhered to in all practical relationships and in the entire work of the party." [1]

This was typical of the attitude of party members like Molotov and Kaganovitch. The election of officials was dying out, and the organisational principles of Bolshevism were being violated at every step. There was only one question in the party—Opposition or anti-Opposition. Three groups, however, were clearly defined. The Centre, consisting of Stalin, Molotov, Kaganovitch, Kirov, controlled the Secretariat, dominated the administration, the State apparatus, etc., with numbers of worker bureaucrats who had lost all connection with the toiling masses. To the right was a group headed by Rykov and Kalinin with kulak tendencies, supported by Tomsky who was heading towards closer co-operation with the Second International. Bucharin wandered about between these two groups.

The third group was the Left Opposition. The Platform demanded the unity of the party. "Our task is to preserve the unity of the party at all costs, to resist decisively the policy of splits, amputations, exclusions, expulsions, etc. —but at the same time to guarantee to the party its right to a free discussion and decision, within the frame of this unity, of all debated questions."

The party should be conducted according to the spirit of the following words of Lenin: "Every member of the party should begin to study dispassionately and with the

[1] Speech of the Second Secretary of the Northern District Committee of the Russian C.P., reprinted in *Molot*, May 27, 1927.

utmost honesty; first, the essence of the disagreements, and second, the course of development of the conflict. . . . It is necessary to study both the one thing and the other, unconditionally demanding that absolutely accurate documents should be printed and open to verification on all sides." All this Stalin and his apparatus had destroyed. Instead they persecuted the Opposition, and used their control of the Secretariat to circulate lies about the Opposition's policy and its personnel.

Finally the Platform demanded the unity of the party. That they wanted a new party was only a Stalinist lie. The dangers were great, and it was to the party that they were appealing. To cut off the Opposition and to continue to destroy its membership was to weaken the party against the very dangers which threatened it. The fact that the party had a monopoly in the political field, a thing unconditionally necessary to the revolution, created special dangers. Lenin, at the Eleventh Congress, had pointed out that there were already in the party persons who under different circumstances would have been Social Revolutionaries or Mensheviks. Through specialists and the upper categories of the clerical workers and intelligentsia, and these were absolutely necessary, there penetrated a stream of non-proletarian influences. In contending for a definite tempo of industrialisation, in contending against the growth of the kulak and his aspiration toward rulership in the country, in contending for an improvement in the living conditions of the workers and for democracy within the party, the Trade Unions and the Soviets, the Opposition was contending for ideas which would bring the working class nearer to the party and re-enforce the foundation of unity. If the opportunist mistakes were not corrected there would be nothing but a show unity which would weaken the party and in the case of war compel it to reform its ranks on the march and under fire from the enemy. The attempt to introduce into the party methods of direct physical violence would ultimately re-act against its own organisers. " The most important, the most militant question, and the one which troubles all the members of our party, is the question of party unity. And in truth it is upon this question that the further fate of the proletarian revolution depends. Innumerable class enemies of the proletariat are listening intently to our inner-party disputes and, with unconcealed delight and impatience, are awaiting a split in our ranks. A split in our party, a formation of two parties, would mean enormous danger to the revolution.

"We, the Opposition, unqualifiedly condemn every attempt whatsoever to create a second party. The slogan of two parties is the slogan of the Stalin group in its effort to crowd out of the All-Union Communist party, the Leninist Opposition. Our task is not to create a new party, but to correct the course of the All-Union Communist Party. The proletarian revolution in the Soviet Union can win through to the end only with a united Bolshevik Party. We are struggling within the Communist Party for our views, and we decisively condemn the slogan 'two parties,' as *the slogan of adventurers*. . . .

"We will struggle with all our force against the formation of two parties, for the dictatorship of the proletariat demands as its very core a united proletarian party. It demands a single party. It demands a proletarian party —that is, a party whose policy is determined by the interests of the proletariat and carried out by a proletarian nucleus. Correction of the line of our party, betterment of its social composition—this is not the two-party road, but the strengthening and guaranteeing of its unity as a revolutionary party of the proletariat."

THE FATE OF THE PLATFORM

This was the Platform. When it appeared it was met with derision inside and outside the Soviet Union. This was the policy for which the Opposition was expelled from the Stalinist party in November, 1927. The Stalin régime, of course, condemned it root and branch and said it was an anti-party document, accused the Opposition of wishing to form two parties, and meanwhile kept the document away from the party and the masses. What is more important to remember to-day is that the policies it outlined were met with derision and contempt not only by the Stalinists but by some very learned bourgeois. Paul Scheffer, the Russian correspondent of the *Berliner Tageblatt*, had spent many years in the Soviet Union. Let us see what he thought of it: "The book sounds to our ears like a dirge over lost illusions, a lost paradise, the end of a dream. One could not think of it as poetry, exactly," [1] and much rubbish of the same sort. To all these people Stalin was the realist, practical, level-headed. Trotsky was the romantic revolutionary, harking back to the gallant days of 1917. For them the Permanent Revolution in the sense of the permanent economic reconstruction of Russian economy was mere theorising.

For Trotsky and the Marxists it was a question of the life and death of the revolution. Russia would embark on a great campaign of industrialisation or perish. Trotsky has written, and his whole career before 1927 and since is evidence of the truth of the words, that he and the Opposition had realised long before the fate that awaited them, but nevertheless had decided to spread their ideas without compromise and with all their energy. To do this they were driven to all sorts of subterfuges which laid them open to the charges of anti-party activity, imprisonment and exile. The majority never flinched. If only their ideas could but penetrate deeply enough, objective circumstances which they knew were coming, might enable enough in the party to see the correct line and save the revolution. Nor were they disappointed. When N.E.P. broke down in 1928 it was the fact that a policy consistently fought for during three bitter years was ready to hand that enabled Russia to make the turn, even though the clumsy régime went to the opposite extreme, caused deep and needless suffering and suffered heavy loss. When Stalin did make the turn, the Liberal bourgeois pundits and friends of the Soviet Union blinked, groped, and then faithfully trotted behind their new Messiah. There are other aspects of the Permanent Revolution which many of these followers of Stalin against Trotsky and Trotskyism will have an opportunity of studying in the flesh before very many years have passed.

[1] *Seven Years in Soviet Russia*, by Paul Scheffer, p. 186.

But in 1927 for Stalin and the bureaucracy the Platform and all it stood for was not only nonsense but mutiny.[1] It was necessary to act quickly, for the Stalinist policy had had a resounding defeat in the Anglo-Russian Committe and in China, while Moscow and Leningrad were restless under the pro-kulak policy. Further, despite the years of slander, Trotsky's popularity with the great masses outside the party, though diminished, was not killed, could not be killed. In October, at a demonstration led by the Central Executive Committee in Leningrad, Zinoviev and Trotsky and other Oppositionists found themselves on one platform with the Stalinists on another. The crowd, the crowd of the days of October, recognised them, shouted greetings and surged around, deserting the official platform so completely that its occupants had to come and stand with Zinoviev and Trotsky.

STALIN SUPPRESSES THE PLATFORM

Stalin ensured victory in the ideological struggle by suppressing the Platform. While his henchmen in speeches and articles condemned it, the Platform itself was refused publication as an anti-party document. When Opposition members tried to duplicate it on a hectograph, they were imprisoned and exiled for fractionalism and underground activity.

On September 9, 1927, the first American Labour delegation questioned Stalin about the differences between himself and the Opposition. He referred them to speeches by Rykov and Bucharin. With this crude subterfuge one delegate was not satisfied. He asked for the Platform itself. Stalin replied: "I did not sign that platform. I have no right to dispose of other people's documents (laughter)."[2] Two months later he was telling a delegation of foreign workers that "if it is a question of freedom of the press for the proletariat, then I must say that you will not find another country in the world where such broad and complete freedom of the press exists as in the U.S.S.R."[3] But Stalin is a genius in his own line and would not lay himself

[1] Molotov actually used the word in polemic against the Opposition.
[2] *Leninism*, by Joseph Stalin, Vol. II, p. 61.
[3] *Leninism*, by Joseph Stalin, Vol. II, p. 82.

open to the charge of suppressing a document entirely. He merely wanted time to inoculate the party with arguments against the Platform and against Trotskyism. It was the custom before a party congress to publish theses and counter-theses for discussion in the party. Stalin kept the Platform until the discussions in the party locals had begun and delegates in the outlying districts of Russia had already left for the Congress. He then published one section of it in *Pravda* of November 5, 1927, with copious annotations. On the 15th November the Opposition were expelled from the party for fractional activity, underground work, having an illegal party press, etc., with the whole Government apparatus in full blast against Trotskyism. Two days after, on the 17th November, Stalin published in *Pravda*, another small section of the Platform, again with copious notes. Thus the proprieties were observed and the way was prepared for a smashing victory over the Opposition at the Conference. Zinoviev and Kamenev, true to type (how well Lenin knew them!), capitulated, confessed their sins, were put on probation, denounced Trotskyism as counter-revolution and were later re-admitted to the party, to be expelled, to confess, be re-admitted, etc., etc. Trotsky and the other leaders took the road to exile, while the Stalinist terror fell on the worker Oppositionists.

The Opposition Vindicated

We may seem to have devoted a disproportionate amount of time to the Platform. In reality, after Lenin ceased to write in 1923, no document in the history of the Soviet Union is of more importance and shows more convincingly the superiority of Marxist analysis over bourgeois empiricism and Stalinist ignorance. The Fifteenth Party Conference, which rejected the Platform and sanctified the expulsion of its authors, took place in December. One month afterwards, in January, 1928, the first danger against which the Opposition had warned so unceasingly shook the whole fabric of the Soviet Union. Throughout the winter there had been difficulties in the grain collections from the peasants, and as soon as their main enemy, the Opposition, was out of the way the kulaks made the famous bloodless revolution.

283

They challenged the whole power of the proletarian State by refusing to give up their grain except at the prices that they demanded, and unless goods were sold to them at prices equal to those of the far cheaper goods of capitalist countries. The proletariat in the towns, the Red Army, could not get the necessary supplies, and the dictatorship of the proletariat had either to collect the grain by force or, in Stalin's own words, "face the inevitability of a profound crisis in the whole of our national economy." What, asked Stalin, had to be done in order to make up lost ground? "It was necessary, first of all, to strike hard at the kulaks and the speculators who were screwing up the price of grain and creating the danger of famine in the country. . . ." This was his statement to the Plenum of the Central Committee of the C.P.S.U. on July 13, 1928.[1] It was to this dangerous pass that his ignorance, his ideological victories and organisational measures, his long persecution of the Opposition, had led the country. Long before July he had been eating every one of his words. The Central Committee had met in March and diagnosed the causes of the crisis—the increased income of the kulak, too low a rate of taxation on the kulak, the aggravation of the political situation by the capitalist elements in town and country, kulak and nepman. It is from this time, with the gulf at their feet, that dates the beginning of the industrialization. In May Stalin was thundering against the kulak: "All talk about the kulak being 'no worse' than the capitalist of the town, that the kulak is not more dangerous than the town nepman, and that therefore there is no reason now to fear the kulak—all such talk is sheer Liberal chatter which lulls the vigilance of the working class and of the great mass of the peasants. . . . To fail to understand the significance of large-scale kulak farming in the countryside, to fail to understand that the specific gravity of the kulaks in the rural districts is one hundred times greater than the specific gravity of the capitalists in urban industry, is to have lost one's senses, to have broken with Leninism and deserted to the side of the enemies of the working class."[2]

[1] *Leninism*, Vol. II, p. 128.   [2] *Leninism*, Vol. II, p. 105.

THE STALINIST POLICY EXPOSED

The Stalinist régime from 1924 to this day in national and international affairs foresees nothing and is aware of a wall only when it bounces its head upon it. It had denied the permeation of the party apparatus by bourgeois elements. The accusation of Thermidorean degeneration had been the most fiercely resented of all the Opposition attacks. In 1928 the Shakhty trial, whatever elements of a frame-up distinguished it, revealed that in the very highest offices of the Soviet Union there were representatives of the counter-revolution actively plotting for the overthrow of the Soviet Union in close collaboration with world Capitalism. Stalin himself told the Central Committee: "What did the Shakhty trial reveal? It revealed that . . . our economic, Trade Union, and, to a certain extent, our Party organisations failed to observe the undermining operations of our class enemies, and that it is essential, therefore, to reinforce and improve our organisations by every means and method in our power and to develop and strengthen their class vigilance."[1] During the next two years events were to show how far the Thermidorean process had gone, while Stalin had been busy destroying the Opposition. On January 1, 1930, only nine per cent of the apparatus of the All-Union Central Council of T.Us. were of working-class origin. In this Council there were 41.9 per cent formerly members of other parties, in the Central Committee of Metalworkers there were thirty-seven per cent, in the Central Committee of Printers there were twenty-four per cent; on the staff of the newspaper *Trud* there were nineteen persons of alien class origin, originating from merchants, nobles and priests; there were eighteen descendants of nobles and merchants in the apparatus of the Central Committee of the Soviet of Trades Union Employees, in eleven central committees of Trades Unions fifty-three persons were found who had been actively alien and hostile to the proletariat in the past. In 1930 Centryosus was employing 136 former Mensheviks, Social-Revolutionaries, Cadets, etc., eleven ministers of former governments, 109 former merchants, and eighty-two

[1] *Leninism*, Vol. II, p. 185.

ex-officers of whom thirty-four had served in the White Army.

The Opposition had condemned the timid five-year plan. Before three months had passed the Central Committee had met and hastily embarked on another revision, and the 460 millions for industry in 1928 had grown by 1929 to 1,600,000,000. Hasty plans were drawn up for the collectivisation of one-fifth of the twenty-five million peasant farms on the countryside.

In speech after speech Stalin proclaimed the danger of a restoration of Capitalism in the Soviet Union, the danger of the growing bureaucracy of the Soviet Union, the criminal policy of Bucharin in suggesting that the kulak would grow into Socialism.[1] By October, 1928, he was aware of the danger of a Capitalist restoration. "Do the conditions exist in our Soviet country that make the restoration of Capitalism possible? Yes, they do exist." And to an audience that for the past three years had been hearing him prove by all sorts of statistics that this was impossible and that the Trotskyist Opposition had been slandering the party in saying such a thing, he had the grace (a rare thing with him) to say, "That, comrades, may appear strange, but it is a fact";[2] he quoted Lenin extensively to prove the dangers of the N.E.P. And he who, in the previous December, had fulminated against the Opposition charge that the centrist group of Stalin and Molotov was acting in close collaboration with a Right Wing of the party and had sworn that never had the party been so united, now in October sounded a tentative note. "Is there a right opportunist danger in our party?" The long cold vistas of Siberia opened before Bucharin, Rykov and Tomsky.[3]

[1] *Leninism*, Vol. II, p. 197.   [2] *Leninism*, Vol. II, p. 142.

[3] Professor Laski writes: "That, on the whole, he (Stalin) was right, and Trotsky wrong, in the great debates of 1924–7 most students would now agree" (*New Statesman and Nation*, Nov. 2, 1935). Students of what? Of the Stalinist refurbishings. There is no shadow of justification for Professor Laski's statement. The evidence given above is only a small selection of what is there for those who want to know the truth.

By great good fortune within the covers of one small volume costing sixpence the whole controversy between 1924 and 1927 is summed up and can be definitively judged. The Opposition being expelled in November, on February 7, 1928, the C.P.G.B. published in English *Where is Trotsky Going?* consisting of quotations from the Platform and official replies. The dishonesty of the editing does little to mitigate the shattering refutation by events of every major point on which the Stalinists condemned the Platform.

THE BUREAUCRACY STRENGTHENS ITSELF

The British General Council had broken off the Anglo-Russian Committee, Pilsudski had established a Fascist régime, first Chiang Kai-Shek and then Wang Chin-Wei had destroyed the proletarian movement in China. Stalin could not pursue these Leninist policies any longer because there was no one to pursue them with. Those who had told him that his line would end just there were in Siberia for their pains. Stalin still held the power. Now, however, to add to the external failures came the revolt of the kulak which threatened the whole structure. The Stalinist régime was in serious danger. Something had to be done.

Despite the difficulties under which they had laboured, Trotsky and the Opposition had done their work well. The party and the masses could be partially bluffed and befuddled about the Anglo-Russian Committee and the Chinese Revolution. But the grain crisis could not be hidden. Stalin turned rapidly, and the bureaucracy prepared a new five-year plan and set itself to adopt a large-scale programme of industrialisation. Some of the Left Opposition in exile hailed this change as a sign of the regeneration of the régime and made their peace with Stalin. Trotsky and the more experienced Marxists, while welcoming the change, knew that the Stalinist clique had shifted to the Left to save its own skin. It had been leaning more and more on the kulaks and nepmen inside the country, the Social Democrats and the colonial bourgeoisie in its struggle against its own Left Wing. Now outside, and far more dangerous inside, Russia, these allies had grown strong enough to threaten and, if swift measures were not taken, destroy. The bureaucracy therefore mobilised the proletariat against kulak and nepmen on the basis of the five-year plan. But one thing the Stalinist bureaucracy could never do—restore the party to health. The colossal failures abroad had been hidden by lying on an unprecedentedly vast scale, as a preparation for the physical removal or destruction of opponents. The new turn could only be safely undertaken by the régime if all who had advocated it a few months before were silenced, and the policy made to appear as Stalin's special contribution, carefully thought out, to meet a situation long foreseen. The party was therefore thoroughly purged of every vestige of Trotskyism. But Stalin knew that he could not take his Right Wing over towards the Left with him. He had to disembarrass himself of Rykov, Tomsky and Bucharin, his allies for four years, who viewed the scale of the new turn with distrust. A campaign, slow and cautious at first but soon all over Russia and in the International, in the best anti-Trotskyist manner, was launched against them. Rykov, Tomsky and Bucharin, their supporters expelled and exiled, were accused of Right Wing deviations; and later Stalin, losing all sense of respect for the cause he represented, ultimately accused them of wishing to restore Capitalism in the Soviet Union. So complete was Stalin's ideological victory that Bucharin and his friends made it unnecessary for him to use the organisational. They capitulated, recognised their errors, confessed their sins, were put on probation. Thus Stalin and his clique, Molotov, Kaganovitch, Manuilsky, Ordjonikidze, even in making the turn, had tightened their grip on the apparatus.

To bind the bureaucracy still closer to themselves, Stalin, as soon as Trotsky was exiled, introduced a system of allowances which gave extra privileges to the upper bureaucrats, and made the principle of the party member (however highly placed) having equal pay with the workmen a fiction. Later he abrogated the law altogether, and party members were allowed to draw whatever pay the party might decide. Trotsky for years continued to believe that the extension and strengthening of the proletariat which would result from industrialisation would be sufficient to restore the Bolshevik Party to its natural function as representative and protector of the masses. It was a vain hope. The process of bureaucratisation had gone too far. Industrialisation strengthened the proletariat but created hundreds of thousands of skilled technicians who fortified the bureaucracy. Stalin was their man. Their interests were safe in his hands and they supported him; and he, with the O.G.P.U., manipulated the party, using it as the instrument of his personal power, through its means making himself and the ever-growing bureaucracy more and more independent of both peasantry and proletariat. Granted the almost ridiculously easy capture of the apparatus by Stalin in 1923, even before Lenin died, we have here a perfectly understandable historical process. The backwardness of Russia, the lack of education and experience of the workers who, after ten years of the revolution, found themselves persons of authority, all this was reflected in the singular ignorance and incompetence in great problems of Stalin himself. The German defeat of 1923 had fortified the national Socialist tendencies of the bureaucracy and strengthened it against a weakened and disheartened proletariat. Stalin's economic policies and mastery of inter-party manoeuvring had resulted in a still greater strengthening of the bureaucracy as against the proletariat. The defeat of the General Strike in England, the ghastly failure of the Chinese Revolution, all drove the Russian proletariat still further from hopes of the world revolution towards putting its faith in the national Socialism of the bureaucracy. The drive against the kulak and nepman seemed to promise a restoration of the proletariat to its rightful place in a Workers' State. But even while mobilising the proletariat against its enemies, the bureaucracy, with promises of the class-less society in ten years, still further concentrated power in itself through Stalin and the manipulated party. Thus the industrial programme, and, as we shall see, its partial realisation, could not and did not emancipate the Russian proletariat, but resulted in a tightening of its chains. The division into rulers and ruled, developing into privileged and oppressed, with its inevitable consequences on property relationships, that problem Lenin and Trotsky knew could never be solved within the boundaries of a national State, least of all a state which, despite its natural resources, was and for a generation would remain a backward agricultural country.

Chapter 11

INDUSTRY AND THE PLAN

Six Years too Late

Official Stalinist history, retailed with a childlike confidence by the Webbs and all the learned Friends of the Soviet Union, is that the division of the land in 1917 had checked the development of large-scale capitalist farming. The existence of twenty-five million small farms was not only leading to Capitalist differentiation, but had also definite limits as far as production was concerned. Stalin had foreseen all this, but had allowed the kulaks to develop until the State-farms and the collective farms were sufficiently advanced to fill the gap which the loss of kulak production would cause. During 1927, however, chiefly through the initiative of Stalin, the party decided that the time had come to initiate a large-scale campaign of collectivisation and the Fifteenth Conference marked the official launching of this policy. The Trotskyist Opposition had intemperately demanded the destruction of the kulaks (or alternatively the tickling of the kulaks; Stalin accuses them of both on the same page)[1] when the kulaks were necessary. It is not only historically useful but politically necessary to expose this plausible packet of lies.

True, at the Fifteenth Conference one can point to bits of Stalin's speeches where he talked about large-scale farming as the only way out for Russia. But he had made similar statements before, and at that time less than one per cent of the farms were collectivised. More to the point is a special report on agriculture by Molotov at that very conference in which he said that the offensive against the kulak for the construction of Socialism was actually going

[1] *Leninism*, Vol. II, p. 271.

on at that time in the growing Socialist construction, and he saw no need to talk about it.[1] Stalin himself tells us that it was only in April, 1928[2], that the Political Bureau of the Central Committee adopted a decision to organise in the space of three or four years a number of new Soviet (State) farms. Stalin himself tells us that it was in July, 1928,[3] that the Central Committee decided to carry out "unswervingly" the intensive construction of collective farms decided upon at the Fifteenth Conference.

And, most conclusive of all, in the midst of the crisis which followed the breakdown of N.E.P., Bucharin, Stalin's right-hand man for four years, summed up the blindness and incompetence of the régime and destroyed this legend of collective farming carefully undertaken, at the right moment. "We did not tackle the problem of our specialists until after the Shakhty affair; the problem of the Soviet and collective farms was practically left till after the grain supply crisis and its resultant convulsions, so that it had then to be attacked from a dead point. We have, in a word, acted pretty much in accordance with that characteristically Russian proverb: 'Unless it thunders, the peasant does not cross himself.'" And for one moment he gives us an indication of what the Leninist leadership of the party and the country had been. "At the time of our transition from War Communism to the New Economic Policy, we began to regroup our ranks in the most courageous and decided manner. This gigantic regrouping of forces, combined with the determined propaganda of such slogans as: 'Learn commerce,' was the prerequisite for our economic successes.[4] . . ." In April, 1929, Stalin had at last been battered into recognising what Trotsky's theses had stated six years to a month before. "*The key to the reconstruction of agriculture is the rapid rate of development of our industry.*"[5] Russia under any leadership was destined to many crises and upheavals. But they could have been foreseen and mitigated. The Opposition had foreseen them. The party

[1] *XV Conference of the C.P.S.U.*, C.P.G.B., p. 75.
[2] *Leninism*, Vol. II, p. 339 and again on p. 341.
[3] *Leninism*, Vol. II, p. 342.
[4] *International Press Correspondence*, Oct. 19, 1928.
[5] *Leninism*, Vol. II, p. 217. Italics his own.

and the proletariat could have been educated, and although of necessity with many mistakes and set-backs, the country would have been far more developed, far more powerful than it is to-day, and its political life, even if harsh and backward, not the thing of terror and disgrace to the Socialist ideal that it is.

THE SUCCESSES OF THE PLAN

Let us at once make one point clear. The amended five-year plan saved the Russian Revolution. By 1932–1933 collective ownership had demonstrated its capacity for increasing production on a scale unprecedented in the most expansive periods of capitalist economy. The world knows the successes. The capacity of electric power stations has increased sixfold since 1913. The total production of electricity in 1936 is over 32 million kilowatt-hours, or seventeen times as much as in 1913. Coal production, 29·1 millions in 1913 and 35·5 millions in 1928, was 108·9 millions in 1935. Oil, 9·2 million tons in 1913, 11·7 in 1928, was 26·8 millions in 1935. Iron, 4·2 million tons in 1913, was 3·3 millions in 1928 and in 1935, 9·4 millions. These are the basis of the modern State. If even the Soviet Union goes down, that is to say, back to Capitalism, collective ownership has demonstrated how much Capitalism retards the possibility of production. But Trotsky and the Left Opposition, though fighting for a large scale plan and intensive industrialisation, never had any illusions that these would bring the millennium, or could do more than strengthen the proletariat in its position as dominant class in the Workers' State.

Stalin first opposed industrialisation, and then, driven to adopt it, encouraged extravagant hopes about what it would bring. The illusion spread to Western Europe. Official Stalinists and friends of the Soviet Union pointed to the rising indices of production and encouraged the belief that they were an infallible indication of the near approach towards the classless society. The health of a society depends not only on a rising economy: in the last analysis the Socialist society depends on a productivity of labour far beyond anything that we have yet seen.

But for many years the decisive factor will be not an absolute standard of economy, but the constantly shifting relationships between the different social groups in the State. When the social and political tension in the Soviet Union were revealed in the last half of 1936,[1] it came as a grievous shock and disillusionment to many quite sincere well-wishers of the Soviet Union in Western Europe.

Not only is Socialism, a "balanced, harmonious" economy, impossible in backward and isolated Russia. To-day the country moves and will continue to move from crisis to crisis, whatever the successes of collective ownership. Collective ownership "works," it wins great successes, but the struggle between collective and private ownership continues. Crises, as great as capitalist crises, shake the country, and to-day collective ownership is on the retreat. It is these things that lay behind Lenin's ceaseless warnings against the dangerous illusion of a national Socialism. The attempt to put Socialism in a single country into practice cost the lives of millions.

THE ECONOMIC BLINDNESS OF SOCIALISM IN A SINGLE COUNTRY

Planned economy, much more than the actual overthrow of Capitalism and the political seizure of power, is the most difficult task that faces a revolutionary party. In the Soviet Union in 1928 it would, under the best of conditions, have been difficult to plan and difficult to carry out. The Stalinist régime inevitably turned it to chaos.

To begin with, Socialism in a single country, at first chiefly a weapon for use against Trotsky's theory of the Permanent Revolution, now formed the basis of all the

---

[1] "When we hear that so close and trusted a friend of Stalin as Radek is suspected, and that one of the ablest of Soviet generals is recalled for examination, and that a hunt is going on for men and women who may have some time said something critical of official policy, we are compelled to wonder whether there may not be more serious discontent in the Soviet Union than was generally believed." Editorial article, *New Statesman and Nation*, 5th September, 1936. This belatedness comes from reading Stalinist propaganda, listening to the conscious or unconscious falsifiers who "have been and seen for themselves" all those who cannot or will not understand that not only Russia's safety from external aggression but also her internal development depends on world economy, in political terms, on the world revolution.

economic and political plans of the Stalinist bureaucrats. They had determined, in defiance of all economics, Capitalist or Marxist, on the building up of an economy absolutely independent of the rest of the world. Yet every word they spoke about international Capitalism, the rivalries of imperialism, the international division of labour, proved the falsity of trying to separate the economic destiny of one part of the modern world from the rest. Molotov solved the difficulty in the best Stalinist manner. He said at the Sixth International Congress that the Soviet Union would build its Socialism on an independent economic basis, but after the world revolution (presumably coming all at one stroke) they would rebuild it on an international economic basis. Dangerous nonsense as this was in words, it was trebly dangerous when embodied in plans. Stalin aimed in the two five-year plans at establishing the classless society, the first to lay the foundation, the second to achieve it. The result was a plan not so much beyond the capacity of the country, but a plan that refused to understand that Soviet economy was still a part of world economy. Says Arthur W. Just, Moscow correspondent of the *Kölnische Zeitung*, "There is every reason to believe, for instance, that the Government bodies entrusted with the task of formulating the foreign trade plans were so misinformed about economic conditions abroad that they were completely taken by surprise when the sudden shrinkage of values occurred in 1931 and when, later on, Russia's foreign trade slumped badly. Right down to the spring of 1931 the Soviet press and official quarters were still quite convinced that the U.S.S.R. would be relatively untouched by the world trade depression."[1]

It was not misinformation. Since 1928 in the International the Stalinists had been announcing a world crisis and coming revolution. That was the basis of the new theory of Social Fascism. But at the same time all who insisted, with the Platform, that in the last analysis Soviet economy was subject to world economy, were Trotskyists, and risked peace and liberty.

The plan was based on exports of 923 million roubles

[1] *Soviet Economics*, a symposium edited by Dr. Gerhard Dobbert, 1933, p. 69.

and imports of 880 million roubles for 1929, steadily increasing to imports of 2,627 millions and exports of 2,040 millions in 1932–33. But by 1931 exports were only 811 million roubles, imports, 1,105.

The catastrophic fall in world prices which followed the crisis vitiated the whole scheme of the plan and, to make matters worse, while the prices of heavy machinery which the Soviet imported were comparatively unaffected by the crisis, it was the prices of agricultural products, which paid for this machinery, that fell by fifty per cent. Thus while Russia was continually increasing exports it was getting less and less in return. Then in 1930–31 war threatened from Japan. The Stalinist régime was compelled radically to recast the plan and build war-factories in territory strategically safe both from Western Europe on the one hand and Japan on the other, territory hundreds of miles away from the industrial centres and lacking means of communication. Money had immediately to be appropriated for armaments. World economy and world politics which rest on it were teaching Stalin some simple but costly lessons in the elements of Marxism.

While on the one hand it was simple Marxism to govern the plan always in the closest relation to world-economy, on the other such a plan could be adequately realised only in co-operation with the masses, and particularly the proletariat working through its Soviets and Trade Unions, exercising a constant check and test by the effect of the plan on its living conditions and the qualities of articles it used. The plan both on paper and in propaganda aimed at improving the living conditions of the masses. A Workers' State rests on the workers, and any plan which did not in actual fact improve their conditions from year to year was thereby condemned. The masses themselves were the best judges of this, and a Soviet régime should have boldly drawn their full strength into co-operation. For a system of planned economy embarked upon by a Socialist State involved such dangers of bureaucratic rigidity and consequent error, that it demanded a ceaseless and vigilant check from below. But the Stalinist régime was based on bureaucracy; its only idea of fighting bureaucracy was to admit workers into its ranks and create more ill-educated and incompetent bureaucrats. Stalin has never understood the rôle the workers must increasingly play in a Workers' State. An early step of the swollen bureaucratic régime was to take the plan as an excuse for destroying the few remaining privileges of the workers so as to ensure control over them in the difficult days that were ahead. The Trade Unions were deprived of the status they had at least nominally enjoyed since N.E.P. and made mere appendages of the State; the remnants of workers' control were wiped away.

Stalin found that the workers of 1930 wanted to give up their privileges. "The workers again and again complain: There is no master in the works, there is no system in the works. We can no longer tolerate our factories being transformed from productive organisms into parliaments. Our Party and Trades Union organisations must at length understand that, without ensuring one-man-management and strict responsibility for work done, we cannot solve the problems of reconstructing industry." For the moment, however, under the barrage of propaganda promising the millennium, the workers in the factories submitted and girded themselves for what seemed the final sacrifice. Hitherto wages had varied between fixed proportions in an effort to lessen inequality. Stalin introduced a system of shock-brigades, bodies of workers who received better pay and valuable privileges for more intensive effort. It was, in a country still so backward as Russia, quite justifiable, though a retreat. He announced it as a step forward towards Socialism, and the requisite quotations and interpretations from Lenin were loosed on the workers. Yet such is the vitality of collective ownership and planned economy that in many respects industrialisation triumphed over all these handicaps. In the first year of the plan the success was such as to astonish even the Stalinists themselves. The low quality of production, due not only to the backwardness of the country but to a vulgar haste for achieving paper records, the bureaucratic methods, added to the inevitable confusion which so vast a scheme under the best auspices

must inevitably bring,[1] the systematic lying for the glorification of the régime, when all these are discounted, not
only the first year but all the years of the five-year plan
have proved that the Socialist methods, even in the difficult
internal and external circumstances of a backward country
like Soviet Russia, are incomparably superior to capitalist
economy. Stalin was jubilant. "We are becoming a land
of metals, of automobiles and tractors; and when we put
the U.S.S.R. into a motor car and the muzhik into a
tractor, then let the reverenced capitalists who pride
themselves on their 'civilisation' try to catch up with us.
It is still to be seen which country will then have to be
considered backward and which advanced." This, for
the time being, might be considered by those who knew
him as the crude boasting of a fundamentally ignorant
and commonplace mind. He forecasts the catching and
outstripping of the most advanced capitalist countries
in ten years.[2] As long as this remained words, it did not
much matter, but by 1930 there was nothing in the Soviet
Union to prevent these absurdities being translated into
immediate practice. In late 1929 the ominous signs of the
world-crisis were already clear. The International was
heralding the crisis as the beginning of doom. Under
those circumstances it would be all that Russia could
do to accomplish the five-year plan in the time set for
it. Instead Stalin decided to accomplish it in four.
The culmination of this hysteria was reached in his report
to the Political Report of the Sixteenth Congress in July,
1930. He now seemed seriously to be expecting Socialism,
or some tolerable substitute, in 1932–33. Whereas to the
bourgeois expert in 1928 the Platform seemed a romantic
gesture, this 1930 report seemed to indicate that the strong,
silent man and the clique who surrounded him had lost
their reason. "I will not speak of the bourgeois writers
whose eyes simply bulge out of their heads at the very

[1] We do not underestimate this.
[2] There are many astonishing statements in Strachey's *The Theory and Practice of Socialism*. But surely the most astonishing is the following: "They had to build up, in a decade or so at the most, a Socialist system which should surpass the Capitalisms of Britain, America and Germany, with their century and more of development behind them," p. 432. So it seems that this miracle has been achieved. Can idolatry go further?

words Five-year Plan. . . ."[1] They boasted that they would soon abolish the market and begin the Socialist exchange of goods. Russia's troubles were over. "It must be admitted," said Stalin, "that the Soviet Government is the most stable in the world."[1] Russia, he said, had entered into Socialism, and he gave warnings to all who thought otherwise. Trotsky in 1926 had suggested that industrial growth in the Soviet State should be twelve to eighteen per cent yearly in comparison to the average six per cent of capitalist countries. Stalin abused Trotsky as a defeatist and enemy of Socialism. The "reactionary character" of Trotsky's eighteen per cent he proved by the figures of 1929–30 which he said were thirty-two per cent.

Trotsky and the Opposition in exile, while welcoming the drive, were now warning against the exaggerated tendencies which had so soon appeared. From his exile for Trotskyism, Rakovsky, after Lenin and Trotsky perhaps the ablest and certainly the most brilliant of all the Bolsheviks, in one of the most masterly surveys of Russian economy ever published by the Opposition,[2] summed up the Marxist view. He told the Stalinists that they were overstepping their limits, that there were no resources for this catching up and outstripping, that industrialisation could and must be continued, but that this mad attempt to build Socialism was piling up incalculable dangers and would bring a heavy retribution. Stalin in his report wrote many pages condemning the right-wing deviation of Trotskyism, hailed the unprecedented rates of development, set forty-seven per cent as the increase of industrial growth for the coming year, and met argument with terror. Once more the errors of the bureaucracy were paid for by the workers.

Deprived of means of defence, the full weight of the unprecedented rates of development fell on them in cut wages, low standards of living and remorseless speeding-up. Their resistance was met by terror. On January 25, 1931, *Isvestia* published the decree giving up to ten years of prison, not to class enemies but to Socialist workmen for infraction of discipline which provoked or caused "deterioration

[1] *Leninism*, Vol. II, p. 365   [2] *La Lutte des Classes*, May, 1932.

of the rolling stock," "delays in the departure of trains or boats" and "all other incidents which might impede the execution of official plans for transport or compromise the regularity and security of traffic." In case of premeditation the penalty was death. But no brutality, no terrorism could check the steady fall in prices in Western Europe, where it took almost two tons of Soviet raw material to buy what one had bought before. The Platform had demanded that the one concrete check on the confusion inevitable in this initial experiment was a stable monetary unit. But as soon as the Stalinist régime felt the pressure, dishonest to the core, it let the rouble go. At the end of 1933, according to the Plan, the circulation of roubles was to have been 3,200,000,000. At the end of the first year there were 2,642,000,000 roubles in circulation, at the end of the next year, 4,263,900,000, in November, 1931, 5,181,700,000. By means of wage statistics calculated in these roubles the Soviet Press proved to the starving workers the steady improvement in their standard of living. The Japanese menace followed, and then on the groaning country came the final burden—the collapse of agricultural economy under collectivisation so long neglected and now carried out in the Stalinist manner.

THE LIQUIDATION OF THE KULAK

Since the days of Engels it had been Socialist policy that the collectivisation of peasant agriculture was never under any circumstances to be forcibly carried out. At the Fourth Congress of the International, speaking of the crisis which had led to N.E.P., Lenin told the delegates of the disaffection not only of the peasantry, but also of large numbers of workers: "It was the first and I hope the last time in the history of Soviet Russia that we had the great masses of the peasantry arrayed against us, not consciously, but instinctively, as a sort of political mood." Lenin understood the backward millions of ignorant peasants. Ruthless against all whom, as Spain has once more recently proved, are far more ruthless than he in pursuit of privilege and property, he was permeated by a deep humanitarianism, as unlike the sickly frothings of Liberalism as his revolutionary doctrine is different from their bleatings about democracy. "We are in favour of communal farms, but they must be run in such a manner as to win the peasants' confidence. And up to that time we are not their teachers but their pupils. Nothing can be sillier than the mere thought of forcing the average peasant to change his economic relations. Our task is not to expropriate the average peasant, but to take account of the special conditions of their lives, to learn from themselves the methods that may lead them to a better social order and least of all to order them about." It was electrification, by which he meant large-scale industry and all the benefits it would bring to the countryside, which could make the peasant change his immemorial habits, realise the inadequacy of peasant civilisation, and willingly take the road to Socialism. Nothing else could ever do it.[1]

But after the kulak offensive in 1928, as we have seen, the Stalin régime revised its plans and announced that twenty per cent of the peasantry would be collectivised at the end of five years.[2] Huge sums were apportioned and, on the basis of the coming industrialisation, the provision of tractors and other forms of mechanised assistance, it was planned that there would be a steady rise in Soviet agricultural economy by 1932 from 73.7 million tons in 1927 to 106 million tons in 1932.[3] The plan itself was, with due regard to the national and international situation, not unworkable. But Stalin was now seriously trying to transform Socialism in a single country from a propaganda weapon against Trotskyism into economic reality. What should have been carefully and persistently carried out during four years was now being rushed through without preparation. With that brutality which Lenin had noted

[1] Never by "plundering the peasant." That is purely and simply a Stalinist lie of the old days when the necessity for basic capital was pronounced a chimera and co-operation was to bring Socialism. In no single writing at any time did Trotsky, Zinoviev and Kamenev, the leaders of the Opposition, ever hint at or tolerate any suggestion of extortion for the benefit of industry from peasant production. Even in the years when they saw the kulak peril approaching, they demanded only political restriction of the kulak, heavy taxation of the richest, and gradual collectivisation on the basis of industrialisation.
[2] *The Soviet Union Looks Ahead*, 1930, p. 83.
[3] Ibid., p. 251.

and feared so many years before, and which now characterised the whole terrorist régime, the poorer peasants, having nothing to lose, were mobilised against the kulaks, and under the guidance of party members from the towns collective farms were created by the simple method of violence against all who resisted. While the whole Soviet Press screamed of the miraculous turn of the peasants to Socialism, millions of peasants were being forced into the commune—that highly-developed form of collective production and co-operative living which can come only on the basis of the very highest development of production. Despite all subsequent denials, Stalin's speeches show that he gave his authority to this irreparable folly.[1] In little more than a year fifteen million peasants poured into the collectives, while Stalin announced a series of brilliant victories on the grain front. The kulaks were deported to Siberia or driven off to swampy land. Stalin celebrated the success of his new policy of liquidating the kulaks, "the last capitalist class," and by so doing ushering in the class-less society. He would accomplish by administrative decree and terror what only an industrialisation beyond the strength of Russia for the next fifty years could accomplish. Just for a moment an inner party struggle checked the mad race. The pressure of the proletariat, combined with the pressure of the peasantry, strengthened the old Right Wing, and in early 1930 Stalin's position was in serious danger. He had to retreat, wrote an article called "Dizzy with Success" in which he rebuked his astonished janissaries for carrying out his orders, and quoted Lenin amply to prove that there should be no forcible coercion of the peasantry. There were torchlight processions in the villages, the peasants cut out the article and pasted it in their homes. Collective peasantry dropped from fifteen million to five. But Rykov, Tomsky and Bucharin in helping to destroy Trotskyism had forged a perfect weapon which Stalin knew how to use. Setting the machine to work he cleared the party of his enemies, and by July the old hundred per cent collectivisation and the

[1] *Leninism*, Vol. II, p. 252. "And that is why the middle peasant has turned towards the 'communia.'" Soon, however, the middle peasant or Stalin found that a mistake had been made and the middle peasant discovered, or was discovered to have, a preference for the artel.

liquidation of the kulak policy was again in full swing, except that the main form of collectivisation was to be, not the commune, but the artel where only the land and the cattle are held in common. In his report to the Political Conference in July, in the section dealing with agriculture, Stalin reached the summit of his career as an economist. After the dreadful exposure of all his forecasts which soon followed, he ceased to pontificate on the economic prospects of the Soviet Union; before the end of the plan he had confined himself to vague and extremely cautious generalities, and for years he has been as silent about the future of economic schemes as the Chinese Revolution has made him about the prospects of any revolution.

Socialism Round the Corner

To-day, this July, 1930, report reads like delirium. Stalin told the Soviet people of the State farms. "The programme is surpassed 100 per cent.

"It turns out that the people who laughed at the decision of the Political Bureau, of our Central Committee were actually laughing at themselves. . . . *The Five Year Plan in three years.*[1] Let the bourgeois scribblers and their opportunist imitators talk now about it being impossible to carry out and surpass the Five-Year Plan of Soviet farm construction in three years.

"(b) As regards *collective farming*, we have an even more favourable picture. . . ."[2] Followed a flight of statistics. "It turns out that the people who laughed at the decision of the Central Committee were laughing at themselves. . . . This means that we have already surpassed the five-year programme of collective farm construction in two years, and by more than fifty per cent (applause). . . . *The Five-Year Plan in two years*[3] (*applause*). Let the opportunist old women mumble now about it being impossible to carry out and surpass the Five-Year Plan of collective construction in two years."[4] Following the chief builder, a frenzy of collective-farm building seized the country. Bands of armed Stalinists descended on the countryside to help

[1] Italics his own.   [2] *Leninism*, Vol. II, pp. 341–342.
[3] Italics his own.   [4] *Leninism*, Vol. II, pp. 345–346.

those peasants who were still unconvinced by Stalin's speeches. Kulaks and their families were deported by millions. Then the fiction of the kulak was dropped. At the Congress of Soviets in 1931 Molotov told the peasants that all henceforth had to decide "for or against the collective. Against the collective means supporting the kulak against the Soviet power." By the autumn of 1931 over sixty per cent of the farms had been collectivised. The peasant, said Stalin, has now turned to Socialism. The style of this campaign can be judged by a statement of Molotov's early in 1930 that in the previous thirty days they had made more collective farms than in the previous twelve years.

What happened is known far and wide. The bourgeois Press and publicists have seen to that. Civil war raged on the countryside. The peasants refused to produce; they ate the seed rather than plant it, they slaughtered the livestock rather than take them to the collective farms. Thousands were shot, and these and those deported were the more successful farmers. No economy in the world, Capitalist or Socialist, could stand such maladministration and such brutality. A ghastly famine seized the country. Grain-production, 83 millions of tons in 1930 was 69 in 1932; sugar-beet fell from 14 million tons to 6.56; horses, 34 million in 1929 were 16.6 million in 1932; large-horned cattle, 68.1 millions in 1929 were 38.6 millions in 1932; sheep and goats fell from 147.2 millions to 52.1 millions, a loss of nearly seventy-five per cent; pigs from 20.3 millions to 12.2[1], and to this shrinkage was added the burden of meeting the foreign commitments on the shrinking prices of the world crisis and the factories and armaments against Japan. The Soviet authorities had to take from even the little that there was. Millions died,[2] and long after the famine, until January, 1935, the Russian masses queued

[1] These are the official figures given on pages 36 and 37 of *Socialism Victorious*, by Stalin, Kaganovitch, etc. It is certain that these figures hide about twenty per cent of the decline, in accordance with Stalin's brazen slogan, "Statistics on the class-front."

[2] The official Stalinists, the Webbs and a few others, to-day still deny the famine. The reader should consult W. H. Chamberlain's *Russia's Iron Age*, a review by the Beatrice Webb in *The New Statesman* of March 9th, 1935. Chamberlain's reply in the issue of May 18th, and a letter from E. J. Evans in the issue of April 20th, 1935. That will in all probability be enough.

for bread. On the 8th of August, 1932, *Izvestia* published the decree which imposed the death-penalty on the wretches who stole "Socialist" property from the railway-wagons, or any collective farm property whatever. In case of extenuating circumstances the punishment would be at least ten years, and there was to be no amnesty. The workers and peasants, starving and held in the iron grip of the Stalinist terror, could only make sporadic revolts, but as the régime heaved and cracked, disaffection began to appear in the bureaucracy itself. To the mass shootings of workers and peasants were now added a series of proscriptions against professors, secretaries, collective-farm officials, workers, all who dared to utter a word of criticism, while, in a vain attempt to drown the sombre rattle of the bullets, Stalin and the Soviet Press sang unceasing panegyrics to the brilliant and amazing victories of peasant Socialism. But by the middle of 1932 the country could bear it no longer. In May the amount of grain to be collected from the peasant was reduced by a quarter, the number of cattle to be given over to the State reduced by a half. And far more important, the attempt to abolish the market and introduce Socialist exchange of commodities was abandoned finally and for good. The peasant was allowed to buy and sell. The Russian Revolution was once more on the defensive before the moujik. Then in October, 1933, Fascist Germany left the League of Nations. The defensive became a retreat, and the Russian Revolution is retreating to this day.

Chapter 12

"AFTER HITLER, OUR TURN"

The International Purged

As the Stalinist régime destroyed the Bolshevik party by slander and organisational terror (not against class-enemies, it must always be remembered, which all history proves to be necessary, inevitable and not in the least confined to Communists, but against honest, intelligent and devoted members of its own ranks), so it automatically transferred these methods to the International.[1]

With the final expulsion of the Opposition in 1927 went the expulsion engineered from Moscow of all Trotsky sympathisers. Souvarine had gone before; now Monatte, Loriot, Treint, in France; in Belgium Van Overstraten, in Italy Bordiga, in the United States, Cannon, Swabeck, Abern, Schachtman; in Canada, Spector, member of the Executive of the International, later MacDonald, the party secretary. The method was Stalinist: lies and slander, the ideological preparation; breach of discipline, the pretext; and then ruthless expulsion of the offending Trotskyists and all their followers. For example, Moscow, wishing to clear up the mess in China, published the following in the documents for the Sixth Congress: "Owing to a wrong conception of the tasks of the United Front, the leaders of the Communist Party of China committed a series of vital errors which considerably hampered the preparation of the revolutionary organisations for the fight and which, as later experience has shown, were the

[1] This is not a comprehensive history of the International. Large sections of its activities will remain untouched. We merely show the reasons for its collapse. It will be sufficient to indicate the main lines of development, concentrating on the greatest defeats, since there were no victories.

beginning of a whole chain of opportunist blunders which finally resulted in the bankruptcy of the C. P. leaders. . . .

"They believed that Chiang Kai-Shek had become a national figure, that his desertion of the revolution would weaken the revolutionary movement and that concessions must be made to him, his demands must be satisfied so that he might be preserved for the revolution."[1] Who didn't subscribe to this interpretation had to go. Thus by July, 1928, the way was cleared for the great turn to the Left inside the Soviet Union and the International.

At the Sixth Congress in July, called after four years, Bucharin, already out of favour, still played a prominent part and announced the new policy. He was mainly responsible for the Programme of the International, a document based on Socialism in a single country and therefore valueless. The stabilisation of Capitalism was denounced as ended, which was true enough. The Opposition had been pointing out long before that the General Strike in England and the revolution in China were the precursors of new upheavals. The Stalinists denied it first, then proclaimed it as a new discovery. But from this they drew conclusions, based not on reality and Marxist understanding but solely on the necessities of Stalin's policy and the sycophantic ignorance of men like Manuilsky and Piatnitzky. Comfortable nonentities, their only qualifications for revolutionary leadership were their support of Stalin, to whom they owed all. He, on the other hand, could be sure that their lack of distinction in the days of Lenin, and their personal mediocrity would never aspire to challenge his position as supreme leader and chief theoretician. It is this subservience among his henchmen that prevents any check on Stalin's theories, however fantastic, however ridiculous, however dangerous. The Congress laid down that the world revolution was imminent, that the masses were becoming "radicalised," that they had lost faith in Social Democracy, and the Communists should prepare to lead the masses to victory. After four years the International had met, only to be still further confused and misled. The crisis was undoubtedly

[1] *Between the Fifth and the Sixth World Congresses*, C.P.G.B., pp. 446–447.

coming, and the masses would ultimately seek a revolutionary solution to their difficulties. But the first stage would most certainly be a growth of the Social Democracy. As a crisis deepens after a period of comparative prosperity the first move of the masses is towards the Trade Unions and so under the political leadership of the Social Democracy. The recent rise in France of the Unions from less than two millions to five million is an inevitable phenomenon, predictable and predicted. The Russian masses followed Kerensky first. The Spanish masses from 1931 followed the Republican leaders. Except possibly after the tortures of a Fascist régime, and then not with any certainty, the masses never move straight to a Communist Party but rally to the mass organisations. The Communist Party knows this and fights for its place in the mass movement, warning the workers of the inevitable treachery of the reformist leaders, laying bare the realities of each development, and guiding the growing disillusionment of the masses towards itself. Instead of foretelling this process Stalin, through his mouthpieces, proclaimed the loss of faith of the masses all over the world in Social Democracy (the MacDonald Government in Britain was still to come; millions stuck to the German Social Democracy to the end), the steady swing of the masses to Communism, and the imminent revolution. It is in this way that Lenin's successor, wielding more than Lenin's power without Lenin's brains, step by step, both in broad orientation and day to day direction, wrecked every opportunity of successful revolution. A correct orientation does not mean victory. Incorrect orientations so glaringly false lead to certain defeat. Over the new turn, however, hung the previous three years of revolution with Chiang Kai-Shek and Wang Chin-Wei, Pilsudski and the Anglo-Russian Committee. Resourceful in falsehood, the Stalinists announced that a new period in post-war history—the third period—had begun. The first period was the period which had ended in 1924, the second period had ended with the defeat in China, now had begun the third and final period. The Social Democracy, who had been the chief friends in the second period, were now the chief enemy in the third. The same Social Democracy, the same parties, the same men, were yet to become, as they still are to-day, even better friends than in 1925–27. But behind all this verbiage one solid reality existed— the determination of the bureaucracy to use the International for the defence of the U.S.S.R. That was openly stated to be the first aim. The Conference took this to mean, by means of the revolution. Stalin and the bureaucracy, however, meant, in place of the revolution.

THE INTERNATIONAL PURGED AGAIN

In addition to this ideological confusion the International, wounded already by the long series of expulsions, was now drained again by another organisational onslaught. All who could not pass immediately from the Social Democracy being the chief friend to the Social Democracy being the chief enemy were expelled as Right Wing deviators with abundant personal calumny. In the U.S.A. Lovestone, Gitlow and Wolfe, with the confidence of ninety per cent of the party, were driven out by the purse-controllers in Moscow. In Italy Tasca, Feroci, Santini and Blasco; in Czechoslovakia Hais and Jilek; in Austria Strasser and Schlamm, in France Doriot, then Sellier, with all their supporters; in China Chen Diu-Siu, the founder and leader of the party; in Sweden the bulk of the party and the leader, Kilboom; in Spain Nin, Andrade and Maurin (prominent leaders of the Spanish revolution to-day), in Germany Brandler and Thalheimer, and many good workers. The International has been stabbed and stabbed again by Stalin so that its growth has been stunted, the education (which can come only from experience guided but independently under-taken and independently studied), denied it. And all in the name of discipline, orthodoxy, centralism, Leninism; whereas Lenin, great disciplinarian as he was, understood history and men too well to expect a blind obedience even from men of his own party. If you insist on obedience, he wrote to Bucharin in 1921, about the International, you will get only obedient fools. Unshakable on questions of principle, he allowed a wise laxity except at rare moments when a revolution was in danger. He trusted to events to prove him right, and they generally did, whereupon the offenders were always accepted back on the old terms. Witness his treatment of Zinoviev and Kamenev.[1] If he was wrong he admitted it fully. But Stalin, incapable of correct analysis, was always wrong, has never once in the whole history of the International ever admitted it, but always put the blame for failure on subordinates and covered up the old failures and the preparations for the new by abusing his opponents and then expelling them. He wanted obedient fools, and since 1929 he has had them. The expelled members formed different small groups; a Right Opposition was added to the Left Opposition, both, but more particularly the Trotskyists, being the target of the whole Communist Press, neither time nor money being spared to destroy them. Some, unable to find a footing in revolutionary politics, drifted back to the Social Democracy, others, like Souvarine, to anarchism, some like Doriot even reached Fascism. Some of these men were not of the stuff of which revolutionaries are made, but many of them and their followers would, under a different régime, have added their particular gifts and experience to the revolutionary movement. That they deteriorated was triumphantly pointed out by the Stalinists, though they themselves were the cause of this deterioration.

SOCIAL FASCISM

The new policy of the third period was promulgated in numerous official documents, and the attack on the Social Democracy was crystallised in the once famous phrase, that the Stalinists would give millions to bury to-day—the egregious folly of Social Fascism. In its day Stalin had all the credit for it. But like all his theoretical essays it was stolen from his chief henchman of the time.

Summing up the German failure of 1923 and blaming equally Brandler and the Social Democracy, Zinoviev, deprived of Lenin and therefore theoretically helpless, declared that Fascism had already conquered in Germany

[1] It seems that Stalin is the only leading member of his party whom he ever asked to remove from an important position.

by the aid of the Social Democracy. "What is Pilsudski and the others? Fascist Social Democrats. Were they this ten years ago? No. Of course at that time they were potential Fascists, but it is precisely during the epoch of revolution that they have become Fascists. What is Italian Social Democracy? It is a wing of the Fascists. Turati is a Fascist Social Democrat. Could we have said this five years ago? . . . Ten years ago we had opportunists, but could we say that they were Fascist Social Democrats? No. It would have been absurd to say it then (sic). Now, however, they are Fascists. . . . The international Social Democracy has now become a wing of Fascism."[1] So Zinoviev in January, 1924.

When in September, 1924, Stalin, still expecting immediate revolution, wrote his first article on international affairs, he merely copied Zinoviev in his own way. He paraphrased and elaborated thus: "Firstly it is not true that Fascism is only a fighting organisation of the bourgeoisie. Fascism is not merely a military-technical matter. Fascism is a fighting organisation of the bourgeoisie dependent upon the active support of Social Democracy. Objectively Social Democracy is the moderate wing of Fascism. There is no ground for supposing that a fighting organisation of the bourgeoisie can reach decisive results in its struggles, or in a government of a country, without the active support of Social Democracy. There is just as little ground for supposing that Social Democracy can achieve decisive results in the struggles or in the government of a country without active support by the fighting organisation of the bourgeoisie. These organisations do not exclude but complement one another. They are not poles apart, but immediate neighbours.[2] Fascism is the unformed political block of these two basic organisations, which arose under the critical after-war conditions of imperialism, and is intended for the struggle against the proletarian revolution."[3] Fascism dependent upon the active support of the Social Democracy—Social Democracy being unable to govern

---

[1] The *Lessons of the German Events*, p. 44–45.
[2] Another Stalinist translation is more effective. "They are not antipodes but twins."
[3] *International Press Correspondence*, October 9, 1924.

without the active support of Fascism. This is Stalin. We must emphasise it over and over again; no one will ever understand the history of the Soviet Union and the International since 1924 unless he can grasp (and it is a difficult thing to grasp) this unique combination of economic and political ignorance and stupidity, Tammany Hall ability and ruthless determination.

Stalin wrote this in September, but a month later he proclaimed Socialism in a separate country, Social Democracy became the chief friend, and the Stalinist paraphrase and embellishment of Zinoviev was conveniently forgotten. Now with the new policy of the third period, this discarded folly was fished out and hailed as the summit of human wisdom. The actual phrase Social Fascism seems to have been Stalin's own, and the Stalinist gramophones at home and abroad, Pollitt, Cachin, Thorez and Thaelmann, vied with each other in bringing it in on every possible occasion and paying homage to the master.

In July, 1929, the E.C.C.I. held its Tenth Plenum.[1] On Page 8 the General Staff of the World Revolution analysed Fascism: "In countries where there are strong Social Democratic parties, Fascism assumes the particular form of Social Fascism, which to an ever-increasing extent serves the bourgeoisie as an instrument for the paralysing of the activity of the masses in the struggle against the régime of Fascist dictatorship. By means of this monstrous system of political and economic oppression, the bourgeoisie, aided and abetted by international Social Democracy, has been attempting to crush the revolutionary class movement of the proletariat for many years." Hypnotising themselves with words, they saw millions of workers rushing from the Social Democracy to Communism. Stalin had said it would be so and therefore it was so already: "As a result of their own experience, the German workers are abandoning their illusions concerning the Social Democratic Party." To be quite sure of destroying any liaisons which the left-ward moving sections

[1] *The World Situation and Economic Struggle.* Theses of the Tenth Plenum E.C.C.I. Published by the C.P.G.B.

of the Social Democratic party might seek to make with the Communist Party, the Plenum categorically instructed all sections of the C. I. to pay "special attention to an energetic struggle against the 'Left' Wing of Social Democracy which retards the process of the disintegration of Social Democracy by creating the illusion that it—the 'Left' Wing—represents an opposition to the policy of the leading Social Democratic bodies, whereas as a matter of fact, it whole-heartedly supports the policy of Social Fascism."

Page after page of the report spoke of the radicalisation of the masses, "the coming revolutionary battles," "the upward swing of the labour movement," etc., etc., while under their eyes Social Democracy was in full control of its millions of voters and the millions in the Trade Unions. The Trade Union leadership was described as the "Social Fascist trade union bureaucracy" nearly a dozen times in as many pages; all were warned against the ever-growing "Fascization" of the Trade Unions. The Plenum characterised Social Democracy as "evolving through Social Imperialism to Social Fascism," and dismissing the Trade Union leaders as "sufficiently disgraced," demanded the United Front from below. The leaders were not even to be spoken to.

All over the world the obedient fools rushed to ruin themselves. Thus it was that the British Communist Party, already functioning in an atmosphere traditionally unreceptive, disgraced itself in the eyes of the British workers by reckless talk of insurrection. Pollitt and Tom Mann were charged with proclaiming the imminent revolution. Up to late 1934 the British party continued with this glaring absurdity. In Mexico, in India, in China, in Africa it was the same. The Spanish revolution broke out in 1931. For nearly four years the small Communist Party lost its chances by playing Social Fascism in every key. Revolutionary situations as in Spain, a solid bourgeois-democracy as in Britain, Stalin whistled and his obedient fools danced. Ruinous as it was everywhere, in Germany it reached its highest scope and led the great German proletariat to its doom.

FASCISM

Fascism, say the Liberals and Social Democrats,[1] is provoked by Communism, and therefore they put their trust in democracy. The cowardice of the one and the hypocrisy of the other, are only equalled by their fertility in inventing absurdities. The violent destruction of the leaders and organisations of one class by another is a commonplace of history. The forms in which the different classes organise themselves politically will change according to the period. The reality of the class-struggle remains. Tsarist Black Hundreds, and F. E. Smith and his Ulstermen, were active against their enemies before they knew anything about the world revolution and the dictatorship of the proletariat.

Fascism as we know it to-day originates from post-war Italy, and its development there is instructive.

Italy is that most unstable type of modern Capitalism, a highly-developed industry (in the North) in combination with a poor and backward peasantry. Cheated by Britain, France and Belgium at Versailles, Italy faced the post-war dislocation with resources and psychology closer to the defeated than to the victorious nations. Orlando's Government fell on June 20, 1919, and Nitti came to power, to face the economic and political disorder which all European countries faced after the war. In July there were riots due to the high cost of living in both Northern and Southern Italy. Soviets were formed, and although the movement collapsed after a week, yet the ruling classes had had a warning. The Government re-organised the police, strengthened the gendarmerie, and created a special guard. But certain sections of the bourgeoisie realised quite clearly from what was happening all over Europe that the army and the police could not be depended upon to act against any powerful mass movement, for they, after all, are themselves part of the people. Various nationalist bodies full of patriotic emotion and hysteria, youths bitter at the

[1] Stanley Baldwin has joined them. This is one of his favourite themes. Englishmen shall have neither Fascism nor Communism, he says every day, as if it is a matter of men preferring beer to vodka, or potatoes to spaghetti. Meanwhile the National Government gives every possible protection to Mosley. It knows that British Capitalism may need him.

degradation of Italy by Clemenceau, Lloyd George and Wilson, the excitement in view of the annexation of Fiume and Dalmatia, all thriving on the economic confusion in the country, could easily be organised into nationalists, futurists, arditi. Socialism was the enemy and a mass Press-campaign resulted in the sacking of the offices of *Avanti*, the Socialist paper. Economic and social forces express themselves through men. Italian reaction was fortunate enough to find Mussolini, ex-Socialist, of great organising ability, gifts for demagogy and yet utterly unlike Stalin in that he has exceptional political intelligence and judgment.[1] He formed the Fascist Party in 1919 and Fascist propaganda, a potent political force in our time, made its appearance. We can see its origins quite clearly.

The old type of reaction, Kaiserism, Tsarism, House of Lords Toryism, has had its day, and will never deceive the working-class again. Capitalism, therefore, had to find itself a mass-basis among the petty-bourgeoisie and take on the protective colouring of a people's party. Yet lavish funds, the most intensive Fascist propaganda and all the weight of bourgeois society can never break or even seriously shake a working-class movement. It takes the cowardice and treachery of Liberals and Social Democrats to do that. At the first elections held by the Nitti Government the Socialist vote was 1,840,593 against three and a half millions for all the other parties put together; and properly organised, the social weight of workers and peasants in a nation-wide struggle for power is always immensely greater than its electoral representation. Electoral victories are heady. In the presence of the King at the opening of parliament the 156 Socialist deputies shouted, "Long live Socialism— Long live the Socialist republic!" When they left the building they were attacked by nationalists and army officers, and the masses, ready for action, replied with a general strike in Rome, which spread to Milan and the industrial cities of the North. In Milan the army fired on the demonstrators. In Mantua the masses held

[1] Mussolini is without a shadow of doubt the ablest reactionary post-war Europe has produced.

the city. Thenceforward it was a question ultimately either of the victory of the proletariat and the peasantry or the victory of the ruling class; but the masses could find no leadership. In April, 1920, there was a general strike in Turin which lasted for ten days. Nitti was succeeded by Giolitti, but parliament could not govern. In September, 1920, the Italian metal-workers, who had been negotiating with the Federation of Industrialists for the right of collective contracts, were threatened with a lock-out. To prevent this they seized the factories, and soon the movement had spread to the whole industrial region. The workers ran up the red flag and covered the walls with posters, "Long live the Revolution," but with the inherent discipline of an industrial proletariat they set up technical committees, administrative committees, organised militia which guarded the buildings and kept order, doing their best to carry on the work. From there the step towards an attempt at the revolutionary seizure of power could not have been too difficult, given the political requisite of party, policy and organisation. But all these were absent.

The Italian Socialist Party was split. On the 10th and 11th September it held a conference to decide whether they should make this movement a starting point of the struggle for power. By 591,241 votes to 209,569 it decided that the occupation was merely for economic purposes, and in so doing it signed its own death warrant. The astute industrialists promised to grant some form of workers' control, on paper, just as the Blum government to-day has given a forty-hour week, a rise in wages and other advantages to the workers, duly certified by law and passed through both houses. In addition to checking the onward movement of the masses, the Socialist party split into two parts, the revolutionary and reformist. The Third International, though exercising a powerful influence, could not through the inexperienced Italian Communists combine the necessary organisational and programmatic independence with the flexibility of tactic which wins the masses.[1]

[1] Easy enough to write on paper, in this is summed up the whole profoundly difficult task of revolutionists to the actual approach of the armed uprising

It was at this period that Mussolini and his Fascists hitherto negligible, gained their opportunity. He had formed his society in March, 1919. And much as Hitler was to disguise his reaction by calling himself a National Socialist (a significant testimony of the future social organisation of mankind), Mussolini's programme had the workers and the middle classes in mind—women's suffrage, abolition of the senate, constitutional reform, eight-hour day ratified by parliament, minimum wage, sickness and old-age insurances, workers' control of production, progressive income tax reaching to confiscation in some cases, confiscation of war profits to eighty-five per cent, confiscation of the wealth of the clergy, abolition of the standing army and its replacement by a people's militia, etc., etc. But the big agrarians and industrialists who supported him knew quite well what this programme meant. It is quite true that the Bolsheviks, for reasons which we have explained, were not able to carry out much of their programme, have not been able to do so to this day. But the difference between them and Mussolini is the difference between a political movement that is hindered by economic and historical circumstances on the one hand, and on the other the crudest deception. And it is in this difference that lies the inevitable success of the one and the inevitable collapse of the other.

Once the Italian proletariat had decided not to move forward to political power, members of the lower middle classes, and even many of the proletariat itself, turned to the Fascist promise of immediate action which Mussolini was obviously ready to take. Other sections of the proletariat which did not join the Fascists fell into indifference. Yet even the 1921 elections showed 1,569,553 votes for Socialists and 291,952 for the Communists. The General Confederation of Labour had grown from half a million in 1919 to two million. But the Fascist militia were allowed to destroy the advance-guard of the proletariat and peasantry with system and thoroughness. The Communists

which is in itself a strictly subordinate matter. Trotsky has stated that the actual resort to arms is one-tenth of a successful uprising and is merely the climax to the main business—the political preparation. Nine-tenths of the Stalinists think the opposite way.

were too few to fight and could not work the United Front tactic. The Social Democrats and the Liberals trusted to democracy, in this case the King of Italy and the Italian constitution. To their horror the King deceived them and Mussolini in 1922 marched on Rome in a railway carriage. But his position as Prime Minister was far from secure, and the brutality and corruption of his régime, culminating in the open murder of Matteoti, the courageous Socialist deputy, on June 10, 1924, roused millions of working-men and women and their petty-bourgeois allies. On June 27 in Rome there was a commemoration of Matteoti's death. Let a Social Democrat[1] speak: "Revolt was in the air and in the minds of men. The merest trifle would have been enough to make it break out in the streets. The parliamentary opposition had announced its secession. Filippo Turati had spoken of the murdered man before the hundred and twenty-six deputies elected by the people. Immortal words had been uttered. A stroll in the streets of Rome was enough to convince anyone that some decisive action was looked for. All the roads leading to the Tiber were black with people, all waiting for the Opposition members of Parliament to leave the Chamber in a body, to betake themselves to Lungo Tevere Arnaldo de Brescia, where Matteoti had been kidnapped . . . whither for a fortnight humble peasants, working-men and women had been coming to say a prayer and to strew the symbolic tombstone with flowers.

"But the parliamentary section of the party was of opinion that its struggle lay in keeping within the law, that law that was trodden underfoot by the Government."

Parliament, Parliament, Democracy, Law, Order—it is these words in the mouths of Social Democrats that demoralise workers, not Fascist propaganda.

The immortal words did not harm Mussolini. He consolidated his position on the backs of the battered working-class movement; then came the settlement with the petty-bourgeois dupes (not so spectacularly as Hitler on June 30, 1934; the case was not so urgent). There was civil war in the Fascist party. In Rome each of the two groups marched

[1] *Ten Years of Tyranny in Italy*, by Pietro Nenni, 1934, p. 171.

against each other with machine-guns and conflict was avoided with difficulty. In Turin, Genoa, Slavona, they fought openly. As early as September, 1923, Mussolini wrote in the *Corriero Kalrano*: "Should we be unable radically to rejuvenate the Fascist Party, then it would be better to destroy it and to permit the healthy and fresh forces which live and work within it to merge powerfully into the freer and broader national stream." The lower middle-class elements were weeded out. To-day industrialists, landlords, militarists, flourish in Italy. They have to submit to restriction and regulation by Fascism, but that is a trifle to pay for the destruction of the working-class movement. Italy's rates of wages and living standards are lower than they have been for fifty years. But deprived of their organisations the workers are helpless.

HITLER

Hitler in Germany in 1924 had aimed at doing for German Capitalism what Mussolini had done for Italian. But the pusillanimous capitulation of the German Communist Party had ruined Hitler's chances. The big bourgeoisie, the militarists, have no love for these demagogic parvenus with their uncouth hordes of mercenary toughs. It is only when capitalists see that the workers, disillusioned by capitalist bankruptcy, may seize power that they turn to Fascism as a last expedient. Five years passed before Hitler got another chance. But he had the first requisite of any leader—belief in his cause. He continued with his agitation and his propaganda. He attacked Capitalism, but got few workers to join him. He attacked Marxian-Socialism and substituted his own brand which, when explained to capitalists, induced some rich and influential ones to give him millions. He could not have published dozens of daily papers and kept some half-a-million Brown-shirts without their help. Only an economic crisis would give him his opportunity—and it came in 1929.

The world economic crisis seized Germany first in Europe, because of all the great countries of Europe Germany was the most vulnerable. Since 1924 Germany had existed and been able to pay reparations chiefly by loans from

America. In addition, trustification, monopoly Capitalism, which had gone further in Germany than anywhere else, the consequent domination of the Government by finance-capital, rationalisation, with its consequent increase of unemployment and loss of purchasing power by the masses, the whole historical development of Germany between 1914 and 1929, all these meant that in Germany terrific class-battles would be fought with fateful consequences for Europe and the world. The clash had been avoided in 1924. Now nothing could stave it off.

It would be as well here to point out at once the issues at stake. If the German proletariat were victorious, it meant the almost immediate victory of the Austrian proletariat. Fascism in Italy would receive a most serious blow. In Spain the revolution which had broken out in 1931 would receive an enormous impetus and an enthusiastic ally. Most important of all, the bogey of German invasion, which is the main threat that French Capitalism uses to the French workers, would disappear at a stroke, and the French bourgeoisie would be jammed between the German working-class movement and its own. The difficulties of economic construction in the Soviet Union would have been solved by the combination of Soviet natural resources and Germany's marvellous industrial organisation—that alliance which Lenin had so hoped for. There was the possibility of an invasion of a Soviet Germany by France and Poland, of an invasion of a Soviet Austria by Italy. The Soviet army, ready to oppose intervention, would be a powerful barrier to this, and (given a certain development of the national class-struggle) to suppose that the working-classes of Britain and France, Belgium and Holland would idly allow a Soviet Germany to be crushed by imperialists is a mirage existing only in the minds of Tory diehards and (we know it to-day) the rulers of the Soviet régime. If the Communist International functioned as it could on the basis of the world-crisis, every development in Germany would be followed by the world working-class movement and their responsibility to a Soviet Germany put clearly before them. It will be difficult enough for the imperialists to get whole-hearted participation in an ordinary imperialist war. They would imperil their own existence if they tried to interfere openly in the affairs of a Soviet Germany.[1]

On the other hand the defeat of the German proletariat would be a catastrophe for Europe. The greatest anti-war force under Capitalism was the German proletariat. As long as it was powerful the war against the Soviet Union would have to begin in Berlin. But the victory of Fascism in Germany would mean (we see it to-day) the victory of reaction all over Central and Eastern Europe. It would weaken the Spanish Revolution and the French. It would mean inevitably war against the Soviet Union, it would mean all the things that face us to-day. This is not wisdom after the event. In the very first stages of the struggle they were clearly set down by the expelled Left Opposition, the existing state of parties in Germany estimated, the course of action to be followed outlined.

THE WARNING

The first intimation of danger was the Reichstag election of September, 1930. In May, 1924, the Nazis polled 1,918,310 votes, in May, 1928, 809,541 votes. Then came the crisis. Hitler had at last persuaded important sections of German Capitalism that he could be depended upon to smash the German working-class movement. Backed not only by German but by international capital, he and his party drew to it the threatened middle classes by promising them to destroy the big chain-stores, etc., the lumpen proletariat by bribery, and every unattached voter by playing on nationalist sentiment and promising everything to everybody. Now in September, 1930, after one year of the crisis, he gained 6,406,397 votes, an increase of over five million. The blindest of the blind could see that not only the whole world but even the builders of Socialism in a single country would have to concentrate on the developments in Germany during the next few years. The workers of Germany, whom Fascism was aimed against and who alone could break Fascism, were organised in the Social Democratic Party and the Communist Party.

[1] Under Fascism the situation is of course entirely different. But in pre-Fascist Germany, the sending of soldiers to help a Franco would have meant an internal upheaval.

The Social Democratic Party during the stabilisation had developed a huge bureaucracy. With the failure of the Communist Party in 1923 the workers had quite inevitably gone back to the Social Democracy, which had strengthened itself all over Europe on the basis of the temporary stabilisation of 1924-1929. The Social Democrats had control of the Prussian Government and thousands of posts in the Government service. Two-thirds of the police chiefs of Prussia were Social Democrats. There were nearly a hundred Social Democratic members in the Reichstag and many in the other parliaments of Germany; they had jobs in State banks, there were thousands of Trade Union officials, workers in the Party Press, right down to posts that were much smaller but yet, in post-war Germany, safe. It has been estimated that the Social Democracy had actually at its disposal in 1931 nearly 290,000 actual posts.[1] Anyone with the slightest experience of workers' organisations knows that this bureaucracy, basing itself on the layers next to it, with the organisation, propaganda and finances of the party and Trade Unions in its hand, could exercise an enormous influence on the millions on which they rested.

But below these were nearly twenty millions of the German working people in town and country. In May, 1924, the Social Democrats had had only six million votes, the Communists 3,693,000. But by December, in spite of the imminent revolution foretold by Stalin and Zinoviev, the Communist Party had lost 974,000 of these votes, and the Social Democracy had gained 1,881,000, making them 7,881,000. The revolutionary problem is to turn enough of these away from their leaders. Wels, Leipart, Otto Braun, Severing, Noske and the large majority of the German Social Democrats, no more than Citrine, Bevin, Attlee, Morrison, Jouhaux, Léon Blum and the others, would not prepare workers for any sort of struggle with Capitalism. Before 1933 they were willing to come to terms with Fascism if allowed. Now that Fascism is exposed, they pretend that capitalists, faced with a choice between social revolution and Fascism will choose parliamentary democracy. They

[1] Another estimate puts it at 400,000.

321

can always escape abroad. But the vast millions of Social Democratic workers have no choice but to fight Fascism or be crushed by it. They listened in Germany as they will always listen to the speeches of their leaders, they hope that these will do something, they have faith in the organisations that they have built up with so much sacrifice. Their leaders teach them to have faith in democracy, in the King of Italy, in Hindenburg, in the Popular Front, in God[1] (Walter Citrine), in everything except their own organised strength. It is usually only when the enemy is upon them that they realise that their Social Democratic leaders have scattered to the four winds and never intended to fight Fascism at all.[2] It was the business of the Communist Party of Germany to expose these Social Democratic leaders for what they were, and win enough of the Social Democratic workers, or at least neutralise the others, so as to be able to make the attack on Fascism. Whatever Hitler said, Mussolini in Italy had shown that Fascism aimed at destroying the workers' organisations and bourgeois parliamentary democracy, leaving the workers defenceless. The army and police cannot be trusted to do that, the bourgeoisie can no longer trust the bourgeois State, so it organises its bands. But it is this very factor which makes the Social Democratic worker under skilful leadership ready to fight. He is not a revolutionary. If he were he would join the Communist Party. But he, in certain circumstances, will fight in defence of what he considers to be his lawful constitutional rights. Whenever a ruling class has to take away by violence these rights, the revolutionary situation becomes a possibility.

The German Communist Party votes in 1930 had jumped from 3,300,000 to 4,600,000, nothing in comparison to the Fascist increase. But in Germany, with twenty-five large towns of over 500,000 people, with the workers dominant in the economy of the country, the combined Communist

[1] T.U. Conference at Brighton, 1933.

[2] Under one condition only will they ever fight: if, as in Spain, the Liberal bourgeois is placed in such a position that he must defend himself, and gives battle to Fascists. Your Social Democrat will always follow a bourgeois. In Austria in 1934 Bauer was on his knees before Dolfuss to the end. The workers began the fighting; the bureaucrats could not help themselves. This does not mean that some Social Democrats are not physically courageous men, as many revolutionaries, e.g. Zinoviev, are physical cowards. It is a political attitude that is in question here.

and Social Democratic vote represented the dominant social force in the country. In highly industrial countries like Germany and Britain the organized workers hold the fate of the country in their hands. The other political parties in Germany, Nationalists, Catholic, Centre Party, etc., might be numerically imposing, as they were in Russia even after October, 1917. Lenin did not fear all their votes, contemptuously dismissed the Constituent Assembly in 1918, and held the power. The ruling class v. the working class is the issue, both fighting for the lower middle-classes. Even the big capitalist parties were not homogeneous. In a crisis the Catholic Party, for instance, would split, probably to the advantage of the workers, who, were their leadership strong and decisive enough, could count on drawing the bulk of the Catholic workmen to their side. In unity for action the workers in the factories, transport and other essential services would be masters of the situation. With the policy of the United Front against Fascism, the Social Democratic worker, step by step, could be led on the basis of his own experience to fight against Fascism; and the victorious struggle against Fascism, not in parliament, but in the streets, would lead directly to power.

That was the task in the Germany of 1930. It is the task in France to-day, and ultimately, excepting the complications of a war, the task in Britain to-morrow. The German Communist party had to point out every manœuvre of Hitler and the capitalists and at the same time prove to the workers that their leaders would not fight; not by telling them this but by challenging the leaders to fight. At the same time they had a quite special responsibility, to give the workers confidence that the Communist Party was not only willing but able to lead that fight. For a very noticeable thing in the elections of 1930 was that, though the Communist vote had increased by over a million and a quarter, the membership of the party had not correspondingly increased, which meant that, though many workers believed in the necessity of revolution and accepted the line of the Communist Party, they doubted the capacity of the Communist Party to carry out that line; 1923 remained in their minds.

Trotsky, in an article written from his exile in Prinkipo just after the elections, warned them that the situation demanded careful handling.[1] The six million voters for the Social Democracy did not mean that the voters were unalterably attached to the Social Democracy. Millions of these could be won by the Communists as the Bolsheviks had won millions for the October Revolution, and the German Communist Party in 1923 had been able in a few months to get the majority of the German proletariat behind it. But the Communist Party would have to drop its exaggerations and absurdities and base itself solely on realistic estimations of the political situation. With the position as it was, to take the offensive would be disastrous. The Communist Party, with the advance-guard of the workers, would be smashed to pieces, leaving the road clear for Fascism. He suggested defensive battles and an unwavering struggle for the United Front. The Social Democratic leaders would clamour that they wanted to fight. What did they propose? The Communist Party would not ask the Social Democratic worker to leave his party. Let him demand of his leaders that they take joint steps for defence, each party its own banner, its own flag, but a simply-defined programme. If the Social Democratic Party leaders accepted, so much the better. The fight would go on and the Communist Party would apologise for having misjudged them. But they would refuse. Then as the Fascist danger grew they would have the task of explaining to their members why, in face of the growing threat, they continued to refuse the quite reasonable offers of Communists who, after all, were fellow-workers and were not proposing immediate revolution, but merely common defence against an immediate danger. "There is no doubt that the leaders of the Social Democracy and a very small stratum of workers will prefer, in the last analysis, the victory of Fascism to the revolutionary victory of the proletariat." But it was precisely this preference which gave the Communist Party an opportunity to break the ranks under the control of the Social Democratic bureaucracy. "We must conclude agreements against

[1] *Les Problèmes de la Révolution Allemande* par L. Trotsky, Paris, 1931.

Fascism with divers Social Democratic fractions and organisations, while placing clearly before the masses precise conditions for their leaders." This was in 1930.

THE UNITED FRONT

So that there might be no misunderstanding of the colossal blundering and treachery which gave us a Fascist instead of a Soviet Germany with all that will mean for Europe, we cannot do better for the English reader than use the example of the present tactics of the Communist Party of Great Britain in its effort to get into the Labour Party.

The gentlemanly leaders of the Labour Party do not want them, for harmless as the Communists are to-day, the very word Communism compromises the Social Democrats with the bourgeoisie. The Communist leaders know this as well as anybody else. But they make an open application to the Social Democratic leaders. It is true that they want to get in merely to agitate for an alliance of the Soviet Union with Britain and France against Germany and Japan, under the guise of the League of Nations and collective security. But we can leave aside their aims, which do not concern us for the moment. Naturally Morrison, Citrine and the other Labour Party leaders refuse. But, small as the British party is, it has, as every party always has, influence among the Social Democratic workers in certain districts where Communists and militant Social Democratic workers have fought many fights together in the days when the Communist Party was a fighting party. Furthermore at the present moment the politically-minded workers everywhere are profoundly stirred by the war danger and the unsettled state of Europe. The British Communists are not asking for revolution. There are many good comrades among them. Why then should the Social Democratic leaders turn them down? In Social Democratic districts which are favourable to the Communist Party, resolutions are passed demanding the affiliation. Trade Union conferences do the same, Social Democratic intellectuals like Sir Stafford Cripps and G. D. H. Cole, who have not the typical Trade Union mentality and servility to bourgeois ideas of the Labour leader risen from the ranks, are sympathetic and ask why not. The *New Statesman* comes out in support. In every section of the Social Democratic party on every possible occasion the Communist Party urges its claim. Certain districts not only pass resolutions, but actually begin to take joint action with the Communists in defiance of headquarters. In the powerful South Wales Miners' Federation a Communist, Arthur Horner, is elected president. This is a strong lever. The *Daily Worker* of July 6, 1936, reports that 121 Labour Party organisations are for affiliation. In addition, in Hammersmith the South Hammersmith Co-operative Political Council, the South Hammersmith Divisional Labour Party, in all fifteen organisations in the borough, have voted for unity. This means that in that district unity for action is achieved. The Communist Party consistently offers plans for united action. The Social Democratic leaders consistently refuse. Yet the Communist Party is only recommending the same League of Nations, the same collective security as the Labour Party.

The pressure embarrasses men like Morrison and Citrine dreadfully. The Edinburgh Conference shows a Labour Party split ideologically from top to bottom. And if suddenly the war-crisis were to come nearer, and the Communist Party once more puts a concrete programme for unity before the Social Democratic leaders, these gentlemen have either to accept them or face the possibility of grave unrest and even a serious split in their ranks. For the Communist Party is irreproachable in its demands. It is not asking to make a revolution. It is merely taking the Social Democratic leaders at their word and suggesting that instead of talking they do something. In Germany by October, 1923, the Social Democratic Party was breaking to pieces under similar pressure. And in the Germany of 1923, unlike the Germany of 1930, Hitler's bands did not stalk the streets. Marxism aims merely at foreseeing, foretelling, clarifying and preparing in advance for what the workers will at a high moment of history instinctively respond to. The great millions of workers in Germany wanted to unite to fight Fascism and fought to do so, and if a campaign of the sort the British Communist

Party is waging to-day had been waged in Germany, after the September election of 1930, against Fascism, Hitler could not have passed.[1] The thin layer of the Labour aristocracy would, in the moment of crisis, have been swept away like dust with a broom. How then did it happen that the German Communist Party pursued the exactly opposite policy? First, the German soil was particularly fertile for Stalin's Social Fascist stupidity. A bitter feud had divided the two parties since the murder of Karl Liebknecht and Rosa Luxemburg and the accumulated treacheries of the Social Democracy. Secondly, the expulsion from the party of all who were not prepared to accept the party-line, discipline, centralism, unity, etc., and thirdly and more important than all these, the determination of Moscow at all costs to maintain a division between France and Germany, and to sacrifice the German revolution for this end. The German Communist Party tried to break away from Social Fascism. Sections of the Social Democrats made offers for unity. That the Russian bureaucracy insisted on division, even to the extent of letting Hitler come in, is one of the most criminal blunders in history.

STALINIST POLITICS

As far back as the middle of 1931, Trotsky, watching anxiously the tactics of the Communist Party in Germany, had seen where the Stalinist policy was leading and hoped in vain for a change. Before Hitler came into power Walter Duranty, Russian correspondent, had written in the *New York Times* of November 20, 1932, that "the Bolshevist Kremlin to-day regards the growth of the revolutionary movement in Europe with real anxiety." He was seeing only a fraction of the whole truth—that the Kremlin was prepared to sacrifice the workers' movement thinking thereby to save itself. That the German workers went down without a struggle when they had an even chance of victory was no fault of theirs. They were ruined by the ignorant and treacherous Soviet bureaucracy.

The German Social Democracy had been declared the

---

[1] A campaign similar in intensity, but for united action, not organisational unity; and independence tenaciously guarded. See pp, 170–4.

chief enemy long before the third period, since 1927.[1]
The Soviet bureaucracy feared the German Social Democratic Party for its support of Locarno. In 1922 Germany,
rebuffed by Britain and France, had signed the Treaty of
Rapallo with the Soviet Union.[2] The division between
France and Germany was naturally a very good thing for
Russian foreign policy. But the Treaty of Locarno in 1925
seemed to Stalin and to the world at that time the beginning
of a friendship, and the German Social Democracy, which
pressed hard for this burying of the hatchet between France
and Germany, became the special enemy of the Soviet
bureaucracy. Stalin's second period had prevented this
antagonism developing fully. But with the break-up and
final exposure of the Anglo-Russian Committee and the
tardy realisation that the Social Democracy was no help
against a war of intervention, with the imminent growth
of the war-danger, Social Fascism was directed with special
ferocity against German Social Democracy. In the material
collected for the Sixth Conference we see the Stalinist
bitterness against the Social Democracy: "On question (sic)
of International policy the attitude of German Social
Democracy is in line with that of the rest of the Second
International; recognition of and collaboration with the
League of Nations, and bitter denunciation of the Soviet
Union. German Social Democracy represents the 'Western
orientation,' and it takes advantage of every opportunity
to extend the cleavage between the Soviet Union and
Germany."[3] Hitler proclaimed his hostility to Marxism in
general, but also to France, and for Stalin, therefore,
concerned with Socialism in a single country and not with
revolution, Social Democracy in Germany, with its Western
orientation, was the main enemy. This ruined the German
revolution. Social Fascism in July, 1929, when a year
before Hitler had lost a million votes, was merely another

[1] *The Communist International between the Fifth and Sixth World Congresses,*
C.P.G.B., 1928, p. 98. The Essen Conference had also to fight against Right
deviations. A group of comrades had set its face against the thesis adopted
by the conference to the effect that the Left leaders in the S.D.P. were the
chief enemy.
[2] Ebert, the Social Democratic President, swore he would never speak to
Stresemann again.
[3] *Between the Fifth and Sixth World Congresses,* p. 94.

Stalinist folly preventing the Communist Party of Germany from exercising the influence it should. But after the elections of September, 1930, it was criminal. For the responsibility of leading the masses against Fascism rested and will always rest with the revolutionary party. The Social Democratic leaders are what they are, and for the revolutionary party to lay blame on them for what it knows they will do is the merest childishness. But lacking Marxist training, dead in the International since 1924, ignorant and bureaucratic, the Communist Party, under Moscow's firm guidance, professed itself quite untroubled at the results of the September elections and prophesied Hitler's early doom. On September 15, 1930, the *Rote Fahne* told the German proletariat: "Last night was Herr Hitler's greatest day, but the so-called election victory of the Nazis is the beginning of the end," and on the following day: "The 14th of September was the high point of the National Socialist movement in Germany. What comes after this can only be decline and fall."

THE ECONOMIC CRISIS

During 1931 the crisis steadily intensified.The Communists could not see and the Social Democrats would not see that parliamentary government was doomed in Germany, and that this political crisis would end in a dictatorship either of the Right or of the Left. This had long been obvious to the shrewdest capitalists inside and outside Germany.

Germany's creditors began to call in loans, bank crisis followed bank crisis. The downward trend of production and trade was intensified, and Germany, instead of sliding, began to plunge. More and more groups of German capitalists began to see their way out in Hitler. The Social Democrats prated of democracy, the Communist Party redoubled their attacks upon the Social Fascists. The violence of the Fascists grew daily with their increasing financial and popular support, and in the face of this the bewildered Social Democratic worker was told a dozen times a day that the Social Democratic Party, Social Fascism, and not Fascism, was the main enemy. He was invited to form the United Front only from below, in other

329

words, an ultimatum to leave his own party simply because the Communists told him so. Red Trade Unions, an experiment already tried and a proved failure, were started again in opposition to the Social Fascist Unions and served only to accentuate the division between the workers.

In March Bruening tried to unite Germany and Austria in a complete customs union. This would have helped German trade, given some moral confidence to Germany, and allayed for a time the spectre of German Communism. But it would have threatened the ill-gotten gains of France and the Little Entente. They forbade it. The Hoover moratorium on German debts could not check the disintegration. The Bruening Government, armed with Article 48 of the Constitution, by dictatorial decree after decree made the workers and salaried employees bear the brunt of the crisis. But the Social Democrats clung desperately to Bruening and Hindenburg. Support Bruening against Hitler, they urged the workers. He is the lesser evil.

The workers had organised themselves into the Reichsbanner, ready to fight for the defence of the republic. It was all that the Communists needed. They, while not identifying themselves with the fight for the republic, could fight side by side with the Social Democrats against Fascism. That road, as we see in Catalonia to-day, could lead only to the struggle for the dictatorship of the proletariat, the Social Democratic workers being driven to take it, not by propaganda but by the very logic of events. But for the Communists Hitler was the lesser evil. Destroy the Social Democracy, the dirty Social Fascists. Most probably unrealised by themselves, Moscow had shifted their propaganda slogans to compete with the Nazis in inciting all Germany to an antagonism against France, just as Moscow to-day has the French Communist Party inciting all France to antagonism against Germany. The Nazis claimed to be fighting for the national liberation of Germany from the Treaty of Versailles by war. The Communists, instead of opposing this typical imperialist slogan with the slogans of International Socialism, reinforced by the whole International, were made to compete with the Fascists by putting forward the slogan of a popular revolution for national emancipation from the Treaty of Versailles. Adventurers of the officer type, men like Scheringer and Count Stenbock-Fermoy, thinking of nothing else but an imperialist war with France, fraternised with the Communist Party on the basis of this fight for national emancipation, and brought only further disorder and confusion into the Communist Party without the slightest gain; in this field the Nazis were invincible. All this, however, had nothing to do with the struggle of the German workers, but with Moscow's foreign policy. Then in August, 1931, came an astounding interference from Moscow in the policy of the German Communist Party.

THE RED REFERENDUM

The great stronghold of the Social Democrats was Prussia, where since 1919 they had ruled. They had had the uninterrupted command of the police, and Prussia, with Berlin, was the most powerful State in the Reich. But by the middle of 1931 the Prussian Government was in serious danger, for the Nazis were sweeping everything before them, and it was certain that at the coming elections they would be the largest single party in the Prussian Landtag. The Social Democrats, therefore, with revolutionary courage, manœuvred and manipulated so as to continue governing if no party gained an absolute majority. The Nazis were furious and demanded a referendum, their only legal means of turning out the Social Democratic Government.

Despite three years of Social Fascism the first instinctive reaction of the German Communist Party was to side with the Social Democrats against the Fascists. The Party leadership in Germany started to fight against the Referendum. That, however, meant support of the Social Democrats with their "Western orientation." Stalin made them stop their opposition to the referendum and support the Fascists against the Social Democrats. Luckily we have the evidence of Piatnitzky himself, Secretary of the Communist International. "You know, for example, that the leadership of the party opposed taking part in the referendum on the dissolution of the Prussian Landtag. A number of party newspapers published leading articles opposing participation in that referendum. But when the Central

Committee of the party jointly with the Comintern arrived at the conclusion that it was necessary to take an active part in the referendum, the German comrades, in the course of a few days, roused the whole party. Not a single party, except the C.P.S.U. could do that. . . ."[1]

Thaelmann and his Central Committee are not entirely to blame for the German catastrophe. They meant well. The tradition of obedience and discipline, the faith of the German party leaders, were mercilessly exploited against the cause. On July 21 the Communist Party, suddenly forgetting Social Fascism, addressed a letter to the Social Democratic ministers, Braun and Severing, demanding a United Front for struggle on behalf of the workers' living conditions and threatening to form a United Front with the Fascists against them unless they agreed. The Social Democratic Government had shot down workers demonstrating on May Day, had passed savage repressive legislation against the Communists, banning the Communist military organisation, the Red Fighting Front, and saying openly that these actions were directed against the Communists and not against the Fascists. Like Walter Citrine and Herbert Morrison, Braun and Severing did not want any United Front. They therefore refused this proposal, as it was certain they would refuse. Social Democrats never form United Fronts because of proposals addressed to them by revolutionary parties. These proposals only assume importance when backed by the mass agitation initiated by the revolutionary party among their own party-members. On this refusal the Communist Party called on its members to support the Fascists in their referendum. During the campaign there appeared in the Communist journal, *Fanfare*, on the 1st August, a portrait of Scheringer, the rabid nationalist, with the following message: "Whoever opposes the popular revolution, the revolutionary war of liberation, betrays the cause of those who died in the World War and gave their lives for a free Germany." The same words could have been used by Hitler in the Fascist campaign. Thaelmann himself tells how workers, miserably confused, came to the Communist

[1] *Guide to the XII Plenum*, E.C.C.I., *Modern Books*, p. 42.

Party and asked if after all a Braun-Severing Government was not better than a Hitler-Goebbels Government. Thaelmann told them they were not class-conscious enough.[1] Had everything depended on them the Moscow-driven Communist leadership would have succeeded in getting the Fascists into power in Prussia since the summer of 1931. But the common sense of the German workers revolted against the blind bureaucratic stupidity above. They refused to vote, and where twenty-five million votes were required to ratify the plebiscite, the Fascists did not get half that number.

In the autumn, with the Fascist danger growing every day, and Bruening mercilessly slashing at the workers, as was inevitable, a section of the Social Democrats began to turn tentatively to the Communist Party. Breitscheid, a Social Democratic leader full of revolutionary words (a kind of Stafford Cripps), proclaimed openly that if things went on as they were going (the Social Democratic Party had been trying to negotiate with the centre, which, however, was drawing to the right) the Social Democratic Party would have to form a United Front with the Communist Party. Here was a chance that had come unasked, and in spite of all that had gone before. Faithful to Moscow, Thaelmann rejected the offer with scorn and warned the workers against it. To those who suggested that the Braun-Severing Government was better than a Hitler-Goebbels Government he said: "This influence exercised over revolutionary workers by the treacherous ideology of the lying Social Democrats, these relics of Social Democratic thought in our ranks, is, we declare, in full agreement with the decisions of the Eleventh Plenum, *the most serious danger that confronts the Communist Party*.[2] How great that danger is, is shown at the present time, among other things, by the latest manœuvres of Social Fascism. . . . It is therefore undertaking a new demagogic manœuvre, it is 'threatening' to form a united front with the Communist party. . . . We have not conducted our fundamental struggle against Social Democracy with sufficient sharpness and clarity.

[1] "Some Mistakes in our Work," by Ernst Thaelmann. *The Communist International*, December 15, 1931, p. 717.

[2] Italics his own.

Let us take a few examples. . . ."[1] And his first example was, the neglect of exposing, as the most dangerous type of reformism, some thousands of workers who, disgusted with Social Democracy, had decided to split off from the party and form a party of their own. It was not yet Communist but was heading in that direction. Social Fascism demanded that they should be violently repelled.

STALIN SABOTAGES THE REVOLUTION

Moscow, seeing that the Red Referendum manœuvre had failed, threw all pretence aside and came openly out for letting Hitler in.

On October 14, 1931, Remmele, one of the three official leaders of the Communist Party, with Stalinist effrontery announced the policy in the Reichstag. "Herr Bruening has put it very plainly; once they (the Fascists) are in power, then the united front of the proletariat will be established and it will make a clean sweep of everything. (Violent applause from the Communists). . . . We are the victors of the coming day; and the question is no longer one of who shall vanquish whom. This question is already answered. (Applause from the Communists). The question now reads only, 'At what moment shall we overthrow the bourgeoisie?' . . . We are not afraid of the Fascist gentlemen. They will shoot their bolt quicker than any other Government. (Right you are! from the Communists) . . ." The Fascists, so ran the argument, would introduce inflation, there would be financial chaos, and then the proletarian victory would follow. The speech was printed with a form asking for membership of the party attached, and distributed in great numbers all over Germany.

Stalinist parties are led from above. Their leaders get the line and impose it. Disobedience is labelled Trotskyism, Right deviation, and what not, and the dissidents expelled. But the situation in Germany was too tense, and violent protests from the Left Wing caused the policy to be withdrawn. But from that moment it was certain that the Communist Party leadership would never fight, and the

[1] "Some Mistakes in our Work," by Ernest Thaelmann. *The Communist International*, December 15, 1931, p. 717.

"After Hitler, our turn"[1] was the line on which they led the party. The German leadership did not follow blindly. Some of them carried on a ceaseless struggle to the very end. But built on Moscow they faced isolation if they broke with Moscow, and the organisational vice silenced or expelled them.[2]

THE BUREAUCRAT AND REVOLUTION

October, 1931, is the actual turning-point in the history of the International and therefore in the history of post-war Europe. It is usual to date this last intense period in which we live from the early months of 1933 when Fascism came to power in Germany. From October, 1931, however, we can see to-day, is the time when it was certain that Fascism would come into power. For if the revolutionary party in Germany would not give the lead to the great body of workers, then nothing could stop Hitler; the German proletariat, after the Russian the greatest anti-war force in Europe, would be stripped of its organisations and its leaders, and the greatest of imperialist wars would be unavoidable.

The question is: Why did Stalin persist in this policy? How could the Soviet bureaucracy possibly conceive that any useful purpose could be served by letting Hitler come into power? No question is more important, not only for the past but for the present. In the answer to it lies the whole complex problem of the relationship between the international working-class movement and the Soviet bureaucracy.

The root of this suicidal policy, which has had such catastrophic consequences, lies in the very nature of a workers' bureaucracy, inside as well as outside the Soviet Union. And we shall understand the Soviet bureaucracy best by noting how closely it resembles the workers' bureaucracies with which we are more familiar.

A Social Democratic bureaucracy believes first and foremost in a national Socialism. It does not consider that

---

[1] The Communists could not popularise this as a slogan, but under the guidance of the leadership, many of the rank-and-file used it among themselves, no doubt sincerely believing in this as Marxism.

[2] See a one-sided but revealing account of this struggle in *International Press Correspondence*, May 17, 1934, p. 744.

the success of the workers in other countries is vital to its own. The basic doctrine of the Soviet bureaucracy, Socialism in a single country, is essentially the same. Each is the ideology of a caste that is well satisfied with its own position. Each Social Democratic bureaucracy is far more hostile to its own Left Wing, the revolutionary Socialists, than to its own imperialist bourgeoisie. Citrine will stand on the same platform with Winston Churchill but will not do the same with Pollitt.[1] The Soviet bureaucracy is to-day far more murderous against Trotsky, Zinoviev and Kamenev and revolutionaries in Russia, than it is to the bourgeoisie of France and Britain. The reason in both instances is the same. They wish to live on good terms with the bourgeoisie, if allowed, but the revolutionaries are enemies of their prestige, privileges and perquisites. Most important for the German policy, however is the fact that the workers' bureaucracies of Western Europe, from the very positions they occupy as administrators of the affairs of millions of docile workers, are incapable of conceiving that the workers whom they dominate can achieve anything, least of all the overthrow of Capitalism and the establishment of a Workers' State. To-day the Soviet bureaucracy believes exactly the same. For both, the revolution of October, 1917, was due to exceptional circumstances. The Soviet bureaucracy has not reached this position all at once, any more than the pre-war German Social Democracy reached its position of 1914 other than by a gradual process. In 1923 Stalin met opposition to his policy for the German Revolution. He manœuvred by saying: Let the Fascists attack first, though they are weak. Two years later, China offers an opportunity for a victory of the world revolution. China seems to the Soviet bureaucracy a field where a revolution can take place without the immediate complications that would ensue in Germany. Stalin is sincerely desirous of guiding the Chinese Revolution to victory. But the very qualities which make him so acceptable to the bureaucracy are the very ones which unfit him for leading a revolution. His

---

[1] Pollitt, of course, is to the right of Citrine to-day, but the aura of the October revolution still hangs around his party.

stubborn stupidity prevents him correcting the policy, even after the disastrous experience with Chiang Kai-Shek. He has to experience the defection of Wang Chin-Wei before at last he turns to the workers and peasants. The failure is complete and henceforth the bureaucracy, as the Sixth Congress shows, with its defence of the U.S.S.R. as the first task, has lost all hope in the world revolution. The expulsion of the Opposition, the consolidation of bureaucratic power by the administrative activity of the five-year plan, intensifies the process of ossification. By 1931 the bureaucracy is fully mature. Every shred of the revolutionary ardour of 1917 has completely disappeared, driven ruthlessly out as Trotskyism. Incapable of visualizing a successful revolution in Germany, the choice appears to the bureaucracy to be between Fascism and the Social Democracy. Given Stalin's foreign policy it cannot be the Social Democracy, with its Western orientation and League of Nations policy. It can only be Fascism.

To do Stalin justice, the leader of the world proletariat is so incapable of independent theoretical analysis that he had no idea of what a Fascist régime in Germany would mean. He had decreed that Fascism could not rule without the support of the Social Democracy. They were not antipodes but twins. It could not much matter which twin was in power. But even this apparently characteristic Stalinist stupidity was shared by the Social Democratic bureaucracy. When Hitler came to power Wels and Liepart, the German bureaucrats, offered to support him. They thought that they could accommodate themselves somehow to Fascism. Citrine, at the Brighton Trade Union Conference in 1933, gives us the view of the British bureaucrat not before but after the catastrophe. "All I can say is that a general strike was definitely planned and projected, but the German leaders had to give consideration to the fact that a general strike after the atmosphere created by the Reichstag fire and with $6\frac{1}{4}$ million people unemployed was an act fraught with the gravest consequences which might be described as nothing less than civil war." The only thing, therefore, was to let Hitler in. The attitude of the Soviet bureaucracy was

337

exactly the same, both before and after the catastrophe. In January, 1934, at the Seventeenth Party Conference in Moscow, though Hitler had been in power one year, Stalin explained his policy. " Of course, we are far from being enthusiastic about the Fascist régime in Germany. But Fascism is not the issue here, if only for the reason that Fascism, for example in Italy, did not prevent the U.S.S.R. establishing very good relations with that country." He hoped to establish good relations with a Germany hostile to France. Almost at that very moment Otto Bauer in Austria was crawling before Dolfuss, "We declared that we would be prepared even to make concessions to the notion of a 'corporative' organisation of society and of the State, in order to make an understanding possible. It was all in vain—Dolfuss refused to enter into any negotiations." Bauer had to fight, but the workers forced it. "Why wait?" they said. ". . . Let us strike now, while we are still ready for battle. Otherwise we shall share the fate of our comrades in Germany."

One year after Hitler, Stalin and Otto Bauer were still hoping to come to terms with Fascism. Being what they were it is clear that before they had had actual experience of Hitler, the idea of the German workers fighting Fascism would not have crossed their minds. "After Hitler, our turn," is the concentrated expression of bureaucratic inertia, cowardice, ignorance and short-sightedness. Stalin could not say openly what he meant. He had to dress it up in revolutionary words, to promise the deluded German workers that the revolution would come after Hitler had come to power. The foreign policy he pursued from that same October showed that nothing was further from his mind. One final difference between 1923 and 1931 should be noted. In 1923 Stalin could almost certainly have carried the bureaucracy with him for a forward policy in Germany. In China he could have abandoned Chiang Kai-Shek at any time without the slightest change in the stability of his position, except loss of prestige to Trotskyism. But by 1931 it is most probable that any attempt to encourage revolution in Germany would have resulted in an internal upheaval. Not that Stalin would ever have suggested any such policy. But it is necessary to emphasize that after 1931 Stalin leads the International along a pre-destined and acknowledged road. To expect a change is to expect Citrine and Bevin to become revolutionary Socialists.

THE MARXIST AND REVOLUTION

The Left Opposition was a small group incapable of exercising influence against two such powerful bureaucracies as the Communist Party and the Social Democratic Party. Trotsky at Prinkipo, branded as a counter-revolutionary, offered directive after directive and uttered warning after warning. Handicapped as he was by being unable to keep his finger on the pulse of events from day to day, yet his collected writings on the German situation are perfect examples, forever to be studied, of Marxism applied to a living situation. On November 26, 1931, he finished a pamphlet "Germany—the Key to the International Situation."[1] He had not yet learnt of the Remmele speech, but that Moscow had been counselling retreat was already clear.

"The coming into power of the German 'National Socialists' would mean above all the extermination of the flower of the German proletariat, the disruption of its organisations, the extirpation of its belief in itself and in its future. Considering the far greater maturity and acuteness of the social contradictions in Germany, the hellish work of Italian Fascism would probably appear as a pale and almost humane experiment in comparison with the work of the German National Socialists.[2]

"Retreat, you say, you who were yesterday the prophets of the 'third period'? Leaders and institutions can retreat, individual persons can hide. But the working class will have no place to retreat to in the face of Fascism, and no place where to hide. If one were really to assume the monstrous and improbable to happen: that the party will actually evade the struggle and thus deliver the proletariat to the mercy of its mortal enemy, this would signify only one thing; the gruesome battles would unfold not *before* the seizure of power by the Fascists but *after* it, that is: under conditions ten times more favourable

[1] Pioneer Press, New York, 1932.
[2] No one who knows, however casually, Trotsky's writings, could countenance the stupid accusations made by the Stalinists against him of being "leader of the counter-revolutionary bourgeoisie", ally of Fascism, etc. Yet Karl Radek wrote these things.

for Fascism than those of to-day. The struggle of the proletariat, taken unawares, disorientated, disappointed and betrayed
by its own leadership, against the Fascist régime would be
transformed into a series of frightful bloody and futile convulsions. Ten proletarian insurrections, ten defeats one on top of
the other, could not debilitate and enfeeble the German working
class as much as a retreat before Fascism would weaken it at
the given moment, when the decision is still impending as to
the question of who is to become master in the German house-
hold. . . . "

Trotsky was a great executive, an organiser and adminis-
trator of the first rank. But the revolutionary temperament,
fortified by intense study, is as strong as in 1917. We are
in the presence of imponderables here. Some men have
it and some have not. But the workers will find such leadership again. The times are propitious. It is Stalinism that
blocks the way.

Trotsky, in the same pamphlet, showed the relationship
of forces in Germany and the overwhelming superiority
of the proletarian forces to the Fascist.

"In the meantime, the main strength of the Fascists is their
strength in numbers. Yes, they have received many votes. But
in the social struggle, votes are not decisive. The main army of
Fascism still consists of the petty bourgeoisie and the new
middle class: the small artisans and shopkeepers of the cities,
the petty officials, the employees, the technical personnel, the
intelligentsia, the impoverished peasantry. On the scales of
election statistics, one thousand Fascist votes weigh as much
as a thousand Communist votes. But on the scales of the
revolutionary struggle, a thousand workers in one big factory
represent a force a hundred times greater than a thousand petty
officials, clerks, their wives and their mothers-in-law. The great
bulk of the Fascists consists of human rubbish. . . . "

But the petty schemers in the Kremlin, intent on building
Socialism in a separate country and engaged in the life
and death struggle with proletariat and peasantry, the fruit
of their long neglect and terror against Trotskyism, with
Japan threatening them on the Eastern frontier, wanted
only to be left alone. Trotsky made demand after demand
for the United Front. The Communist Party should cease
its babble about Social Fascism and offer to the Social

Democratic leaders proposals for a concrete struggle against Bruening's decrees, for united committees to sweep the Fascists off the streets, and for mutual protection. *Rote Fahne*, the Communist paper, and *Vorwærts*, the Social Democratic paper, were bitter enemies. The party should propose to every Social Democratic worker in his district and openly to the Social Democratic leaders the formation of a defence corps. Much as the Communists detested *Vorwærts*, yet if the Fascists attacked *Vorwærts* they would fight valiantly in its defence. Conversely they would expect help from the Social Democratic workers if the Fascists attacked *Rote Fahne*. Every day, on every issue, in every conceivable manner, they should struggle for the United Front, and agitate among the Social Democratic workers to demand the United Front from their leaders, while themselves offering it. The Communist reply was, as always, a stream of abuse against the counter-revolutionary Trotskyists. The Social Democrats did make offers. All are not Citrines and Bevins. The Communists brushed them aside. In the *Communist International* of March 15, 1932, Piatnitzky wrote: "The Social Democrats too sometimes put forward the slogan of unity. And in this the renegade Trotsky hastens to their aid with his proposal for a 'bloc' between the Communists and the Social Democrats. . . . How is it possible to deduce . . . the necessity of establishing a 'bloc' with the German Social Democrats, say, for the struggle against Fascism, when the Social Democrats are doing nothing but helping the Fascists?" To-day, without a tremor, the members of the International will swear that they repeatedly offered the United Front to the Social Democracy and that the defeat was due to their refusal.

THE LAST PHASE

On March 13, 1932, at the first ballot for the election of President, Hindenburg received 18,661,736 votes, Hitler 11,338,571, Thaelmann five million. The Social Democrats voted for Hindenburg as the lesser evil. Hindenburg had not polled a majority of the total votes and a second ballot was required. Before this second ballot the Nazis terrorised Germany. Evidence transpired that despite Hitler's repeated assertions of coming to power by constitutional means, plans had been made for a *coup d'état*. On April 10, Hindenburg was re-elected with over nineteen million votes, Hitler's vote had increased by two million, but Thaelmann had lost a million votes. Three days after Bruening dissolved Hitler's Brownshirt organisation, but left the Nazi Party untouched, the same kind of dissolution that the Popular Front Government has recently applied to the Croix de Feu in France. On April 24 the Nazis won great victories in the State Parliament elections, and on May 30 Hindenburg dismissed Bruening and made Von Papen chancellor. It was a warning that the President was going to the Right. Sooner or later he would reach to Hitler. Sections of the bourgeoisie were still hoping to hold power without Hitler, or subordinate him to their own purposes. Some of them still feared the Socialism in his programme. All parties were hoping for an alleviation of the crisis to fall from heaven. Ultimately the bourgeoisie would have to come to Hitler, and the whole Communist agitation now could have centred round that single point: We struggle for the United Front, but Hitler means the destruction of the working-class movement, and the day the bourgeoisie place him in power we shall lead our workers and call on the Social Democrats for a mortal struggle.

On June 16 Von Papen, the aristocratic Junker, allowed the Brown-shirts once more to resume their activities, along with the Stahlhelm and the Republican Reichsbanner. We do not intend to go into the intrigues between Hitler, Von Papen and afterwards Schleicher. We have no time to spare for those who were horrified at Hindenburg, the old Prussian Field Marshal, "betraying the Republic" and making Hitler chancellor. Trotsky, in the middle of 1932, summed up the situation in words that ought to be branded on the foreheads of all Social Democratic, Liberal and other progressive persons: "A bloc of the Right Wing with the Centre would signify the 'legalisation' of the seizure of power by the National Socialists, that is, the most suitable cloak for the Fascist *coup d'état*. What relationships would develop in the early days between Hitler, Schleicher and the Centre leaders, is more important for them than it is for the German people. Politically all the conceivable combinations with Hitler signify the dissolution of bureaucracy, courts, police and army into Fascism. . . ."[1]

By the middle of 1932, under the stress of the crisis, German production was fifty-five per cent of what it had been in 1928. Nearly seventy-five per cent of industry was at a standstill. Between January, 1930, and January, 1933, imports declined by two-thirds and exports by nearly half. In three years £1,500,000,000 had been taken from the incomes of the workers. The average weekly wage in eighteen months had been reduced from £2 2s. 2d. to £1 2s. 6d. Unemployment benefit was 37s. a month. Tax after tax crippled the workers and poor, Crisis Tax, Occupation Tax, Head Tax, Salt Tax, Turnover Tax to the small trader. But on the other hand the big magnates had been granted financial aid amounting to £144,000,000. By this time the unemployed were nearly seven million, and there were 300 suicides per week. But with Germany breaking up under their feet the Social Democracy and all their kith and kin of the Second International stood firmly for their democracy; while the Third International persisted in its United Front from below and assured the workers that they need not be worried about Hitler because Fascism was there in Germany already.

The workers were joining the Communist Party, but the absence of discussion, the stifling of criticism, the Stalinist unity of the party which had ruined the C.P.S.U. had the national Communist parties in its grip. In the first quarter of 1932, 94,365 new members joined the party, but 53,879 left it.

Elections to the State Parliaments took place on April 14, 1932, and gave the Nazis 162 seats in Prussia, the Socialists 93, the Centre 67, the Communists 57. The Nazis seemed all-powerful, but the workers, in the face of the opposition of both bureaucracies and the increasing terror of the Nazis, were forming battalions of proletarian defence, and wherever they were formed they drove Hitler's mercenaries off the streets. In the Prussian Diet, however, the Communists joined with the Fascists and other reactionary

---

[1] *The Only Road*, Pioneer Publishers, New York, p. 19.

343

parties to pass a vote of censure on the Coalition Government, led by Braun. This Government nevertheless still continued to rule as an interregnum Government. The Communists, still in alliance with the Fascists, called for a new government. This obviously could only be the Fascists with their 162 seats. In the Reichstag Von Papen, having no power behind him, but still hoping to manœuvre without Hitler, had only one force to fear, the working-class movement. He knew, as all the bourgeois know, the stuff of which Social Democratic leaders are made. Yet the unity of the workers might be achieved over the heads of the makers of speeches and passers of resolutions, under the determined leadership of the Communist Party. The workers were fighting for it. But the Communists were striving to turn a Social Democratic Government out to put a Fascist Government in. Von Papen's road was therefore clear and he determined to take control of Prussia before the elections of July 31. The bitterest satirist of Social Democracy could not have invented what happened then.

Social Democracy Militant

On July 20, 1932, Von Papen sent for Severing and told him that the Prussian Government would be dissolved and a Commissar of the Reich, responsible to Von Papen and Hindenburg, placed in command. Severing said grandly that only force would make him submit. Basing his action on Article 48, Papen dissolved the Prussian Government and proclaimed martial law in Berlin. Grezhinsky, the Berlin police president, a Social Democrat, was informed of his dismissal by General Stuelpragel and refused to accept it. The German General knew the dirty cowards he was dealing with. He sent a lieutenant and four men, who arrested Grezhinsky and his assistant, and while their subordinates stood around in tears, carried them off. They had had the Prussian police under their command for twelve years; they could depend on them. Berlin was over seventy per cent Red, and not only in Berlin, but in all the great towns, the industrial workers were only waiting for the word. But before these two doughty warriors (how bravely they had shot down the Communists!) had spent

344

two hours in prison they had promised in writing not to perform their duties. So much for the police. Next was the Government itself. The new deputy-commissioner with less than half a dozen soldiers went to Severing, who, before this manifestation of force, surrendered at once. And that was the end of the twelve years of Social Democratic Government in Prussia.

The masses were stupefied; they could not understand it. The workers in the large works waited all night for a general strike.[1] During the night the Communists distributed an illegal leaflet calling for a general strike. But they had called for numerous general strikes before, and which Social Democratic worker would disobey his party and join them in a general strike for a Social Fascist Government, which was the chief enemy, and which they had just joined with the Fascists to weaken? In similar circumstances, in Russia between April and October, 1917, every disillusionment of the masses with the Soviet leaders resulted in a doubling and trebling of the influence of the Bolsheviks, so close did these stand behind the Soviet leaders, kicking them forward, and ceaselessly showing the masses who were responsible for the failure to implement the workers' demands. July 20 had opened the eyes of the German workers. Say the Petroffs: "A storm of indignation raged through the masses. They felt themselves to be shamefully misled, betrayed. But having been for long years bereft of any initiative of their own, these masses could not take action without their recognised leaders. So no hand moved, no shot was fired, not a single factory closed. July 20 passed, and it had brought to the masses only a boundless discouragement. But many a fist was clenched in the pocket—it was not quite clear against whom. . . . The dismissed Prussian Government later on appealed to the State Court. But it aroused among the workers only a smile of contempt."[2] It is at such moments that a revolutionary party which has followed a correct policy reaps its reward. That Braun and Severing had shot Communists made no difference to the necessity for the United Front.

---

[1] *The Secret of Hitler's Victory*, by Peter and Irma Petroff, 1934, p. 80.
[2] *The Secret of Hitler's Victory*, by Peter and Irma Petroff, 1934, p. 80.

Lenin in hiding and Trotsky in prison offered it all the more.

With every failure of the Left the Right increases in audacity. The Nazi terror increased. There were twenty-five murders during the election week-end of July 31. This violence and assurance on the one hand, the grievous failure of Social Democrats and Communists to supply anything like a lead on the other, resulted in a great increase of Nazi Votes—13,700,000 and 239 seats. The Social Democrats still had 7,000,000, the Communists 5,300,000. In Parliament the Papen Government was so openly dishonest and so reactionary that it aroused the indignation of the sorely-tried German working people, and the Nazis, by voting for it, compromised themselves in the eyes of their poorer supporters. Their violence during the election drove the proletariat still further to organise anti-Fascist defence corps. Many workers, in spite of the bureaucracy, were fighting to organise themselves as workers, but Social Democrats and Communists fought to keep these on party lines. "The workers had at last recognised that their disunity was the cause of their weakness. They energetically demanded the tearing down of all barriers. But their leaders always met their demands with dishonesty, hypocrisy, and sabotage. So it was with the Social Democrats; so it was with the Communists."[1] One can no more quarrel with the Social Democratic leaders than one can quarrel with parasites for sucking the blood of the animals on which they live. That is their nature. But the Communist action was unnatural. Stalin had analysed the situation. Let Hitler come in; he will soon collapse and then will be the revolution. In September, 1932, the Twelfth Plenum of the E.C.C.I. was held, a Plenum which should have had one subject on the agenda—the coming struggle in Germany. The Executive studiously avoided giving prominence to Germany. "Only by directing the main blows against Social Democracy, this social mainstay of the bourgeoisie—will it be possible to strike at and defeat the chief class enemy of the proletariat—the bourgeoisie."[2] That the whole future

[1] *The Secret of Hitler's Victory*, by Peter and Irma Petroff.
[2] *The Twelfth Plenum. Theses and Resolutions* (in English), Moscow.

fate of the International was trembling in the balance was far from the minds of these bureaucrats. One section of the report is grandiloquently headed, "The Development of the Revolutionary Upsurge and the Preparation of the Struggle for the Dictatorship of the Proletariat." But Germany is not even first among equals. China has two lines, Poland two-and-a-half lines: Germany two-and-a-half lines, as follows: "an increase in the mass influence of the Communist Party; Social Democratic workers, in spite of their leaders, have begun to resist the terror of Fascist gangs"; Belgium and India have more space than Germany. On the specific tasks of the major Communist parties, Germany has just one more line than France, and Germany, France and China are equally treated. The Plenum was much more concerned with a resolution on the war in the Far East, and the Tasks of the Communists in the Struggle against Imperialist War and Military Intervention against the U.S.S.R.

In the official Guide to the Plenum it is the same. True they say, "Of exceptional importance to the fate of revolution in Europe and the whole world is the revolutionary upsurge in Germany." But Poland has more space than Germany, and we are informed that "the growth of the revolutionary upsurge in Poland, along with the growth of the revolutionary upsurge in Germany, is *the decisive factor for preparing the revolutionary outburst in the chief Capitalist countries.*"[1]

Stalin and his minions in September, 1932, put Poland on a level with Germany, and told the International that the revolutionary upsurge in these two countries was a factor for preparing outbursts elsewhere.

The Guide warned against exaggerations, but explained in detail why the chief blow should be directed against Social Fascism, and why the United Front be formed only from below. No call to the masses of the world, especially in Britain, France, Poland and Austria, to stand by in defence of the German proletariat, as had been done in the first part of 1923 and when Chiang Kai-Shek was leading the Chinese workers to victory.

[1] Italics theirs.

Independent thought having long been destroyed in the International, all its writers had developed the complementary quality of embellishing Stalin's great contribution to Marxism with loving and respectful ingenuity. The MacDonald Government was Fascist, so was the Government of Hoover, and the Government of the Gaekwar of Baroda. Anarchists were Anarcho-Fascists, Syndicalists were Syndicalo-Fascists, the Trotskyists were Trotskyo-Fascists.[1] All these puerilities, off-shoots of the Oriental idolatry Stalin demanded from all in the Soviet Union, could only harm the movement everywhere. In Germany, however, it was helping to push the working-class into the jaws of Hitler. The German Communist Party had been calling the Bruening Government Fascist, the Papen Government Fascist, later they were to call the Schleicher Government Fascist also. In Germany Right Opposition and Left had been urging that this nonsense should cease; the Left Opposition wanted the various forms of government clearly analysed before the workers, always pointing out that Hitler's coming into power would mean the destruction of the movement and should therefore be the signal for a nation-wide struggle beginning with the general strike and ending, come what might, in revolution. Said the Guide to the Twelfth Plenum: "The Social Democrats and their Trotskyite and Brandlerite agents, while utilising this clever manœuvring of the German bourgeoisie, deny the Fascist character of the Papen-Schleicher Government, attempting to implant among the masses deceptive illusions that the victory of the Fascist dictatorship is impossible unless Hitler comes to power, unless the Fascist domination is openly proclaimed, unless there is a German edition of the 'march on Rome.'" From between the lines peeped hints of Stalin's curious ideas on German class-relations and international politics. The German bourgeoisie, said the Guide, were afraid of Hitler. "In addition they are afraid that if Hitler comes to power it will create an extremely intense *international* situation for Germany, and will hasten the maturing of a revolutionary crisis." Further-

[1] This list is taken from the introduction by Max Schachtman to *The Third International after Lenin.*

348

more, why argue about names. Hitler was already in power. "In Germany Social Democracy has called on the workers three times in six months to smash Fascism at the ballot-box. The result is the Hitler Government and the establishment of the Fascist dictatorship."

The voice might be the voice of Manuilsky, but the ideas are unmistakable. That is the mentality of Stalin from his very first writings to the present day.

The Masses Betrayed

In that very September Trotsky finished *The Only Road*. It was one long plea for the United Front. "How much time has been lost—aimlessly, senselessly, shamefully! How much could have been achieved, even in the last two years alone! Was it not clear in advance that monopolistic capital and its Fascist army would drive the Social Democracy with fists and blackjacks toward the road of opposition and of self-defence? This prognosis should have been unfolded before the eyes of the entire working class, the initiative should have been retained firmly in our hands at every new stage. It was not necessary to shout, nor to scream. An open game could have been played quietly. It would have sufficed to formulate, in a clear-cut manner, the inevitability of every next step of the enemy and to set up a practical programme for a united front, without exaggerations and without haggling, but also without weakness and without concessions. How high the Communist party would stand to-day if it had assimilated the A.B.C. of Leninist policy and applied it with the necessary perseverance!"[1] Millions were disillusioned with the Social Democratic Party, but for them to leave it or at least turn elsewhere there must be another party, and every action of the Communist Party drove them away instead of bringing them nearer. There was still time. If, however, the party did not mend its ways, then the Third International was doomed and the international proletarian movement would have to begin all over again. It was then that he forecast the new Fourth International, the very idea of which is such a thorn in

[1] *The Only Road*, p. 35.

349

Stalin's side and which he is striving to destroy. "Should the worst variant materialise; should the present official parties, despite all our efforts, be led to a collapse by the Stalinist bureaucracy; should it mean in a certain sense to begin all over again, then the new International will trace its genealogy from the ideas and cadres of the Communist Left Opposition."[1] But that was still to come.

But the workers of both parties, so treacherously misled, were taking action together. Between September and November the united proletarian front in the streets grew. In September the Reichstag was dissolved. The reactionary nature of the Nazis, proved in the last Reichstag, and the instinctive strivings of the proletariat struck a great blow at Fascism. In the elections of November 6 the Nazis lost nearly two million votes and thirty-four seats. The vagaries of history had given the Communists one more opportunity to rally the forces of the proletariat. The Right were conscious of the danger to themselves. Some of them had been opposing Hitler, but they realised that if the process of disintegration continued German Capitalism would lose its only mass support, many of the lowest ranks of the Nazis would swing to the Left, and capitalist Germany would be in serious danger. Hitler, playing for position, moved to the Left, and Nazis and Communists led a great transport strike in Berlin, against the wishes of the Social Democrats. They also fought the police side by side.

At the elections in November the Communist Party increased its vote by twenty per cent, and the bourgeoisie made yet one more move. On December 2 Von Schleicher became chancellor. In addition to trying to win over the Trade Unions to his side, Von Schleicher was careful to give free play to the Nazis, and granted them permission to hold a demonstration in the east of Berlin, the working-class district. The Social Democrats asked their followers, as usual, not to take part in the resistance organised by the Communists. But many of them came out, and the Nazis with all their bluff and bluster had to be heavily protected by a huge force of police, armed with machine-guns and armoured cars. The workers, aware of

[1] *The Only Road*, p. 91.

the danger, were getting closer and closer together on the streets. But the Communists, rooted in their Social Fascism and the United Front only from below, continued with their slogan of Social Democracy as the main enemy, and the Social Democrats were only too glad to point to the Communists as the real enemy of working-class unity, and shelter their own cowardice behind it. Then on January 30, 1933, Hindenburg appointed Hitler chancellor. To the Communist Party it was not a matter of great importance; merely another Fascist Government. They issued one of their rhetorical appeals for a general strike. It failed, as it was bound to fail. A general strike cannot be called for at will. As a deliberate act by a revolutionary party it is the fruit of a long preparation among all classes of workers, revolutionary and otherwise. But they did not mean the general strike. Long before Hitler they had been preparing to go underground. In December, Stampfer, a Social Democratic editor, had written in *Vorwærts* suggesting united action between the two parties. The Communist Party took no notice. In March Hitler burnt the Reichstag. In those desperate days Stampfer went to the Russian Embassy asking for assistance, seeking ways and means to form some sort of United Front. The Communist leaders ridiculed the idea. Telegrams, letters and resolutions poured in from all over the country asking them to resist. They had never had any intention of resisting. They left the masses leaderless. "After Hitler, our turn." Meanwhile the Social Democracy was still the chief enemy. Let the workers watch and see how the Social Democracy would be the chief support of Hitler. They said it when Hitler came to power and for one year afterwards. Hitler out-manœuvred his nationalist allies, and using the Reichstag fire as the basis of his propaganda, threw the whole force of the State into a new election. The results testify as to what was the strength of the working-class movement in Germany. All Hitler's propaganda, his violence and intimidation, could not shake it. Losses were negligible. But Fascism has its duty to perform. At the last election in September Hitler had had only one-third of the votes. But he was powerful enough to begin and conclude the systematic extermination of every organisation that was not Nazi. Power, it was once more proved, does not depend on an election majority.

THE EBB TAKEN FOR THE FLOW

Then began the most dreadful part of this dreadful record of stupidity and crime. The Social Democratic leaders, proverbially stupid, had no idea of what was about to happen to them, and even if they had it would have made no difference. They were quite prepared to serve Hitler, and in the Reichstag had declared the Hitler Government to be a "constitutional and parliamentary Government." Leipart, the Trade Union leader, was quite prepared to hand over the Trade Unions to Hitler and accept their reorganisation "on the Italian model." He offered "the knowledge and experience" of himself and his colleagues to Hitler. They had sent the funds abroad. Hitler asked them to bring them back—they obligingly did so. Wels, in the Reichstag, offered to support Hitler's foreign policy—a good beginning. It should be noted that the democracy these gentlemen defend is to be defended only from the Left. Given their jobs and the opportunity to "protest," they can accommodate themselves to any amount of inroads on democracy from the Right. But the Fascist boot they bent so dutifully to kiss was only seeking to consolidate its stance before kicking these worthless turncoats from the jobs and pensions to which they clung so desperately. On May 1 Hitler ordered a National Socialist Labour demonstration. The Social Democractic leaders recommended the workers to go. On that night Hitler began the raids, the mass arrests, the murders, the confiscations of buildings and funds, directed especially against the Trade Union movement. The bureaucrats fled for their lives.

But all through and right up to early 1935 the International learnt nothing, understood nothing, and literally sent thousands of German workers to torture, imprisonment and death. This must be traced in detail, for it shows that Stalin, working out his tortuous policies, had had no idea of what Fascism meant, of what it would do in Germany. Stalin and the Stalinists really and honestly thought that Hitler was just such another as Schleicher or Papen. It was not only the demoralising defeat without a struggle that has so crushed the German proletariat and broken the faith of all Marxists in the International. It was the policy of the International after the defeat which ruined German Socialism for perhaps a decade, and started the movement to break with the Stalinists once and for all and build the new International.

On April 1 Fritz Heckert, as representative of the Communist Party of Germany, made his report to the Executive of the Communist International. Stalin's prestige came first. "As far back as 1924, the leader of the international proletariat, Comrade Stalin, gave an estimate unsurpassed in its exactness and perspicacity of the evolution of Social Democracy towards Fascism—an estimate which lies at the basis of the programme of the Comintern and the policy of the Communist Party of Germany. . . . Fascism, said Comrade Stalin . . ."[1] and Heckert quoted in full the passage in which Stalin had proved to the satisfaction of the whole International that Social Democracy is a wing of Fascism, and they were not antipodes but twins. "Everything which has happened in Germany has fully confirmed the correctness of Comrade Stalin's prognosis. Hitler does not reject the support of Social Democracy." Never in history has been such degrading fanaticism.

The first law of Stalinism is to praise Stalin. The second is to abuse Trotsky. It was on Trotsky that Heckert's wrath chiefly fell for the heinous crime of proposing the United Front, and writing in the *Manchester Guardian* that it was the refusal to form the United Front on the basis of defence of parliamentary democracy and of the mass Trade Unions which had caused the defeat. Trotsky, said Heckert, was a "Social Fascist," Leipart was "Trotsky's ally," Trotsky was "the confederate of Hitler." "The Welses and Leiparts, however, do not come alone. They come to Hitler with Trotsky. It was he, Trotsky, who, carrying out the social orders of Hitler, tried to sling mud

[1] *Why Hitler in Germany?* Report of Fritz Heckert, representative of the C.P. of Germany, to the E.C.C.I., with Resolution Adopted, Modern Books, p. 24.

at the only party which is struggling against Fascism in the most difficult conditions."

The Praesidium, having heard the report, declared: "that the political line and the organisational policy pursued by the Central Committee of the Communist Party of Germany, led by Comrade Thaelmann, before and at the time of the Hitler coup, was quite correct." Then came a typical feature of Stalin's Leninism. Exactly as in Germany in 1923 and in China in 1927, having proved their previous follies, which had ruined the revolution, correct, the International called upon the German workers to prepare for the coming revolution. "The revolutionary upsurge in Germany will inevitably grow in spite of the Fascist terror. The resistance of the masses to Fascism is bound to increase. The establishment of an open Fascist dictatorship, by destroying all the democratic illusions among the masses and liberating them from the influence of Social Democracy, accelerates the rate of Germany's development towards proletarian revolution. . . . It is necessary to strengthen the Party and strengthen all the mass organisations of the proletariat, to prepare the masses for decisive revolutionary battles, for the overthrow of the Fascist dictatorship by an armed rebellion."[1] This desperate folly, approved by the Praesidium and persisted in for nearly a year, cost the lives of hundreds and the imprisonment of thousands of the finest and bravest German comrades. That Stalin and Litvinov did not believe a word of all this will, however, soon be made clear.

All through that year of 1933 the E.C.C.I. led the German workers to believe that Hitler's defeat was near. The more Hitler battered the workers and concentrated power into his own hands, the more the International sent them into the open on strikes and demonstrations, delivering them to their enemies. In the middle of 1933 Piatnitzky published a document called "The Present Situation in Germany."[2] Hitler had already launched his attack on the Trade Unions, and Piatnitzky, still encased in the armour-plate of Social Fascism, explained why. It was merely a matter of jobs. "The Fascists needed for

[1] Ibid, p. 24.   [2] Modern Books.

their own supporters the 400,000 soft jobs occupied by Social Democrats." This, however, was "no easy task. . . . In order that this might be achieved, it was necessary to implicate the Social Democrats in the Van der Lubbe affair, even if but for a few days, so as to provide the Fascists with a pretext for closing down their Press during the excitement—for they might possibly think of exposing the outrageous Fascist provocation. . . . At the same time the Fascists made use of the Social Democrats to penetrate through them into the working class, and this could be done much more easily if they thrashed them soundly first. . . . "

Until Stalin gave the word that Fascism and Social Fascism were no longer twins his bureaucrats were physically incapable of seeing the wholesale destruction of Social Democracy going on before their very eyes. "But it would be a great mistake to think that the Social Democratic party has already been destroyed in Germany. Gradually the Fascists will let it have its Press back and will then permit it to continue the demagogy which it carried on before Hitler came to power. . . . The C.P.G. will have to put in a great deal of work to convince the Social Democratic workers that the Social Democrats are responsible for the fact that the Fascists came to power in Germany. Anyone who thinks that the objective conditions will themselves do this work without systematic, bold and self-sacrificing effort on the part of the C.P.G. is making a great mistake." A long experience has taught all Stalin's servants that the safest policy, the only safe policy, is to go on saying what he has said until he changes his mind. It is not facts, but what Stalin says, that matters. Piatnitzky claimed to see that the German proletariat was recovering from the Fascist blows. "The German Communists have shown that they know no fear. They go out into the streets. They allow their names to be openly put forward as candidates at factory committee elections in spite of Fascist terror, etc." One after another, still waiting for the Communist revolution, the German comrades were driven straight into the concentration camps and the torture chambers.

He admitted that there was a temporary retreat, but

355

"that, however, did not imply the collapse of the process of the maturing of the revolutionary crisis." The German bourgeoisie was turning and twisting like an animal wounded though not yet fatally. "In proportion as the C.P. of Germany liberates the majority of the workers from the influence of Social Democracy and leads them to the struggle against the Fascists, the conditions will mature under which armed insurrection will be converted from a slogan of propaganda into a slogan of action, under which the Party will pass on to the direct realisation of this slogan." So it went on all through the year.

In December, 1933, the Thirteenth Plenum of the E.C.C.I. was held. By this time the working-class organisations in Germany had been crushed except for a nucleus of Communists fighting magnificently but misguidedly for revolution. In its official report[1] the Plenum still harped on Social Fascism: "German Social Democracy was and still remains the banner-bearer of all the parties of the Second International which follow the steps of German Social Democracy. Social Democracy continues to play the rôle of the main social prop of the bourgeoisie also in the countries of open Fascist dictatorship. . . ." In Germany, said the Plenum, "enormous revolutionary energy is being accumulated among the masses and a new revolutionary upsurge is already beginning." A special section was headed "Against Social Democracy and for a United Front from Below." The Plenum confirmed that the policy had been correct. But here there was a hitch. Of the three leaders of the German Communist party whose tactical line was held up as correct, Thaelmann was in prison, and Remmele and Neumann had escaped. These two men, less docile than the well-meaning but too loyal Thaelmann, had opposed the line before Hitler came to power. Now, their eyes fully opened at last by the fate to which they had led their followers, they stated that the movement in Germany was defeated, that Hitler was firmly in the saddle, that it would take a long period to rebuild the movement, and that only on an honest and realistic investigation into the causes of the defeat. Others

[1] *Thirteenth Plenum of the E.C.C.I. Theses and Decisions.* Modern Books.

356

in the International were saying the same. This for Stalin would have been a disaster. The Plenum condemned them and called on "all sections of the Comintern to ruthlessly root out opportunism in all its forms, and, above all, Right opportunism (Remmele, Neumann, the defeatists in other countries in their estimate of the prospects of the German revolution), for unless this is done the Communist parties will not be able to lead the working masses up to the victorious struggles for the Soviet power.[1] Social Fascism remained and when it went it was not on account of the working-class movement but because Moscow's foreign policy had changed.

[1]P. 23. Ibid.

Chapter 13

THE GREAT RETREAT

Inside Russia the bureaucracy had made its first concessions in May, 1932, and the rightward swing was accelerated by the German defeat.

Beginning first with the peasantry, it spread to the proletariat, gathered strength and permeated the whole economic, social and political life of Russia. Stalin now ruled supreme. Every rival had been disgraced, the party was his docile instrument. The bureaucracy, welded by the combined fight against peasantry and proletariat, was now a distinct caste of millions, through Stalin and the apparatus controlling all the organs of politics and economics. Deprived of Trade Unions and Press, their Soviets being merely a screen for the manipulation of Stalin's monolithic party, the workers were helpless.

The Placation of the Peasant

The first business of the régime was to placate the peasantry. Despite the entering into Socialism Stalin had realised even before the bombastic report of 1930 that the abolition of the market and Socialist exchange would have to be put off for some little time. Early in 1930 the Central Committee had issued a circular prohibiting the closing down of markets, re-opening the bazaars and warning party members, in large letters, "NOT TO HINDER the sale by peasants, including members of collective farms, of their products in the market." As the Fascist menace forced itself upon their consciousness the Stalinists had to restore production and take measures to unify the nation. The peasant is not interested in statistics of collective farm construction. If collectivisation had given him such a standard of life, such facilities for education and culture

358

as would make him see that it was better than private property, he would have cheerfully given up his private ownership. But only Stalin could believe that Russian industry could do this for over a hundred million peasants in five years. There was only one thing to be done— stimulate peasant production by encouraging him to sell. This meant the restoration of the market. The collective farms gave the State a broader basis from which to fight private ownership, but the struggle between the two continues, as it will continue to do until the socialised industry of Germany or Britain is thrown in the scale against the backwardness of the countryside.

In January, 1934, Stalin and Molotov signed a decree giving permission to the Central Consumers' Co-operative and its chain of subsidiaries to buy 100 million poods (about sixty million bushels of grain) from collective and individual farmers. The decree established the principle that such purchase of grain should "serve the interest of the sellers. . . .

"Collective farms, collective farmers and individual peasants retain the right to sell their grain at the market price in city and village markets and at railroad stations. . . .

"Administrative pressure to influence the collective farmers and peasants to sell their grain is categorically forbidden."[1]

In that same winter, in the far-Eastern region most threatened by Japan, collective farms were exempted from delivering grain and rice to the State for ten years, individual farms for five. In a number of other districts the quota of products was reduced by fifty per cent.[2] Exemptions were given all over the Soviet Union for 1934 to encourage trade-plants, cattle-trading and collective farm-trade. Collective farm-trade became the slogan of the day, and was proved to be Socialism. But it is deeds and not words that count with the peasant, and in January, 1935, came the new decrees restoring private property on the countryside. The collective farms were given to the owners for

[1] *Moscow News*, January 27, 1934.
[2] *International Press Correspondence*, December 22, 1933.

ever and ever. It was a last desperate attempt to assure the embittered peasantry that never again would the Soviet régime interfere with them. Before the growing wrath of the proletariat the bureaucracy needed some mass support. Socialism was defined anew. "It is a deliberate attempt to mislead the working peasantry in the capitalist countries when they are told that the collectivisation of the working peasantry deprives them of anything they have owned. On the contrary: it leaves them in possession of all their property and adds much more to it."[1]

The collective farmer was given a plot of land for himself and allowed to cultivate it for his own profit. He need only do two days work on the collective farm and that on the basis of piece-work. After the Government tax is paid the Socialist peasant receives his share of farm-produce, not in money but in kind, which he may sell where he pleases. The peasant may own one cow, two calves, two pigs with their litter, ten sheep, twenty bee-hives, and an unlimited quantity of poultry. Such yearly surplus as he may have over this he will certainly sell to his own private benefit. But this is only the lower limit. The private property allowed by law proceeds by upward stages to the districts occupied solely in rearing live-stock, where the collective peasant will own eight to ten cows, 100 to 150 sheep, ten horses, five to eight camels, and unlimited quantities of small livestock.[2] On the depleted countryside this is a fortune. Behind the façade of the collective farm, the kulak, liquidated at such enormous cost, is on his way back. Nothing can stop him, and Stalin has learnt another lesson in Marxism—that only an industry far beyond the capacity of the Soviet Union for another generation can liquidate the kulak. His whole policy for five years, which brought so much loss and suffering, has not been able to prevent a process of differentiation which is growing and will grow with every succeeding year. But there is not only the differentiation between individual collective farmers. There is the differentiation between collective farm and

[1] *International Press Correspondence*, March 30, 1935.
[2] *International Press Correspondence*, March 30, 1935.

collective farm. Great or lesser fertility of soil, distance from or proximity to industrial centres or easy transport, the free play of the market, means that certain collective farms are making rapid progress while other are falling behind. *Pravda* of September 30, 1935, has already spoken of millionaire collective farms. These can buy better equipment and thus increase their production. They can invest in State-loans and draw interest, they can speculate on the market. Early in 1936 the State, in order to corner the market against the speculators, had to issue a decree offering inducements for sale to itself. From 50 to 100 double centners, the increase in price is fifteen per cent, from 100 to 150, twenty per cent, and on a graduated scale to an increase of ninety per cent for sales to the State of from 800 to 1,000 centners; every collective farm which sells to the State over 1,000 double centners of wheat will receive double price for the entire quantity sold. Individual farmers will receive similar bonuses, but on a smaller scale. Speculation is rife. The division into rich and poor goes and will go ceaselessly on, with the inevitable social and political consequences.

The downward trend in grain production has been checked by the large-scale organisation of the collective farms, and there has been an increase since 1932. But the amount produced per hectare is still little more than it was in 1913, and even the Webbs hesitate to say with certainty that the food position is safe for the future. Actual achievement can be easily measured. The original plan in 1927, envisaging a collectivisation of twenty per cent of the farmers by 1932, forecast 106 million tons of grain as the probable production. Thousands of millions of roubles have been spent on agriculture. Hundreds of thousands of tractors have been distributed over the country-side. The sown area has been increased by millions of hectares. The kulak was liquidated at the cost of an administrative devastation such as has no equal in modern history. Yet the grain production for 1935, with ninety per cent of the countryside collectivised, is 92[1] instead of the 106 million tons which Stalin, in July, 1930, promised

[1] *International Press Correspondence*, Nov. 14, 1936.

to achieve in less than a year. While the pigs have increased, the cattle are still fourteen million less than they were in 1929, the horses still little more than half what they were in 1929, the sheep and goats still less than half. The Soviet Union is still an agricultural country, and a very backward agricultural country. It is on the basis of increasing class differentiation within low production, bitter disillusionment after fantastic hopes, that arise the present and future troubles of the Stalinist régime.

THE SUCCESSES OF THE PLAN

And yet the five-year plan won great successes. In the actual achievements the Stalinists in their propaganda have as usual shamelessly lied, and their claim to fulfilment of over ninety per cent is so flagrantly false as not to be worth repeating. In addition to the monumental failure in agriculture, the plan was twenty-eight per cent short in coal, sixty-two per cent short in pig-iron, seventy-four per cent short in steel, eighty-two per cent short in rolled steel, twenty-eight per cent short in oil, fifty-eight per cent short in electric power, ninety per cent short in motor cars, eighty-one per cent short in tractors, eighty-six per cent short in copper, forty-eight per cent short in housing, and sixty-two per cent short in railway-building. It must be remembered too, that Russia, a backward country, offered more scope for increased industrialisation than a country already highly developed. Nevertheless when every allowance has been made, the fact remains that in a world-crisis, with an economy steadily falling, the Soviet Union, from its own resources, has shown a progress that has not been equalled by any Capitalist country in its most expansive period. Whereas, if we take production in 1929 as 100, the industrial output of the U.S.A. in 1934 was 67, that of Great Britain 96, that of Germany 86, France 71, Italy 80 and the world as a whole 76, Russia went from 100 to 239. Had the Social Democrats had the courage to make Germany a Soviet State in 1919, the compensating economy of both these countries under collective ownership and the leadership of the German proletariat would have produced results which would have astonished the world.[1] But the average production per head of the population is still low. Follows inevitably competition, between the unskilled labourer and the skilled, between the skilled labourer and the petty bureaucrat, between these and the upper bureaucracy and the highly-skilled technicians. Nothing can stop this, and a rise in productivity can intensify instead of lessening the economic and therefore political divisions in the population. The Bolshevik Party intended by Lenin to regulate economics and politics in the interests of the workers was now the instrument of the bureaucracy against workers and peasants, but chiefly against the advanced workers seeking to make Leninism a reality. And this was taking place in a country bearing the scars and deep wounds and festering sores of the most turbulent twenty years in all history. The social contradictions, and the contradiction between the promises of the bureaucracy and its actions, all could only be met by an increasing terror.

THE TERROR

The economic upheaval, the social crises, had been overcome, could only have been overcome by increasing terror and the grip of the ruling caste. Nothing could stop that process now. The fate of Trotsky, Zinoviev, Kamenev, Radek, Bucharin, Rykov, Tomsky, warned all who dared to oppose: their personal supporters would be ruthlessly cut away, they themselves would be accused of counter-revolution in the Stalinist-controlled Press, Stalin's majority would condemn them, and they would have to take the road to exile or make humiliating confessions of penitence. In 1928 it was still possible to argue with Stalin at a congress. But after his crushing of opposition in early 1930 the party itself sat and listened to his pronouncements in silent terror. Through cynicism or because a pretence cannot be eternally maintained, there were times when his speeches showed the true state of affairs. Announcing the return to 100 per cent collectivisation in July, 1930, he showed to what a pitch of terror-stricken servility he had already reduced the

Mr. Lloyd George knows that very well. This great Liberal was one of the first to welcome Hitler's coming to power. These Germans, he said in effect, will know how to manage their Communism.

party: "Here and there voices can be heard to the effect that it is necessary to abandon the policy of mass collectivisation. We have information to the effect that even in our Party there are some who support this 'idea.' But such things can be said only by those who, willingly or unwillingly, have joined forces with the enemies of Communism."[1] Party members, it was clear, not only dared not speak at the congress. If they criticised even among themselves Stalin was aware of it. And the phrase, "joined forces with the enemies of Communism," was not rhetoric. The critic, whoever he was, would be accused, like Rykov, of counter-revolution and wishing to restore Capitalism. If that was the lot of party members, it could be imagined what scope was allowed to the ordinary worker. Through the years of revolution and civil war Lenin had held the yearly congresses, with fierce debates for the clarification of policy and the education of the party and the country. But during the critical four years after 1930 Stalin held no congress. Then in January, 1934, came the Seventeenth Congress. He delivered a long report: "It must be admitted that the toiling peasantry, our Soviet peasantry, has completely and irrevocably come under the red flag of Socialism." There were thousands of delegates there from all over Russia, who knew the state of the countryside. The decrees restoring private property were still to come. But no man dared speak. Stalin reviewed the work of the Central Committee. The privileges of the bureaucracy, now all-powerful, had been causing discontent among the masses, and Stalin explained the Marxian conception of equality. We need weary the reader only with the conclusion: "To draw from this the conclusion that socialism calls for equality, for the levelling of the requirements of the members of society, for the levelling of their tastes and of their personal lives, that according to Marxism all should wear the same clothes, and eat the same dishes and in the same quantity—means talking banalities and slandering Marxism." What mortal had ever thought so! But this explanation sufficed.

The report was typical, including the usual shrill abuse

[1] *Leninism*, Vol. II, p. 327.

of Trotskyism. But what was most significant is that after this exhibition the delegates, meeting to discuss the economic political and social results of the five-year plan, the greatest economic experiment in history, made no single objection to Stalin's lies and evasions. Many spoke, but after the debate, in a speech lasting three minutes, Stalin summed up: "As you know, no objections whatever were raised against the report. Hence, an extraordinary ideological political and organisational compactness of the ranks of our Party has been displayed." He modestly begged to be excused a reply. The delegates shouted: "Long live Stalin!" and all standing sang the International. Nothing in the history of the Soviet Union so completely sums up the internal situation as this incredible session.

Those who like H. G. Wells are begging the Soviet authorities to introduce free speech seem to think that free speech is introduced or withdrawn at the caprice of rulers. There was a moment in 1923 when the party stood at the cross-roads. It took the wrong turning, and the session of 1934 was the culmination of an inevitable process. Stalin does not introduce free speech because he dare not. The cult of the leader in Italy, Germany and Russia is to-day due to the same cause, the unbearable social and political tension in the country. Fascism is bankrupt. With the help of revolution in the West Russia has a great future, and even without that revolution has won and still wins great successes. But that vast difference does not alter the proved quality of the Stalin régime, the reasons for it, the immense dangers it holds for international Socialism.

TROTSKYISM RESURGENT

The first plan was safely over, the solid industrial foundations had been laid. The remorseless economic pressure on the masses could be eased. More provision could be made for consumption goods. The standard of living began slowly to rise again to what it had been before the 1928 crisis. There are numerous indications that Stalin and the bureaucracy, imperialist war excluded, looked forward to the steady building of some sort of Socialism and the liquidation of Trotskyism in an era of prosperity

365

and internal peace. To their horror they once again had to learn another elementary lesson of Marxism. The masses during the last years of the five-year plan, half-starved and shivering, had been too cowed to fight. But as their standard of living began to rise they gained strength and started on the inevitable struggle with the bureaucracy; for their political privileges, destroyed by the bureaucratic domination of the Soviets, for their industrial privileges stolen from them by the merging of the Trade Unions with the State. Stalin regularly purged the party, and then announced that it was united as never before. But the discontent among the masses continually forced itself even into the bureaucratised party. And this mass discontent, as it realised what Stalin's Socialism meant, began to centre around Trotskyism. It was not surprising.

For Stalin, haunted by Trotskyism, had never ceased to besmirch it and he had done all he could to degrade Trotsky's name in the eyes of the Russian people. Ever since 1923, and indeed long before, Stalin's curious mind had conceived the idea of rewriting the history of the October Revolution so as to eliminate the part Trotsky had played in it and substitute himself instead. Year by year the history of the party, of the revolution, of the whole country, was rewritten. Trotsky's picture was taken out of the composite photographs where he stood side by side with Lenin. Year after year Stalin's meagre contribution to October became more and more; year after year Trotsky's less and less. Trotskyism had been finally liquidated in 1927, but every year saw the campaign against it steadily increasing. The bourgeois empiricists, who have seen in this nothing more than a personal vendetta, have once more proved their incapability to understand history and particularly Russian history. Never was a campaign more solidly based on a political issue. Trotsky was expelled from the party in 1927, but all through 1928 the failure in China and the failure of the kulak policy had to be covered up with louder and louder blasts against Trotskyism. Industrialisation and collectivisation had to be purged of every memory of Trotskyism, which had advocated them so long. When Trotsky condemned the over-stretched tempo of industrialisation and collectivisation and the lie of having entered into Socialism, Stalin, confident of success, derided Trotskyism, but as party and masses recognised the limitations of Stalin's Socialism he of necessity had to detroy Trotskyism once more. Trotsky had ridiculed Social Fascism as the crowning example of Stalin's ignorance and stupidity and had fought for the United Front in Germany. The press of the whole International had condemned him. But when Social Fascism had to be dropped, and it became clear that the United Front might have saved Germany from Fascism, the only thing to do was to fulminate against Trotskyism.

Had Stalin been more cautious in attacking Trotsky and boasted less of all he intended to do after the five-year plan, his control of the Press would have kept Trotsky's name from the Russian people. Had Stalin's policy at home and abroad been successful, Trotskyism would have died a natural death. But, as it was, the masses were never allowed to forget Trotskyism. The Permanent Revolution seemed to haunt Stalin. Like so much of Stalin's policy this reaped its own reward. Abuse of Trotsky had been drummed so steadily by Stalin into Russian ears that now at least one thing was certain—Trotskyism was the direct antithesis of Stalinism. Thus it was that the mass discontent in Russia, the opposition to tyranny in the party, the protest against the ceaseless terror, began to crystallise round Trotskyism. The Left Opposition had traced this process carefully. The first hint the outside world had was the terror after, Kirov's murder in 1934.

Marxism, Leninism, Trotskyism, condemn terrorism, Marxism being concerned with mass movements and political and social revolutions, not with murder. This has been revolutionary policy for nearly a hundred years. No single word of Trotsky or any Trotskyist can be found in all their writings advocating terrorism. The first reports of the trial spoke of White Guards and a Latvian Consul. The conjunction of Trotsky and terrorism might seem to be fantastic. But the Left Opposition knew the situation in the country and knew Stalin. As far back as 1929 Trotsky, after his expulsion, had warned the

367

Opposition that sooner or later Stalin would draw a trail of blood between the Soviet régime and the Trotskyists. He needed it for his campaigns.[1] Stalin ordered mass shootings and arrests of all whom he suspected of opposition, under a general charge of Trotskyism. An Opposition Circular of December 10[2] warned Trotskyist groups every where to be on guard against a frame-up, and it followed within a few days. Trotsky was directly accused of organising the murder, Zinoviev and Kamenev were implicated, banished, confessed to "moral responsibility" and were sentenced to long terms of imprisonment. Stalin feared them as old associates of Trotsky who might form a rallying centre for the militants in the masses and dissentient elements in the party. Ultimately thousands of persons were deported from Leningrad, where Zinoviev had formerly been president of the Soviet, and people could not be bluffed with lies about Trotsky and the great part Stalin had played in October. To whoever had eyes to see it was clear that the proletariat was on the march again and that the advance-guard was pressing the régime.

The mass-arrests, the shootings, would have been meaningless otherwise. January, 1935, brought the abolition of the ration-cards for bread. The last privilege of the Socialist worker was now gone, for his few roubles a month now had to buy bread at the same price as that paid by the officials with thousands. In that same January came the decrees re-establishing private property on the countryside, and the announcement of the new Constitution giving equal voting power to the peasantry—destroying the Soviets by making the unit of representation territorial instead of being based on the factories; and by direct election to a parliament placing the function of government as in bourgeois countries out of even the nominal control of the masses. The face of the Stalinist régime was now turned definitely to the right. The fate of Zinoviev and Kamenev, the terror in Leningrad, had shown that there was no legal way out of the tyranny and terror of the régime. More militant sections of the proletariat, and

[1] See *Fight*, the organ of the Marxist Group, Vol. I, No. 1, October, 1936, p. 16.
[2] See *The Kirov Assassination*, by L. Trotsky, Pioneer Publishers, New York.

particularly the youth, began to fight the régime openly. So violent did the struggle all over the Soviet Union become[1] that in April, 1935, Stalin published the decree instituting the death penalty for children from twelve years of age and upwards. The régime, on the defensive against the proletariat, leaning on the peasantry, but cheating both proletariat and peasantry, could meet opposition only by terror. In May came the Franco-Soviet Pact, and Stalin gave his blessing to French war-preparations. Three hundred thousand were purged from the party to make the party united on this extension of Leninism.

The decree in April had not checked mass dissatisfaction among the youth. Now after this purge Stalin struck at the whole youth movement. The Consomols, the famous youth organisation, over five million strong, fourteen to twenty-three years of age, the Soviet citizens of the future, at one stroke of the pen were ordered not to concern themselves too much with production and were forbidden to take any part in politics.[2] Henceforth they were to concentrate on education and read the classics. That sure barometer of discontent in Russia, the campaign against Trotskyism, rose higher and higher as Stalin began determinedly to sweep away the whole ideology of revolution, and create an atmosphere which would give confidence to his new allies abroad and guarantee at home the peaceful enjoyment of their privileges by the millions of technicians, specialists, administrators, officials, secret police, etc., whose man he was. The army had been a Socialist army under Socialist discipline. The bourgeois paraphernalia of field-marshals, generals, etc., had no place in it. Off duty there was no saluting, in the early days officers and men had drinks together and fraternised in Socialist fashion

[1] The English Press is singularly deficient in serious studies of the social and political developments in the Soviet Union. For the struggle of the youth against the Stalinist terror see "Ou vont l'enfance et la jeunesse Soviétiques," *La Revue Hebdomadaire*, September 21, 1935, p. 346. The writer hopes to translate and publish this article soon. Based exclusively on a mass of Soviet material, it is the kind of exposure which silences even Stalinist bluff and abuse.

[2] The Webbs, on p. 395 of their book, *Soviet Communism*, give a detailed account of this typical piece of Stalinist tyranny. But so petrified is their political judgment by admiration for the Soviet Union that they do not spend on it a note of exclamation, far less a word of explanation.

despite the strict discipline when on duty. Stalin abolished this. As in bourgeois countries regiments are the Duke of York's Own or the Prince of Wales' Own, so in the Socialist State many regiments were linked to factories, knitting together army and people instead of striving to keep them apart as the bourgeois have to do. Despite all the bureaucratic distortions some contact between army and people remained. It was the distinguishing characteristic of a Socialist as opposed to a Capitalist régime, one of the precious legacies from the days of Lenin and Trotsky. Stalin abolished it. There was no doubt now as to where he was tending. The Society of Old Worker Bolsheviks was abolished. The Old Political Convicts Association was abolished. The Communist Academy, the famous association for the study of Marx and Engels, was wiped away by a decree. The Stalinist bureaucracy was not only going to the Right, it was seeing to it that there would be no means of turning to the Left except by a violent overturn of the régime.

The bureaucracy was assuring its privileges. In the academies the students were given uniforms, and the Tsarist methods of discipline, including semi-military supervision, were restored, so as to keep them under psychological and physical control. The cult of the family was reintroduced. It made for stability, it sanctified the privileges which the better paid bureaucrats could give to their own children. Laws dealing with abortion and marriage, that could have been signed by Mussolini or Hitler, were clamped on Russia by decree. Stalin's crude mentality, which for so many years has lain like a huge shadow over Russia, dwarfed every healthy growth, did not leave even art or history untouched. The magnificent early films were replaced by jazz-comedies. Shostakovitch, the brilliant young modernist composer, was disgraced for writing "leftist" music, and instead a rival who wrote an opera with Cossack folk-melodies was elevated in his place with Stalin's special approval. Pokrovsky, that clumsy but able and devoted Stalinist historian and stalwart arsenal of historical arguments against Trotskyism, was excommunicated, and his works written in an earlier and more revolutionary period were put on the index. Bucharin who, as he had written and said a thousand times, wrote that Russia had been a backward country before the war, was pulled up so sharply that he had to apologise. All history books had to be once more rewritten to suit the new nationalist conservative Russia. And side by side with this burying of the revolutionary ideas went the concentration of all power into the hands of the bureaucracy and the reduction of the workmen to units of labour.

In the resolution on organisation submitted to the Seventeenth Conference by Kaganovitch, covering fourteen pages,[1] orders for concrete leadership, personal responsibility, and one-man management occur no less than twenty times. The fiction of workers' control, after twenty years of the revolution, is dead. But the bureaucracy fears the proletariat. It knows, none better, the temper of the people it so mercilessly cheats and exploits. Furthermore it was necessary to raise the productivity of labour. At these manœuvres Stalin and his group are matchless. In August, 1935, the Stakhanovite movement was hurled upon the Russian people as the greatest discovery of centuries. By means of a system of co-ordination of work, a commonplace under Capitalism, certain individuals in industries were enabled and encouraged by careful manipulation to achieve record-breaking output. Norms of production doubled, trebled and quadrupled. And as a reward, the Stakhanovites received fantastic sums with which they bought fur-coats (like one a miner saw in a picture of King George V), gramophones, silk underwear, two-horse droshkies, etc., etc. But the rank and file workers knew what this would mean ultimately—a general raising of the norms demanded. Fierce fights broke out in the factories; Stakhanovites were attacked. The Stalinist overlord of the Ukraine says in *Pravda* of November 13: "The struggle against the sabotageurs and those who are resisting the Stakhanovist movement . . . is now one of the main sectors of the class struggle," and Zhdanov, ruler of Leningrad, in *Pravda* of November 18 warned the recalcitrant: "In certain industries, the Stakhanovist movement

---

[1] *Socialism Victorious*, p. 673.

has met with a certain resistance, even on the part of backward workers. . . . The party will stop at nothing to sweep out of the road of the victory of the Stakhanovist movement all those who resist it." Economic realities cannot be entirely suppressed by terror. The workers continued to beat up the record-breakers, to wreck their tools, even to murder some.[1] But the Stalin régime has achieved one important aim. By giving the Stakhanovite workers not only high wages but privileges, such as special schools for their children and special seats in the cinema, it is splitting the workers and creating a labour aristocracy, thus helping to stabilise the position of the bureaucracy.

And as the Right turn inside the Soviet Union far exceeded the bounds that had been reached in 1924–1927, so the corresponding turn in the International, taking the Social Fascists of yesterday in its stride, has hailed Liberalism as the ally of revolution and offered the hand of friendship to Fascism.

[1] *Trud*, November 18, September 24, October 23, November 1, November 12; *Isvestia*, November 28; *Pravda*, November 3. For murders *Pravda*, October 19; *Isvestia*, October 30 and November 2. See *New International*, February, 1936.

Chapter 14

THE REVOLUTION ABANDONED

WE HAVE NOTED WALTER DURANTY'S OBSERVATION IN November, 1932, as to the attitude of Stalin and the bureaucracy to revolution in Western Europe. Stalin had been actively preparing for the German defeat before that. On August 27–29, 1932, the International engineered the world Anti-War Congress at Amsterdam under the patronage of Henri Barbusse. It was the first of those futile peace congresses with which Stalin, using bourgeois men of letters, pacifists, and all and sundry have dragged the working-class movement more and more away from the only method of struggle against war—the struggle against Capitalism. This congress, however, did condemn the League of Nations and call upon the workers to turn imperialist war into civil war. Marcel Cachin and other Communist speakers followed official Communist policy. But a foundation had been laid for the future Right turn. It would appear also that Stalin had been preparing the way with the bourgeois governments since November, 1931, that is to say, one month after Moscow had announced capitulation in Germany. While he assured the International that Hitler's coming into power was merely a preliminary to the revolution, he and Litvinoff were acting in a way which showed that nothing was further from their minds.

THE ROAD TO GENEVA

In that same November Molotov, in Moscow, had for the first time expressed the Soviet faith in international capitalist law. "Our policy of non-interference in this Manchurian question arises from our respect for the international treaties to which China is a party, from our

373

respect for sovereign rights and the independence of other nations, and from our unqualified rejection of any policy of military occupation and intervention."[1] This, not at Geneva or to the bourgeois, but to the Russian proletariat.

Now as soon as Hitler came into power, Stalin hastened to edge himself still further into the capitalist camp and disclaimed publicly any further connection with revolution. On February 6, 1933, at the Disarmament Conference, Litvinov submitted a definition of an aggressor and made an attack on Japan such as any League of Nations delegate might make against another. That in itself was of little importance. For all revolutionary Socialists have realised that a Soviet diplomat or statesman might have to do or say things to bourgeois statesmen which are obvious lies, such as, for instance, the time-honoured fiction that the Soviet Government has nothing to do with the Third International, but merely gives it a home. What is of importance, however, is what the Soviet Government tells the Russian people and, through the International, the world proletariat. In March, 1931, despite all the journeyings and diplomatic courtesies of Litvinov, Molotov was still preaching revolution, "Our purpose is the establishment of Socialism in the U.S.S.R. and the carrying on of the world struggle for the cause of Communism, for the complete victory of the causes of Marx-Engels-Lenin"; a statement met with thunders of applause. But to Litvinov's declaration about international law Stalin now gave whole-hearted corroboration inside Russia. Said *Isvestia* of February 8, 1933: "Litvinov's declaration not only is aimed against intervention in a country where there is a revolution, but in the name of the U.S.S.R. undertakes the obligation not to intervene in a country where there is a counter-revolution." Neutrality in regard to Spain was therefore no surprise. Stalin had three years before openly joined the upholders of the status quo, that is to say, ultimately of the counter-revolution. The later stages followed with monotonous inevitability. In October

---

[1] For this section see *World Revolution and the U.S.S.R.*, by M. Florinsky, pp. 219–248; the writer, though bourgeois in outlook, has grasped the essentials of Russian history since 1924.

Germany left the League of Nations, and three months after Litvinov told the Congress of Soviets that the League, to which the Soviet attitude had never wavered since Lenin called it a thieves' kitchen, might now be a force for peace. He was preparing the country for the entry and the subsequent alliance with France. In September, 1934, Russia joined the League. In May, 1935, the Franco-Soviet Pact was signed. It was an open military alliance, of doubtful value because France's adherence is subject to the approval of Great Britain. Yet none but a fool can object to the Soviet Union making non-aggression pacts (for what they are worth), making an alliance with France or even entering the League of Nations; and revolutionary policy on this point should be made quite clear.

PACTS WITH THE BOURGEOIS

Both Lenin and Trotsky in 1918 fully endorsed the acceptance of help from the British and French against the Germans. Let us accept the help of the British and French brigands against the German brigands, said Lenin quite openly, but never ceased to call upon the proletariat of France, Germany and Britain to carry on their revolutionary struggle against the bourgeoisie. Lenin never moved from that position. In 1920 he was in process of coming to arrangements with Britain. The British demanded the cessation of revolutionary propaganda in the East. Lenin agreed. But before the agreement was signed the Eighth Congress of Soviets met and Lenin told the delegates of the negotiations: "But we are now prepared to make the utmost possible concessions and we think that it is in our interests to obtain a trading agreement, and as quickly as possible buy some of the main things that are necessary for the restoration of our transport, i.e., locomotives, for the restoration of industry, for electrification. This is the most important thing for us. If we get this, then in the course of a few years we shall strengthen our position to such an extent that, even if the worst comes to the worst, if in a few years military intervention takes place, it will break down because we shall be stronger than we are now. The policy of our Central Committee

375

is to make the utmost possible concessions to England. And if these gentlemen think they can catch us on any promises, then we declare that our Government will not carry on any official propaganda, that we do not intend to touch any British interests in the East. If they think they are going to get anything out of that let them try, we shall not suffer."[1]

The British Foreign Office could read it if they liked. He was anxious for such support as the Liberal bourgeoisie might give to a trade agreement with Russia. But he knew that any arrangement that the bourgeoisie entered into was for its own benefit. He could tell them anything, but never would he deceive the international proletariat of which the Russian proletariat was a part. He was always ready to manœuvre, with a political judgment and souplesse that Stalin's crude cunning has tried in vain to ape. But however much Lenin might manœuvre he would never deceive the masses, because he always knew that Fascists, Conservatives, Radical or Liberal bourgeois, Social Democratic bureaucracy, were all, in the ultimate test of war and revolution, "one bloody lump," and that Soviet Russia could be saved by the proletarian revolution and the proletarian revolution alone. He would have entered the League of Nations and signed a pact with France, but the International would have remained a revolutionary force. Was this impossible? The International did, for one year after the entry, continue its revolutionary propaganda. Russia was many months in the League when the British Labour Party met in conference at Southport and decided that if necessary it would fight a League of Nations war. The British Communist Party violently attacked this reactionary policy. Said R. F. Andrews (in emphasised print), "The Soviet Government is in the League of Nations to pursue the working-class objective of fighting for peace and exposing imperialist war plans. British imperialism (whether working through a Labour Government or not) is in the League to pursue its own imperialist ends, which enormously increase the peril of war. If Socialists ought to support the Soviet

[1] *Lenin on Britain*, p. 291.

Union s work in the League, for that very reason it follows that they should expose the Labour Party's conception of the League as a 'collective peace system.'" Andrews asked himself the question: "But supposing Fascist Germany attacks the U.S.S.R.: are you not in favour of the workers supporting the British or French Governments in an attack on Fascist Germany?"[1] The emphasised reply was, "Under no circumstances." "Such action," said Andrews, "would help the German Capitalists to represent the war as one of self-defence, it would strengthen British Capitalists and weaken British workers, it would put British imperialism in the event of victory in a favourable position for attacking the U.S.S.R., it would mean suppressing the inevitable revolts in India and the Empire. On the contrary, by supporting the workers in their struggle against exploitation, profiteering and oppression in war-time (a struggle which is unavoidable in any case), and developing it into a struggle against the war itself, the British workers would undermine Hitler's own front which would be the most effective assistance British revolutionaries could give to the U.S.S.R. in such circumstances." Harry Pollitt in *Labour and War* took the same line, ridiculed the notion of aggressive and defensive capitalist countries. Capitalist countries fought for markets by intrigue and peaceful means, until when peaceful means no longer served they used arms. Up to March, perhaps April, 1935, Stalin's obedient fools were still on the line of the proletarian revolution. They know as well as any Trotskyist that what they wrote in 1935 is still true to-day, is an iron-truth. But when their master spoke they turned. To-day they are shamelessly telling the British workers to fight with the British bourgeoisie if Britain allies itself with the Soviet Union. While fighting with the British bourgeoisie the workers must in some miraculous way maintain an independent class policy. "This," says J. R. Campbell, "would clear the way for the defeat of our own Capitalist class once the main Fascist aggressor was defeated."[2] As always, it is Stalin's foreign policy and not the workers'

[1] *The Labour Party and the Menace of War*, by R. F. Andrews, C.P.G.B.
[2] *Peace—But How?* by J. R. Campbell, C.P.G.B.

revolution that guides these paid agents. It is in France that we can see most clearly the results of Stalin's new manœuvre, heading as always to the destruction of yet another working-class movement.

FEBRUARY 6, 1934

The crisis seized France late. There was a steady decline but relative stability in French economy up to 1932, but by that time the country was in the throes and set out on the roach which leads either to the Fascist dictatorship or the dictatorship of the proletariat. One by one every European country falls in line behind Russia, Italy and Germany. The French struggle was the last opportunity that the International would have on the continent. The odds were against it. The German defeat and a Fascist Germany were an almost irreparable blow. But France is a country with a great revolutionary tradition, and in addition the French workers had before their eyes the example of what had happened to the German workers. Success or failure, however, lies with the revolutionary party, and for one year the French Communist Party continued with the theory of Social Fascism. The International was tactically bankrupt. It had nothing to say. In the spring of 1933 it had made one hysterical effort to form the United Front. Without intense previous preparation such an effort is doomed to failure. It failed, and the Social Democracy was again proclaimed the enemy.

Trotsky, in this period of ebb, called for a programme based on a demand for a single chamber, lowering of the voting age to eighteen, and full political rights for the army. He was abused as a counter-revolutionary. And all through 1933, while the class-conflict in France sharpened, the French Communist Party remained blind as only the functionaries of the Third International can be blind. On the 6th February, 1934, the French bourgeoisie, using the Stavisky frauds as a pretext, struck for power, aiming at taking the working-class by surprise. Daladier, the Radical, was at the head of the Government, supported by Socialist votes. The bourgeoisie wanted to break not Daladier but parliament altogether. "Down with the thieves," shouted the Fascists. If they could succeed in entering the Chamber and murdering some of the deputies, parliamentary government in France was finished, and a Fascist régime would have the chance to rivet itself in the offices of government and destroy the French working-class movement. The utter imbecility of all Stalinists was never more completely shown than in the actions of the Communist Party of France in this grave crisis.

The Jeunesses Patriotes, the Croix-de-Feu, the Solidarité Française, all the Fascist bands were preparing for the event by demonstrations in the Place de la Concorde and the Champs Elysées. Their aim was to set fire to the Palais Bourbon. High officers in the Government and the police knew. The Fascists demonstrated for one solid month, building up their forces and preparing the public. The revolutionary party must see and prepare. But the Communist Party, with its eyes on the Social Fascists and its ears cocked towards Moscow, ridiculed all warnings. André Marty, a member of the Political Bureau, told the French workers to be calm and not to concern themselves about the Fascist demonstrations. Stoppage in a factory for a few minutes or leaving it in a body before the closing hour, wrote Marty in *Humanité*, have for the workers an importance a thousand times greater than constant impulsive manifestations in a bourgeois neighbourhood.

He wrote this on February 3. Three days after, on the morning of the 6th, the day of the attack, the Communist Party suddenly called on the workers to demonstrate in the Champs Elysées, not, however, against the Fascists, but with them. The U.N.C., the Union Nationale des Combattants, is a Fascist organisation. The A.R.A.C., the Association Républicaine des Anciens Combattants, is an auxiliary ex-servicemen's organisation controlled by the Stalinists. Let us quote verbatim. Said *Humanité*: "The war veterans of the U.N.C. will be at the side of the veterans of the A.R.A.C. to defend their lawful rights and arrest all the corrupt, all the robbers." *Humanité* therefore called on the workers to demonstrate and attack with the Fascists against the Daladier Government.

The Daladier Government, trembling in its shoes, shot down the demonstrators, and after one of the most critical street clashes in modern European history, beat them back. But the Fascists were only checked, not defeated. They raised the slogan, "Down with the shooters," striving to get rid of the Daladier Government. *Humanité* joined them again, calling on the workers to demonstrate and to demand the arrest of Daladier and Frot, and the downfall of their Government for shooting Fascists. The Social Democrats will always fight behind a bourgeois. Blum offered to stand by Daladier and sought a United Front with the Communists. The C.G.T.U., the Red Trade Union, refused. The Communists referred the Socialists to the Amsterdam-Pleyel committees, some vague offshoots of the Anti-war Conference under Barbusse in 1932. For the struggle against Fascism Stalin's theory still held good, and condemned the Socialists as Social Fascist outcasts. God only knows what was in the minds of Cachin, Thorez and the other Stalinist heroes of the Central Committee in those few fateful February days. It is clear that when Stalin conceived the idea of "After Hitler, our turn," he had no idea of what Fascism in an industrialised country really meant. But by February, 1934, the whole world knew. It is possible that the French Stalinists had Stalin's orders to down the Daladier Government, for Daladier was known to be favourable to a rapprochement with Germany. It is, on the other hand, possible that they had said Social Fascism and adopted the revolutionary pose so long that they instinctively acted on the absurdities they had so often repeated. Whatever the reason, *Humanité* for the 6th, 7th, 8th and 9th February and the directives of the Communist leaders are convincing testimony of the malignant influence which Stalin's monolithic methods, especially since 1929 had been exercising over the whole International. Bureaucratic stupidity, enthroned in the Kremlin, now has its little counterparts in every national Communist Party.

On the 8th Cachin and Thorez woke up to what was happening, and called for a Communist demonstration for the 9th at the Place de la Republique. There could not have been a more criminal blunder. For the Communists by themselves were too few to fight. They had rejected the Socialist offer of the United Front. If the advance-guard of the workers demonstrated without sufficient support the police could break them and decapitate the working-class movement at a stroke. Their own workers had not been prepared for struggle; not a week before these revolutionaries had been preaching that there was no need for alarm. It was the sure instinct of the Paris workers which saved them. There was fierce fighting that night and men were killed. The proletariat, the stock of 1789 and the 10th August, 1792, of 1830, of 1848 and 1871, came out in their thousands, whether Socialist or Communist. It was in the streets that French parliamentarism was saved. The coup had failed.

Marshall Lyautey threatened to march on the Chamber with troops if Daladier did not resign, and Daladier crumpled. Doumergue took office to screen the preparations for the second assault. But the masses were on the alert. On August 12 Socialists and Communists called for a one-day protest strike, and got, all things considered, superb response. But instead of building on this, the Communists once more withdrew into Social Fascism. The Stalinists claim to-day that after February 6 they began to fight for the United Front. Never was such a lie. Stalinists never see anything until Stalin tells them. As late as April 13, 1934, in the *International Press Correspondence* Thorez, oblivious to what was happening under his very nose, was as fierce an opponent of Social Fascism as in the days before Hitler. "At this moment some opportunists of the C. P. of France are proposing to the Party that it abandon its policy of the United Front from below and carry out a policy of a bloc with the Social Democracy. At this moment there are forces demanding that the C. P. of France shall finally abandon the positions of Bolshevism in order to return to the Social Democratic rubbish heap," etc., etc. They might have gone on with it to this day. The terrible blunder of it was that the Social Democracy had had its eyes opened by what Fascism had done in Germany. Its workers were on the alert to fight. After February 6, they formed thousands of United Front Committees, in spite of both Communist and Socialist leaders. Blum and Jouhaux were in a position from which they could not extricate themselves if a revolutionary party had put itself at the head of the mass desire to struggle on a programme of action. What the Stalinists did was to form a pact with Blum and restrain the masses, so as to facilitate the new foreign policy of the Soviet bureaucracy.

STALIN BLESSES IMPERIALIST WAR

Suddenly in the middle of the year the French Communist leaders set out with a will to fight for the United Front. It was a United Front against the Fascist danger. To-day, when they are offering friendship to sincere Fascists, the French masses can see how scurvy a trick has been played upon them. But for two years the Communist Party raged against Fascism. In June, 1934, the National Conference of the Communist party officially announced the new turn, began to work for it below in the ranks of the Socialist Party, and above by offers to the Socialist leadership. The French masses, now growing more militant day by day, responded. Ultimately on July 27, 1934, the Pact for Unity of Action was signed. But those who in March, 1934, considered the Social Fascists the chief enemy now displayed a suspicious friendliness. The Socialists, those incorrigible word-mongers, wanted the word Socialism put into the agreement. The Communists refused. They proposed also that there should be no criticism by either side, breaking an unalterable principle of Leninism. The Socialists, who had not expected this, agreed. Léon Blum was not deceived by them, and wrote in his paper that he could see what they were after— they were preparing mass-support for Russia's new non-revolutionary foreign policy. Herriot went to see Stalin that summer; Pierre Cot the air-expert visited Stalin, the Franco-Soviet Pact had been discussed, and Russia's foreign policy was now the Social Democratic foreign policy, and the Communists were therefore ready to embrace Blum, and Blum had no objection since they obviously would now be as devoted servants of French Capitalism as any Social Democrat. The Communists had insisted on Socialism being left out of the joint pact. They were after bigger game than mere Socialists. They wanted the Radicals, particularly Herriot, who was the sponsor of the Franco-Soviet Pact. Still making the masses believe that they were fighting Fascism, they launched the slogan of the People's Front. And while they were looking to the Radical bourgeois the masses began to turn to them. Against the flagrant arming of the Fascist Croix-de-Feu and the savage decree-laws passed by the Laval Government, the proletariat, drawing hundreds of thousands of the petty-bourgeoisie in its train, began to turn to the Communist Party, that is to say, to look to direct action instead of parliamentary manœuvring. Demonstration after demonstration showed the rising temper of the French people. But though the strength and influence of the Communist Party grew and grew, Cachin and Thorez, faithful to Stalin, were fighting to rope in the Radicals.

In May, 1935, they succeeded and welcomed everybody except the Fascists. The invitation to the Fascists was to come later. But so little were they concerned with the class-struggle that they offered the alliance to Flandin in his capacity as President of the Alliance Démocratique. Flandin, however, refused. Then in May Laval went to Moscow to cement the one-sided alliance, and he and Stalin issued the famous declaration: "M. Stalin understands and fully approves the measures of national defence taken by France to raise its armaments to the level of its security." It was the end of the Communist struggle against Capitalism. For if France was to be strong against the foreign enemy, the class-war at home could only weaken it. Henceforward the French workers were to be fed with propaganda, but carefully restrained from action.

It is the belief that this came like a bolt from the blue to the Communists in France. The confusion they were in for a few days was lamentable. But the declaration was a surprise only in the sense that Stalin had not informed them that it was coming so soon, and they had not made their ideological preparations for deceiving the masses.

Months before they had been laying the foundations. The first move came late in March, and it seems that the Communist rank-and-file (perhaps the leaders themselves) did not know the reason for the new turn. In early March the Stalinist youth signed a pact with the French Socialist youth, which under the leadership of Fred Zeller was very much to the Left. They agreed to form a United Front to fight against the Doumergue Government, against the sacred union of the nation, and the whole military apparatus of the bourgeois State. Both declared that the Soviet Union was to be defended by the revolutionary action of the international proletariat. To win the Socialist youth of Paris and the Seine district to a revolutionary policy was a great victory for the Stalinists. For in this very month of March Léon Blum, like all Social Democrats in this uncertain age, not being able to risk his workers having any illusions about his internationalism, was making his own pro-war policy unmistakable. "In case of Hitlerite aggression," he told the Chamber, "the workers will rush to the frontiers." Against these and similar declarations Socialists and Stalinists organised a campaign. But before that month was ended the Stalinist youth began to draw out of the pact. The French Communist Party ceased to struggle against the two-year military service law and Circular 3084, also dealing with military service. They refused to demonstrate in front of the barracks, they refused to fight the Fascists by independent working-class action. The Stalinist youth declared that it was not necessary to fight the Fascists. In the 3rd and 4th arrondissements they made pacts with the Fascist youth and the Jeunesse Patriotes. They formed the Grand Youth Community, "in order to struggle against war." They abandoned Turn Imperialist War into Civil War.

Early in April came Kossarev and Chemodanov, President and Secretary of the Russian Communist youth, sent to Paris by Stalin to turn the Socialist youth against the pact they had signed a month before. Chemodanov, a typical product of official Stalinist Russia, impudent, brazen and with specious arguments to prove his policies true Leninism, argued as follows: "If there is a war it will undoubtedly be against the U.S.S.R. This will not be a war between classes. . . . If Hitlerite Fascism wages war against the U.S.S.R. it will be a war of Fascism against Communism. Your duty, comrades, is at the front. If in this period you make your revolution in France you are traitors." Kossarev warned the French Socialists against the Trotskyists, "whose policy is at the present moment of great danger for the international proletariat." Léon Blum and the hardened Social Democratic schemers could accept all this. It made their own position much easier. But the French Socialist youth rejected Chemodanov's advances. "If in this period you make your revolution in France, you are traitors," was for them counter-revolution, and they repelled this Stalinist interpretation of Leninism. All this took place weeks before the Stalin-Laval communiqué, showing that Chemodanov had not been making any mistakes but knew quite well what he was about. Before a few months had passed Zeller and his followers had joined the Trotskyists.

The Communist Party now had its People's Front against Fascism. In Czechoslovakia there was no Fascist danger, but there was need for a pact with Russia. There, too, the Communists[1] became ardent lovers of their country, and having tied the revolutionary proletariat to the bourgeois war-machine, Stalin called the Seventh Congress in August, 1935.

The Seventh Congress

Seven years had passed since the previous Congress. The German proletariat had gone down, and Stalin had called no congress. But the obedient fools turned up in Moscow, and the new policy was consecrated in a series of resolutions with which we shall not weary the reader. By great good fortune Dmitrov, the hero of the Reichstag trial, was available for the post of secretary. Sufficient to say that henceforth monopoly Capitalism did not lead inevitably to imperialist war, war could be prevented, the world was divided into peace-loving democratic Capitalisms

---

[1] It is obvious that these people are Communists no longer. The reader does not need inverted commas to remind him of that.

like France and Czechoslovakia, and war-making Capitalisms like Japan and Germany, Russia's enemies. The Congress, without debate, unanimously passed a resolution which declared the final and irrevocable victory of Socialism achieved in the Soviet Union according to the Bolshevik theses of Lenin and Stalin against the counter-revolutionary theses of Trotsky and Zinoviev. There was method behind this madness. For while previously a Communist had to fight to turn imperialist war into civil war, now the circumstances had changed. Socialism was achieved in Russia, it was a Communist duty to save this curious Socialism, even at the cost of sacrificing his own revolution. "The defence of the U.S.S.R." had reached its apotheosis.

It would be diverting but useless to follow the confusion into which this transparent stupidity threw the International. Italy for attacking Abyssinia was a war-making Fascism, but when Italy was being sounded as to whether she would join with France and Britain to guarantee Locarno there was for a few weeks a possibility of her becoming a peace-loving Fascism. But she joined Germany and it seems has now become a definite war-loving Fascism. Britain was a war-loving country under Baldwin. But she might become a peace-loving country under Eden. Sir Samuel Hoare came out for sanctions against Italy, and the French Communists greeted this with joy and called upon Laval to do likewise, so that in France the International hailed Britain as a peace-loving country. But the British Communists did not trust Sir Samuel, and were carrying on a campaign against the National Government. They put their faith in Eden whom they thought would fight for a League policy. Then Eden came out for a Western pact with Germany, omitting Russia. The Communists dropped him and Britain has remained a war-making country. Only thoughtful revolutionaries, however, realise how the International, following Stalin, missed the greatest opportunity in years of at best striking a powerful blow against the colonial policy of imperialism, and at worst rallying round itself the vanguard of the working-class movement in preparation for the coming war. Nothing was more certain than that the capitalists would ultimately do a deal at the expense, large or small, of Abyssinia. Liberals and Social Democrats will always follow Anthony Eden or any glib Conservative behind whose words they can shelter and then claim to have been deceived. Communists have nothing to gain by such practices. The International from the first moment could have pointed out that nothing but working-class action could have saved Abyssinia, and as the whole dirty record of lies and greed and hypocrisy unfolded itself could have driven home nail after nail into the coffin of the League. The Liberals, Social Democrats (particularly the Social Democrats) and pacifists, with their desires to help, could have been challenged every time they opened their mouths with proposals for supporting action by the working-class. Every day that the League further exposed itself the emptiness of their words would have been made more manifest. Abyssinia might not have been saved—Abyssinia is not saved to-day—but the International would have had a chance to build up around itself a mass-resistance to wars for collective security and international law and democracy and all the shibboleths, new and old, which would have given it a firm base for the internal class-struggle and the international complications that were bound to ensue. Instead they followed the new line, driven by the Russian bureaucracy's hope that a successful sanctions policy might be a useful precedent against Germany for Russia in the future.

Could short-sightedness go further than to expect a British Government to impose sanctions against Germany on behalf of Russia? The whole adventure ended in ignominious failure. The Communists, however, retain unchecked their faith in the League. But there is one important episode, not generally known, which shows the Soviet bureaucracy approaching the end of the road which leads to the counter-revolution. In August at Brussels the International Federation of Trade Unions was holding a congress. The Abyssinian question filled all minds. Eugen Jagot, of the War Resisters' International, determined to make an effort to persuade these Social Democrats to make this last attempt to stop war, by calling on their own workers instead of continually begging

387

capitalist Governments. He found sympathetic response among the lower ranks of Trade Union officials, but men like Citrine, Jouhaux and the other leaders were, of course, scared of doing anything which their capitalists did not approve of. Still Jagot was making some progress. Soviet Russia might have turned the scale. If the Soviet Union, the Workers' State, had come out clearly for a boycott against all war-material to Italy or any other country which interfered in Abyssinian affairs, the hand of those working at Brussels would have been strengthened, and Soviet Russia would have been in an immensely powerful position, the centre of the whole anti-imperialist struggle. As in the General Strike of 1926, while the Soviet Government maintained the formal diplomatic proprieties, the Russian Trade Unions could have expressed solidarity with the Reformist Trade Unions, collected millions and offered concrete proposals to stop imperialist intervention by international workers' action. The Soviet workers could have put an instant embargo on the oil that Russia sent steadily to Italy all through the dispute. The mass feeling that had been aroused all over the world would have been directed into a single channel under the direction of the Third International. It was that pressure alone which could have checked Mussolini and weakened him at home, while the self-motivated protests of British Imperialism could only strengthen him. It would then have been an urgent matter for British and French imperialism, and French imperialism in particular owing to the internal situation, to press for a solution, in order to quiet the unrest at home. Abyssinia might have escaped with a certain loss of territory. At worst the International would have doubled its influence for revolutionary struggle and the Soviet Union would have stood higher than ever as a basis for the struggle against Imperialism. But a workers' bureaucracy cannot think in this way.

Jagot and those others who were striving at Brussels for international working-class action counted on Soviet support. The Third International in good Stalinist fashion had been clamouring for unity of the workers, of the two Internationals, etc., etc. Now when there seemed a possibility of its realisation, Stalin showed the real nature of the Government he represented. From Moscow came categorical instructions to the Communist delegates under no circumstances to support any kind of action except sanctions by the League of Nations. The scheme collapsed. Socialism in a single country had reached the stage where the leader of the international proletariat was as nervous of the action of the world proletariat as any Fascist dictator. Stalin cannot stop now. The day is near when the Stalinists will join reactionary Governments in shooting revolutionary workers. They cannot avoid it. For in the great crises of imperialist war there is only one choice, with Capitalism or with the revolutionary workers. There is and can be no middle way.

THE FRENCH REVOLUTION APPEARS

The revolutionary wave in France mounted steadily. The French workers, believing in the Communist Party tradition of action, determined to fight Fascism, and ready for a large-scale offensive against the decrees of the Laval Government, rallied around the Communist Party, followed the Communist Party line, joined the Communist Party. Following the 6th of February the membership tripled in the course of two years, rising from 30,000 to over 150,000 in the middle of 1936. The Young Communist League, 4,000 in February, 1934, was nearly 100,000 two years later. The circulation of *Humanité* reached a quarter of a million copies daily. The Communists gave currency to the slogan, "The Soviets everywhere." It became the most popular slogan in the whole of working-class France, and for all workers Soviets mean the direct challenge to the bourgeois State. One feature of the workers' meetings which told an unmistakable tale was that the workers were ready for Soviets, they had come out for the general strike as on February 12, they were ready always to pour out in hundreds of thousands to make a counter-demonstration against the Fascists. But they would not respond to any talk about immediate demands or partial strikes. They were worn out, they had no resources, strikes for higher wages would mean long-drawn out struggles when they might be defeated in sections, or win small victories at great cost. They felt that they must move together in a united effort. It is such mass feeling that produces a revolutionary situation.

Not that these millions were thinking in terms of revolution, millions of workers rarely do, but a revolution is made on the slogan of the day, and when the millions of workers are determined, if they feel above them the correct leadership, they will go to the end. But the Communists were not thinking of revolution. They complained that both Radicals and Socialists would not support extra-parliamentary action against the decree laws. Herriot and Léon Blum were quite prepared to attend peaceful demonstrations, however. So the Communists organised demonstration after demonstration, but in all their propaganda and agitation were strictly subordinated to the policy and ideology of the Radicals, chiefly Herriot, the supporter of the Franco-Soviet pact. The Communists sang the Marseillaise, they carried the Tricolour, they became ardent defenders of the Republic, that very republic which was allowing La Rocque's armoured cars and aeroplanes openly to prepare for the assault on the workers. In addition to the fight against Fascism they were supposed to be fighting the decree laws. But Herriot was a member of the Government which had passed those laws. In the conflict between Herriot and the decree-laws Herriot was easily victorious. The Communists grovelled before the Radicals. For the great demonstration on July 14 the Socialist Youth decided to march in their uniforms of a workers' militia. At the co-ordination committee of the Socialist Youth and the Young Communist League, Ancelle, secretary of the Paris district of the Y.C.L., threatened them: "If on July 14 you insult the Radical leaders, the Tricolor and the Marseillaise, we'll break your necks." In the typical style of Stalinist polemic, perfected in the many campaigns against Trotskyism, they called all who insulted the Tricolour and the Marseillaise, agents of the bourgeoisie, traitors, criminals and counter-revolutionaries. The Socialist Youth, under Trotskyist influence, would not give way. The matter went to the Organising Committee, where the Stalinists complained. The Radical leaders, quite astonished at this zeal on their behalf, replied, "How can these young men marching in uniform affect us? Not at all. It's quite all right with us and does not embarrass us at all." The Socialist Youth marched in uniform, shouting revolutionary slogans, and had a great reception. Late in 1935 the Fascist leagues were dissolved by parliamentary decree, a hollow fiction which deceived nobody. Meanwhile the ferment among the masses continued. Negotiations were set on foot for the unity of the Communist and Reformist Unions, the Communists making all the concessions. Under the slogan of unity, every principle of the United Front was being broken. Whereas the United Front is designed to stimulate action, this Stalinist manœuvre aimed at exactly the opposite.

How great the temper of the French workers was is proved by their reaction to Hitler's marching into the Rhineland. The Communists raised the loudest scares, "The defence of the country," "Collective security through the League." But so indifferent were the French workers that Flandin and Sarraut did not feel themselves able to take the counter-measures that they otherwise might have done. The Right tried to exploit the Hitler scare at the elections. The workers, intent on the class-struggle at home, ignored them. But despite the loud acclaims over the victory of the Popular Front, the elections were a serious blow to the Communists. The results were too good. They had not wanted so many Socialist votes. They did not want Blum as premier. They wanted Herriot, nailed irretrievably to the Franco-Soviet Pact. Blum they knew was favourable to an agreement with Germany, every Social Democrat being always ready to make an agreement with capitalists. So was Daladier, the Radical of the Left. Had the Radicals gained enough votes to be the dominating influence in the Government, the Communists might have gone into it, but they did not trust Blum and Daladier. That was their first disappointment. The second was what no one except a revolutionary of years of theoretical learning and practical experience could have foreseen in the years that had elapsed since February 6—the sudden, mighty explosion of the revolutionary force that had been generated in the masses of France. With that instinctive discipline which any revolutionary knows is always to be found in the organised masses at the moment when they decide to act, the French workers went into the factories, refused to come out until their demands were satisfied, and by so doing challenged the whole force and pretensions of the bourgeois State.

The Stay-in Strikes

It was not yet revolution, but it was a revolutionary act of the highest importance. The Government, the Communist bureaucrats in France, practically the entire world except Leon Trotsky and the Left Opposition, were taken entirely off their guard. For over two solid years Trotsky and the Left Opposition had been warning the Communist Party that France was approaching the revolutionary stage, that they should build a workers' militia, and ideologically and organisationally prepare the workers for the inevitable armed struggle. The Communists called all this Trotskyist provocation, and continued with their pro-Herriot demonstrations and complaints in parliament about the Fascist Leagues. Now the workers were in the factories, and the suddenness, the cohesion and the mass-weight of the movement, paralysed the Government.

The workers received reinforcement. As always happens when the workers show courageous and decisive action, large sections of the petty-bourgeoisie, the bank-clerks, insurance-clerks, waiters, the girls in the Galeries Lafayette, all the "Yes, sir" and "No, Madam" elements of the population who are, from the very circumstances of their employment, strongly subjected to the whole bourgeois régime, followed the proletariat and joined in the strike. "The Soviets everywhere." The words shouted at meetings for years now acquired an immediate practical significance. On the countryside the agricultural workers began to invest the farms. A Communist Party that had used the two previous years in adequate preparation would have been master of the situation with all its potentialities. The stay-in strike was spontaneous only in a limited sense. It was the product of the whole previous historical period which began on February 6. If a Communist Party had placed openly before the workers the ultimate necessity of armed struggle, had prepared for it, but had at the same time given critical support to a Popular Front, their votes would have been no less and, though the suddenness of the workers' movement might have surprised them, the Soviets so thoroughly popularised would have been formed at once, and workers and State would have faced each other with the workers holding the initiative. Even as it was, despite all the previous misdeeds and treacheries, the Communist Party of France had the leadership of the nation in its hands. The revolutionary impulse of the united masses, always stronger on the day than all but the greatest of revolutionaries can hope for, had transformed the relationship of forces in a day. Breaking at once with the Popular Front the Communist Party could have even then called for the formation of Soviets. The response would have been instantaneous. "Les Soviets partout." The words were ringing through all France as Liberté, Egalité, Fraternité had resounded in the days of July, 1789.

Still more easy would it have been to demand the expulsion of the bourgeois from the Government. The Soviets could have dealt with the economic demands as a whole, and linked with them political demands, the immediate arrest of the leaders and the disarming of the Fascist leagues, the dismissal of the most reactionary officers, the improvement of the living conditions of the soldiers, and the democratisation of the army, which would have split it for and against the workers at one stroke. The Government was powerless. So it was on July 14, 1789, so it was in the early days of 1848, so it was when the Commune began, in the great strike in the revolution of 1905, in the March days of 1917, in Germany in November, 1918, in Germany on August 11, 1923, in Spain in August, 1931, as it always is in the first spontaneous outburst of the masses in a revolutionary period. The masses act and create a situation. Revolutionary leaders must recognise it and act on it, for such chances come very very rarely in history. In France in June, 1936, the particular method of attack chosen by the workers, seizure of the factories, had made the situation absolutely impossible for the bourgeois.

They could not send the soldiers into the factories to shoot a million workers out of them. How many factories would have survived the wreck? And in such circumstances no army can be trusted. It was not only the million and a half men in the factories and the middle-class strikers. The whole working-class of France was supporting the strike. We have statistical evidence of that, for a few weeks after the Trade Union membership had moved from less than two million to over five million, "joining up for the class-war," as they told each other. Any movement so vast as to affect over six million of the population would inevitably have serious repercussions in the army, which would only show itself, however, when the army had been called upon to shoot the masses and these had refused to give way.

The petty-bourgeoisie could have been bound to the movement by linking the demands of their strikers to the workers' demands and refusing to treat separately. Blum, not to say Daladier, would have had to make an early choice, with the workers or with the bourgeoisie, and either supported the Soviets or exposed himself at once to all his followers. The bourgeois Press, frightened at what it saw, lied voluminously about the strike. The workers were polite to the employers, but in many factories always had one of them as hostages. In the warehouses for perishable foodstuffs, the food rotted while they went out and bought what little they could afford, such was their scorn and contempt for the class they were fighting. And how ready for drastic action the men in the basic industries were can be judged from the following. On June 9, 537 factory delegates in the steel industry, representing 243 factories, met at Mathierin-Jaureau Avenue, discussed the situation with great passion, and sharply rebuked the Trades Union leaders who had negotiated the settlement of June 7. These delegates passed a resolution in which they specified that they could not accept the application of the agreement without a real upward readjustment of their salaries. They gave the owners forty-eight hours to accede, failing which they would demand the nationalisation of the factories.[1] On June 12 the general settlement for the steel industry

---

[1] "Que Faire," *Communist Review*, July, 1936, p. 15.

all over France was to be signed. The factory delegates had entrusted the agreement to Trade Union delegates, nearly all Communists. When they saw the terms, however, they refused to sign and immediately four evacuated factories were re-occupied. From there to revolution is but a single step. The bourgeois gave in. They had to, for this was a very different thing from a British Labour parliamentarian threatening the Tories in the House of Commons with nationalisation of this or that industry unless the employers do this or that.

To have led this movement towards revolution would need enormous courage, audacity and fortitude. But how else was any revolution ever led? And Thorez, Cachin, Marty, and the rest were fortunate in that they were not unknown, shabby men who had been to prison, as were Lenin and his band of Bolsheviks. All France knew them. They had a journal which was widely-distributed and whose circulation would have doubled or trebled itself if they had taken the lead. Outside of France there was Hitler, but every modern revolution will have to face the possibilities of intervention, and the Spanish Revolution was waiting to help them; the proletariat of Belgium was to follow the French almost overnight. If a general European war were ultimately to develop, then it could not begin under better conditions for the Soviet Union and Socialism than with the international proletariat in actual conflict with its bourgeoisie in three countries so closely linked as France, Spain and Belgium. Lenin, in 1917, worked on just such a scale, and because of that was successful. For Marxists the Permanent Revolution and international Socialism are not propaganda phrases. They must form the basis of all revolutionary strategy. That is the reason for the existence of an international. Otherwise the revolutionary words are not only meaningless; they are a positive danger. Only the actual development of events under the whip of their activity and their slogans could have told the French Communists how far they could have gone. Agitation, says Trotsky, is always a dialogue with the masses. The party gives the slogans, and according to the response of the masses knows how far it can go. Such were the possibilities of the situation which developed in June. Ultimate conflict is inevitable, and whether it comes soon or late, the workers' leaders should have taken the initiative at once. But what they actually did, these infamous scoundrels, was to carry out to the letter the commands of their counter-revolutionary leader in Moscow and fight their hardest to break the strike and demoralise the masses. They did not want the workers to act, and they and the Trade Union leaders sabotaged from the first day.

THE STALINISTS BREAK THE STRIKE

Humanité of June 2 came out with: "The Trade Union militants, as they have indicated, are using all their strength to achieve a rapid and reasonable solution of the conflicts that are in progress." What this meant the bourgeois knew. Powerless before the masses, they received unexpected help from these renegades. *Paris Soir* on the same day wrote: "Will they be able to stop the development of events? Those responsible for the Trade Union movement are undertaking this task with the hope of succeeding in it." The Communists and the Trade Union leaders were not responsible for the movement. It had come from the rank-and-file, but thus early the bourgeoisie could see what they were after. When some eager workers began to run their factories themselves, the Industrial Editor of *Humanité*, for merely reporting it in the paper, was publicly dismissed from his post. But the strike continued, and on June 6 *Humanité* began to fear a possible insurrection. "It is a question neither of demagogy nor of insurrection," they pleaded. "It is simply a question of making the bosses give back a little of their purchasing power to the men who have for four years lost up to thirty per cent of their purchasing power, and in some cases even more." They knew that at any moment the movement might overflow from economic into political channels and the struggle for State-power begin. They fought to prevent it. "It is in the interests of the entire nation," said Vaillant-Coturier in the same issue. Thorez, the general secretary, raised the slogan, "One must know when to end a strike." Every word weakened the workers and strengthened the frightened bourgeoisie. By June 7 they were almost frantic, seeking to drown the class-struggle in the whole nation, Fascists and all. Vaillant-Coturier, in *Humanité* of that date, said: "What is outstanding in this movement, which grows from hour to hour, is . . . the reconciliation of the opinions and religious beliefs, from the Communist and Socialist to the national volunteer, from the Catholic to the unbeliever, and the speed which characterises the work taken up again after victory." The national volunteers are Fascists. Even the bourgeoisie were laughing at them: "The inspirers of the People's Front," said *Paris Soir* of June 7, "suddenly in the face of the fire that has broken out have adopted the rôle of extinguishers."

But nothing could hold back the French workers from the satisfaction of their immediate demands. Blum, more active in those few days than any Social Democratic minister has been in all its life, passed bills hastily through parliament, and, peace being restored, the capitalists began quietly to sabotage by raising prices and at the same time preparing for the second clash which they knew must come. But to the Communists the strike was a warning. The workers' movement was certain to break out again. Stalin did not want that. He wanted a strong, free and happy France to fight against Hitler. The French workers might go down, but Stalin does not pay the expenses of the International for the benefit of the French workers. The Communists therefore began to find the Popular Front too narrow, and to look beyond Radicals to those on the Right, who were unalterably anti-German. Since January, 1936, they had thrown out the slogan, "The unification of the French nation." Now they began to fight for it. Blum and Daladier were sympathetic to an understanding with Germany, and in opposition to them, Communist propaganda and agitation became one long incitement to hostility between France and Germany. They put forward the new slogan of a Front of Frenchmen. "Unity, unity, unity! It is on this unity that the future of our country depends," wrote Vaillant-Coturier on July 12.[1] On July 15 they hailed the army: "It is to the honour of the people of Paris to have, in

[1] All the quotations are from *Humanité*.

dignity, saluted its soldiers and its army." They paid tribute to the Senate: "The Communist Party does not intend any more to yield to the popular custom of attacking the Republican Senate." And on July 29 these anti-Fascists, who had all these years so exploited the French workers' desire to fight against Fascism, offered the Fascists the United Front. "We shake hands with the sincere Croix-de-Feu and with the sincere National Volunteers, with all those who really wish the well-being of the people." They began to attack the Socialist Party. It was Germany and the Red Referendum and "After Hitler, our turn" all over again.

The workers had followed with trust and confidence all the way. The advance-guard had begun to recognise, immediately after the strike when prices had begun to rise again, that Capitalism offered them no way out. Next time they would go further. They had submitted restlessly to the class-collaboration policy, and accepted the explanation that it was only a manœuvre to gain the sympathy of the middle classes. But the hand of friendship to the Fascists began to open the eyes of some. For the moment the Spanish Revolution had carried the Communist Party to its peak. But the Communist Party did not want independent action by workers. It could have armed a battalion of thousands of men, organised public subscriptions for guns and ammunition, and marched them to Spain. The Blum Government dared not ask the army to shoot civilians who were going to fight against anti-Fascists in defence of a Popular Front Government. At that time any attempt at a Fascist coup d'état would have been met by the full force of the workers, and the revolution would have been on the order of the day. The Communist Party, however, wanted the Blum Government to intervene so as to provoke the conflict with Germany at once if possible. Blum stuck to neutrality, the inevitable Social Democratic policy. Then in late August Dr. Schacht visited France, bringing Hitler's proposals for getting a free hand against Russia. The Communist leaders, now frantically anti-German, threatened to break the Popular Front if Blum and Daladier so much as sat down to discuss with Schacht. It was becoming clear to more and more workers what were the real motives behind their policy. They continued to invite all who were anti-German, Fascists and all, to their Front of Frenchmen. The current of dissatisfaction began to flow more strongly, and on September 4 Léon Blum moved openly against them. On that day the Permanent Administrative Committee of the French Socialist Party passed a unanimous resolution:

"Roused by the campaign undertaken by the Communist Party in favour of a 'French Front,' which would be none other than an attempt at a National Government, it declares that the Socialist Party has never been called upon to give an opinion upon such a formation. . . . As a class-party the Socialist Party never hesitated to help in the constitution and success of the People's Front.

"The Commission believes that it would be dangerous for the very aim thus sought after to seek alliance with the Groups that fought and are still fighting democracy and peace, the defence of which constitutes the reason for the existence of the Popular Front.

"It calls upon all Parties and Organisations of this Popular Front to maintain their union and their confidence in a form of action which is far from having exhausted the results that it should yield."

The Stalinist bureaucracy despite all its clamour for the unity of the workers, was ready to make the International destroy this unity for the sake of its foreign policy.

Fascism in France has not developed for three reasons. First the bourgeoisie made a bad choice. Colonel La Rocque and Sir Oswald Mosley are aristocrats, and can never build a mass movement in the way that Hitler and Mussolini, sprung from the people, could do. Secondly, when the French Communist Party abandoned the revolutionary struggle, the initial cause of Fascism, the threat to bourgeois property was temporarily removed. Thirdly, the French bourgeois, always sensitive to the international situation, know that war may break out at any minute. The Popular Front Government, or some variant either to the left or to the right, will lead the masses into the war more easily than a Right Government. A Fascist attempt would bring civil war, and they would rather not risk that now. The Stalinist version of the United Front is not unity for action, but unity to lead all workers into Imperialist war.

The politically-minded of the workers at this moment when the situation is so tense have been thrown into confusion. The petty-bourgeoisies, without even the nominal gain of the rise in wages, are disillusioned. Doriot, an ex-member of the Communist Party, has turned Fascist and with the support of the whole bourgeois Press is seeking to pull the petty-bourgeoisie away from the Left to the Right. Trained in the Stalinist school of mendacious propaganda, and knowing the cesspool of corruption which the International is, he can supplement his attacks with documents, and is a formidable opponent. With the Stalinists sacrificing everything to anti-German agitation, with Doriot pulling at the petty-bourgeoisie and La Rocque and his armoured cars and planes waiting their chance to strike, the French workers are in serious danger. If they fight a defensive battle for democracy, they will lose. But organised for the Socialist revolution they can win a great victory. Will they reform their ranks in time? There is an even chance that they may. That the chance exists is due to Trotsky and a band of followers, young, inexperienced, with all the odds against them, but fighting the most difficult and critical revolutionary battle of our time. It is not only the bourgeoisie they are arrayed against. Stalin is using all the forces of the Soviet State and the Third International to crush them and their leader. He hopes to conciliate the bourgeoisie, but these implacable revolutionaries he knows he cannot conciliate. And he knows that if they succeed it is the end of him and his régime.

THE FOURTH INTERNATIONAL

During the years since 1928 the groups of the Left Opposition could not form a successful party. In Germany they were only 750 strong in 1933, and were almost swept away in the debacle which followed the coming to power of Hitler. In Spanish-America they had made considerable headway, and in Canada, Cuba, China, France, Spain and Britain there were small or large groups, hounded always by the Stalinists, and unpopular in the working-class movement generally, because their criticisms of Stalin seemed anti-Russian and formed a suitable background for the unending mud-stream of abuse against Trotskyism. Trotsky, however, continued to write, to explain, to give advice. The Left Opposition always considered itself a section of the International until after 1933. Trotsky hesitated for a few months, but when Stalin declared that the policy of the International had been correct all through in Germany, and ruthlessly broke the German comrades who wanted to rebuild the International on a sound foundation, he realised (even then reluctantly) that the Third International was past all hope and set out on the task of laying the basis for a Fourth International.

In 1934 he gained asylum in France and came into contact with the French section. It was a small group, not quite a hundred. They published a weekly journal, *La Verité*. In it Trotsky wrote articles, but the group could not make much headway. Both the bourgeois press and the Communists joined in demanding Trotsky's expulsion, and *Humanité* ran a campaign against Trotskyism. February 6 brought home to the old Opposition that the revolutionary period had begun in France. They set out on a lone fight for the United Front. When it did come they welcomed it, but quickly realised what the Communists were after. As far back as June, 1934, they began to press for a workers' militia and a revolutionary programme. Revolution was on the way. The only way to meet it was by placing the perspective openly before the masses and, step by step as the class conflict developed, preparing for the inevitable climax. The Communists called these demands provocations. From that time on "Trotskyist provocations" have been a feature of the International's propaganda. In August, 1935, the revolt of the workers burst out at Brest and Toulon. The Communists damped it down. The Trotskyists put out posters in Paris calling for demonstrations and action on behalf of the fighters in Brest and Toulon. Side by side with the police the Stalinists went around Paris tearing these down.

In June, 1935, still less than a hundred in number, the Trotskyists decided to take the step of entering the Socialist Party, in order to make contact with the masses. The Stalinists, now working in close harmony with the Social Democratic bureaucrats, persecuted them ceaselessly, but their influence grew. The growth of the movement helped them. In America the grouping for the Fourth International, though relatively small, consolidated itself. A strong Dutch party stood for the Fourth International. In Belgium a large grouping inside the Social Democratic Party and a smaller one outside began to wield influence. In Spain, never a stronghold of Stalinism, Trotskyist literature had a wide sale, and a Spanish group with Trotskyist principles was formed. The new groupings began to make their voice heard. In May, 1936, the French, now 500 strong and with great influence over the Socialist youth in Paris, were expelled from the Socialist Party, and formed a new party of its own, publishing a weekly paper, *La Lutte Ouvrière* (The Workers' Struggle), while the Paris youth published a monthly, *Révolution*.

In the June strikes they came suddenly into prominence. Alone in France they issued the slogan of Soviets and sought to drive the movement forward instead of turning it back. The bourgeoisie realised where the real enemy was, and the Stalinists initiated a prosecution against them. Their paper was suppressed and warrants of arrest were issued against the leaders. What gave them significance was not so much their own strength but the storm of abuse which filled the Paris bourgeois press against them in this period. *Le Temps* ran three successive articles describing the Trotskyists and the Fourth International. *Echo de Paris*,[1] *Paris Soir*, and all the Right Wing papers wrote articles on Trotskyism and the Fourth International. Paris workers began to listen to them, and young workers began to join the party. To-day they are over a thousand strong and increasing every day.

In Belgium the group in the Social Democratic Party put up a candidate in the elections, had 6,000 at an eve of poll meeting, polled 10,000 votes, and were within 300

[1] 10th of June, 1936.

of winning the seat. They were, of course, expelled, and a party is now being formed in Belgium over a thousand strong. All this has reacted on the French party. But of more immediate importance than all these things is the probable split in the French Communist Party.

Their shameless betrayals had been causing more and more dissatisfaction among the rank-and-file, which broke out when Ferrat, a member of the Central Committee, challenged the policy. He was forthwith expelled for Trotskyism. But he published the reasons for his expulsion, and Cachin and Thorez had to fight down the discussion in their own ranks. The revolt may be stifled, but given time, and time is all important, it must ultimately break out. The Stalinist policy is too flagrant and has reached its limit. Should, as is expected, some twenty or thirty of the younger Communist deputies in the Chamber break away, as they have threatened to do, they will bring thousands with them, and will not have to search for a road. The French section for the Fourth International is always in the public eye, has the ear of an ever-growing section of the younger workers. The Zinoviev—Kamenev trial has accelerated the process of Stalinist disintegration. Should the dissident Communists and the Trotskyists come to an agreement while the dissident Communists are still in parliament, a new perspective opens for the French revolution. The first few thousand members will be difficult to win, but once those are won, the Trotskyist party will play the leading part in the coming struggle and put the new International in the forefront of the revolutionary movement. All this Stalin knows, and knows too that he must at all costs prevent. He has openly abjured world-revolution. He is murdering the old revolutionaries in Russia. He is striving to make the Third International as innocuous as possible by making it shout for democracy, for love of country, for the League of Nations. He may even liquidate it altogether to assure the bourgeoisie that he will leave them alone, if only they leave him and his bureaucracy in peace. But he dare not do this while Trotsky guides the Fourth International. Organisationally the Fourth International is pitifully weak.

But the work of preparation goes steadily on. Slowly but surely workers understand Stalinism. Many parties have declared for a new International, but are in opposition to the harsh principles of the Fourth. The various groups quarrel and dispute among themselves. But for Stalin, Trotsky's name as ideological leader of a new International spells disaster. For too long Stalin, and the Stalinists inside Russia and outside, have abused Trotsky and Trotskyism as counter-revolutionary. They cannot turn back now. Should Stalin liquidate the Third International by merging it with the Second, Trotsky's case will be overwhelmingly proved and the revolutionary movement in Europe despite its bitter disagreements must ultimately regroup itself around the Trotskyist Fourth International. The huge fabrication of lies and slander against Trotsky and Trotskyism in Russia will tumble to the ground, and Stalin and Stalinism will face the masses inside and outside Russia naked.

Chapter 15

A FOURTH INTERNATIONAL THE ONLY HOPE

THERE IS A LOGIC IN HISTORY AND DESPITE ALL THE
rich and strange episodes of historical evolution there is a
consistent line which can be followed. We can see the
future of the Third International in the role it plays in the
Spanish revolution.

THE SPANISH REVOLUTION

When Franco launched his attack on the Popular Front
Government, that hybrid showed exactly what is to be
expected from these political combinations of bourgeoisie
and workers in a revolutionary period. Two Governments
seeking to negotiate with Franco fell in quick succession,
and but for the workers and peasants the Popular Front
would have been swept off the stage. But instead of calling
upon the workers to lead the peasants in the Socialist
revolution, the Third International, in and out of Spain,
has continued with an intensive propaganda for Spanish
democracy. The drive of the revolution in Spain has
thrown the bourgeois one by one out of the Popular Front
Government in Madrid. In Catalonia, the industrialised
section of Spain, the workers, though not knowing Marxian
economics, had instinctively seized bourgeois property in
the very first days of the counter-revolution—as clear an
indication of the future course of proletarian revolutions
as the stay-in strikes in France—and Companys could remain
in the Government only by pretending to be a Socialist.
The Third International, however, continues to hold up
the revolution with its new love for democracy. The
Stalinists to-day do not want a Red Spain. It will only
ail. Worse still a Red Spain will start the revolutionary
movement surging in Europe again. It would mean an

upheaval in France. Not only do they not want a Red Spain, they will fight to prevent it. The Stalinist bureaucracy was willing to support non-intervention at first, just one stage beyond its German policy of letting Fascism come in. But the workers in Western Europe could not understand the neutrality of the Soviet Union; then came the tardy realisation of the fact that Fascism in Spain might weaken the free, strong and happy democratic France, which the Soviet bureaucracy needed so badly as an ally against Germany. Stalin and the bureaucracy decided to assist Spain.

Bourgeois democracy is doomed in Spain. It is the breakdown of parliamentary democracy which breeds Fascism. Before the actual conflict the Social Democratic workers can be rallied on the slogans of the defence of their democratic rights, yet to attempt to crush Fascism by the maintenance of parliamentary democracy is to lead the workers to ruin. The choice lies between the capitalist Fascist dictatorship, or the Socialist Workers' State. If the workers are to win against Franco and his German and Italian allies, they can win only as the Bolsheviks won, on the slogans of the land for the peasants, the confiscation of bourgeois property, and the revolution of the Moors in Franco's rear. The war must be a revolutionary war by workers and peasants organised in Soviets or other workers' organisations. But the Soviet bureaucracy made the fight for a democratic Spain a condition of assistance; and the bureaucracy and its agents, though active against Franco, are now preventing Spanish workers and peasants from doing the very things that created Soviet Russia. They want no change in Europe. The Third International pushes yet another revolution to disaster. Blum also supports Caballero against Franco.

The United Front between Spanish Social Democracy, French Social Democracy and the Soviet bureaucracy controlling the Third International is established in defence of bourgeois democracy, i.e. Capitalism, in Spain. But the Soviet bureaucracy with more to lose is much the most reactionary of the three. In Catalonia the P.O.U.M., a centrist party, has taken a leading part from the early days of Franco's attack. It had committed the error of joining the Catalonian Government, but it stood for the Socialist revolution, it issued revolutionary slogans. Such danger as there was of a Red Spain came from the P.O.U.M. leadership. P.O.U.M. was not Trotskyist but held the Trotskyist view of the Soviet bureaucracy and the Third International. The Stalinists in Spain instigated a murderous attack on P.O.U.M. as Fascist provocateurs.[1] Not content with using all their force to keep the revolution within the bounds of bourgeois democracy, they are and will henceforth be the implacable enemies of the Socialist revolution and all those who fight for it. The masses in Spain may push them further but they will resist and hamper and impede the progress of the revolution, and that to-day is their rôle in Europe.

Everywhere they are carrying on strenuous propaganda for unity, one large unified party. Stalin is ready to sink the identity of the Third International into the Second, if only he can get Trotsky and his great reputation out of the way. The lesser Trotskyists can be dealt with, their voices have no international significance. But Trotsky, the man of October, and his Fourth International bar the way. The Stalinists want him silenced. He may be murdered in Mexico. And once he is out of action the Stalinist struggle for the League of Nations and collective security calculates on being able to ignore the Fourth International, the workers can be led into the coming war for democracy and the defence of the U.S.S.R., and the Third International will assist the capitalists to crush colonial revolts, the sign-manual of the counter-revolution. Only the determined opposition of the capitalist bourgeoisie to forming or implementing a Soviet pact will prevent the Soviet bureaucracy and the Third International from this course, the traditional path of the Social Democracy. But the road has a gap, a gap across which at present there is no bridge—for while the workers' bureaucracies of Western Europe are based on a capitalist system, the bureaucrats of the Soviet are based on a Socialist

[1] See *The Red Flag*, January, 1937.

system. The Russians may get their alliances, and Cachin and Pollit will stand on the recruiting platforms side by side with Laval, Daladier, and Blum, Churchill, Lloyd George and Citrine. La Rocque will be there and Mosley also. For when war does begin, Fascists and Social Democrats will sink their different views of foreign policy and fight the common enemy of the system they support. But the policy of the Soviet bureaucracy will break owing to the very nature of the Soviet State. For British Capitalism may, despite all its efforts, be drawn into a war against Germany side by side with the Soviet Union. But all Capitalists, German and British, know what happened after the last war and what will happen after this one. They know that if Russia survives the confusion and ruin of the war as a Workers' State, the Socialist revolution in Europe is half-way to victory before it has begun. For them, victor and vanquished, however the war ends, the Soviet Union must be destroyed. And as soon as the war enters a decisive phase, and one side has established a claim to domination, perhaps before, a capitalist coalition will destroy the common enemy. The two systems cannot live side by side for any extended period, still less can they fight side by side. Cannot Stalin and the bureaucracy see this? The wisest bureaucrat remains a bureaucrat, and the bureaucrats have their policy whose roots lie deep. They will follow it until it breaks in their hands. To-day nothing can change that. What is of far more importance is the corrupting influence they exercise on the workers of Europe through the venal Third International.

Abyssinia taught the workers a great lesson, Spain taught them more. The advanced workers of the Social Democracy, slowly, as workers do, are beginning to see the real nature of Imperialism, to see what democracy, constitution, law and order means in the mouths of capitalists. The Edinburgh Conference of the Labour Party shows the ferment. But as the workers turn to the Left, instead of meeting a revolutionary party, firm and uncompromising in doctrine, clear in theory, but fighting for the clarification of ever greater masses of the workers on the common experiences of the United Front, they meet the Third International backed by all the resources of the Soviet State and the revolutionary traditions of October, driving them back to collective security, back to democracy, back to the illusions of Socialism through the Social Democracy. It is the crying shame and tragedy of our age. Only at the moment of violent repudiation of the Stalinist bureaucracy by the bourgeoisie will the policy of the International undergo any change. But that moment will be chosen by the Imperialist bourgeoisie who will use Stalinism or discard it at their will. It is to this that the Stalinist bureaucracy has led the Third International, in its time the greatest revolutionary force that history has ever seen.

RUSSIA TO-DAY

But if all this is so, does there remain any justification for the theory of the Permanent Revolution which this book maintains? Under the ablest Marxist leadership would the position of international Socialism have been much better? Has the Revolution on the world-scale justified itself? Why should we still pursue this course? These questions must be answered.

Let us look rigorously at the Soviet Union to-day.

After nearly twenty years of unparalleled effort, turmoil and suffering, the Workers' State presents a spectacle which is a caricature of Socialism. Grain production is little more than it was before the war, and the twelve millions of tons exported before 1914 is more than accounted for by the increase of population. Livestock is actually less than before the war, and the amount of food per head of the population is less than it was in 1913. The production of cotton goods is only twenty-one per cent more than it was in 1913, while the population is nearly forty per cent more. Housing accommodation is incomparably worse than it is in the advanced capitalist countries, and prospects are not good. As any municipal councillor knows, with a fast growing population and limited resources, housing schemes fall behind, old houses decay as fast as new ones can be built, and the excess of population, greater in the Soviet Union than elsewhere, throws the plans for re-housing still further behind. Road mileage is roughly one to three in comparison with advanced capitalist countries, railway mileage is less. We have paid full tribute to the industrial progress. But a society is founded on production and not on percentages of increase. There were 11,000 motor cars in the Soviet Union in 1926. This year the plan aims at building 161,000. This in percentages is a triumph. A chart will show how between 1929 and 1935 the production of cars in the U.S.A. has declined. But the Soviet pro-pagandist does not state that the U.S.A. production declined from over five and a quarter million to over four million. The consumption of petroleum and related fuels in the U.S.A. in 1935 was 970,000 thousands of barrels, in Russia it was 123,000. Production in the U.S.A. was 1,020,500 thousands of barrels, in Russia it was 168,000. Steel pro-duction in the U.S.A. fell from 56·43 million in 1929 to 33·43 million in 1935. Russia hopes to produce sixteen million tons in 1936.

The Soviet Union remains a backward country, and it cannot be too often repeated that the level of law and justice can never rise higher than the technical level of production. The idiocy of Stalin's overtaking and out-stripping should not need to be demonstrated. To-day a huge armament bill drains the country. Europe will go up in flames in a few years, perhaps months. When will Soviet Union production approach that of the U.S.A., far less rise to such a pitch as to give that standard of life to the worker without which all talk of Socialism is a mockery? "God grant that our children or perhaps our children's children will see Socialism in this country,"[1] said Lenin. He had confidence in collective ownership but he knew its limits. Long before the Soviet Union can approach even advanced capitalism, its fate will be decided by the results of the class-struggle in Europe.

The average worker is still dreadfully poor. True he has the seven-hour day, but excessive overtime makes this merely

[1] This immensely important statement is quoted by Trotsky in his *History of the Russian Revolution*, Appendix II, p. 1240, the single volume edition. It was made in the spring of 1920 at a congress of Agricultural Communes. Lenin was not a sanctimonious person, but his earnestness to impress his hearers that Russia's economic and therefore social development would remain backward for many, many years, was undoubtedly the cause of his slipping into the traditional expression.

a nominal advantage. He has educational and cultural facilities far beyond anything that was dreamed of under Tsarism. But when the most generous allowance is made for all that the State provides him with, "the Socialised wage," the worker's average income is no more than sixty shillings a month. And he lives under a political tyranny without parallel in Europe. A hierarchy of bureaucrats exploit him, with superior wages, privileges, better houses, better education for their children, and such power in economics and politics as no other rulers in Europe wield. The whole country must think as the bureaucracy demands. Stalin will say that the Social Democracy cannot rule without Fascism and Fascism cannot rule without the Social Democracy, make it party policy, and the worker must swallow it. The secret police, whose budget was increased by thirty per cent in 1936, is supreme. Disobedience in production or politics can be punished by dismissal, with loss of housing and all other prospect of employment. The gross inequality is proved to be Socialism and the worker must accept it. The bureaucracy changes the divorce laws by decree, so great is its contempt for the worker. He must obey or perish. On August 11, *Pravda* reported the arrest of some young Communist workers who had been "impudent" enough to discuss the theory of Socialism in a single country. We could multiply instances of this revolting tyranny. Let us for a moment neglect the possibilities of victorious revolution that have been so ignorantly and wantonly thrown away. Let us admit that under the best leadership and administration they might have failed, and Socialist Russia left still solitary. Under the best internal administration the standard of production after twenty years in a hostile capitalist world could have been far higher, but even at the very least, there would still have been scarcity as compared to Britain or France, with the resulting social and political tension. But whereas Lenin aimed at making the Bolshevik Party, based on the working-class, the mediating factor between workers, peasants and bureaucracy, Stalin from the very start aimed at making the party the servant of the bureaucracy, and has systematically destroyed its working-class basis. To-day it is no more than a militia of the Stalinist clique, and so long as he protects the privileges of the bureaucracy, the bureaucracy is well content. The new constitution is liberal in appearance. Actually it destroys the Soviets, the chief political gain of the revolution. It proves that, far from withering away, the State is more omnipresent than ever. It ensures the rule of the party by restricting nominations to the organisations it controls.

Finally there is the intellectual life which has grown out of this regimentation of a whole population The hopeful visitor to Moscow is charmed by the independent attitude of the workers and the spirit of camaraderie that exists between all classes of society. Though it will diminish with time nothing, not even a return to Capitalism, will ever change that, as nothing, not even the return to Capitalism, will ever give the land back to the landlords. It is the heritage of the revolution, and has passed into the life of the nation. Nearly a hundred and fifty years after 1789 something similar pervades the atmosphere of France, and even Fascism there will not be able to destroy it.

But it is Russian intellectual life which is one of the most dreadful features of the Stalinist régime, and bears the impress of his insecure position and his personal limitations. What other mind could have conceived the rewriting of the whole history of Russia from 1905 to the present day to prove that he and Lenin prepared the Russian Revolution, led it between March and October, and that the Red Army victories in the civil war were due to him? His laboured absurdities are hailed in the Russian press as models of Russian prose. If you wish to write model Russian, model your style on Stalin's, is the recommendation of a literary journal. He is mentioned with Hegel and Spinoza in articles on philosophy. Trotsky, in an article written while Lenin was alive but ill, compared Lenin to Marx and has recorded the satisfaction that the dying leader felt at that comparison coming from a pen so profound and a character of such integrity as Trotsky's. But Marx-Engels-Lenin-Stalin is the new hierarchy in the Soviet Union. *Pravda* of February 1, 1935, carried a report of a speech made by one Avdeyenko at the Seventh Congress of the Soviets. Molotov greeted it with joy in his summary. "Centuries shall elapse and the Communist generations of the future will deem us the happiest of all mortals that have inhabited this planet throughout the ages, because it is we who have seen Stalin, the leader-genius, Stalin the sage, the smiling, the kindly, the supremely simple . . . !

"When I met Stalin, even at a distance I throbbed with his forcefulness, his magnetism and his greatness. I wanted to sing, to shriek, to howl from happiness and exaltation." He concluded: "Our love, our devotion, our strength, our heart, our heroism, our life—all these are thine, great Stalin! Here take them, all this is thine, chief of the great fatherland! Dispose of thy sons, capable of heroic feats in the air, under the earth, on the waters, and in the stratosphere. . . . Men of all time and of all nations shall call by thy name all that is beautiful, strong, wise and pretty. Thy name is and shall remain on every factory, every machine, every bit of land, and in the hearts of every man. . . . When my beloved will bear me my child, the first word I shall teach him will be—*STALIN!*" (Frenzied applause.)

That is the intellectual level of Stalin's Socialism. All men in the Soviet Union are reduced to it. The articles of Rakovski, Radek and Piatakov after the trial, when they stood in fear of their lives, tell the history of Stalin's Russia as clearly as the official documents. These men, the revolutionaries of 1917, two of them among the most gifted men of this generation, cringed and crawled and grovelled in the dust before Stalin, called him the greatest and best and most brilliant of men, and called Trotsky mad dog, Fascist, and conspirator with German, Japanese and Fascist. Sidney and Beatrice Webb, Romain Rolland, André Gide, Sir Charles Trevelyan and all these staunch supporters of Stalin's Socialism should live there and enjoy this new society for a year or two. History would be enriched by some of the documents they would sign their names to.

The Gains of October

All this is gloomy enough. But there is the other side. A semi-mediæval country has been brought into the circle of the modern world, the accumulated dust and impediments and superstitions of centuries have been swept away, and this has been possible on so sweeping a scale by the economic revolution in October, 1917, and the changes it brought in its train. Much less has been done than the Stalinist megaphones persistently blare, but a basis has been laid, and scores of millions stirred out of the slough of backwardness and ignorance by the two five-year plans. The heritage of Tsarism, the historical developments we have described, have prevented the effort from being translated into corresponding widespread and concrete improvement in the living standards of the great millions. One-fifth of the budget devoted to unavoidable war-preparations, the increasing privileges of the bureaucracy, will continue to retard this. But the new towns that have sprung up, the construction and use of the turbo-generator, the aeroplane, the tractor and the motor-car, it is on these that a modern civilization rests. We have said enough to show how much the October Revolution has justified itself. But these things, valuable as they are, are not the ultimate significance of the Russian Revolution. It is not that which makes it the centre of attention of hundreds of millions of exploited people all over the world. Its significance lies in the attempt to build and maintain a Workers' State, to lay the foundation of the Socialist society, resting on an economy in which private ownership was abolished. The solution of that problem, the biggest question-mark of our generation, is still hanging in the balance. It is not that there is inequality. That was to be expected. It is that the inequality is growing. The *International Committee of Employees Bulletin*, published in Moscow, for June, 1936, shows that a typist gets 175 to 250 roubles a month, the head of a department 700 to 1,000; the workman's pay is about 250 roubles, allowances and all included. A recent report of Ordjonokidze, Commissar of Heavy Industry, derides the very idea of equality of pay among the workmen and openly glorifies higher pay for better work. The Stakhanovite Movement is based on the same non-Socialist principle. Inequality is inevitable in a society based on a low economy. But it must be seen for what it is and fought, not discussed as

Socialism. Chamberlain tells us that he has seen, at one of the great official parades, a Commissar's wife wearing a dress that cost the pay of a Russian worker for four months. She could not have passed safely through the streets in Leninist Russia, far less mount the platform. Every honest visitor from Moscow brings back the same tale. The Stalin motor-plant will for 1936 make seven thousand limousines, triumphantly announces the Stalinist régime. For what and for whom? And there are the far more ominous financial indicators. Deposits in the Savings Banks rose from 1,700 million roubles in 1935 to 2,500 million in 1936. It is not the sixty shilling a month workman who is saving money. The public debt service rose from 1,300 millions in 1935 to 2,000 millions in 1936. The peasant on the basis of low production fights for his individual personal property and slowly but steadily is gaining. The Russian proletariat, after its Herculean efforts, seems to have exchanged one set of masters for another, while the very basis of the proletarian State is being undermined beneath its feet.

That is the position to-day. Where is it going to end? The Zinoviev–Kamenev Trial, and not so much the trial but the purge, shows us clearly. For it shows that in however disorganised and confused a form the international Socialist revolution is still alive in Russia and gathering strength.

THE TRIAL

Late in 1935 the campaign against Trotskyism had passed from the stage where Trotsky had made mistakes on every front, to be rectified only when Stalin came, to histories by Marshal Voroshilov in which Trotsky was shown to be the planter of counter-revolutionary nests in the Red Army during the civil war, which were exposed only by the vigilance of Comrade Stalin. And, inevitable concomitant of these ideological victories, went the organisational terror. No other way was now open to Stalin. There were in 1935 well over five million men in concentration camps in the Soviet Union.[1] The budget for 1936 showed the increase

[1] Walter Duranty, whose Stalinist sympathies must be borne in mind, wrote in the *New York Times* of Feb. 3rd, 1931, that in 1929–1930, the number of kulaks and others exiled was two million; and the "liquidation of the kulak" continued without relaxation for years after. Souvarine also relates

of thirty per cent in the funds for the secret police. Some such explosion as the Zinoviev–Kamenev trial was inevitable.

The Left Opposition had lost contact with Russia for two years. The repression of international Socialism in the first Socialist State was too great, a cruel irony of history. But its strength was seen by the violence with which it was denounced and the numbers of Trotskyists purged from the party. On June 5, 1936, *Pravda* announced the new constitution. This constitution destroyed the workers' Soviets, giving power to a parliament which would consist of persons nominated by Soviet officialdom. It gave the vote to priests, white guards, ex-nobles and ex-merchants. Of all this *Pravda* approved. Classes had been abolished (or nearly abolished), and these were not dangerous. But against the Trotskyists *Pravda* breathed fire and slaughter.

"The struggle continues. Too weak for a direct attack, the remains of the counter-revolutionary groups, the White Guardists of all colours, *especially the Trotskyists and Zinovievists*, have not given up their base, *spying, sabotaging* and *terrorist* work. With a firm hand we will continue in the future to strike down and *destroy the enemies of the people, the Trotskyist reptiles and furies*, however skilfully they may disguise themselves."

The Left Opposition, now organised into sections working for the Fourth International, knew what this meant. At its conference in the last week in July, 1936, it issued an appeal to the toilers of the whole world, demanding an international commission of enquiry into the charges against the Trotskyists in Russia. It was not too soon. Less than one month after, Stalin had murdered sixteen, including Zinoviev and Kamenev, for Trotskyism. The strength of the movement against the crimes and incompetence of the Stalinist régime was shown by the greatest purge in the

that a brochure of B.- Chirvindt, director of prisons, incautiously revealed the number of the various punishments meted out in 1929. It was 1,216,000 against 955,000 for the preceding year. This was for the republic of Russia alone, excluding the Ukraine, the Caucasus, etc., and excluding the penalties inflicted by G.P.U. The sentences of death had increased in one year by 2,000 per cent. The reader can consult Bilan de la Terreur en U.R.S.S. (Faits et chiffres). Librairie du Travail, 17, rue de Sambre-et-Meuse, Paris X.

history of Russia since 1918.[1] Thousands were arrested, many holding high official position and for months *Pravda* has been a curious compound of loyal addresses and mass arrests for Trotskyism. Two significant examples will suffice. Long after the trial, *Pravda* of Jan. 4th reported that (despite ten years of purgings), the Communist Party organisations of the great cities of Kiev and Rostovdon had been captured by the Trotskyists; four Soviet generals were arrested, despite the critical international situation and the inevitable ruin to discipline and morale.

In the face of these things, the cry of "why did they confess?" loses significance. Furthermore, confessions are a feature of Stalinism. Friedrich Adler has proved, in *The Witchcraft Trial in Moscow*, that Abramovitch in a trial in 1931, confessed to committing crimes in Russia at a time when he was being photographed at a conference of the Second International. On June 9th, 1934, *Isvestia* published the decree by which, if a soldier left the country, not only the members of his family who knew about it would be punished, but "the other adult members of the family of the traitor, living with him or at his expense at the time of the treason are deprived of electoral rights and deported for five years to the distant regions of Siberia." Under Stalin a child of twelve is liable to the death penalty. That is the published law of the land. What crimes against innocent relations would the G.P.U. not threaten in the secrecy of a prison?

A conspiracy of thousands to murder Stalin is an absurdity, but it is not impossible that some were guilty of plotting to change the régime. Stalin knew, however, that they had all broken with Trotsky, that the Trotskyists con-

[1] "What, really, is the meaning of this new drive in the U.S.S.R.? Is it that 'Trotskyism' is more widespread and more serious than we had been led to suppose? That seems to be the implication of an article a day or two ago in *Pravda* by Mr. Roginsky, who prosecuted the wreckers at the recent trial." *New Statesman and Nation*, Editorial paragraph, Nov. 28, 1936. For years in its various journals and in the writing of Trotsky, the Trotskyists abroad had been tracing this growth with unimpeachable evidence. The Moscow Trial itself is dealt with in *Le Livre Rouge du Procès de Moscou* by Sedov Trotsky (Paris) and *Behind the Moscow Trial* by Max Schachtman (New York). Both books are obtainable through the offices of *Fight*, the British Trotskyist Journal, 97 King's Cross Road. See also, *The Witchcraft Trial in Moscow* by Friedrich Adler, the Secretary of the Second International.

demned the Stalinism of Zinoviev, and the rest. But he took the opportunity to slander the growing Fourth International abroad and the spectre which haunts him at home, the return to Leninism, which he calls Trotskyism. His position is desperate. A political crisis was inevitable. The second five-year plan was drawing to a close. There had been progress, but the great hopes raised in 1928–1929 and again in 1933, when the Second Plan began, were now seen to be only Stalinist lies. In October, 1932, Manuilsky at the Twelfth Plenum of the E.C.C.I. had told the world "Do not forget that we shall enter class-less society only with the completion of the second Five-year Plan." The Russians had been choked with these promises. Now they were spitting them out. Where was Stalinism leading Russia? The discontented youth were responding to Trotskyism, the only alternative to Stalinism. Mass discontent might even be anti-Trotskyist but would rally in a crisis round the old associates of Lenin.

Stalin struck fiercely at all who might form a rallying point for the opposition that has forced its way into the party itself. And by this very means he only ensures that the dissatisfaction will next time be more organised. For no man is safe in Russia to-day. Radek lied faithfully for years, only to be struck at like the rest. And these experienced revolutionaries know now, and every thinking man in Russia, that Stalin is far more insecure than could possibly have been thought by those who were not Trotskyists. And the cleavage grows wider. To-day the right of inheritance has been legally restored. But the advanced workers of Russia see these things clearly, as they must. Isolated as they are, the bureaucracy can scarcely hold them down. A revolution in Germany, relieving them of external pressure and giving them allies, would give them the chance to conquer Stalinism, lessen inequality, ensure that collective ownership remains. The battle in the Soviet Union has entered a new phase and will be solved, as Lenin knew it would be solved, by the revolution in the West. That battle must be won by the Russian workers. If the Soviet Union goes down, then Socialism receives a blow which will cripple it for a generation. And therefore, though seeing the Soviet Union as it is, the Trotskyists, uncompromising enemies of Stalinism, will defend the Soviet Union in peace-time as in war.

THE PERMANENT REVOLUTION

The economy of the Soviet Union is based on collective ownership and therefore, despite Stalinism, the Soviet Union must be defended. It is a basis for the international State, for the abolition of war, for possibilities of existence as yet undreamed of. Alone in the world to-day it is a force for peace. Tsarist Russia, with more territory, embroiled itself in imperialist competition on every frontier. The Soviet Union has a huge army, but for self-defence only. Britain, France, Japan and America, if they remain capitalist, have no choice but imperialist war after imperialist war. They know its dangers, yet move steadily to it. Never was a civilisation so glaringly and humiliatingly bankrupt. But a proletarian revolution, in Germany for instance, will at once remove another great country out of the imperialist scramble, broaden the basis of Socialism, drive the economy of both countries forward, relieve the internal tension, and strengthen the force for peace.

Permanent Revolution or permanent slaughter, Trotsky has written. What other prospect is there? The Tories accept the permanent slaughter. The international Socialists accept the Permanent Revolution. Liberals and Social Democrats are the comedians of the modern political world. They are on the side of the permanent slaughter, but want it dignified by the League of Nations or Collective Security or some such twaddle. Their special technique lies in being deceived. They were deceived by Grey before 1914, they were deceived by Lloyd George and Wilson in 1919, they were deceived by John Simon over Manchuria in 1931, they were deceived by Samuel Hoare, by Baldwin, by Anthony Eden. If Beelzebub stood on the Treasury Bench without troubling to disguise his horns and tail in coat and topper, and swore to them that this coming war would be a war fought for Christianity, they would rush to support it, to bewail after that they were deceived.

He is a credulous fool indeed who accepts this transparent subterfuge. They support the capitalist system. In imperialist war one must go either with the capitalists or with the revolution. They go with the capitalists, but seek moral justification for doing so. They see the war coming and they will fight for Capitalism. But to fight with Nazi Germany will be gall and wormwood for them. They could not justify that even to themselves; the Social Democrats will find it difficult to line up the workers to fight side by side with Fascists. Hence these gentlemen want an alliance with the democratic countries. But the British capitalists pursue their intrigues abroad unbothered by these noisy salvationists. British Capitalism knows that these moralizing politicians will come to heel. They always have, they always will. Here and there a few, out of personal integrity, will refuse to fight or save their consciences by some equally brave and futile gesture. But organised Liberalism and Radicalism and the Social Democratic bureaucracy rose with Capitalism and will stick to it and go down with it, doing their best to bring the workers in their train.

Despite Stalinism, despite everything, the Russian workers still love their revolution, and will fight for it and the revolution in the West or the East. Neutrality in the Spanish struggle was not the policy of the Russian proletariat but the policy of the Stalinist bureaucracy. As in the beginning so it is to-day. The Russian Revolution depends on the revolution in Western Europe. The Stalinists seek to kill Leninism. It cannot be done, for it draws its strength not from the memories of the October Revolution, but from the economic, social and political chaos of the modern world. Capitalism will solve this and live or perish before the Socialist Revolution. Cowards and cynics talk of an age of barbarism, as if mankind will destroy itself in the coming war for Hitler, for Mussolini, or for king and country. Let 80,000 civilians, one per cent of the population of Greater London, be massacred in war, and the revolution is on the order of the day, and the same applies to every other great European city. The result it is impossible to foretell, but the conflict is certain. Stalin may try to discipline the Russian proletariat and the Russian army to fight with this or that bourgeoisie. But the peril of war will imperil the bureaucracy. It will fight as the leader of a revolutionary people or it will go under. And the possibilities are that after months or years of war, Europe will have the unprecedented phenomenon of an army of a million highly-trained men, equipped with arms, trained in a revolutionary tradition, offering their help to the armies on the opposite side to wipe Capitalism off the face of Europe. The will and courage of a few men will make history within the given circumstances, but the people will be ready. If the ideological basis of the new International is so quickly ready it is due not only to the objective circumstances, but to the energy and determination and courage of one man who has given his life to the movement. But it would have come all the same. Fascism may win in France and Spain, and throw back humanity for decades. But if even it does, what then? The Liberals and the Social Democrats, cowering in Iceland or sitting under the trees in some desert island, will continue to write their theses on Democracy. But the proletariat will have to lift itself, as the Italian proletariat is already lifting itself to-day. It is a sea of blood and strife that faces us all, and shrinking from it only makes it worse. Turn the imperialist war into civil war. Abolish capitalism. Build international Socialism. These are the slogans under which the working-class movement and the colonial peoples will safeguard the precious beginning in Russia, put an end to imperialist barbarity, and once more give some hope in living to all overshadowed humanity.

APPENDIX ON
SIDNEY AND BEATRICE WEBB'S
"SOVIET COMMUNISM."

THE REPUTATION OF THE AUTHORS MAKES THIS THE MOST dangerous of the unofficial Stalinist books. It is necessary to expose it thoroughly, and this is very easily done. We are not concerned with factual slips. These are inevitable in any large and comprehensive book, may be quite serious, and yet not invalidate the book as a whole or a particular argument. We are concerned with basic structural errors.

1. *The Webbs do not understand the agricultural question in the Soviet Union.*

They say (p. 246) that "only 20 per cent of collectivization had been contemplated during the first year." Elsewhere (p. 565) they say again that collectivization was planned to take place at the rate of 20 per cent per year. This is completely wrong. On page 300 we give the references which show that 20 per cent was the programme for five years. This double mistake is no accidental slip. Every line of their account shows that they have accepted completely the great change from 20 per cent in five years to Stalin's "liquidation of the kulak as a class," without a thought for the industrial resources which the change demanded, and which made it certain to be the ruinous experiment that it was. You cannot collectivize 20 per cent or 80 per cent at will. But you can try, with the results that we have seen.

Of the Left Opposition and the kulak they say (p. 243): "This faction demanded the most drastic measures for the suppression of the kulaks, but failed to make clear by what means it proposed to increase the agricultural output of the minute holdings of the majority of poor peasants otherwise than by the slow spread of one or other form of voluntary co-operation."

Every fact is wrong. On pages 271-272 we summarise the Platform on agriculture, with a long quotation. The Opposition did not demand drastic suppression of the kulak, but "an all-sided limitation of the efforts of the kulak to exploit." The Opposition made it quite clear that collectivization on the basis of industrialization was the only road towards Socialism.

The Opposition explicitly condemned the idea of Bucharin and Stalin that voluntary co-operation could bring Socialism. We have quoted Stalin on page 211 laying it down in 1925 that re-equipment of factories and expansion of industrial capital had nothing to do with Socialism. We have shown at length that for four years the Opposition fought this costly stupidity. We have shown on page 291, that it was only in April, 1929, that Stalin announced as a new discovery what had been hammered into his head for six years. Only space prevents us giving more evidence. The Webbs do not understand this controversy at all. Those who look askance on the Trotskyist criticism of the Soviet Union should ponder why those who support Stalinism as against Trotskyism can do so only by propagating the most grotesque blunders.

2. *The Webbs juggle with Socialism in a Single Country.*

If the peasantry and industrialization was the great practical question of the Soviet Union, Socialism in a single country is the theoretical question which cannot be avoided. The Webbs are believers in Stalin's theory. By Socialism, say Stalin and all the Stalinists, Lenin meant what exists in Russia to-day. The Webbs go one better. "What the proletariat of every country means by Socialism is the suppression of the landlord and capitalist, together with the profit-making motive, by collective ownership, in a condition of social equality, with the universalization of security by the appropriate organization of social services" (p. 1103). So it is not Lenin according to the Webbs, but the proletariat. Doubtless the proletariat of Western Europe and America will be glad to know that that is what it means by Socialism. But the Russian proletariat has some experience of Stalin's Socialism. The Russian worker, with his sixty shillings a month, watching the technician or high official pass by in one of the limousines, or hearing of the collective farmer with his 100 to 150 sheep, ten cows, ten horses, camels, etc., does he think as the Webbs do? We can only guess. For Stalin sees to it that nobody discusses an alternative view. Do the Webbs know of the workmen, who, says *Pravda* of August 11th, were arrested for having the "impudence" to discuss Socialism in a single country? And, if so, what sort of Socialism is this that does not allow itself even to be discussed? And why all the trials and the shooting and the thousands of Trotskyists arrested? Why do the Trotskyist "conspirators" capture the Communist Party organisations of Kiev and Rostovdon (*Pravda*, January 4th)? Is it that the Russian proletariat has other ideas of what Socialism should mean than those Stalin presents them with? Stalin at least passes the baby on to Lenin to hold. The Webbs pass it on to the proletariat.

But this subject, too, has a history. The Webbs cannot evade it, and the subterfuge they adopt is painful even to point out. They say (p. 1101) that neither Marx nor Engels nor Lenin, "no one had directly and explicitly grappled with the particular problem in the light of all the facts, economic, social and political, even as they were in 1845 or in 1905; and, of course, these great authorities were none of them conversant with the state of things in 1925, which alone was relevant to the issue."

Marx and Engels had not grappled with the problem. Neither had Lenin in 1905. We will not argue about that. The Webbs are entitled to their opinions once it is understood that these are their opinions. But they have to deal here with history. If even Lenin, poor man, had not examined the question as he ought, at least he had ideas on the question. He had them in 1905. But he had them in 1923 when he ceased to write. Stalin had the same ideas in 1924. The Webbs have not the nerve to say, as Stalin does, that Lenin always said that Socialism could be built, so they stop at 1905. Lenin died in 1924. Stalin produced his theory in autumn 1924. The Webbs skip all that and begin in 1925 "these great authorities were none of them conversant with the state of things in 1925, which alone was relevant to the issue."

Lenin's whole position held to his death, Stalin's crude volte-face the Webbs simply put 1905 and hop over to 1925. It is a very poor case that needs such defence.

Now for the actual arguments they use as to why Socialism in a single country is possible. Even with the definition of Socialism which they fasten on to the proletariat, they have a heavy field to plough. They claim that Marx and Engels did not dream of the monopoly of foreign trade. Do they really believe that Marx and Engels thought that collective ownership would come all over the world at once? Or that if it came in any one country they would calmly advocate free trade, and allow Capitalism to ruin the nascent Socialist industry? To support Stalinist history and politics you have to make ignoramuses and fools of Marx and Engels.

They say (p. 1102) that another of the objections to Socialism in a Single Country is the fact that if it were established it would be destroyed by hostile Capitalisms. Who made that argument we do not know. The Webbs say that it is irrelevant to the issue. Every Trotskyist will agree fervently. We who deny the possibility of something have little time to argue as to what would happen if it took place. But the Webbs go on (p. 1102): "Unless the objectors wished all attempts at industrial reconstruction of the U.S.S.R. to be abandoned, and the penury and periodical famine to be continued, whilst waiting for the socialist revolution to take place in the capitalist countries. . . ." This of Trotskyists, with their long fight for the plan, sneered at as super-industrialists for years. Let the reader turn to chapter VIII, particularly pp. 202–208.

But the limit is reached in what they term is the final Trotskyist objection. "It was, so Trotsky alleged, the policy of a narrow nationalist egoism, unworthy in the successors of Lenin, Engels and Marx. Better, far, it was said, devote all the energies of the U.S.S.R. to the tasks of the Comintern." It is difficult to restrain oneself at this malicious slander. "Better far, it was said." Whoever said that? When? Where? We are accustomed to this, coming from all sorts of nondescript Friends of the Soviet Union. What is it doing in a book of this kind? The mere phrasing, "it was said," shows what the authors think of the validity of the argument, but again, this is where you land, whatever your gifts, whatever your training, when you set out to defend Stalinism against Trotskyism. The best way is to put on a pair of blinkers, get the loudest megaphone possible and shout "Socialism victorious in the U.S.S.R."

"Trotskyism is Fascism," etc., as insistently as possible. One gets to believe it in time if it is shouted long and loudly enough. But reasoned, historical argument, no. It cannot be done.

The Webbs end with an argument that the Stalinists do not use, for obvious reasons. They say that the world revolution was a proved failure, and therefore it was the only thing left to do, this building of Stalin's Socialism. Bourgeois nationalism, bourgeois empiricism, the shallowness of bourgeois political thinking are here amply demonstrated. For the Webbs, Socialism could always have been built. Lenin and Trotsky wanted the world revolution, probably because it was a fine thing. But once you saw that you couldn't have it, then you naturally turned back to the building of Socialism; that is neither Marxism, nor Leninism, nor Stalinism. Marxism, Leninism, Trotskyism, preach the interdependence of world economy and therefore of world politics. The world revolution was and is a necessity for Russia. Over 1,000 million pounds is being spent on armaments this year in the Soviet Union. Socialism can only come when that money, for instance, is going into production for use and not for destruction. Such expenditure means poverty for the population, necessary though it is. The necessity proves the folly of Stalin's theory. Russian economy could have been developed without cultivating idiotic and costly illusions. The world crisis played havoc with Soviet economy in 1930–1933. A world war may shatter the basis of collective ownership. The Webbs switch over from world revolution to national Socialism more easily than they cross the road. Even Stalin took a little more trouble. Show the workers of the world what Socialism can do, and that will bring world Socialism infinitely quicker than revolution. That is their argument. The workers and peasants of Catalonia found other more urgent arguments. Franco and not Soviet statistics stimulated their desire to emulate the Soviet Union. The Webbs should found a society for converting Hitler, Japanese Imperialism and Baldwin to the theory of Socialism in a single country. They and the classes they represent need conversion—by those who have the time.

These are the principles on which the book is based. It has much useful detail. But on major issues its history is wrong in a score of places, and its political insensitiveness (we have given an example on p. 369) is a thing to wonder at. Of the arrest for the Kirov murder of Zinoviev and Kamenev, they say (p. 560) that it was "open to misconstruction." The penalties of Soviet secrecy on such matters is that the "world at large puts a bad construction on everything" (p. 560), and the arrest and summary execution of so many persons "could not but excite adverse comment," etc., and much in the same strain, like the *Times* whitewashing some brutality of the British Imperialists in India. And for the same reason. The ice is so thin that the skaters do not even wish to pretend that they have crossed it. Stalin, they argue, is no dictator. The proof they give is irrelevant. Such a statement needs no proof. Finally (p. 1042) there is this priceless passage: "When, however, the Soviet Government feels itself as secure as the British Government does, there seems no reason why popular lectures and speeches at open meetings and discussions in cheap pamphlets and newspapers, should be any more restricted than they are in England," and "We may hopefully expect that, with the Soviet characteristic of universalism in all its administration, those in authority in the U.S.S.R. will, in due season, take this view." The only answer to this piety is Amen.

Is this what the proletariat (according to the Webbs) mean by Socialism? So the British Government, with its Sedition Bill and Public Order Bill, is the standard of security of Stalin's Socialism. André Gide has dropped his Stalinism at last. The Webbs have performed eminent services to the working-class movement by their sociological studies. But nothing will be so valuable as a book from them on the lines of Gide's *Return from the U.S.S.R.*, recanting their Stalinist follies. Support of the Soviet Union? Yes. It is to their credit that they align themselves on the side of the Workers' State. But in the last analysis their book does infinitely more harm than good, for the simple reason that it is false; and falsehood has no place in the Socialist movement. If they wish to help Lenin's work they must use Lenin's intellectual methods. He never spread any fables about the Soviet Union. Why should they? That is bourgeois and Stalinist. But workers do not need it. The workers must beware of all these new recruits to Stalinism. The Webbs transfer their discredited "inevitability of gradualism " to a new field. Its discredit there will be swifter than it was in Western Europe. The Soviet Union depends on the world revolution, and not all the authority of the Webbs, Stracheys and Maurice Dobbs can alter the laws of history, though they can confuse the workers striving to see the light, and thus bring nearer the catastrophe which we all wish to avert.

Index

431